THE ARMY AND DEMOCRACY

The ARMY *and* DEMOCRACY

MILITARY POLITICS IN PAKISTAN

AQIL SHAH

Harvard University Press

Cambridge, Massachusetts
London, England
2014

LIBRARY OF CONGRESS CATALOGING-IN-PUBLICATION DATA

Shah, Aqil, 1973– author.
The army and democracy : military politics in Pakistan / Aqil Shah.
pages ; cm
Includes bibliographical references and index.
ISBN 978-0-674-72893-6 (alkaline paper)
1. Pakistan. Army—Political activity. 2. Pakistan. Army—History.
3. Civil-military relations—Pakistan. 4. Pakistan—Military policy.
5. Democracy—Pakistan. 6. Pakistan—Politics and government. I. Title.
UA853.P18S53 2014
322'.5095491—dc23 2013037070

To my late father, S. M. Jan Shah,
poet and idealist

CONTENTS

PREFACE   ix

ABBREVIATIONS   xiii

Introduction   1

1   Waging War, Building a Nation   31

2   Marching toward Martial Law   72

3   "Revolution" to Revolt   94

4   Recapturing the State   119

5   From Zia to Musharraf   150

6   Musharraf and Military Professionalism   186

7   The Military and Democracy   215

Conclusion   254

NOTES   289

ACKNOWLEDGMENTS   379

INDEX   381

PREFACE

On May 2, 2011, American Special Forces killed al-Qaeda leader Osama bin Laden in the Pakistani garrison town of Abbottabad in an early morning raid when much of Pakistan, including apparently its army and air force, were fast asleep. The raid also laid bare Pakistan's perennial civil-military pathologies. For one, it shattered, once again, the military's carefully constructed myth of invincibility and raised the hopes of many Pakistanis, including some members of parliament, that the military would finally be held accountable because it was caught sleeping at the wheel. But as tensions between the army and the government flared, there were also fears and rumors of an impending coup. Through all this, the Pakistani army's putative civilian boss, Defense Minister Chaudhry Ahmed Mukhtar, remained clueless. He later told a government inquiry commission that he found out about the incident when his daughter called him from New York the next day. This would be unimaginable in a democratic state. In Pakistan, it is business as usual.

It would be tempting to blame it all on corrupt or self-serving politicians. They have not covered themselves in glory. But there is an even more compelling reason: Pakistan is a garrison state, one of the last ones in the world still standing. It is the military that has directly or indirectly ruled Pakistan for most of its existence. The military is at the center of the international community's three most serious and interlinked concerns about Pakistan: the war-prone conflict with India, the jihadi threat, and the security of its nuclear weapons. The army sustains the ruinous security competition with India, directly or indirectly facilitates Islamic extremism and terrorism by harboring militant groups as a tool of foreign policy, and exclusively controls the country's nuclear weapons.

The impact of these roles warrants a fine-grained study of the institutional underpinnings of the Pakistani military's power in the making and execution of state policy. This book is a small step in that direction.

I must readily admit my own biases. Amartya Sen has famously noted, "Democracy is a universal value." In the same vein, I firmly believe that any country can become democratic. Contrary to what many in Pakistan and elsewhere think, social science research shows clearly that the emergence of democracy in a country does not necessarily require a certain level of economic development or a particular class structure, let alone a specific culture or a waiting period. Civilian control of the military—that is, control of the military by democratically elected officials—is a universally applicable concept and a basic principle of democratic governance.

The story I tell in these pages has been a long time in the making. Growing up in Pakistan under the repressive, right-wing military government of General Ziaul Haq, I found it hard to imagine Pakistan's return to democratic rule. Zia's death in August 1988 paved the way for a transition from military to civilian government. But democracy in Pakistan, however imperfect, has never been allowed to stand on its feet. Civilian factors, such as perceived misgovernance and corruption, may be important in providing the military with the opportunity and the pretext to bare its fangs. But why does the military exploit that opening? After all, military coups happen when armed men want them to happen. Armies retract from power when they want to. I have long been convinced that unless one builds an informed understanding of how members of the military think, perceive, judge, evaluate, and choose one course of action over another, any analysis of the military in politics will be insufficient.

This book is my interpretation based on the facts as understood, experienced, and expressed by military officers and civilian elites, including politicians, bureaucrats, scholars, and journalists. It does not address the lived experience of ordinary Pakistanis. No matter how much public support military dictators claim to enjoy, the choices and preference of the amorphous people usually do not directly determine the actual decision, planning, and execution of military interventions and of military extrications from power. The same is generally true for other major policies or decisions typically made in the name of the people, especially in authoritarian contexts. This is not to say that the people do not matter, but to acknowledge that military decisions can matter as much or more and tend to have a significant impact on the lives of the people. Therefore, they deserve separate treatment.

ABBREVIATIONS

AL	Awami League
CGS	Chief of General Staff
CJCSC	Chairman Joint Chiefs of Staff Committee
COAS	Chief of Army Staff
FATA	Federally Administered Tribal Areas
FSF	Federal Security Force
IJI	Islami Jamhoori Ittehad
ISI	Inter-Services Intelligence
ISPR	Inter-Services Public Relations
JI	Jamaate Islami
MMA	Mutahida Majlise Amal
MoD	Ministry of Defense
MQM	Mutahida Qaumi Movement (known as Mujahir Quami Movement until 1997)
MRD	Movement for the Restoration of Democracy
NDC	National Defence College
NDU	National Defence University
PML-N	Pakistan Muslim League (Nawaz)
PML-Q	Pakistan Muslim League (Quaid Azam)
PNA	Pakistan National Alliance
PPP	Pakistan People's Party

THE ARMY AND DEMOCRACY

INTRODUCTION

The third wave of democracy that swept military authoritarian regimes out of power from Latin America to Asia in the 1970s and
1980s heralded the declining political role of the armed forces. Like
militaries in the Middle East and Burma, however, Pakistan's military bucked that trend. In fact, Pakistan has been one of the main
military authoritarian exceptions to the global pattern of democratic
resurgence.[1] The country experienced its latest military coup in 1999,
which was followed by eight years of military government, a situation that led one prominent scholar of democracy to wonder whether
Pakistan was reversing the third wave.[2]

Since Pakistan's birth out of the bloody partition of British India on August 14, 1947, its political history can be summed up as a
story of repeated coups followed by protracted periods of military
government, briefly punctuated by elected civilian rule. Until 2013,
Pakistan did not experience even one democratic transfer of power
from one democratically elected government that had completed its
tenure to another. All its previous democratic transitions have been
aborted by military coups.

This book illuminates the classic paradox—"Quis custodiet ip-
sos custodes?" (Who guards the guardians?)—that has long puzzled
philosophers, political scientists, and policy makers through an examination of the political role of the Pakistani army. Achieving the
proper relationship of the military to civil authority is not only an
academic matter. It also constitutes the central conundrum of state-
craft, whose successful resolution is the very essence of any political
system. In addition to its scholarly value, studying this question in
the context of Pakistan has policy implications. Pakistan's civil-
military imbalance affects the prospects of its own security, survival,
and development. Given its strategic location at the crossroads of
South and Central Asia (bordering Iran, Afghanistan, China, and
India), its possession of nuclear weapons, its tense standoff with India, its increasing fragility as a state, and the existence and growth
of transnational Islamist militancy on its territory (in good part due
to the Pakistani military's patronage of violent nonstate actors as a
counterweight to India), what happens in Pakistan does not usually
stay in Pakistan.

Military intervention and authoritarianism first reared their ugly
heads in the decade following independence. It was in those crucial
years that the Pakistani military developed peculiar understandings
and interpretations of its proper organizational role in state and society that have since inclined its members to resolve political problems through the application of military solutions, skills, and methods. Hence it is important to investigate not just why and how but
also when the authoritarian seed was sown.[3] Therefore, this book
examines the key historical conditions, events, and decisions that set
in motion the process of military involvement in politics in the decade after independence—an involvement that has left a lasting imprint on the political trajectory of Pakistan.[4] My central argument is
that the military's tutelary beliefs and norms, a legacy of its formative experience under conditions of geopolitical insecurity[5] and
nation-building problems,[6] have profoundly shaped its political in-

terventions and influence by justifying the authoritarian expansion of its role in state and society.

Stepping back in history to locate the sources of military authoritarianism does not imply that Pakistan's fate was preordained, as some scholars argue.[7] Admittedly, the founding Muslim League under its ailing leader, Mohammad Ali Jinnah, inherited the state of Pakistan with all its colonial institutional structures while confronting serious financial, logistical, and administrative difficulties, including the mammoth task of creating a coherent political unit out of a country divided into two noncontiguous wings separated by a thousand miles of Indian territory. Hence the League's leadership could not completely wipe the slate clean and create a state de novo. Despite this, Pakistan was not destined to go down the authoritarian path. In fact, the country's persistent inability to establish democratic civil-military relations stands in sharp contrast to neighboring India, which attained statehood in the same world-historical context and with a similar colonial institutional inheritance. India is a consolidated political democracy with firm civilian control of the armed forces, however.[8]

Although these two countries differed in many aspects (for example, geography, population size, and the dominant religion), they also had several political and institutional commonalities. Both had high levels of economic inequality and low levels of per capita income and were ethnically heterogeneous. The two new states were born with a common constitutional framework, the civil service, the judiciary, and the military. The two militaries inherited the same organizational structure, bureaucratic norms, fighting doctrines, training regimes, and, above all, a belief that the military and civilians had separate jurisdictions of responsibility that neither should breach. The critical juncture of decolonization and independence provided the nationalist elites in both states with the rare (even if differently restricted) opportunity to remake the colonially bequeathed state or at least restrain its coercive apparatus with the rule of law.[9]

In order to understand why Pakistan failed to turn this burden of newness into sustainable democratic political institutions and processes, it is necessary to discard "the myth of exaggerated continuity between the late years of colonial rule and the early years of independent power."[10]

The perceived security threat from India combined with the internal conflict arising from nation-state building to increase the salience of coercion in governance. This reliance on coercion spurred the early development of the military institution at the expense of civilian political institutions. The process unfolded in at least two overlapping stages. First, the perceived threat of imminent war from militarily stronger India led the founding political leaders to subordinate the needs of society to the needs of the soldier.[11] As they diverted precious resources away from national economic development to warfare and granted the military professional autonomy, the institutions of civilian oversight languished while the otherwise inchoate ex-colonial military rapidly reconstituted, unified, and modernized itself, a process enabled by Cold War security assistance from the United States.

Second, the founding fathers attempted to craft a viable nation-state (partly out of the fear that India would seek to undo Pakistan) by imposing a policy of national homogenization on a multiethnic society, which quickly politicized ethnic and linguistic cleavages. Rather than finding a constitutional power-sharing solution for peaceful accommodation of these cleavages, they retained the highly centralized viceregal system, with an unelected governor general wielding emergency powers, a centralized and powerful civil service, and a weak legislature,[12] ostensibly for reasons of state. The result was the suppression of regional demands for cultural recognition, political representation, and equitable resource distribution, especially in East Pakistan. But the more the state centralized and concentrated its authority, the more it diminished provincial autonomy, which prompted demands for radical decentralization that, in turn, fomented center-province conflict and delayed the process of constitution making.

The Pakistani military had inherited an apolitical professionalism from the British Indian Army. Professionalism stressed high standards of discipline, strict hierarchy, regimental loyalty, and obedience to legally constituted authorities. But military officers (and civil servants) had also imbibed the colonial officials' view of nationalist politicians as untrustworthy, good-for-nothing agitators.[13] Another associated legacy was their strong preference for the viceregal system as the guarantor of internal security and social order.[14] However, these authoritarian colonial attitudes were not sufficient in themselves to have caused the military to intervene in politics. After all, the Indian army had inherited identical beliefs about the nature of professionalism and politicians. To understand the origins of the Pakistani army's involvement in politics, we need to look at the interaction of military institutional variables with the political system. As I explain in Chapters 1 and 2, it was the military's swift institutional evolution within the context of a divided polity under external duress that reinforced its members' inherited distrust of politicians and led senior officers to question the feasibility of the norm of strict aloofness from politics. As they became better organized, better trained, and better equipped, military officers started to contrast their professional achievements with what they saw as the laggard pace of political development and deepening internal divisions. In other words, the military's success in overcoming its acute organizational problems sharpened the difference between its self-image as a cohesive professional institution and its pessimistic view of politics as divisive and parochial.[15]

Samuel Huntington held that by definition, professionalism enhances military political abstinence because it gives the soldiers the autonomy needed to focus on the state's external enemies, which fosters apolitical attitudes and behavior in the officer corps.[16] But as Samuel Finer and others have noted, professionalization provides militaries with internal cohesion, distinct ideologies, and a corporate identity as the servants of the permanent state rather than the government of the day. The professional military's belief in this manifest destiny motivates it to intervene and save the nation whenever it deems that corrupt or incompetent civilian authorities are under-mining the national interest—a set of beliefs that clearly attenuates the scope of control by temporary civilian politicians.[17]

In other words, professional development did not depoliticize the Pakistani military. Instead, it aroused the military's interest in civilian affairs and spurred members of the senior officer corps, led by the commander in chief, General Mohammad Ayub Khan (1951–1959), to voluntarily assume the obligation of properly organizing political society and the state. The military was initially content with playing the role of the stabilizing power behind the throne.[18] Put simply, its main goal was to prevent politicians and a parliamen-tary form of government from destroying the only "focal point of authority"—the viceregal executive—which Ayub and his generals thought would be a prelude to national disintegration. Much like its counterparts in Asian and Latin American militaries during the Cold War, the Pakistani military leadership believed that central-ized authority was key to nation building because it could ensure uniform political and economic modernization of society, which would then deprive venal politicians of the opportunity to exploit people's ethnic sentiments. The military finally set aside constitu-tional government and seized control of the state in October 1958 when it determined that continuing with parliamentary government would only bring more chaos rather than solving national prob-lems.[19] The military subsequently established a government, which was justified in its members' eyes, "in support of modernization and against political confusion."[20]

An Institution of the State

At its core, this book is about institutions, particularly the military as an institution of the state. Within that institution, it is about the officer corps and its senior leadership, which makes the most impor-tant institutional decisions during both war and peace, which the rank and file are, at least in theory, duty bound to carry out. No less important, the high command is the public face and voice of the institution because it "represents the military as a whole . . . [and] articulates its views and conveys its needs to state and society."[21]

In general, institutions wield and distribute power among political and social groups, creating winners and losers who act in their self-interest.[22] But institutions are also agents of assimilation and socialization. They can incorporate and socialize individuals into norms, or "shared expectations about appropriate behavior amongst a community of actors."[23] Thus, institutions can exercise considerable power by shaping their members' interpretations of the world and by identifying both the members' collective ends and the proper means to pursue them. These "logics of appropriateness" can often act as rules that guide the behavior of the members of a group or organization by making certain actions or choices appear legitimate while constraining others or simply filtering them out as improper.[24] Because institutions control these codes of conduct, they can align individual preferences with institutional priorities and thus minimize the scope for internal division and contradictions.

When the institution is as disciplined, regimented, and total as a modern professional military, these behavioral norms can play an even larger role in guiding its political behavior.[25] To varying degrees, a "pervasive characteristic of the military is that it is a profession which regulates the total life cycle and the daily cycle of its members."[26] More than any other organization, modern professional militaries have the capacity to resocialize recruits into a new worldview. This involves changing their behavior and ideas by creating a break with past experience and imposing the learning of new norms and standards of behavior. Hence recruits are stripped of their individuality and given a new institutional identity (represented by identical uniforms, haircuts, and other symbols) that comes with a set of mutual expectations. Typically, professional militaries inculcate a strong sense of nationalism, institutional loyalty, and cohesion.[27] In the words of Elizabeth Kier, "Few organizations devote as many resources to the assimilation of their members. The emphasis on ceremony and tradition, and the development of a common language and *esprit de corps,* testify to the strength of the military's organizational culture."[28]

This process of assimilation is continuous. Militaries invest an enormous amount of resources and effort in constantly reinforcing dominant institutional beliefs and values. Throughout soldiers' careers, and especially through advanced training at the senior levels, "politically relevant attitudes are purposefully learned, implicitly instilled, and latently internalized,"[29] creating incomparably strong pressures for conformity with the established institutional thinking. Put differently, modern, hierarchically led militaries restrict deviance not just by the threat or use of punishment and sanction but also by producing voluntary compliance through identity or role-based obligations and expectations.

Hence I aim to examine and explain military politics in Pakistan from the neglected viewpoint of the military's belief system, what is commonly known as the military mind-set or the military mentality.[30] What beliefs do members of the military hold about their proper role and function in the state and civilian politics? Do they perceive democratic institutions as inherently or as conditionally legitimate? Do they consider military intervention in politics an appropriate response to perceived civilian failures or threats to military interests? How do these norms or codes of conduct, in turn, shape the military's relationship with elected governments and condition its institutional responses to major political events, regime changes, or crises?

To examine these questions, I use valuable but underutilized military sources, including extensive interviews, professional publications,[31] and, notably, the professional journal, training curricula, research papers, and strategy documents of the military's premier war college, the National Defence University (NDU).[32] The NDU is significant for understanding the institutional norms of military tutelage in Pakistan because it constitutes the "highest forum where the military leadership comes together for common instruction."[33] Without graduating from the NDU (or a foreign equivalent), no officer can become a general.[34] Besides, the NDU training program represents a radical shift from the emphasis on operational and staff functions in the training of junior officers (for example, majors at the Staff College) to educating colonels and brigadiers about a broad range of strategic political, social, and economic factors as they affect national security.[35] In that sense, it constitutes the senior officer corps's baptism into a shared ideological framework about the military's appropriate role, status, and behavior in relation to state and society. These shared values affect how these officers perceive and respond to civilian governmental decisions, policies, and political crises.

By peeping inside the black box, we can assess how the military's particular conceptions of professionalism shape its involvement in politics. Except for Stephen P. Cohen's classic study,[36] very rarely have scholars illuminated military politics in Pakistan from the perspective of the military institution.

In this book I also discuss and contribute to the literature on civil-military relations. First, I apply insights from sociological institutionalism to the study of military politics, typically studied either through rational choice or institutionalist theories, which ignore the "logics of appropriateness" that define bureaucratic-organizational interests and shape how organizations interact with their larger institutional and social surroundings.[37]

Second, scholarly analyses of the linkage between external threats and civilian control of the armed forces fall into two contrasting camps. The first one is based on the Lasswellian garrison-state argument that security threats and crises can "subdue civilians and pass all powers to the generals,"[38] which foreshadows my analysis of the Pakistani military's formative organizational experience. However, drawing on the work of Stanislav Andreski,[39] the conventional wisdom in the more recent political science literature is that external security threats result in civilian supremacy over the military. According to Samuel Huntington, "From the standpoint of civilian control, happy is the country with a traditional enemy."[40] The logic is that when a mortal enemy is knocking on the gates, civilians and the military unite to fight it. As a result, the military focuses exclusively on external defense as long as civilians supply it with the resources necessary to carry out its mission.[41]

How are we to reconcile these two divergent interpretations? Pakistan's experience suggests that these two threat-based theories of the relationship between the soldier and the state might lack a crucial intervening variable: national unity. I contend that especially during the early stages of state formation, external threats can be unifying or divisive depending on the degree of antecedent domestic cohesion.[42] Put simply, the greater the shared sense of political community, the more likely it is that harsh security environments will unify civilian and military elites across the board and focus the military outward and away from society.

This investigation also has implications for civil-military politics in new or fragile democracies. Pakistan's experience suggests the importance of making a distinction between removing the military from politics and "removing politics from the military."[43] It underscores the negative importance of entrenched military traditions of tutelage as a barrier to any process of sustained democratization in countries that are making the difficult transition from militarized authoritarian rule, such as Egypt and Burma. Besides other political or institutional factors, the nondemocratic values, norms, and beliefs of the officer corps pose a serious danger to the prospects of democracy in these countries in the long haul.

I also address issues that have profound implications for regional and international security. To compensate for Pakistan's conventional military weaknesses, the Pakistani military has long provided material assistance and training to Islamist militants to fight India in Kashmir and to gain regional influence in Afghanistan. Although this policy may have provided some illusory military dividends by tying down Indian security forces in Kashmir, because it has given militant groups the space, resources, and autonomy to operate freely inside Pakistan, its costs have been much higher, and its presumed utility has sharply declined.[44] Not only has this policy triggered a more offensive Indian military buildup, but also terrorist attacks by Pakistani militant groups in India have raised the risk of a wider interstate conflict. Besides, militant groups like the Tehrike Taliban Pakistan have undermined the Pakistani state's monopoly over coercion and have terrorized Pakistani society. Over 45,000 Pakistani civilians and security personnel have been killed in terrorist attacks since 2004.[45] However, military officers' writings—solicited and published by the high command—continue to advocate the utility of asymmetric warfare[46] through using mujahideen as a necessary bulwark against Indian military superiority,[47] clearly demonstrating that institutional wisdom can be resistant to change even after returns on a policy start to diminish and the costs of pursuing it become high.

Controlling Coercion

If democracy is a governmental form whose necessary (but not sufficient) condition is the exercise of popularly delegated power by elected officials who are accountable only to the people, the military must be subordinate to the democratic political leadership.[48] It is possible for a country to have civilian control of the military without democracy (for example, China, Cuba, and the former USSR). But democracy is impossible without civilian control.[49] Civilian democratic control is rooted in a set of norms and institutions that designate the proper functions and missions of the military and the conditions under which it may exercise those functions.[50] The point of civilian control is to make "security subordinate to the larger purposes of the nation, not the other way around."[51] Together, the rules and norms that constitute civilian control are meant to act as a barrier to block military interference in politics.[52] In practice, this means that democratically elected leaders exercise de facto and de jure control over the military in matters of national policy, including external security (defense policy, weapons acquisition, and force structure) and military corporate autonomy (budgets, personnel policy, and training). But there is no obvious or inevitable reason that those who are lethally armed with guns must obey those without them.[53] Any armed force that is strong enough to deter external aggression or an internal insurrection against a state is strong enough to capture it.[54]

Hence, in addition to the structures and rules that regulate the military, civilian democratic control is predicated on voluntary military allegiance and subordination to the democratically elected government. As Robert Dahl observes, "Polyarchy is impossible unless the military is sufficiently depoliticized to permit civilian rule," and "The chances of polyarchy are directly dependent on the strength of certain beliefs . . . among all ranks of the military . . . [namely,] political neutrality, constitutionalism and obedience to civilian authority."[55]

In an important wide-ranging study that examines civil-military relations in Asia, Africa, Europe, and the Americas, Zoltan Barany reaffirms the importance of voluntary military restraint, arguing that "democracy cannot be consolidated without military elites committed to democratic rule and obedient to democratically elected political elites."[56] Similarly, as Richard Kohn has noted, "Civilian [democratic] control requires a military establishment trained, committed, and dedicated to political neutrality, that shuns under all circumstances any interference with the constitutional functioning or legitimate process of government, that identifies itself as the embodiment of the people and the nation, and that defines into its professionalism unhesitating loyalty to the system of government and obedience to whomever exercises legal authority."[57]

In a democracy, militaries can be trained to obey civilian authorities or prevented from interfering in politics by subjecting them to the certainty of legal accountability or the threat of countervailing force. But because it is often the most lethally armed organization in the state, its members cannot always be forced to submit to the will of the unarmed politician. Instead, armies "obey their civilian masters for the simple reason that they consider them to be the legitimate rulers of the state, and believe this to be, quite simply, the right thing to do," regardless of the way in which "state and society treat the military."[58] In other words, "Whether or not military officers would face dismissal or prison, they choose to submit, to define their duty as advice to civilian bosses rather than advocacy, and to carry out all lawful orders effectively and without complaint."[59] If Dahl, Kohn, Barany, and others are right, the exercise of civilian democratic control ultimately depends on the military's willingness to submit to democratic norms rather than the actual mechanics of civilian control.

History, Politics, and the Military in Pakistan

Because of a bitter rivalry in the decade before independence, Pakistan's founding Muslim League leadership, led by Jinnah, suspected that the Congress government of India viewed the creation of Pakistan as a "temporary recession of certain territories from India which would soon be reabsorbed."[60] The onset of the territorial conflict between the two countries over the princely state of Kashmir, which sparked military hostilities in 1947–1948, turned this suspicion into deep insecurity, further complicated by irredentist Afghan claims on Pakistan's northwestern territories.[61] More than any other factor, the conflict with India shaped the initial trajectory of Pakistan's civil-military relations.[62] It spurred the militarization of the Pakistani state in the early years and thus provided the context in which the generals could increase their influence in domestic politics and national security policy without leaving the barracks. As state building and survival became synonymous with the war effort, the civilian leadership diverted scarce resources from development to defense[63] and abdicated its responsibility of oversight over the military, thereby allowing the generals a virtual free hand over internal organizational affairs and national security management. Thus, to paraphrase Charles Tilly, war made a war-making state.[64]

Reinforcing the emergence of this warring state was an equally crucial political handicap: Pakistan lacked the background condition that makes democracy (and, by implication, civilian democratic control of the military) possible: national unity.[65] In the words of

Christophe Jaffrelot, Pakistan's was a "nationalism without a nation."[66] Pakistan emerged from British colonial rule with a deep ethnic diversity that overlapped with its geographic division into two wings, West Pakistan and East Pakistan. West Pakistan (or, more precisely, the Urdu-speaking migrants or Muhajirs from northern and western India and the Punjabis) dominated the central government and its institutions, while East Pakistan had a territorially concentrated Bengali majority that was excluded from the armed forces and the civil bureaucracy.[67] But the Bengalis were intensely proud of their linguistic heritage and had an established tradition of seeking cultural autonomy through agitational politics.[68] Independence provided "a brief moment of political unity."[69] However, as I explain later, the West Pakistani elites' desire to integrate the Bengalis and other smaller West Pakistani ethnic groups (Pashtuns, Sindhis, and the Baloch) into the nation-state by using coercion while denying the legitimacy of all claims for political representation, participation, and regional autonomy based on subnational identities led to the centralization of power, which decreased provincial autonomy and further strained the internal cohesion that can facilitate the crafting of democratic institutions.

Scholars have argued that external danger provides a powerful stimulus for internal unity by strengthening group consciousness and the awareness of separateness.[70] But as Lewis Coser pointed out decades ago, "when cohesion is weak, when there is little willing acceptance of authority because of the weakness of internal solidarity," conflict is unlikely to have an integrative effect on society.[71] In other words, the unifying effect of conflict with out-groups may depend on some degree of prior internal cohesion, integration, and identification with the state. In the absence of national solidarity, especially at the early stages of state formation, external conflict is less likely to unite elites in defense of the nation and keep the military away from politics because some institutions or groups may perceive the threat differently than others. Under such conditions, elites in control of the state will have the incentive to resort to repression to achieve regime or state consolidation, thus creating early precedents for justifying actions that violate democratic political procedures, which undermine state legitimacy and make achieving national cohesion even more difficult. In fact, as I show in subsequent discussion, ethnic divisions between West and East Pakistan (as well as within West Pakistan) limited the prospects of a unified response to external danger, which raised fears among civilian and military elites that external enemies could exploit internal disunity, which spurred the imposition of emergency measures to maintain what they perceived to be national security, which in turn alienated the Bengalis and ultimately led to the breakup of the state in 1971. It would be reasonable to argue that had Pakistan's civilian and military leaders not followed these myopic authoritarian policies and managed to hold on to East Pakistan by democratically accommodating Bengali grievances, the country's political history would likely have been quite different.[72]

Political scientists have long considered strong political parties crucial to regime stability and consolidation. In particular, parties with stable societal support and robust organizational structures have the capability to moderate and mediate social conflict peacefully.[73] The Muslim League had weak social and organizational roots in Pakistan.[74] Hence its leadership's ability to govern by consent was complicated by the existential political threat stemming from the numerical logic of electoral democracy that favored the Bengalis.[75] Rather than pursuing state-nation policies that could help the development of "multiple and complementary identities" and accommodate distinct ethnic and cultural groups within a democratic federal framework, Pakistan's founding elites followed nation-state policies designed to create a single nation congruent with the political boundaries of the state, albeit for reasons of state or political expediency.[76] However, this national unification project only exacerbated "the chasm between the ideology and sociology" of Pakistan, especially by politicizing Bengali identity.[77] For instance, even though 98 percent of the majority Bengalis (54.5 percent of the total population) spoke Bengali, the central government denied that language the national status it deserved and imposed Urdu (the first language of roughly 4 percent of the total population) as the sole state language immediately after independence, thus sparking a language movement in East Pakistan as early as 1948.

The colonially inherited ethnic imbalance in the military further exacerbated the sense of Bengali exclusion. Before independence, the Punjab accounted for more than 77 percent of military recruitment from the areas that became Pakistan, the North-West Frontier Province for 19.5 percent, and the Bengalis for less than 3 percent.[78] After independence, the government tried to enhance Bengali recruitment in the army but abandoned its efforts primarily because "there was strong resistance within the Pakistan Army to greatly expanding East Bengali representation," based on a pervasive "distaste for the qualities of the [nonmartial] Bengali officers and other ranks."[79]

Seeking to consolidate state authority, Jinnah and his successors found a ready-made governing formula in the iron fist of viceregalism. Backed by the military, the viceregal executive sacked noncompliant civilian cabinets (1953), delayed constitution making, disbanded the central legislature (Constituent Assembly) when it crafted a federal democratic constitution (1954), removed an elected government in East Pakistan (1954), and ultimately amalgamated the provinces of West Pakistan into what is called One Unit to create parity with East Pakistan (1955–1956). As governmental legitimacy was eviscerated under the heavy burden of authoritarian centralization, especially in East Pakistan, the emerging guardians of national security in the military developed serious doubts about the appropriateness and feasibility of parliamentary democracy in a fragile polity threatened by external threat and internal dissension. By the early 1950s, the military under its first Pakistani commander in chief, General Ayub Khan, had dropped its pretense of political neutrality and was no longer concerned merely with protecting its autonomy or budgets. Instead, the generals (and influential civilian bureaucrats) began to envisage a new form of "controlled" democracy "suited to the genius" of the Pakistani people.[80]

Institutional developments within the military had important consequences for civilian politics because they reinforced the officer corps' emerging tutelary mentality. Starting in the early 1950s, the military underwent a formative process of institutional transformation from an ex-colonial army into a national army with its own corporate identity and ethos. This process of institutional development was further spurred by military training, expertise, and armaments Pakistan received for allying with the United States to contain the threat of Soviet expansionism. This aid increased the capabilities of Pakistan's small army, including its firepower, mobility, capacity for multiterrain operations, and command and control, and thereby boosted the military's already high confidence in itself.[81] This rapid military professionalization also conflicted sharply with the perceived failure and instability of civilian politics, especially the inability of politicians to craft an appropriate political system that would ensure national harmony and economic development. The high command believed that only a united and prosperous Pakistan could stand up to India and blunt the chances of the external (Indian) abetment of internal strife.[82] Thus American Cold War security assistance contributed to fanning the army's tutelary ambitions by rapidly modernizing it. This modernization reinforced the soldiers' belief in the superiority of their skills over those of civilian politicians and was crucial to the high command's decision to expand into an array of civilian roles and functions. Initially, the military called the shots under the cover of a Janowitzian civil-military coalition formally headed by the governor general.[83]

After Pakistan's first constitution came into force in March 1956, the military feared that it was only a matter of time before national elections installed a government of autonomist Bengalis and their West Pakistani allies.[84] In October 1958, the military demolished the constitutional order and established a "preventive autocracy"[85] to put an end to what it described as irrationality, chastise the selfish politicians, and set Pakistan on the right path of political development and modernization. In the words of one former army chief of general staff, the "concept of takeover to improve the country" had become part of the "army's DNA" by 1958.[86]

Ever since, the Pakistani military has evinced only conditional acceptance of political processes or democratic norms, has viewed itself as the balancing wheel for keeping the system in alignment, and has frequently intervened to seize control of the government when civilian politicians undermine the supreme national interest as defined (vaguely) and defended by the army. Since independence, the military has ruled directly for more than three decades (1958–1971 under Generals Ayub Khan and Yahya Khan, 1977–1988 under General Ziaul Haq, and 1999–2007 under General Pervez Musharraf) and has wielded decisive political influence behind the scenes for the rest of the time, thus practically making civilian control nonexistent. In fact, it has acquired and exercises prerogatives over an expansively defined national security arena that includes military personnel policy, professional training, budgets, arms procurement, force structure and deployments, nuclear doctrines, and intelligence gathering. Not only does the military claim a large chunk of the national budget (4.5 percent of GDP on average between 1995 and 2009)[87] without any meaningful civilian oversight, but it has also used its privileged position in the state to appropriate public resources (for example, in the form of concessionary land grants for officers' housing societies and subsidies for its welfare foundations) and to expand its commercial and business interests into vital sectors of the economy.[88]

The military's key institutional instrument for exercising and maintaining its prerogatives in national security and domestic politics is its premier intelligence agency, the Inter-Services Intelligence Directorate (or, more commonly, Inter-Services Intelligence, ISI).[89] Its known political role dates back to the Ayub Khan era (1958–1969), when he placed his "total reliance on ISI for internal as well as external intelligence" and used it to keep a "watch on political activities" and evaluate public opinion.[90] The ISI's organization, resources, and influence received a major boost in the 1980s during its cooperation with the US Central Intelligence Agency (CIA) in the jihad against the Soviets in Afghanistan. Ever since, it has evolved into a feared and formidable organization with deep influence over and involvement in civilian politics, which has impaired the rule of law, undermined the development of civilian intelligence institutions, and distorted civilian-military relations.[91]

Unlike the relatively autonomous Chilean Directorate of National Intelligence (Dirección de Inteligencia Nacional) under Augusto Pinochet[92] or the National Information Service (Serviço Nacional de Informações) under authoritarian rule in Brazil, which became centers of power parallel to the military institution, the ISI is part of and works on behalf of the army high command, led by the chief of the army staff. The other difference is that these other intelligence agencies were created for the explicit purpose of dealing with internal subversion and were disbanded after the end of military rule. The ISI's official purview, on the other hand, includes both external and internal threats. Headed by an active-duty army officer of the rank of lieutenant general (or, previously, brigadier or major general), the ISI has advanced the political agenda of the high command by destabilizing elected governments, inducing defections in political parties through bribery and blackmail, creating kings' (or progovernment) parties for military governments to organize their supporters, and rigging elections to legitimate military rule. The Afghan jihad also taught the ISI the "effectiveness of covert warfare for bleeding a stronger adversary, while maintaining the element of plausible deniability."[93] Since the outbreak of the insurgency in Indian Kashmir in 1989, the ISI has redirected its skills, resources, and allied militant groups to fight a low-intensity conflict against Indian security forces in the disputed state.

The Pakistani Military's Professionalism and Politics

Like other professional armies, the Pakistani army is a disciplined institution with a clear chain of command and fairly standardized bureaucratic criteria for the recruitment and promotion of officers. It also has a well-organized schooling system with dedicated staff and specialized syllabi that trains officers for promotion to the next stage of their careers,[94] well-planned annual training cycles, and a well-developed general staff that supervises, coordinates, and controls these activities. Passing through this highly structured professional cycle of training and development tends to instill a sense of professional accomplishment in army officers that, they consider, is unmatched by civilian institutions or politicians.

Taught identical curricula at each stage of their careers, officers tend to hold fairly predictable views about the army's proper institutional role in domestic politics, national security, and nation building. Although these views may be colored by an officer's ethnic origins, social ties, political affiliations, or even personal ambition, the history of the Pakistani military in politics and the uniformity of views expressed by officers show that the sense of institutional unity, loyalty, and purpose instilled by professional indoctrination, especially against the threat from India, and the guardian role in which it casts the army can often be a more powerful indicator of officers' political preferences and behavior than other factors. Crisis situations, like periods of political disorder or perceived threats to institutional integrity that might precede a coup, can also generate pressures for total conformity with command decisions and subdue any residual differences of opinion in the interest of the institution. Once the perceived crisis conditions dissipate, these differences can reemerge and are typically expressed in divisions between the military government and the military institution (for example, the clear disunity between members of the officer corps and senior officers of General Yahya Khan's military junta due to the defeat in the 1971 war with India and the creation of Bangladesh out of East Pakistan).

However, given the conjuncture of such factors as the precedent of past intervention, frequent military socialization into civilian governance (from direct participation in government to conducting the national census and police training when out of government), well-articulated and enforced regimens of professional assimilation and indoctrination, and a clear and present external security mission, members of the officer corps have come to internalize norms that support the army's dual role as a permanent guardian and an interim governor when certain exceptional conditions, such as political disorder, economic crises, or perceived direct threats to its organizational integrity justify the latter. By rationalizing and legitimizing the role of the armed forces as the ultimate arbiter of the national interest, these norms make military role expansion standard and appropriate for its members. By the same token, they militate against permanent army rule. Like military organizations elsewhere, the Pakistan military is not immune to disagreement in its ranks. It is much easier to rally the military by invoking threats to the national or institutional interest posed by, say, incompetent politicians. However, it is relatively more difficult to indefinitely maintain a consensus regarding a sustained stay in power when the military is directly governing the state.[95] Therefore, whenever the military's public reputation and prestige are in jeopardy on account of its direct control of government, the institutional imperative of self-preservation drives the military back to the barracks. In other words, there is no organizational ideology that supports permanent control over politics because that orientation not only lacks broader legitimacy in society but also conflicts with the military's primary mission: fighting wars.

As stated earlier, these tutelary norms are continually reinforced through professional socialization and selection processes that consistently communicate an institutionally approved or correct interpretation of the military's purpose and mission, as well as critical past and current events affecting the institution and the country. Like members of many other professional militaries, Pakistani officers typically see the army and Pakistan as interchangeable, and any civilian challenge or affront to the military is almost instinctively perceived as a threat to the national interest. In other words, the interests of the military become inseparable from those of the nation.[96]

By the very nature of the military profession, army officers have nationalism drilled into them and are trained to fight the enemies of the nation. The security threat from India has long been an important source of institutional cohesion in the Pakistani army that has helped it avoid the factionalism that typically engulfs militaries during or after interventions in politics. With rare exceptions, Pakistani officers have traditionally perceived India as the primary external enemy, officially portrayed in military publications and other officer writings as a venal and hostile Hindu power that seeks to establish its hegemony in the region and remains unreconciled to the existence of Pakistan.[97] For instance, at the NDU, officer students typically characterize Pakistan as a unique, strategically located Muslim state under threat from a belligerent India (with the growing collusion of extraregional forces, that is, American troops on the country's western border seeking to undermine Pakistan's integrity and deprive it of its nuclear arsenal).[98] In this scheme of things, the military is the center of gravity that ensures the survival and stability of Pakistan through a tripartite defense policy: conventional force, nuclear deterrence, and asymmetric jihadi warfare.[99]

The NDU, unlike the higher war colleges of other politicized militaries, such as the National Defense Institute in Indonesia under Suharto, does not impart an ideology of enduring military control of domestic politics.[100] When the military is directly ruling, however, the institutional environment for discussing and writing about military participation, control, and reform of civilian government is relatively more permissive.[101] In fact, during Musharraf's government, the teaching staff at the NDU encouraged officers to formulate a national reform agenda to implement the army's seven-point formula for salvaging Pakistan, which included such items as creating national cohesion, removing provincial disharmony, devolving power to the local levels, and depoliticizing the bureaucracy.[102]

Most officers are prone to view politicians as knaves or fools. They are also generally skeptical of the appropriateness of majoritarian parliamentary democracy in an illiterate society where "conniving" and "self-interested" politicians can simply dupe, bribe, or coerce the common Pakistani to vote for them. Therefore, they tend to strongly favor proper checks and balances on popularly elected prime ministers, especially via presidents with discretionary powers. Beyond formal socialization, these opinions demonstrate the legacy of the organization's formative experience, which was shaped and interpreted by its first Pakistani commander in chief, General (and later Field Marshal) Ayub Khan, who was able to imprint his negative assessment of traditional parliamentary politics and the virtues of presidential government on the army in the first two decades of independence, with profound consequences for subsequent generations of officers. A more recent interpretation of the proper institutional mechanism for organizing civil-military relations, traceable to the Zia period, is that civilian politicians and institutions lack the capability to lead and to anticipate threats; hence Pakistan requires institutionalized arrangements for defense policy management, such as a National Security Council.[103] The council, in the opinion of Musharraf and many other senior officers, can also check military intervention by giving the military a seat at the table—in other words, keeping them out by keeping them in.

Besides the effects of the institutionalized process of total socialization, the bureaucratic system of army promotions also encourages the dominance of certain institutionally enforced ideological perspectives on politics, which generally coincide with the current political role of the army (that is, whether it is in or out of government). Although impersonal criteria of merit and performance constitute the formal bases for promotions after the rank of major, informal influences, such as personal, family, or cohort connections and fealty to senior officers, are not uncommon, especially in the higher ranks.[104] Moreover, officers who are promoted select and promote others like them and thus perpetuate a "zero-error syndrome" that leaves little room for dissent, initiative, or creativity as yardsticks for upward mobility.[105]

Indoctrination and selection, in turn, aid in the coordination of collective action by providing templates for proper behavior.[106] In other words, they act as "uncertainty absorbers,"[107] especially under such crisis conditions as military coups, because there are "fewer distortions in the flow of information as both the sender and the recipient of the message share common understandings."[108] Although different officers or groups of officers may have diverse (or even mixed) motives for supporting a coup, such as ethnic loyalties, social background, or fear of retribution, the underlying glue in an institutional coup is the broad agreement that things have gone haywire in the political system or society, that irregular or nondemocratic political change is legitimate, and that the military has the duty to act as the final arbiter of the national interest. In many Latin American countries, for instance, the military's position as the ultimate defender of both national security and the constitution legitimized the belief among the military (and many civilians) that the soldier could not simply wait on the sidelines when an elected president or the government abused its powers or failed to uphold the constitutional order.[109] A recent example is the Egyptian military's ouster of the country's elected president, Mohammad Morsi, in July 2013. Backed by secular opposition parties and their supporters, the chief of the Egyptian army, General Abdel-Fattah al-Sisi, attributed the intervention to Morsi's violation of the public mandate, alleged abuse of power, and clashes with state institutions, including the armed forces, pleading that the armed forces could not be silent spectators and had to side with the Egyptian public in standing up to a regime that had lost its legitimacy.[110]

When asked about the motives behind active or passive individual participation in the 1999 military coup, the Pakistani officers I interviewed invariably replied that disobeying orders was not an option that crossed their minds. In fact, some two-thirds claimed that they were performing their professional duty to the nation and saw nothing wrong with the military uprooting a corrupt and inefficient, if popularly elected, government that had, in their view, abused public authority, had undermined national institutions, and wanted to do the same to the armed forces of Pakistan because of political motives. Moreover, they knew that their comrades in arms would not hesitate for a second to implement the orders of their superiors.[111] Military coups in Pakistan have succeeded only when they have been led from the top. The soldiers have respected the military chain of command even when they have repeatedly violated the constitutional one.

Pull and Push

Because of the Pakistani army's pivotal position in the US-led fight against Islamist terrorism, it has received considerable attention from journalists, government officials, policy analysts, and scholars. For instance, Pakistani journalist and former ambassador Husain Haqqani has skillfully analyzed the military's role in both domestic politics and foreign policy in the context of its ties to Islamic extremism and Islamist parties.[112] Similarly, the police officer–turned-scholar Hassan Abbas has framed his useful study of growing Islamic extremism in Pakistan in relation to the army's well-known policies and US-Pakistan relations.[113] The political analyst Shuja Nawaz's tome on the Pakistani army is rich in historical descriptions of its nature and role in both war and politics.[114] British journalist and author Anatol Lieven's book rightly dispels the notion widespread in Western media and policy circles that Pakistan is on the brink of an Islamist revolution, but he also grossly understates the army's role in enfeebling Pakistan's political, administrative, and economic institutions in order to advance the view (shared by the generals) that theirs is the only organized and stable state institution holding this "hard" country together.[115] Although each of these studies has its merits, none of them are grounded in a coherent theoretical framework about the political role of the military institution.[116]

Scholarly explanations of military intervention in politics involve both pull and push factors, or opportunity and motive. Explicitly theoretical analyses of the Pakistani military's political role suffer from two general problems. First, most studies typically privilege nonmilitary factors that neatly map onto variables identified in the social science literature, such as colonial legacies,[117] culture,[118] social structure,[119] and political decay due to politicians' infighting, performance failures, or a weak founding party.[120] Some of these factors, in varying degrees, no doubt play an important part in military politics. For instance, it is difficult to dispute that fragile or unstable political institutions create the opportunity for military forays into politics.[121] But these constant structures cannot sufficiently explain military behavior, or, more precisely, variation in military behavior, that is, why militaries capture and then yield power. If, for instance, Islam or the presumably feudal social structure in Pakistan supports authoritarian rule, or if the military protects the class interests of repressive Punjabi landlords, why does it ever extricate itself from government, given that these structures and objective class interests are not readily mutable?

It does so because the label *Homo politicus* applies to the soldiers as much as it does to the politicians they overthrow.[122] Like other professional militaries, the Pakistani army is a corporate entity with identifiable ideas, distinct interests, and specific organizational goals that clearly separate and distinguish it from politicians and even society at large. If nothing else, the military's control over the most lethal coercive resources of the state endows it with the capability to advance those ideas and interests in the political arena, for instance, by setting the political agenda or vetoing policy decisions and thus shaping the incentives and inclinations of other social and political groups.[123]

The point is that the military institution is an "actor in its own right, which cannot be understood as a reflection of societal characteristics and preferences."[124] However, scholars like Ayesha Siddiqa and Mazhar Aziz, who concede the Pakistani military's relative autonomy, typically and unproblematically conceive it as a utility-maximizing agent, and in the case of Siddiqa, even a predatory class, that meddles in politics mainly to protect or advance its financial autonomy and expansive commercial interests.[125] Although militaries in many countries (for example, Nigeria, Thailand, and Indonesia) have owned companies and provided opportunities for personal enrichment, military professionals are "neither capitalists nor workers."[126]

In fact, they are more accurately identified as, and see themselves as, classless. In Pakistan, the military has no doubt developed extensive commercial and economic stakes that contribute to its political meddling and influence. However, the greedy-general story says little about the historical origins of the Pakistani military's involvement in politics since the early 1950s. What Siddiqa calls "Military Inc." was at best in rudimentary form in that period. Aziz admits the role of the subjective perceptions of the armed forces in conditioning its interventions but ultimately turns to rational-choice theory or "the safeguarding of institutional interests of the armed forces" as "a central factor in triggering military intervention."[127]

A less convincing but by no means less common argument favored by army officers, popular writers, and some analysts is that military interventions in Pakistan result from the ambitions or interests of individual coup makers because the office of the chief of staff has too much power over the rank and file.[128] In other words, in the hands of a general inclined to carry out a coup, the army is an infinitely malleable instrument of personal will. Although individual interests may play a role in military intervention, "their explanatory importance is sharply reduced because they generally coincide with, and can often be realized through the activation of corporate interests."[129]

There is no denying that all modern militaries have certain minimum corporate interests and privileges they seek to preserve or enhance, including institutional survival and integrity, monopoly over force, adequate budgetary allocations, and autonomy in internal matters (such as promotions and appointments). But not all of them go about achieving their goals in the same way. It is the military's collective definition of its interests in a particular domestic and external setting that can make a difference in how it behaves. For instance, at the time of the first coup in 1958, the Pakistani army was well funded, well armed, and free from executive or parliamentary controls over its budgets and internal affairs. There were no rival armed militias threatening its monopoly over organized coercion. But it intervened anyway. In contrast, the Indian military remained politically quiescent despite unmet demands for equipment during the Sino-Indian War in 1962, the open politicization of military promotions and appointments (for instance, during the tenure of Defense Minister Krishna Menon from 1957 to 1962), and the creation or expansion of paramilitary forces. In fact, analogous conditions have triggered military interventions in other contexts, including closer to home in Bangladesh (1975) and beyond in Egypt (1952), Brazil (1964), and Ghana (1966).

In other words, military interests cannot be presumed a priori. Instead, military officers' understandings of what those interests are and the appropriate methods of pursuing them in a particular internal or international context can also shape their behavior.[130] In this book, I stress the neglected role of institutional norms and views. These condition military officers' responses to both the pull of broader structures and the push of corporate grievances.[131] Creating a more accurate picture of the military's role in politics warrants an analysis of the relative import of these different pull and push factors as "mediated through the eyes and ears of the men who decide whether to unlock the armory."[132]

Broadly speaking, some armies may stoically tolerate what others find offensive, not because they are indifferent to civilian performance failures or attacks on military autonomy but because their members believe that this is the way things ought to be done. In other words, political crises or budgetary cuts will likely increase the interventionist resolve of those armies, or groups and individuals within them, which consider civilian supremacy an undesirable or disposable principle or conceive of themselves as the permanent state's high priests who do not owe loyalty to transient civilian governments. To put it in the incisive language of E. E. Schattschneider, it is "futile to determine whether men are politically stimulated by interests or ideas, for people have ideas about interests."[133]

This book tells a chronological story, but it is not a history of the Pakistani military and its origins, evolution, or battlefield effectiveness.[134] Instead, its primary focus is the military's institutional role in politics during significant historical junctures, such as periods of regime change to and from authoritarian government. Drawing on new archival sources and interviews, I begin by tracing the origins of military authoritarianism in the formative decade after independence. The founding civilian political leaders made consequential nation-state-building choices as they sought to consolidate state authority under perceived external duress, and these choices stunted democratic development and sparked ethnolinguistic conflict between the center and East Pakistan that, in turn, fomented political instability. The state's preparation for imminent war with India, aided by US Cold War resources, developed and strengthened the military to the detriment of civilian political institutions and thus fostered a sense of superiority and accomplishment in the military that ultimately contributed to its decision to seize power in 1958 to stabilize and rationalize politics.

In Chapters 2 and 3, I examine how military habits of the mind were reinforced during the governments of Field Marshal Ayub Khan and General Yahya Khan in the context of continuing nation-building and security problems to prevent any radical institutional reinterpretation of the military's role in politics despite the bloody civil war in East Pakistan, the army's abysmal defeat in the 1971 war with India, the subsequent decapitation of the state, and the transfer of power from an utterly disgraced and demoralized army leadership to the Pakistan People's Party (PPP) under Zulfiqar Ali Bhutto. Chapter 4 closely examines the military's reassertion of political power when a government-opposition deadlock over the allegedly rigged 1977 election presented an opportunity. It shows how the military high command's interpretations of the actions and intentions of the Bhutto government, especially during the political crisis, shaped its decision to terminate the democratic transition by ousting the PPP government less than six years after Pakistan's first universally enfranchised election.

Chapters 5, 6, and 7 elucidate the role of institutional beliefs and motives in shaping the military's behavior during subsequent moments of transition from and to militarized authoritarian rule, including the military government of General Ziaul Haq (1977–1988), the subsequent transition to electoral democracy (1988–1999), the military's reentry into power under General Pervez Musharraf in October 1999, and its exit in 2007–2008. These transitional moments provide an understanding of the thinking of members of the higher officers corps about the military's appropriate institutional role in national security, governance, and democracy. I also take into account the increased importance of influential new centers of power in both state and society, such as the newly independent media and judiciary, to assess their impact on how the military exercises its political influence in the postauthoritarian context. Finally, I assess the prospects of democratic reforms in civil-military relations in Pakistan in a comparative perspective and briefly discuss the comparative implications of the study.

1

WAGING WAR, BUILDING A NATION

The military's political ascendance became a distinguishing feature of civilian politics in Pakistan within the first decade after independence. Thus any interpretation of the military's repeated and relentless interventions must reckon with that foundational juncture, "during which the state [institutional] structure was cast into an enduring, even rigid, mold."[1]

Pakistan was not originally destined for military intervention in politics. At independence, the Pakistani military was little more than a rump of the British Indian Army (BIA). Consumed by the process of organizational rebuilding in the wake of the BIA's partition into the two armies of India and Pakistan, the relatively young and inexperienced members of the officer corps were hardly in a position to mount a collective challenge to the nationalist leadership. In fact, almost the entire high command was British, and there was only one Pakistani army officer of the rank of two-star major general.[2]

Because of the political and constitutional nature of the nationalist struggle for independence, the Pakistani military—unlike the armies of Turkey and, later, Algeria and Indonesia—had not participated in a war of liberation. In Morris Janowitz's terms, it was an

31

"ex-colonial" army, not a "national liberation army" or a "post-liberation army."[3] In fact, the historical tradition from which the Pakistani (and Indian) armies emerged was not one of military government but of colonial rule, which "implanted a strong sense of self-restraint on the military."[4] Hence there was no precedent or prior legitimacy for the fusion of political and military spheres of the state that the military could use for expansion into politics. Nor was military politicization the result of a "highly articulated and well disseminated" national security doctrine, or what Alfred Stepan calls *new professionalism*, that accorded the military a permanent role in national development and governance, like those adopted by Cold War–era militaries in Brazil, Chile, Argentina, and even Indonesia under Suharto.[5]

Most Pakistani officers who had joined the BIA before independence had been trained at the Royal Military Academy at Sandhurst and, after its inauguration in 1932, at the Indian Military Academy at Dehra Dun, where military education and subsequently professional training stressed military-technical subjects, such as drill, fortifications, military history, and geography.[6] Informal socialization in army messes among senior and junior officers discouraged political discussion. After independence, military training institutions, such as the premier Command and Staff College in Quetta for midlevel officers, inherited strictly military professional curricula and training regimens from the British, initially taught under the supervision of British officers. In fact, as W. F. Gutteridge described them, "The armies of India and Pakistan were essentially British in pattern. The officers were united by their ability to speak English, by their contact with associated British regiments, and by the successful adoption of the regimental tradition and the life of the officers' mess with its in-built codes of behavior."[7]

Furthermore, the British colonial tradition of civil-military relations, inherited by both Pakistan and India, was based on "separate spheres of civil and military influence."[8] This division of labor was amply reflected in the organization of the colonial state in India: a civilian viceroy as the boss of the military commander in chief. During the chaotic partition of India in 1947, the Indian officers and enlisted ranks of the BIA stayed more or less loyal to the departing colonial authorities except for a few localized mutinies (for example, the naval mutiny of 1946). In fact, the soldiers' code explicitly forbade participation in politics. Indian and Pakistani officers inherited a "belief that civilized politics required civilian control and parliamentary processes. Furthermore, under the Raj, Indian officers learned the prudence of having no political views."[9]

This apolitical professional ethos was inherited by the two armies and was transmitted to a new generation of officers in both states.[10] But within a few years of independence, the Pakistani army had developed a political orientation, unlike its Indian counterpart. A 1952 report by a Burmese military mission scouting the region for possible models of professional military organization provides telling evidence of this early divergence.

In India, the Burmese soldiers encountered archaic rules of military conduct: "The Indian Army is steeped in red tape, strict adherence to very finely delineated spheres of responsibility and influence, hoary and innumerable traditions, fossilized customs and rules of conduct and a monumental amount of paper work." In Pakistan, they found a radically different breed of soldiers: "The amateurism and politicized orientation of the Pakistan Army" contained "a kind of virility and enthusiasm making up for a lack of experience and material. . . . It cannot give spectacular results but if you put enough material into it, making up for whatever intangible factors it lacks, then one has an impression that it cannot fail you."[11]

As early as March 1951, a group of Pakistani army officers, led by the then chief of general staff, Major General Akbar Khan, was arrested on charges of plotting to overthrow the government of the first prime minister, Liaquat Ali Khan (1947–1951). In 1953–1954, support from army headquarters was crucial to the autocratic coup carried out by the civilian governor general, Ghulam Mohammad (1951–1955). And in 1958, the military finally executed a successful coup d'état and seized the reins of government. Why did Pakistani officers who shared a tradition of apolitical professionalism with their Indian counterparts break it so soon after independence? Why did they develop a political orientation and supplant civilian authorities?

The achievement of independent statehood, especially as the result of a colonial transfer of power, signifies a shift in the political and ideological compass of the military. The Pakistani army, like its Indian counterpart, had to adjust its organizational identity, as well as its raison d'être, from that of a colonial army trained for the protection of imperial interests to one tasked with the preservation of the sovereignty of the new nation-state against its enemies.

The Pakistani army's identity and beliefs were molded in an authoritarian direction during its formative institutional experience. This experience was defined by at least two factors. First, the perceived threat of war from India resulted in the early militarization of the state, a process enabled and reinforced by US Cold War security assistance to Pakistan, which created the context for increased military influence in national political affairs. Second, the early problems of nation building created by the contradiction between the country's multiethnic society and the founding Muslim League leadership's nation-state policies politicized and polarized ethnic (especially Bengali) identities and spurred movements for autonomy that sparked military and civilian elite fears of internal fragmentation and put a premium on assimilation. The army's composition played an important role in exacerbating problems of national integration. As a result of colonial policy, which remained unaltered after independence, Pakistan's army was almost entirely recruited from West Pakistan (or, more accurately, from the Punjab). Hence the centralizing, militarizing state became synonymous with Punjabi domination and a symbol of Bengali alienation from the outset.

As noted earlier, Pakistan's experience in the foundational period after independence offers the opportunity to reconcile two opposing theoretical approaches to explaining the effects of security threats on civil-military relations. Military danger is believed to both reduce[12] and increase civilian control over the military.[13] Threats can surely have different effects on domestic politics. In some countries, geopolitical imperatives may be associated with stable civilian control, such as in the United States during the Cold War. In other states, security threats may have corrosive effects on democratic civil-military relations, for example, pre–World War II Japan or Burma during the Cold War. The initial experience of Pakistan suggests that the association between civilian supremacy and external security threats may play out differently in states with different levels of national cohesion and unity.

The West Pakistani civilian and military elites perceived the threat from India as existential, whereas Bengali and other ethno-nationalist elites considered it of relatively less import because of their forcefully diminished stake in the Pakistan project. These differing perspectives meant that the prospect of war did not have the effect of keeping the devil busy and out of politics or generating the rallying-around-the-flag effect in which the nation unites behind the army to fight its enemies. Some scholars argue that both of these effects render the military politically less meddlesome. Instead, the prospect of war had the effect of making the professional managers of violence in Pakistan the most powerful group in society. The missing link is national cohesion. Shared notions of the nation make for shared notions of the other. At least at the outset of state formation, the effect of threats on civilian supremacy is likely to be conditioned by prior social cohesion.

In the case of India, Stephen Cohen has argued that civilian control was the product of elite institutional design.[14] However, newly available historical materials suggest that Pakistan and India established almost identical formal institutions and agencies for civilian control, but civil-military relations took a sharply divergent path. Like India, Pakistan created a hierarchical structure for civilian oversight and management of the defense sector. The Defense Committee of the Cabinet (DCC) was created in June

1948 as the highest decision-making body on defense policy.[15] Under the DCC, there was a Defense Council headed by the defense minister and a civilian-staffed Ministry of Defense, which became the main institutional channel for civilian administrative and financial oversight over the military.[16] As in India, each of the three armed forces (army, navy, and air force) was assigned its own commander in chief. Like the Indian military, the Pakistani military's status in the official hierarchy of precedence was also adjusted to reflect the supremacy of civilians.[17]

All the civilian oversight institutions established in Pakistan were clearly designed to empower civilians to regulate the military, but they failed to perform their intended function. The crucial difference was that in India these formal institutional structures were embedded within a larger democratic constitutional framework. Indian political leaders also had relatively more latitude to restrain the military because of the country's more benign threat environment. No less important, India's nationalist movement was as much an anticolonial nationalist movement as it was a "nation-building movement." Under the leadership of Mohandas Gandhi and Jawarhalal Nehru, the Congress Party mobilized and deepened mass support throughout India and in the process "turned regionally and locally oriented folk into Indians."[18] The mass base of the Congress Party reinforced the nationalist leadership's political will to craft a democratic constitutional settlement of the multinationality problem on which a stable democratic order could be erected.[19] The Constituent Assembly of India swiftly instituted a consensus constitution in less than three years after independence, which established a parliamentary form of government with a clear chain of authority over the military, culminating in the prime minister. Crucially, the constitution also made provisions for accommodating India's deep diversity by devolving powers to the regional state levels and recognizing language as a legitimate basis for the future territorial reorganization of the state. This balancing act between central and regional power helped legitimize the center and contained the potential threat of internal fragmentation, thus depriving the military and other rebellious groups of the pretext for fatally challenging or seizing the state. Universally franchised founding elections, first held in 1952 and repeated at regular five-year intervals, renewed the legitimacy and mandate of the Congress Party and thus signaled the institutionalization of civilian rule to all politically significant actors, including the armed forces, as the only game in town.

Pakistan's founding nationalist movement, the Muslim League (ML), had acquired the formal mandate to rule the country after winning an absolute majority of the seats reserved for Muslims in the last preindependence elections, held in 1946.[20] But the demand for a separate state of Pakistan was historically rooted in the fear of Hindu political and economic domination felt by Muslim elites in Hindu-majority provinces, such as Uttar Pradesh, Bihar, and Bombay. Hence the ML did not have a strong social base or organizational infrastructure in Pakistan.[21] In 1946–1947, of the twenty-three members of the League Working Committee, only ten belonged to areas that became part of Pakistan.[22] The ML's late nationalist mobilization of mass support for a homeland for Muslims meant that Pakistani nationalism had not struck deep roots in the hearts and minds of the population, notwithstanding Mohammad Ali Jinnah's claim of a primordial Muslim civilizational distinction from the Hindus. In fact, there were serious latent disagreements within the ML about the structure of a future Muslim state that were papered over in the run-up to independence. Many East Bengali politicians interpreted the 1940 Lahore Resolution as an agreement on two states for the Muslims of India,[23] whereas Jinnah and his close associates imagined a singular Pakistan united by the bond of Islam as one nation. Besides, the migrant nature of Pakistan's top leaders put the logic of their political survival in conflict with the logic of competitive electoral politics. Hence the necessary democratic minima of contestation for political power in a universally enfranchised competitive national election became a threat to the founding elites' hold on power. Lacking the democratic mandate endowed by the mass support mobilized during elections, the party's initial nationalist legitimacy dwindled, especially after the demise of its first-tier leadership (Jinnah died in 1948, and Liaquat was assassinated in 1951).

Waging War

Although broader political conditions and decisions were not conducive to establishing democratic institutions, they did not necessarily have to lead to military expansion into civilian politics. In order to understand that process, it is also important to examine the nature of the development of the military as an institution. The key here was the military's fairly fast transformation from a ragtag, ex-colonial armed force into a well-oiled fighting machine. This process of military institutionalization was shaped by the imperative of preparing for warfare.

Seeking security against India has been Pakistan's top priority since independence in 1947. The origins of Pakistani insecurity stemmed from the Muslim League leadership's deep-rooted distrust of what it saw as a Hindu-dominated if professedly secular Indian National Congress, derived from its bitter experience of Congress hostility in the decade preceding the creation of Pakistan. During the period 1937–1939, for example, the Congress had formed ministries in eight out of eleven provinces of British India, and it managed to profoundly alienate Muslims. In the United Provinces, the party refused ministerial positions to Muslim Leaguers who had informally joined the Congress against colonial rule until they renounced their membership in the ML and pledged allegiance to the Congress.[24] The ML also charged the Congress ministries with pursuing anti-Muslim policies, such as the promotion of the Hindi language and Hindi symbols and the institution of "Vande Mataram," an anthem with anti-Muslim themes, in schools, where Muslim children were forced to sing it. The ML fully publicized these excesses of the

Hindu Raj and anticipated the suppression of Muslim rights in a united India.[25]

Before the partition of India, the ML had accepted the British Cabinet Mission Plan (1946), which stipulated a constitutional settlement in India in the form of a union of Muslim- and Hindu-majority provinces. But the League's leadership feared that the Congress could use its majority at the center to control the army and to effectively abolish the autonomy of the Muslim provinces. After His Majesty's Government finally conceded an independent Pakistan in principle, Jinnah and his colleagues pressed hard for the division of the armed forces of British India so that Pakistan could stand on its own. As Khawaja Nazimuddin, a senior member of the League Working Committee from Bengal and future governor general (1948–1951) and prime minister (1951–1953) of Pakistan, warned Viceroy Lord Mountbatten in April 1947, Pakistan without its own army "would be like a house of cards," with "no earthly chance of survival."[26]

His Majesty's Government was initially opposed to dividing the Indian army for strategic reasons, including the need to exercise unified control of the subcontinent during the partition,[27] but it finally accepted the League's demand for a Pakistani army before departing India in August 1947. As a result, the BIA was split in two.[28] Reflecting the Hindu-Muslim prepartition communal balance, military assets were roughly divided between India and Pakistan in the ratio 64:36. Pakistan's share of the army came to approximately 140,000 soldiers of a total strength of 410,000 in 1947. In the end, Pakistan received roughly 30 percent of the army, 20 percent of the air force, and 40 percent of the navy.[29] Because of the lower proportion of Indian officers, especially Muslims, in the BIA, Pakistan was short roughly 1,500 officers. This shortage was met through temporary commissions, rapid promotions, and the retention of some 500 British officers. The first two commanders in chief of the Pakistani army were also British.

When the BIA was divided, Muslim officers from areas that became part of Pakistan were given no choice but to join the Pakistani army, but Muslim officers in India had to choose between Pakistan and India. For a majority of Muslim officers who migrated to Pakistan, the new state promised a "better life" secure from "Indian domination," better career prospects, and the elation of a newly independent homeland for the Muslims of India in which they would play a crucial role.[30] Even though they had worked together in the BIA and had commanded Hindu and Sikh troops, the communal carnage during the partition of India only confirmed the worst suspicions of these officers about the others' untrustworthiness.[31] That bitter experience "was engraved on the psyches of almost all officers in the Pakistan Army."[32]

After independence, bilateral disputes over water sharing and delays in the delivery of British India's cash reserves and military stores were all seen by military officers (and important civilians) as evidence that India was not reconciled to the idea of an independent Pakistan and wanted to bring it to its knees.[33] The onset of a territorial rivalry with India over Kashmir immediately after independence deeply intensified Pakistani insecurity. As the only princely state that had a contiguous border with both Pakistan and India, Muslim-majority Kashmir held enormous strategic importance for both states. For Pakistan, it was prime real estate from a defense perspective: the rivers that irrigated Pakistan's agricultural economy originated there, and its geographic depth could both offset the negative effects of proximity to India and allow Pakistan to flank its frontier in a conflict.[34] Quite apart from its military and strategic benefits, Kashmir was central to the self-image and identity of each state. In fact, by the time the first Kashmir war concluded in December 1948, Pakistan had captured enough territory in Kashmir to meet its strategic needs.[35] But civilian and military decision makers still valued Kashmir because it was central to Pakistan's national identity as the homeland of the Muslims of the subcontinent, as it was for India's professed secular nationalism. Thus, for both states, Kashmir became what James Fearon calls an "effectively indivisible issue" that could not be shared with or surrendered to the other because of conflicting nationalisms.[36]

These competing nationalisms sparked the first Kashmir war in 1948. That war had two crucial implications for the Pakistani military's institutional role in politics. First, it politicized an important section of the Pakistani officer corps, a process that ultimately culminated in the country's first coup conspiracy. Second, it established the military's privileged claim over a large share of state resources as the only way to secure Pakistan and avoid another war with India. By making military force indispensable to the country's survival, this early securitization of the state created the context in which the military could increase its political influence at the expense of civilian institutions even as it displayed obedience to duly constituted civil authorities.

In the chaotic and confused atmosphere after partition, India occupied the Muslim-ruled princely states of Junagadh in September 1947 and Hyderabad a year later.[37] In similar fashion, Pakistan's civilian leadership decided to seize Kashmir by force in order to preempt the state's accession to India.[38] Because the disorganized state of the Pakistani army ruled out a direct invasion, the Pakistani cabinet decided to exploit a revolt by the Muslim population of Poonch against the maharaja that had broken out in July–August 1947 by organizing a deniable attack on the Kashmir valley. For this covert mission, Liaquat and his colleagues co-opted Colonel Akbar Khan, the director of weapons and equipment at army headquarters, thereby circumventing the military chain of command.[39] Colonel Khan planned the attack in September 1947; it was outlined in a document titled "Armed Revolt in Kashmir" that he shared with the prime minister. In Khan's words, "The authorities needed a lot of assistance from the Army in the shape of plans, advice, weapons, ammunition, communications and volunteer[s]. They did not ask for it because the whole thing had to be kept secret from the [British] C-in-C and other senior officers."[40]

41

Khan, in turn, enlisted the assistance of other army officers, including a deputy director of military intelligence, as well as the most senior Pakistani air force officer.[41] Pakistani raiders, made up of Pashtun tribal militias and active-duty and former military personnel, initially captured sizable territory inside Kashmir. But Pakistan's overall plan to annex the state was doomed after the maharaja of Kashmir sought India's military assistance and reportedly signed an instrument of accession to India. On October 26, 1947, India dispatched the Sikh Regiment's First Battalion to stop Pakistani invaders from capturing the Srinagar airport.[42] The Pakistani army formally entered the war in April 1948 to prevent the Indians from seizing what Pakistan called "azad" (free) territory captured by the raiders. The fighting continued for nine months. The two sides agreed to a UN-brokered cease-fire on January 1, 1949, with India retaining control over most of the Kashmir valley and Ladakh.

From the standpoint of civilian control, the employment of the Pakistani army in irregular warfare violated military hierarchy and discipline and gave officers like Akbar Khan direct access to the highest decision-making levels of the state. Before leaving the army, the first British commander in chief (C in C), General Frank Messervy (1947–1948), presciently lamented the early erosion of the military's apolitical tradition: "I am fed up with what is going on in Kashmir . . . all behind my back. . . . Politicians using soldiers and soldiers allowing themselves to be used, without the proper approval of their superiors, are setting a bad example for the future."[43]

Many officers, including Akbar, saw the civilian leadership's ultimate decision to accept a cease-fire that left the Kashmir vale under Indian control as a national surrender that deprived the army of a potential victory.[44] This grievance provided the motivational trigger for the 1951 Rawalpindi conspiracy,[45] the first military coup plot in Pakistan's history. Named after the northern Punjab city of Rawalpindi, where it was allegedly planned, the plot was hatched by a group of about a dozen veterans of the Kashmir war, aided by civilians with leftist leanings, notably poet and editor of the *Pakistan Times* Faiz

Ahmed Faiz and Sajjad Zaheer, general secretary of the Communist Party of Pakistan. It was the brainchild of Akbar Khan, who in August 1950, just three years after independence, had been promoted to the rank of major general and appointed chief of general staff, the key principal staff officer in the army, with control over military operations and intelligence directorates. Khan was a lieutenant colonel in 1947, and his ascent to major general in just three years when it would ordinarily have taken over twenty years is indicative of the rapid promotions given to most Pakistani officers as part of the government's nationalization plan. Some, including General Ayub Khan, who was a beneficiary of the same policy, have held that accelerated promotions were responsible for the politicization of the officer corps.[46] Although rising so rapidly through the hierarchy could certainly have fanned officers' ambitions, it cannot sufficiently account for the genesis of praetorianism among some Pakistani officers. A similar policy of swift promotions does not appear to have had the same effect in India. For the purposes of this discussion, it is more important to recognize that Akbar Khan's strategic position in the army high command made it possible for him to "cast his net widely and unobtrusively."[47] Akbar and his other army collaborators had begun to conspire to overthrow the elected government in July 1949, barely six months after the cease-fire in Kashmir.[48] The plot was foiled with the help of a North-West Frontier Province Criminal Investigation Department inspector in 1951, and the conspirators were put on trial by a special tribunal consisting of superior-court judges, although the proceedings were to remain in camera to prevent the "disruption and destabilizing of the Armed Forces."[49] The conspirators were ultimately dismissed from military service, imprisoned for "conspiracy to commit acts prejudicial to the safety of Pakistan," and tried in secret by a special court.[50] They were found guilty of sedition and waging war against the state and were given sentences ranging from a minimum of four years in prison to a maximum of twelve years for Akbar Khan.

The plot has received little scholarly attention and has generally been considered insignificant.[51] The historian Ayesha Jalal has characterized the coup plot as the beginning of an Anglo-American plan to cleanse Pakistan and its army of "officers imbued with a sense of patriotism" and pro-Moscow leanings.[52] In contrast, Prime Minister Liaquat claimed at the time that Akbar and his collaborators were conspiring to establish a Communist government under military domination with the help of a foreign country.[53] However, the significance of the planned putsch from the perspective of military politics lies not in any alleged Western or Communist conspiracy but in its impact on the nascent military institution. In fact, the declassified record of the trial suggests that it was an important precursor of the crystallization of the army's future role in politics, particularly its collective self-image as the only guardian of Jinnah's Pakistan and its members' belief in the inappropriateness of full democracy in Pakistan. Akbar Khan's close and formative encounter with high politics led him to contrast his unconditional patriotism and dedication to Pakistan with the selfishness and incompetence of civilian leaders. After his first meeting with Prime Minister Liaquat and other cabinet ministers in September 1947, he derided the "complete [civilian] ignorance about the business of anything in the nature of military operations," which created "the serious danger that the whole scheme would lack effective control."[54] A few months later, when he sensed that the political leadership was losing interest in Kashmir, Akbar concluded that "officials and leaders persuaded with difficulty to visit [Kashmir] for urgent administrative [and military] problems were busy cutting private side-deals."[55] In the end, Khan's perceptions of the "weak [Kashmir] policy of the government of Pakistan, its state of indecision on momentous questions, and its bungling on the issue of Kashmir," "corruption," and his opposition to the presence of British officers provided the explosive mix of motives that impelled him to rally support for a coup in the officer corps.[56]

One lieutenant colonel testified during the trial that Akbar Khan had told him in July 1949 that "Jinnah was dead. . . . There was nobody of his caliber who could run the affairs of the state place. . . .

The civil service and police were most corrupt. The bribery and corruption were ripe [*sic*]. The People had very great regard for the army." Therefore, there was "no reason why the government should not be taken over by the army, controlled properly and run on honest lines." Akbar Khan believed that the country needed command and control because it was not prepared for a "100 percent democratic state," and that people are "conscious of their political rights in countries where the form of government is democratic, but our country is about 200 years back in the concept of a democratic state." Under such conditions, "the people needed a government which could take quick decisions. . . . The idea was to develop the public mind" so that they could fully grasp democracy.[57] Because democratic evolution would take a long time, the solution Akbar suggested was the "overthrow of the government" by arresting Prime Minister Liaquat, capturing the Army General Headquarters, detaining civilian and military officials, and assuming control of the government.[58] The alleged plan was to have Liaquat legitimize the coup by announcing that he had voluntarily handed over power to a military council consisting of the commanders in chief of the army, air force, and navy.[59]

In October 1949, Akbar rallied a group of sympathetic officers, at least one of whom agreed with his assessment that "the army was consisting of honest and upright officers who could take over the government and run it on honest lines."[60] Another key conspirator, Brigadier Sadiq Khan, posted in the army's Seventh Division, expressed "enthusiasm about the coup d'etat" and believed that the country needed a drastic change, and that "not only the Pakistan Army but the public of Pakistan" would welcome the coup.[61] By November 1949, Akbar had co-opted several senior officers, including Major General Nazir Ahmed, who commanded the army's Ninth Division, as well as middle-ranking officers on active duty in strategic staff and command positions, an institutionally significant group given the general shortage of senior Pakistani army officers in the early years after independence.[62] The importance of this group was enhanced even further when two senior officers, Major

General Iftikharuddin and Brigadier Sher Khan, were killed in a plane crash the same year.

Among other possible factors, the Rawalpindi conspiracy was driven by the officers' nationalist conviction that civilian politicians were too weak, incompetent, and unpatriotic to create a strong national army and were relying instead on British officers for national defense and ignoring the advice of patriotic Pakistani soldiers.[63] One such officer was Air Commodore M. K. Janjua, the most senior Pakistani air force officer involved in the plot. He wrote several memos to Prime Minister and Defense Minister Liaquat. Claiming to be solely motivated by his "complete identification" with Pakistan, Janjua recommended the creation of a military-led brain trust to advise the government on "international developments, defense policy and the development of defense-related industry."[64] Buoyed by the belief that it was "only the army that saved Pakistan from being wiped off the map of the world in 1948,"[65] the conspirators had developed grave doubts about the existing political leadership's ability to provide good government and properly defend Pakistan and had come to the conclusion that a coup was not only necessary but also an appropriate form of political change.

It is important to acknowledge that the coup plot was not devised institutionally, and that the Pakistani army under the command of Ayub Khan cooperated (however reluctantly) with the civilian government's decision to conduct a trial. The plot also revealed internal military divisions, as well as military disagreements with the civilian government over the conduct of national security policy. But the conspiracy had other important implications for the military's future political role. First, it showed that the army could readily abandon its inherited apolitical professional ethos in favor of a tutelary professionalism, especially if some military officers decided that it was appropriate to contest and supplant civilian authority. Second, it helped germinate in the senior officer corps the idea that the army could establish "a tidier form of government."[66]

The conflict over Kashmir also heralded the initiation of a war-prone territorial rivalry between the two ex-colonial siblings. This militarized competition had pernicious effects on Pakistan's political development. Ayesha Jalal has masterfully narrated the early formation of a domineering Pakistani state of martial rule that undercut political processes.[67] The importance of this profound structural change must be acknowledged, but the analysis must go further. It needs to examine the impact of the peculiar sequence of political development spurred by the perceived security threat from India: military professionalization before the formation of organized civilian political institutions, which added special complications to the process of democratization.[68]

After the cease-fire in Kashmir, the Pakistani military began to shore up its defenses to deter and, if necessary, fight India. Early military threat assessments concluded that Pakistan urgently needed "an additional army division, the balancing of existing four divisions, one armored brigade, and additional military reserve stores."[69] Woefully aware of Pakistan's limited counteroffensive capability, the commanders in chief demanded the urgent purchase of up to 300 new Sherman tanks, in addition to one heavy and two light antiaircraft artillery regiments, six bomber squadrons, two or three naval destroyers, modern radar systems, and other military hardware for a total capital expenditure of about 90 million rupees, excluding funds for new ordnance factories.[70] The July–August 1951 military crisis, triggered by Indian troop mobilization on the Punjab border in advance of the session of the Kashmir Constituent Assembly, only deepened the insecurity of Pakistani military planners, who had only about a dozen "obsolete" tanks with limited "remaining operational life."[71] Such was the state of militarization that by August 1951 the military service chiefs could attend formal meetings of the cabinet whenever it addressed issues related to defense.[72] As a result, the government yielded to military demands for modernization, subordinated the needs of society to the needs of soldiers by relaxing financial controls to meet urgent war needs, and spent almost 70 percent of total government expenditure in the first three years on the military.[73]

Disciplining the Nation

Like his counterparts in India's Congress Party, Jinnah firmly believed in establishing a democratic government in Pakistan, with a politically neutral and democratically supportive military. In an oft-quoted speech to Pakistani army officers at the Command and Staff College in Quetta in June 1948, he responded to the casual remarks of some officers about an expanded military role in nation building by reminding them of the inviolability of the constitutional chain of command:

> During my talks with one or two very high-ranking officers, I discovered that they did not know the implications of the Oath taken by the troops of Pakistan.[74] I want you to remember and . . . study the Government of India Act, as adapted for use in Pakistan, which is our present Constitution, that the executive authority flows from the Head of the Government of Pakistan, who is the governor-general and, therefore, any command or orders that may come to you cannot come without the sanction of the Executive Head. This is the legal position.[75]

Despite the founding father's clearly articulated emphasis on civilian supremacy over the military, why did civil-military relations take such a radically authoritarian turn? It is true that Jinnah died too soon after independence (in September 1948) to have a decisive influence on civil-military relations. However, in his short time at the helm of affairs, he did not convey the importance of the principle of political subordination of the military to elected officials. For instance, in his Staff College speech, the constitutional lawyer Jinnah understandably emphasized the legally correct relationship between civilians and the military. The legal position, as he understood it, was that the governor general was the civilian commander in chief of the armed forces.[76] But this position was problematic from a democratic standpoint. Jinnah essentially told the budding praetorians of the Pakistani army that they owed their unqualified allegiance to the unelected governor general, not the prime minister and his cabinet.[77] One of Jinnah's aides, Sharifuddin Pirzada, argues that "Jinnah was not happy about reports of the political tendencies of some military officers, but he thought the Army under its British commander was unlikely to organize a rebellion."[78] Jinnah's main frame of reference was British India, which had no tradition of military control over government even though it was decidedly authoritarian.

However, as several scholars have noted, some of his actions set dangerous precedents for the future governance of the state. In fact, Jinnah's decision to retain the colonially bequeathed viceregal system by choosing to become Pakistan's first governor general turned out to be democratically corrosive. As governor general, Jinnah had extensive powers. He appointed Pakistan's first cabinet, presided over its meetings, and set its agenda. Jinnah had the authority to appoint provincial governors, the chief justice of the Federal Court, and High Court judges. He was also president of the legislature and controlled several ministries. In Jinnah, Pakistan had a unique head of state who controlled the "executive, the cabinet and the assembly."[79] Derived from the Government of India Act of 1935, an amended version of which (the Pakistan Provisional Constitutional Order, 1947) became Pakistan's interim constitution, the viceregal system had weak (if technically autonomous) provincial governments and a strong centralized bureaucracy.[80] In fact, Jinnah relied on unelected provincial governors and civil servants to closely monitor and report the activities of government ministers.[81] On August 20, 1947, Jinnah used his right to give instructions to provincial governors to instruct the North-West Frontier Province governor, Sir George Cunningham, to dismiss Dr. Khan Sahib's Congress ministry in the North-West Frontier Province (which was part of the Indian National Congress and had opposed the creation of Pakistan), and had it replaced with a Muslim League one.[82] M. A. Khuhro's Sindh ministry was dismissed in similar fashion in April 1948 for challenging the central government's decision to make Karachi the federal capital, which would remove it from the provincial government's administrative control.[83] In July 1948, the central government added Section 92A to the act, which was enacted as a law by the Constituent Assembly, giving the governor general special emergency powers to take over the provincial government in case of a grave emergency.[84] The act was employed in the Punjab to curb challenges to the central government between January 1949 and April 1951 and in Sindh from May 1951 to December 1953.[85]

Ayesha Jalal argues that the new state of Pakistan was crippled by its colonial inheritance, a result of its relatively sparse share of colonial administrative resources and structures in comparison with India, where continuity and a ready-made postcolonial state eased the transition to independent statehood.[86] In this context, she describes Jinnah's decision to opt for the governor generalship as a Hobson's choice. Devoid of a well-knit mass party that could integrate and discipline the provinces in a territorially divided country, Jinnah had to project state authority by temporarily concentrating it in his hands.[87] In the initial months after independence, Jinnah was also afraid that Pakistan might not survive in the face of a hostile India.[88] In other words, Jinnah was doing what any good statesman would be expected to do under such dire circumstances: construct a cohesive nation-state to fend off its perceived internal and external enemies. However, neither Jinnah nor his compatriots made any effort to convey that he was exercising these powers as a temporary measure to consolidate state authority and stabilize Pakistan, and they did not "justify his actions on the ground that he believed the times were exceptional and that in the future, the nation should look to the constitution."[89] Whatever his reasons, the unintended consequence of his choice was to endow that office with extensive powers outside the bounds of normal political procedure, which his successors would use to undermine civilian cabinets and the legislature.

Perhaps viceregalism would have had less pernicious effects in a culturally monolithic society. But in an ethnically diverse society, this heavy-handed process of nation-state building through centralization fomented early ethnic cleavages that, in turn, worsened elite perceptions of threats to Pakistan's unity and gave impetus to the continued need for centralized authority. It was in this ethnically and politically divided context that the threat from India, rather than becoming the glue that should have increased internal unity, became a source of division between East and West Pakistan. The imagined Pakistan of its Muhajir nationalist elites and its Punjabi-dominated military, at war with Hindu India, was not the Pakistan imagined by a majority of the population concentrated in East Pakistan.

The seeds of ethnic conflict were sown in the very notion of the Pakistani state. In Phillip Oldenburg's words, Pakistan was "a place insufficiently imagined" or perhaps very differently imagined by its majority Bengalis. Jinnah and other mostly non-Bengali League leaders imagined the Pakistani nation-state to be "inseparable from the Muslim nation of the subcontinent, locked in combat with Hindu India." In their view, the state's raison d'être was "safeguarding, and strengthening the Islamic heritage, in which Urdu played a major role."[90]

Bengalis contested this idea of one Muslim Pakistan from its inception. The earliest political expression of this fundamental disagreement occurred in 1940. On March 23, 1940, the Lahore Session of the Muslim League passed a resolution to demand the constitution of independent states, carved out of the Muslim-majority provinces in northwestern and eastern India, in which the constituent units were to be autonomous and sovereign. Many Muslim Leaguers from Bengal interpreted the resolution as a demand for two separate sovereign units, whereas the central League leadership headed by Jinnah had a single nation-state in mind. A convention of Muslim

League legislators held in April 1946 passed a resolution that sought to undermine the Lahore Resolution by demanding that Muslim majority wings should be combined to create the state of Pakistan. Bengalis contended that the convention did not have the authority to alter the 1940 resolution, which had been approved at the League's plenary session. If not an independent state, prominent Bengali leaders expected at least a federal arrangement in a future Pakistan, in which Bengali identity, language, and political rights would be protected. The two-Pakistan idea, which directly undermined Jinnah's two-nation theory, presaged the Bengali nationalist movement that ultimately led to civil war and the dismemberment of Pakistan. To quote Oldenburg: "The exploitation of East Pakistan, the failure to build a nation encompassing the two peoples, and the tragic mistakes made in dealing with Bengali demands cannot be called inevitable unless one considers forces centered in West Pakistan which pushed the country apart. . . . The tragedy of Pakistan was in part the result of a failure of understanding by the Pakistanis, a failure to recognize what the meaning of Pakistan was for the Bengalis and a blind commitment by the 'Pakistanis' to their own model of the state."[91]

Pakistan's ethnic and geographic makeup complicated the building of the classic French-style nation-state, defined as one nation in

Table 1.1 Military officers in Pakistan (West and East), 1955

Commissioned officers	West Pakistan	East Pakistan	East Pakistan percentage of total officers	East Pakistan percentage of population (1951 census)
Army	894	14	1.5	
Navy	593	7	1.2	55.4
Air Force	640	60	8.6	

Sources: Dawn, January 8, 1955, cited in Rounaq Jahan, *Pakistan: Failure in National Integration*, South Asian Institute series (New York: Columbia University Press, 1972), 25; the Population Census of Pakistan (Karachi: Office of the Census Commissioner, Government of Pakistan Ministry of Interior, Home Division), 1951.

possession of its own state. The Bengalis constituted Pakistan's ma-jority ethnic group, but they were territorially concentrated in East Pakistan and were separated from the country's western wing by some one thousand miles of Indian territory. This division hampered the League leadership's vision of creating a unified nation, as well as communication and mobility between people in the two wings.

To make matters even worse, the Bengalis were almost com-pletely excluded from the politically influential military and civil ser-vices, which were dominated by the Punjabis and Muhajirs. Of the 133 Muslim officers of the Indian Civil Service and the Indian Political Service who joined Pakistan, only 1 was Bengali.[92] The military was no less skewed. Punjabis constituted 24.9 percent of the population but made up roughly 77 percent of the army, whereas the Bengalis were 55.4 percent of the population but less than 3 percent of the army.[93] Table 1.1 shows the striking inherited disparity in officer re-cruitment between West Pakistan (predominantly Punjabis, followed by the Pashtuns) and East Pakistan. Bengalis were completely absent at the level of general (see Table 1.2). In 1955, there was just 1 brigadier from East Pakistan compared to 34 from the western wing of the country. Bengali representation at the lower levels was no less dismal. For instance, of the 247 officers of the rank of lieutenant colonel and colonel, only 3 were Bengalis. At the level of major, only 10 of the 590 officers came from East Pakistan.

Table 1.2 East Pakistan representation in higher ranks of the army, 1956

Rank	West Pakistan	East Pakistan
Lieutenant General	3	0
Major General	20	0
Brigadier	34	1
Colonel/Lieutenant Colonel	247	2
Total	304	3

Sources: Ian Talbot, "The Punjabization of Pakistan," in *Pakistan: Nationalism without a Nation,* ed. Christophe Jaffrelot (Delhi: Manohar, 2002), 54.

Although the northwestern areas of India, especially the Punjab, had a tradition of military service in precolonial times, the ethnic lopsidedness of the army was largely the result of a considered colonial policy of recruitment from the so-called martial races, including the Punjabis and the Pashtuns.[94] In contrast, the colonial authorities considered the nonmartial Bengalis undependable and disloyal, and for a reason: soldiers of the East India Company's Bengal Army had spearheaded the Great Sepoy Mutiny of 1857, Bengalis formed the early leadership of the Indian nationalist movement and were active in political resistance against colonial rule in the 1920s and 1930s.[95]

After independence, the Pakistani government broadened civil service recruitment to enhance Bengali participation, in part through the induction of an equal number of recruits from East and West Pakistan.[96] However, there was no successful government policy to redress initial disparities in military recruitment. In fact, the Bengali sense of exclusion from the national army of Pakistan emerged immediately after independence. In March 1948, then chief minister Khawaja Nazimuddin demanded that "first, and foremost among [provincial demands] is that as far as Eastern Pakistan is concerned, we must have a fair and proper share in the Armed Forces of Pakistan for the full integration of the eastern part of the country."[97] But "there was strong resistance within the Pakistan army to greatly expanding East Bengal's representation in the military," as well as a martial "distaste for the qualities of the Bengali officers and other ranks."[98] The civilian government entrusted a commission with the task of recommending ways to increase Bengali recruitment, but the military resisted the idea on the grounds that any changes to the social makeup of the officer corps would detract from the urgent task of reconstituting and reorganizing the Pakistan military from its British remnants. Without proper institutional policies to redress the ethnic imbalance, the Bengalis' prospects of participation in government institutions, especially the army, were effectively eliminated.

Put differently, building a viable state might have required the centralization of authority in the central government,[99] but crafting an inclusive democracy that could peacefully manage ethnic divisions demanded power sharing and regional autonomy for the provinces. In other words, the nation-state and democracy became conflicting logics at the outset. The central government's focus on heavy investment in state building not only meant the uneven development of the political system but also perpetuated the ethnic imbalance of power by concentrating it in the hands of the West Pakistanis.[100] Facing external danger and fearing internal fragmentation, the West Pakistani civilian and military elites refused to recognize subnational identities as legitimate, including the Pashtuns and Sindhis in West Pakistan. Their unwillingness to acknowledge and accept politically significant ethnic differences as the organizing principle of the structure of the polity helped irrevocably sharpen interwing political conflict over identity, interests, and institutions. The more the state centralized power and resources for state building, especially via the process of resource extraction for militarization against the perceived threat from India, the more it threatened to reduce provincial autonomy, which only deepened the sense of Bengali alienation and exclusion from the nation-state project.

Although the Muslim League faced no organized political challengers in the initial years after independence, it quickly squandered its nationalist legitimacy through its nation-state building policies. One of the most disastrous decisions was the imposition of Urdu as the sole state language, even though it was the mother tongue of roughly 4 percent of the total population.[101] By denying the language of the majority its deserved status, the state's Urdu-only policy served to polarize and politicize Bengali national identity around language within a few months of independence. When a Congress member from East Bengal tabled an amendment in the Constituent Assembly of Pakistan on February 23, 1948, to allow the use of Bengali as a language of the assembly along with English and Urdu, Prime Minister Liaquat rejected the proposal as tantamount to dividing the country and reminded the Bengalis that "Pakistan is a Muslim State and it must have as its lingua franca, the language of the Muslim nation."[102] These and other provocative actions and statements from the League leadership sparked student protests in Dhaka in February 1948 that culminated in a general strike in East Bengal on March 11 that led to clashes with the police and the arrest of key student leaders.[103]

Pakistan's elites denied Bengali the status of an official language in part because they claimed that it was steeped in Hindu imagery and was a direct affront to Jinnah's two-nation theory, which was predicated on the cultural distinctness of the Muslims of India from Hindus. In this exclusionary view of nationhood, recognizing intra-Muslim differences would mean the symbolic undoing of the Pakistan project. Hence the state's standard response was to dismiss Bengali demands for linguistic autonomy as a Hindu-inspired conspiracy to divide Pakistan.[104] On his maiden visit to East Pakistan in 1948, seven months after independence, Jinnah warned a large gathering on March 21 that "having failed to prevent the establishment of Pakistan, thwarted and frustrated by failure, the enemies of Pakistan have now turned their attention to disrupt[ing] the state by creating a split amongst the Muslims of Pakistan" through "fifth columnists" who are spreading the poison of linguistic provincialism.[105] He categorically ruled out the possibility of accommodating any demand for Bengali as the state language:

> Ultimately it is for you, the people of this province, to decide what should be the language of your province. But let me make it very clear to you that the state language of Pakistan will be Urdu and no other language. Anyone who tries to mislead you is really the enemy of Pakistan. Without one language, no nation can remain solidly tied together and function. Look at the history of other countries . . . so far as

the state language is concerned, Pakistan's language should be Urdu.[106]

Jinnah reiterated his Urdu-only policy at the convocation of Dhaka University on March 24:

> There can only be one lingua franca, that is the language for inter-communication between the various provinces of the state, and that language should be Urdu and can be no other. The State Language, therefore, must obviously be Urdu, a language that has been nurtured by a hundred million Muslims of this subcontinent, a language understood throughout the length and breadth of Pakistan and, above all, a language which, more than any other provincial language, embodies the best that is in Islamic culture and Muslim tradition and is nearest to the languages used in other Islamic countries.[107]

This statement triggered student protests.[108]

In December 1948, the central education minister, Fazlur Rehman, told the All-Pakistan Education Conference that regional language scripts would be changed to Arabic or Urdu to uphold the country's Islamic ideology. Although other regional languages were non-Muslim by the state's definition, Bengali was the only language written in Devanagari script. To erase all traces of Hinduism, the government established adult language centers in East Pakistan to teach Bengali in Arabic script despite Bengali opposition.[109]

Bengali concerns about provincial autonomy in the future constitution were first publicly expressed by the Working Committee of the ruling Muslim League's East Bengal wing. In its December session, it demanded "maximum autonomy for East Pakistan," especially with regard to communications and foreign trade, on account of its geographic separation from the other provinces and the central government.[110]

In March 1949, the Constituent Assembly passed the Objectives Resolution, delineating the basic objectives of a future constitution. The resolution declared that sovereignty rests with Allah and that elected officials could only exercise the authority delegated to them by Him. It was bitterly opposed by some non-Muslim members from East Pakistan for mixing religion and the state. However, the resolution also envisaged the creation of a federal system with full autonomy for the subnational units.

Popular discontent with the proposed constitution came out in the open in October 1950 when the Basic Principles Committee, formed to outline the future constitution, submitted its interim report. The report recommended Urdu as the state language and denied meaningful autonomy to the provinces. It drew sharp criticism from East Pakistan, especially from Bengali members of the Constituent Assembly of Pakistan. According to one of them, "In East Bengal there is a growing belief . . . that there are principles in the Report which, if adopted, will reduce the majority of East Bengal into a minority and it will turn East Bengal into a colony of Pakistan."[111]

In fact, the committee's report unified and mobilized Bengali nationalist opposition to the central government. Bengali Communists and nationalists, spearheaded by Awami Muslim League (a breakaway faction of the ruling Muslim League) leaders, formed the Central Committee of Democratic Federation, which rejected the report, mobilized mass support against it and organized a Grand National Convention in Dhaka that proposed an alternative constitution based on the Lahore Resolution of 1940.[112] This constitution, which presaged Bengali separatism, proposed the creation of a "sovereign socialist republic" and the recognition of Bengali as a state language.[113] It demanded that Pakistan be turned into a "United States of Pakistan comprising the western and eastern regions with parliament elected by joint electorate," in which the center would have authority only over foreign affairs and defense, and provided for (1) two units of defense forces with two regional general officers commanding in the East and the West under supreme command at the federal capital and (2) a regional defense force raised from and manned by the people of the respective regions.[114] The interim report was withdrawn in November because of the fierce opposition it created, especially in East Bengal, but it raised serious questions in West Pakistan about the loyalty of the Bengalis to the Pakistan project. The decentralized and democratized structure of national defense proposed by the Bengali convention was particularly alarming for West Pakistan elites, especially the military, because it directly challenged their vision of a strong center with a strong national army as the only bulwark of defense against both India and the perceived danger of internal disintegration.

However, it was not until 1952 that incipient Bengali nationalism came into direct and violent confrontation with the state. In January, Prime Minister Khawaja Nazimuddin (himself a Bengali, although he was part of the small, conservative, Urdu-speaking elite of West Bengal) publicly reaffirmed the official Urdu-only policy at the Dhaka session of the Muslim League. His statement led to massive student demonstrations and strikes across East Bengal. On February 21, police opened fire on protesters in Dhaka, killing dozens of students and political activists and thus producing the Bengali nation's first national martyrs and symbols of resistance to Pakistani-Punjabi colonialism.[115] But rather than addressing the issue, the Basic Principles Committee's final report in 1952 simply omitted the question of the state language.[116]

Some scholars have suggested that the linguistic conflict was driven by economic motives. The recognition of Bengali as a national language would have increased the access of the Bengalis to the state apparatus and economic resources.[117] For instance, educated middle-class Bengalis feared that they would be excluded from government employment because their language was not on the subject list of the Public Service Commission.[118] But the demand for autonomy went beyond getting the goodies. In fact, it was the call for cultural recognition that gave Bengali nationalism wider emotional appeal and helped create what Benedict Anderson has called an "imagined community"[119] among the other classes of Bengali society, including rural peasants, who subsequently formed the backbone of the nationalist resistance.[120] Although motives of economic gain may have been at work behind Bengalis' collective claim making, the language movement intensified soon after independence when the unequal distribution of administrative power and economic resources was not even on the political agenda. The primary spark that fired up Bengali nationalism was the West Pakistani (Muhajir-Punjabi) elites' refusal to give recognition to "multiple and complementary" identities, which could have fostered the we-feeling or solidarity necessary for the creation of a democratic political system in a multiethnic state.[121]

After Jinnah's death, the Muslim League government under Prime Minister Liaquat Ali Khan (1948–1951) used the threat to an Islamic Pakistan from India to justify centralized control of the state. Liaquat decried parliamentary government as a luxury for a state under external duress, equated the formation of other political parties with treason,[122] and forcefully denied and derided regional demands for autonomy by declaring that Pakistan was only one nation and that "we must kill this provincialism for all times to come."[123] Besides using the threat of or actually implementing emergency powers to chasten or sack provincial governments (for example, in the Punjab in 1949), the central government used specific legal instruments to silence recalcitrant politicians who opposed its policies, including prominent provincial ministers. The infamous Public and Representative Offices (Disqualification) Act of 1949, for instance, empowered the government to disbar anyone from public life for a period of up to ten years if that person was "found guilty of misconduct in any public office or representative capacity."[124]

Liaquat's assassination in October 1951[125] signaled the formal end of the League's founding legitimacy, and it "was unable to present to the public either a convincing program or an inspiring leader."[126] With Jinnah and Liaquat gone, the League also began to fall apart as factional disputes resulted in splits and the creation of new parties. In

East Pakistan, disaffected Bengali Leaguers had already joined other Bengali nationalists and leftists to form the Awami Muslim League in June 1949. In the center's denial of provincial and cultural autonomy to the Bengalis, that party found a powerful argument in its drive to mobilize mass support in defense of the rights of the putative Bengali nation.[127] A declining Muslim League could hardly perform the integrative function of channeling centrifugal tendencies into support for the existing constitutional order, especially in East Pakistan, let alone command the respect and loyalty of the state's key nonelected institutions, particularly the army, whose senior members distrusted politicians' motivations and capabilities and had already begun to form their own opinions about how Pakistan could be most efficiently and effectively governed so as to ensure the internal order necessary to preserve its territorial integrity.

Losing Control over the Military

The failure of nation-state-building policies to adequately address East Pakistan's genuine demands for autonomy interacted with the perceived external threat to Pakistan's physical security to present treacherous challenges to civilian supremacy, which created the context for the assertion of military supremacy over the state in defense of the nation. Having identified India as Pakistan's mortal enemy, Pakistan's founding fathers concentrated on building up the military. Prime Minister Liaquat considered it prudent to hold the dual offices of prime minister and defense minister, ostensibly to exercise direct control over the national defense effort. But his full-time prime ministerial and party responsibilities meant that he could not devote his undivided attention to the Ministry of Defense. This political absenteeism had at least two effects on the military's perceptions of civilian politicians. First, the generals interpreted the lack of strategic political guidance as clear evidence that politicians, including Quaid-e-Millet (Leader of the Nation) Liaquat, were less concerned about national security imperatives than about their own parochial political interests.[128] Second, giving the generals direct access to the prime minister opened the door to the military's institutional circumvention of the norm of ministerial accountability. In fact, Ayub Khan's staff officer and biographer reveals that absent ministerial oversight, the C in C became the sole source for "giving direct advice to the government instead of their receiving it through a Minister." Ayub Khan "was present on every occasion, associated with everything of importance, taking an interest in all national activities," and "his counsel was obtained before any big or vital decision was taken by the government," whether it concerned "commerce or education, foreign affairs or the interior, industrial development or social welfare."[129] In other words, the "tail wagged the dog."[130]

One senior army officer described the state of civil-military relations in stark terms: "All decisions were made in the GHQ [general headquarters]. There was no civilian control from the top, central government, of the Army machine."[131] In sum, formal structures could not secure civilian supremacy in their own right because the civilian opportunity for controlling the soldiers was restricted by the imperatives of "imminent" war and a "state of continuous tension and antagonism" with an economically and militarily stronger India.[132] The military's position was clear: to defend Pakistan, it needed absolute autonomy to pursue its mission without hindrance.[133]

By 1951, even the formal mechanisms of political oversight of the armed forces, such as the DCC, started to atrophy.[134] In this permissive environment, the military could audaciously rebuff any formal civilian scrutiny on the grounds that outside interference would undermine its combat preparedness. As one former senior army officer explains, "From the security point of view, and lack of trust in civilians, in their ability to keep secrets, the [General Staff] dealt with civil departments directly." When the military needed equipment, it would invoke the sensitivity of the war effort to defy or bypass civilian authorities.[135] For instance, between May 1949 and February 1950, Finance Minister Ghulam Mohammad repeatedly alerted Prime Minister Liaquat to the dangerous tendency of the army C in C and the air force commander to "act beyond their powers" and warned him that their "flagrant disregard" of rules and "serious breaches of finan-

cial procedure" risked a potential "breakdown of financial administration" in the country. In fact, in one instance, the air force openly
defied the DCC, which had approved the purchase of six Halifax
bombers, by delaying their transfer to Pakistan for a year because
the air commander considered them to be worthless.[136] A year later,
the Ministry of Defense placed an order for the purchase of twenty-
four Vickers aircraft without seeking the required approval from the
DCC or the Ministry of Finance.[137]

Military Institutional Development

The institutional effects on the military of the early erosion of civilian oversight were magnified by the military's swift organizational
transformation from a disorganized fragment of the British Indian
Army to a well-equipped and trained military. The sources of this
institutional development were both domestic and external. At independence, the Pakistani military's share of the BIA personnel was
set at one-third, which was about 140,000 troops. Pakistan inherited
the western part of the Punjab, home to the martial Punjabi Muslims, who supplied 48 percent of the total combatants in the pre–
World War II BIA.[138] But it lacked the requisite number of officers.
The late Indianization of the BIA's officer corps meant that Muslim
officers constituted just one-fourth of its total officer strength. Officer shortages were initially met by retaining some 500 British officers. The government set up a special committee that was given the
target of achieving complete nationalization of the armed forces by
January 1951.[139] This goal was reached through granting permanent
commissions to short-service and emergency commissioned officers
and expedited promotions to regular officers.[140] With the exception
of technical branches where British officers were retained, the government was able to appoint Pakistani officers to key command and
staff positions in the army by 1951, including the appointment of
Pakistan's first C in C, General Ayub Khan, in January of that year.

The army's main problem was the lack of firepower. Ayub Khan
described the grim state of the army after partition: "Our army was
badly equipped and terribly disorganized. Yet it had to escort millions

63

of refugees, and fought a war in Kashmir. . . . Throughout this period, we had no properly organized units, no equipment and hardly any ammunition."[141] Pakistan did not receive its full share of the military stores of British India primarily because India held them up on account of the war in Kashmir. Nor did it inherit any major ordnance factories, all seventeen of which were located in India.[142] To its advantage, most of the BIA's military cantonments and many of its key air force establishments were in northwestern India, which became part of Pakistan.[143] Pakistan also inherited strategic naval ports at Karachi and Chittagong. However, only nine of the forty-six training establishments were located in Pakistan. Except for the prestigious Command and Staff College at Quetta, the Indian Military Academy at Dehra Dun and many of the principal combat and technical training schools remained in India.

However, the army was able to overcome these organizational shortcomings quickly thanks to its privileged access to state resources, given the perceived threat of war with India.[144] By mid-August 1949, the Pakistani army had begun to transform itself from a paper army into a well-organized one.[145] The army reconstituted, upgraded, or created key combat-training institutions, including the Armored Corps Training School and the School of Artillery.[146] A new officer-training academy, the Pakistan Military Academy, was established in Kakul, Abottabad (in the North-West Frontier Province), in January 1948, and the first batch of army officers graduated in November 1949.[147] The high command under Ayub Khan designed a new uniform combat-training plan that was implemented down to the unit level through the C in C's annual exercise attended by all general officers, field formations, commanders, and senior staff officers and the directors of different arms and services at the general headquarters.

In March 1951, just two months after his appointment as C in C, Ayub Khan created the Training Advisory Staff to "set, coordinate, and conduct [training] exercises" and advise divisional and brigade commanders on training policy. This body was eventually replaced by the Directorate General of Training under a Pakistani major general in 1956. The general headquarters also updated or replaced post-partition operational plans, especially after the massive Indian troop concentration on Pakistan's border in the summer of 1951. Although logistics facilities were nonexistent at independence, the army succeeded in "realigning logistical concepts and doctrines," and as a result, "the organization and establishment of logistical installations and depots" was carried out in anticipation of "the type and duration" of a future war. Armed forces requirements were standardized, and "specifications were modified . . . to accommodate existing capacity and workmanship."[148]

By 1954, the army could hold large-scale, multiterrain maneuvers in the fields and hills of the Punjab, involving some 50,000 troops.[149] In 1951–1952, Ayub Khan had set up a Planning Board in the army general headquarters to create an infantry division.[150] In essence, the swift reconstitution, reconstruction, and reform of the army, involving "tremendous technical and organizational progress," turned the ex-colonial army into the "real Pakistan Army with a distinct personality of its own," infused with "a new spirit and a new pride."[151] This pride in its achievements against all odds was wildly out of sync with the patent lack of perceived efficiency and unity among politicians and gave impetus to the formation of praetorian proclivities in the senior officer corps.

Although the military's inherited apolitical ethos remained more or less intact between 1947 and early 1951 when British officers commanded it, the seeds of politicization were being sown during that period. Immediately after independence, the need to appear loyal to the founding fathers may have required that the army as an institution continue to project itself as subordinate to the civilian government and to observe constitutional mores. Enjoying internal autonomy and unrestricted access to resources, the military had no apparent reason to cross the civil-military boundaries erected under the British. But especially after the deaths of Jinnah in 1948 and Liaquat in 1951, the military under its first Pakistani C in C, Ayub Khan, developed grave misgivings about the feasibility of the parliamentary system of government in an internally divided and externally threatened Pakistan.

Members of the officer corps had inherited the colonial officials' view of nationalist politicians as untrustworthy rabble-rousers and malcontents.[152] Ayub Khan and his general staff held politicians in contempt for their lack of dedication to Pakistan and believed that centralized government, unmediated by populist pressures, could ensure the internal cohesion and sense of purpose that was a prerequisite for strong external defense. As members of the first-class army of a third-world country, the general staff officers began to conceive a wider project of political tutelage in the early 1950s.[153] One senior officer testifies, "A great deal of time was spent in the army headquarters on political discussion" and the lack of probity, stability, and efficiency in administrative and political life. For instance, as a way to create national unity (and, in effect, to blunt the numerical advantage of the Bengali majority), the military under Ayub became firmly committed to the idea of uniting all the provinces of West Pakistan into "One Unit" to rationalize administration.[154]

Secret American documents provide further evidence of the military leadership's determination to "influence and control the trajectory of the political affairs of the state."[155] One declassified telegram written by an American diplomat in Pakistan in 1952 relates a conversation with C in C Ayub Khan about reports that Pakistani army officers were favorably inclined toward military intervention in politics, following the example of Egypt, Syria, and Lebanon. The general's response is revealing on at least two counts. First, he assured the diplomat that he had warned his divisional commanders that "the talk of the Pakistan Army taking over government must be stopped . . . that the Pakistan army did not have trained men in governmental affairs,"[156] thus showing that he was concerned more about "not having trained personnel to run the affairs of the government, as opposed to the acceptance of the civilian supremacy over all governmental affairs, including those of the military."[157] Second, he told

66

the American official that whether the issue was foreign policy or domestic crises, the "Pakistan Army will not allow the political leaders to get out of hand, and the same is true regarding the people of Pakistan,"[158] and if need be, "the army would declare a military government in order to secure stability."[159] Ayub's declared intention of exercising military control to ensure preferred domestic and external outcomes leaves little doubt that as early as 1952–1953, the high command had come to believe that overthrowing a duly constituted civilian government was appropriate and well within the military's professional purview.

In the opinion of Major General Sher Khan Pataudi, then serving as adjutant general in army headquarters, an understanding of civilian problems was considered "essential for the commanders . . . so that they understood the problems in which they may have to play their part as guardians of the country."[160] In these early years, army headquarters regularly monitored civilian government performance. Initially, the high command was content with exercising indirect oversight over the government while it built up its organizational capacity. But as its importance grew in direct proportion to the intensity of the perceived threat from India, it began to acquire institutional bases of power in the policy-making process.

Expanding Military Roles

By 1952–1953, military pessimism about civilian incompetence and lack of interest in nation building deepened to the extent that the army under General Ayub Khan began to participate liberally in, perhaps even to encroach on, nonmilitary missions through the instrument of "aid to the civil power."[161] As early as 1951, the military acquired the confidence and experience to conduct large-scale nation-building activities, including emergency operations during natural disasters, construction of public infrastructure, and, above all, what the army called security operations to preserve the nation. In its purported role as the chief guardian of internal peace, the army's most significant deployment was in Lahore in March 1953.[162] The prevalent account shows that in March 1953, the provincial government called in the military to restore order after the police failed to control riots against the minority Ahmadi Muslims led by the Islamist Majlise Ahrar and the Jamaate Islami.[163] However, days before the military moved in to stabilize the situation, Ayub Khan confidently assured his American interlocutors that as the "only stabilizing force in Pakistan," the army would not let "things get out of control."[164]

As the army's quasi-official account suggests, the local general officer commanding, Major General Azam Khan, had already concentrated and mobilized his troops in anticipation of a decisive military operation. Frustrated by the provincial administration's apathy and "loss of wit," he sought and received direct approval from army headquarters to impose martial law.[165] The military quickly imposed order. But it soon became clear that the high command's interpretation of "aid to the civil power" was rather expansive. The army involved itself in repairing roads, constructing pavements, sprucing up public parks, cleaning up shops, and controlling the prices of essential goods. To "foster a civic sense among the public," Azam Khan sponsored a Healthier Lahore Week and deployed the services of Inter-Services Public Relations, the military's media wing, to organize a publicity campaign against "social evils like excessive expenses on marriages and parties."[166]

It is clear that an apparent civilian failure to reestablish public order presented the military with an opportunity to temporarily supplant the civilian administration. But the army's aggressive and self-initiated "aid to the civil power" operation, its supersession of local authorities, and its self-assumed responsibility to civilize the public and streamline the civilian administration attest to a broader desire to appropriate nonmilitary functions. In fact, the army extended martial law beyond the deadline set by the central government even though the law-and-order situation in Lahore had returned to normal.[167] According to the former head of military public relations, Brigadier A. R. Siddiqi, then working as a captain in the Lahore office of Inter-Service Public Relations, martial law was the army's "biggest exercise yet in the management and application of force in civil affairs."[168] The successful execution of military government (even if local) only reinforced the confidence of senior officers in their ability to provide a more efficient form of government. It also intensified the growing contradiction between a rapidly institutionalizing military and the perceived failure of civilian politicians and bureaucrats to provide public order and governance. In fact, by the end of the period of martial law, "the idea of the superiority of military power over civilian authority had taken root in officers' minds" and had made them "dismiss the grim reality of their political involvement and praetorianism."[169] The generally enthusiastic initial response of the public to martial law only reinforced these beliefs.

Although domestic resources provided the early impetus, Pakistan's defense ties to Washington consolidated and completed the process of military institutionalization. To overcome the domestic resource and technological constraints on effectively balancing the threat from India, the Pakistani military began to seek foreign military supplies soon after independence. For instance, the army sent a top-level mission to the United States in June–July 1949 to solicit US military assistance in return for close cooperation with Washington in "long range defense planning" against the Soviets.[170] In 1952, the military initiated formal efforts to forge a military alliance with the United States without consulting the political leadership.[171] In October 1953, Ayub Khan felt confident enough to visit Washington and urge senior American military and political leaders to provide Pakistan with aid even though the government "had not corresponded with the State Department at all about it."[172]

But despite the Pakistani military's strenuous efforts to court the United States, the Americans could offer only limited aid in the early years because of "legal, supply, and policy priority" constraints. Still, the US Department of State believed that "the final political orientation of Pakistani leaders will be influenced by the responses they receive to these requests. We may desire the use of bases and other facilities in Pakistan in the event of war. Our responses to Pakistan's request for military aid should increase its willingness to make bases available to us."[173]

Despite this recommendation for striking a mutually beneficial bargain with Pakistan, it was not until Washington needed a strategic proxy state in Southwest Asia during the administration of President Dwight D. Eisenhower that a military pact between the two nations became possible. US concerns about maintaining Asian security in the aftermath of the Korean War greatly enhanced the alliance value of geographically important states like Pakistan for America's containment policy. Given Pakistan's proximity to the Soviet Union and the Persian Gulf, American military planners saw the country as an important supplier of strategic bases in the event of a war and later as a staging ground for intelligence operations against the USSR.[174] Because nonaligned India was unavailable, the Eisenhower administration co-opted Pakistan into the Cold War containment alliances it was building in the Middle East (the Central Treaty Organization) and Southeast Asia (the Southeast Asia Treaty Organization).

In October 1954, the army under General and Defense Minister Ayub Khan received a major external boost when the two countries signed the Mutual Defense Assistance Agreement. Under the agreement, Pakistan initially received $171 million in "military equipment and training assistance" in recognition for "its desire to play a role in the collective defense of the free world."[175] American aid also created new infrastructure in the form of military cantonments and airfields, as well as training facilities. Between 1954 and 1965, members of the officer corps were routinely trained in the United States until the second India-Pakistan war in 1965 triggered an American military aid embargo.[176]

Although the aid was not significant in gross financial terms, US military advisory missions and equipment helped transform the army into a well-equipped force armed with modern weaponry and make it qualitatively superior to the Indian military.[177] Between 1954 and 1957, the program strengthened existing Pakistani forces and envisaged the expansion of four infantry divisions, the expansion of an armored brigade into an armored division, the creation of an independent armored brigade, the provision of aircraft to equip six fighter squadrons, and the modernization of air bases.[178] By drastically increasing the size, sophistication, and firepower of the Pakistani army, American military assistance not only reinforced the military's sense of superiority to civilians but also emboldened it to take risky actions in the conflict with India, including the initiation of a war in 1965. Exposure to American concepts and military thought also had a "decisive influence on the ideas of the officer corps" in relation to both strategy and tactics.[179] As documented in the army's quasi-official history, the attitudes imparted by this exposure "broadened its outlook" and "increased its efficiency," adding an extra layer of self-assuredness about the military's institutional capacity to intervene in civilian politics.[180]

In a process similar to that in Guillermo O'Donnell's portrayal of the Argentinean military before the 1964 coup,[181] military officers in top staff and command positions inevitably started making comparisons between the military's rapid institutionalization, marked by its development as a cohesive professional group, and what they saw as divisive civilian politics that retarded the country's political and economic development. Many senior army leaders wondered why the "army as a whole could [not] take on any and every problem of the state."[182] Early deadlocks in constitution making and power struggles between the governor general and the Constituent Assembly would give them plenty of opportunities to test these assumptions.

2

MARCHING TOWARD MARTIAL LAW

In the early 1950s, the central issue of constitutional politics in Pakistan was the proper distribution of administrative, political, and economic power between the center and the provinces, especially East Pakistan. One of the toughest challenges to the Islamic identity of Pakistan championed by the founding fathers was the early emergence of Bengali linguistic nationalism. Key to finding a solution to this problem was evolving a working federal constitutional formula to peacefully integrate the Bengalis into the national mainstream. However, the West Pakistan–controlled central government was loath to concede meaningful provincial autonomy lest a "tendency might develop which would have an adverse effect on the cohesion of the various units of Pakistan."[1]

Although the Bengalis had a majority in the Constituent Assembly of Pakistan (CAP), the military and, to a lesser degree, the civilian bureaucracy were predominantly Punjabi. Hence the more resources the state invested in building the military, the more it perpetuated this gross regional imbalance and attenuated provincial autonomy. From the Bengali nationalists' viewpoint, West Pakistani elites had effectively captured the state and excluded them from power. By the same token, the Bengalis did not share the sense of urgency in the Pakistani state's primary security project of defense against India. As noted in the Introduction, the external threat did not produce the conventional effect of uniting the nation against its enemy and directing the military away from domestic politics, in good part because the very idea of the nation was deeply contested.

The Bengalis' sense of exclusion from the state and the central government was exacerbated by discrimination and inequality in other forms beyond fair representation in the state structures. By 1954–1955, the central axis of the conflict had shifted to economics. Pakistan's highest-earning export crop, jute, was produced in East Pakistan, but its revenues were unfairly appropriated for the military and industrial development of West Pakistan. During the first decade of independence, the central government allocated nearly two-thirds of developmental and nondevelopmental funds to West Pakistan. From 1947–1948 to 1960, 62 percent of foreign developmental aid and loans went to West Pakistan, and only 17 percent was allocated to East Pakistan, with the rest going to the central government.[2] Given their numerical majority, the Bengalis' only hope of getting a fair share in governing the state was through competitive politics. However, a free and fair national election on the basis of population threatened to end the political and economic domination of West Pakistan's unelected elites.

Hence interwing disagreements over political representation and their contrasting preferences over the electoral system helped complicate and delay the process of constitution making and, therefore, elections. There were also fundamental differences on the issue of representation in any future constitutional framework. West Pakistani politicians generally favored interwing parity, but because Bengalis were virtually excluded from the state structures, especially the army, they were firmly committed to a majoritarian democracy in which parliamentary representation would be based on population. The other major point of disagreement was the electoral system. Bengalis wanted a joint-electorate system because of the sizable

Hindu population of East Pakistan (22 percent).[3] The West Pakistan–dominated center preferred separate electorates that would divide Bengali Hindus and Bengali Muslims. In the words of one scholar, separate electorates were "a mechanism of segregation and control rather than multi-culturalism, and would ultimately contribute to undermining Bengali loyalty."[4]

Given the lack of a serious competitor, the Muslim League was dominant in both West Pakistan and East Bengal in the early years. In fact, it won provincial elections held in the Punjab in 1951 and the North-West Frontier in 1952. But unable or unwilling to improve its organization or expand its support base, the ruling League gradually lost its hold over provincial politics, especially in the eastern wing, as Bengali grievances against the central government increased and the central government failed to address them. Hence the League was routed in the March 1954 provincial elections in East Bengal by the United Front (UF), a coalition of major Bengali parties, including the nationalist Awami League and the socialist Krishak Saramik Party, which mobilized the Bengali electorate by promising to implement a twenty-one-point agenda of institutional reforms.[5] This charter of Bengali nationalist resentment included demands for the adoption of Bengali as a state language and as the medium of education and for regional autonomy according to the Lahore Resolution of 1940, which would basically give the provincial ministry control of all state subjects except defense, currency, and foreign affairs, which would be under joint center-province authority. It also advocated the shifting of naval headquarters from Karachi to East Pakistan and the arming of the Ansar (a volunteer civil force created in 1948 to assist the police in East Pakistan in crime suppression) for its defense.[6]

The viceregal executive and the military saw the rise of this ethnoregional elite as a threat to the security of Pakistan. In particular, the demand for the adoption of Bengali as a state language was seen as "the start of the disintegration of Pakistan" and a "triumph for those who wanted to see East Pakistan detach from West Pakistan and bring it near to India."[7] The UF's alleged Communist bent supplied an additional sense of urgency to the problem. Official intelligence assessments of the League's defeat stated categorically that Communists were instrumental in the coalition's victory. This attitude was not restricted to the governor general and the civil-military bureaucratic elites. At one cabinet meeting in April 1954, the country's finance minister explained, "The flight of capital from East Bengal had already started and no assurances given by Central ministers was going to stop it, unless the attitude of the masses in Bengal was changed. The change had to be brought about. . . . The problem was not conceding Bengal a thing but of fighting communism. Making any concession to East Bengal would be really making concession to communism."[8]

By May 1954, Military Intelligence was reporting "disturbing" Communist activity in East Bengal to the defense ministry.[9] A top-secret Ministry of Interior summary for the cabinet, based on reports by the Intelligence Bureau, declared that the UF's twenty-one-point agenda was the agenda of the "Communist Party" funded by the "Hindu capitalists of Calcutta" for the "destruction of Pakistan."[10] It is not surprising that the governor general imposed governor's rule under Section 92A and dismissed the UF ministry (which was the first non–Muslim League government in Pakistan) after barely two months in office, ostensibly for its inability to maintain public order and for engaging in antistate activities.[11] The defense secretary, Major General Iskander Mirza, was appointed governor to effect the needed change in the attitude of the Bengalis with the full might of the state.[12] Mirza's harsh tactics against Bengali "subversive elements inimical to Pakistan," such as the arrest of over a thousand people, including legislators and college professors, further delegitimized the government and inflamed collective Bengali outrage against West Pakistan.

If nothing else, the 1954 elections permanently changed party politics in Pakistan and clearly revealed that the major political axis was regional.[13] The Muslim League was essentially restricted to West Pakistan, and the Bengali parties had no support base in Pakistan.

This fragmented polity and especially Bengali demands for autonomy particularly alarmed the military, trained in the imagined
unity of the nation. Its leadership viewed provincialism as an arti-
fice of politicians' chicanery and as a serious threat to the integrity of
Pakistan. Frustrated with what its members viewed as the lack of
national cohesion and a constitutional formula to achieve administrative and developmental rationalization, General Ayub Khan
drafted a blueprint for a constitution in October 1954 with the title
"A Short Appreciation of Present and Future Problems of Pakistan."
Its main aim was to put the allegedly easily misled people of Pakistan on a path of unity, stability, and development. Democracy in
Pakistan, wrote Ayub, could work only if it "suits the genius of the
people." Hence his plan proposed a "controlled democracy with
checks and counterchecks" to make it work under local conditions. It
advocated a strong presidential system in which the president would
have unfettered executive authority to control the cabinet and the
provincial ministries. Elections to the central and provincial legislatures were to be indirect to avert the dangers of universal suffrage,
that is, the election of unscrupulous politicians by uneducated people. Assuming the natural strategic and economic unity of the area
constituting West Pakistan, it recommended that all its provinces be
welded into One Unit so that it could develop properly and become
a bulwark of defense for Pakistan. This would also create parity
between the two wings, which would harmonize development and
reduce provincialism, thus preventing politicians from misleading
the people by fanning subnational loyalties. Each unit was to have its
own legislature of 150 members, which would appoint a cabinet that
would be controlled by a governor, accountable to the head of state
and empowered to dismiss provincial governments. No less crucially,
the plan called for the fusion of civilian and military authority to rationalize the national defense structure and make it immune to political interference by appointing a military supreme commander who
would head a triservice joint staff and double as defense minister.[14]

With military backing, the viceregal executive actively subverted the norms of cabinet government, thus arresting the normal development of political institutions. During 1953 and 1954, jurisdictional conflicts between Governor General Ghulam Mohammad (1951–1955) and the prime minister or the CAP created an opportunity for the military to insert itself formally into power politics ostensibly on behalf of its civilian supreme commander. In the process, the generals abandoned even the pretense of political neutrality and began to openly intervene in political crises as the dominant component of what Morris Janowitz calls a "civil-military" coalition, in which the military "expands its political activity and becomes an active political bloc," and civilian executives or parties can "remain in power only because of the passive assent or active assistance" of the armed forces.[15]

This pattern of behavior is somewhat similar to what Alfred Stepan calls the moderating role of the military, except that in Stepan's model, the military accepts the inherent legitimacy of parliamentary forms of government and rates its relative capacity to govern lower than that of civilians. It crosses the boundaries of the moderating pattern to seize power only after it develops, articulates, and internalizes an all-encompassing ideology of security and development considered necessary to avoid a societal (communist) revolution.[16] In contrast, the Pakistani military ranked its capacity to govern as higher than that of civilians and had serious reservations about the legitimacy or feasibility of parliamentary democracy.

Between 1954 and 1956, this civil-military coalition exercised tutelage over the cabinet and parliament. In their tutelary role, the generals kept the unelected head of state in power to thwart challenges to centralized rule and an India-centric defense policy. For instance, Governor General Ghulam Mohammad and the military decided to summarily remove the Muslim League cabinet of Prime Minister Khawaja Nazimuddin in April 1953,[17] even though he had a majority in parliament and had recently passed a budget.[18] By his own admission, Ayub "had worked hard to have something along this line accomplished."[19] In defense of the viceregal coup, Ayub deployed his troops at key points in the country, and the threat of military action was used to preempt the legislative assembly from convening an emergency session.[20]

The reasons given by the governor general for the dismissal were the government's inability to maintain order and to provide food security. However, the prime minister's policies violated everything for which the civil-military coalition stood, including a centralized state with a powerful military as the only guarantee of Pakistan's survival against the threat from India. In fact, the *Second Basic Principles Committee Report* (the Nazimuddin report), released in December 1952, included a major concession to East Pakistan by providing it a majority in the national legislature. The Nazimuddin cabinet was also considering a no-war declaration offered by Indian prime minister Jawarhalal Nehru, which would provide "the perfect cover for reducing defense expenditures" to improve "an extremely critical economic situation," marked by precarious wheat shortages. The cabinet did not finally approve the proposed no-war pact with India because it lacked a reliable framework for the resolution of outstanding bilateral disputes.[21] But it did make an attempt to reduce military allocations in the budget, and this action also ultimately contributed to its downfall.[22]

The dismissal of the Nazimuddin ministry and the imposition of governor's rule in East Pakistan in May 1954 prompted the CAP—especially its majority Bengali members—to curtail the extraordinary powers of the viceregal executive. In September 1954, it repealed the Public and Representative Offices Disqualification Act to preempt its use against assembly members. It then passed the Government of India (Fifth Amendment) Act to divest the governor general of his discretionary powers and to prevent the arbitrary sacking of yet another government. In October, the CAP finalized a draft constitutional bill that reduced the president (who would replace the governor general) to a titular head of state.[23] The draft constitution accepted the crucial Bengali demand that Bengali be declared a national language alongside Urdu. The legislature would be bicameral, with representation in the lower house on the basis of population and representation in the upper house on the principle of equality between the federating units. The federal government would have authority over defense, foreign affairs, currency, and communications, while the residual subjects would be reserved for the provinces.

Before the assembly could formally adopt the constitution, Ghulam Mohammad (by now incoherent after a stroke had left him partially paralyzed) declared a state of emergency throughout Pakistan on October 24, 1954, and dissolved the CAP because "it had lost the confidence of the people and can no longer function."[24] The explicit role of the military was even more transparent in the 1954 intervention. Prime Minister Mohammad Ali Bogra was called back from a trip to the United States and was escorted to the governor general's residence under armed guard, where he was threatened with dire consequences: cooperate or face martial law or worse. He was made to agree to continue as prime minister with a reconstituted cabinet. As *Dawn* noted: "There have indeed been times—such as that October night in 1954—when, a general to the right of him and a general to the left of him, a half-mad Governor General imposed upon a captured Prime Minister the dissolution of the Constituent Assembly and the virtual setting up of a semi-dictatorial executive."[25]

The governor general called this autocratic progeny the "cabinet of talents," which was most notable for the allocation of the two most powerful ministries of coercion, interior and defense, to members of the defense establishment: Major General Iskander Mirza and the commander in chief, General Ayub Khan, respectively. In particular, Ayub's elevation to the cabinet left little doubt that the military was the real power behind the throne. Having secured a place in the central cabinet, Ayub could now formally implement the army's grand constitutional scheme, including the merger of the provinces of West Pakistan into One Unit, which had achieved greater urgency after the UF victory in East Bengal. The cabinet of talents initiated the process of that merger in November 1954 and tried to lend it a veneer of legitimacy by seeking formal approval from provincial legislatures. However, there was a "general and deep seated fear in all other units that unification would mean control of West Pakistan by the Punjab."[26] Hence the scheme was imposed on the smaller units by outright coercion, including the threat of military takeover and the sacking of unsupportive provincial governments (for example, in Sindh).[27] The cabinet also devised a draft constitution based on Ayub's blueprint, but it was aborted by a Federal Court ruling that mandated that only a new assembly could make the constitution and ratify the creation of the One Unit in West Pakistan. Hence the governor general had to convene a second assembly.

In June 1955, the new CAP was indirectly elected by an electoral college of the provincial assemblies, like its predecessor. It ratified a new constitution in March 1956 that represented a "reaction of the politicians" against the viceregal-military coalition.[28] The constitution provided for a unicameral legislature consisting of 300 members equally divided between the two wings and reduced the powers of the president (the successor of the governor general), who was to act only on the advice of cabinet ministers, with the exception of the power to declare an emergency under certain conditions. The president no longer had the power to dissolve parliament arbitrarily or veto legislation indefinitely. However, the president could remove the prime minister if he was satisfied that the latter had "ceased to command the confidence of the assembly."[29] This provision left ambiguity that could be exploited by a president like Mirza who believed that only controlled democracy could work in Pakistan. Bengali and Urdu became national languages, and the principle of parity in representation between the two wings was retained.

The military leadership viewed the constitution as a recipe for anarchy. In Ayub Khan's assessment, it was a "document of despair" that "by distributing powers between the president, the Prime Minister and his cabinet, and the provinces" had "destroyed the focal point of power and left no one in a position of control."[30] Two and a half years later, the military seized power and threw the constitution into the dustbin of history.

Constitution to Coup: Instability, Interests, or Ideas?

Between the creation of the second CAP in July 1955 and the military coup in October 1958, four short-lived coalition governments formally ruled Pakistan's central government. Some scholars have attributed the coup to cabinet instability.[31] It is unclear why frequent cabinet changes should directly concern the military unless the military considers such changes to be its business. Barring catastrophic conditions, professional militaries that lack tutelary tendencies are likely to view political discord or government instability as a normal part of the political process. In contrast, militaries that consider their involvement in politics legitimate are likely to respond to political crises as cues for action.

Factional rivalries and shifting coalitions, expedient politicking, and regular changes in government at the national and provincial levels no doubt marked Pakistan's politics at the time, but these teething problems did not constitute a breakdown of the political system. In fact, the 1956 constitution had operated for barely two years, and Pakistan's first universally enfranchised national elections were scheduled to be held in February 1959. Even sympathetic observers wondered whether political instability was really the cause of the ultimate breakdown of representative government, especially given the "remarkable revival of the Muslim League, which was now dominant in West Pakistan and had won significant municipal elections in the East."[32]

In fact, political instability possibly owed as much to civilian deficits as it did to the attitudes and actions of the authoritarian civil-military coalition, now formally headed by Mirza, who replaced Ghulam Mohammad as governor general in October 1955 and was elected president under the new constitution.[33] Like Ayub, Mirza had inherited the colonial officials' distrust of politicians and harbored grave doubts about the appropriateness of parliamentary democracy in Pakistan because in his view the people needed controlled democracy in which "the head of state should exercise control as long as the vast majority of the people remained illiterate and unfit for true democracy."[34]

With full military backing, Mirza repeatedly undermined the working of parliamentary government. One illustrative example was the coalition government of the Awami League prime minister H. S. Suhrawardy (1956–1957), arguably one of the most seasoned political leaders the country had known since Liaquat, who was "fully committed to freeing the political process from the clutches of the civil-military oligarchy."[35] In fact, Ayub was deeply suspicious of Suhrawardy because of the latter's "unnecessarily harsh and undignified" questioning of army officers in the Rawalpindi conspiracy trial as the conspirators' defense lawyer. It was only after Suhrawardy agreed to no interference in the army's affairs that Ayub consented to his appointment.[36]

In the thirteen months during which he was in power, Suhrawardy sought to create a cross-regional coalition of the Bengali Awami League and the Republican Party (a breakaway faction of the Muslim League), a direct threat to dominance of the authoritarian coalition. Although he supported the general direction of Pakistan's pro-US foreign policy and valiantly defended it against the political uproar during the Suez crisis of 1956, he also tried to assert his authority over the military. In particular, Suhrawardy was concerned about the ethnic lopsidedness of the armed forces. In an April 1957 note to the Ministry of Defense, the prime minister officially expressed his displeasure about the exclusion of East Pakistan from "our defense requirements" and observed that "East Pakistan can never be contented until its people get military training and are absorbed in some defense formations." As a way out, he recommended affirmative action for Bengalis in the military by lowering the physical standards of recruitment. In response, the commander in chief, General Ayub

Khan, blamed the lack of army representativeness on East Pakistani youths' lackluster response to army recruitment efforts and noted that although physical standards could be lowered to encourage more Bengali induction, this would be undesirable for combat, and that an official inquiry committee had recommended equal physical standards for recruits from both wings.[37] However, Ayub ultimately lowered these standards just a month after the October 1958 coup.[38]

The prime minister's relations with the military soured further over the growing opposition to the One Unit in West Pakistan and demands for radical autonomy from East Pakistan. Although the Suhrawardy government was able to block the implementation of a resolution passed by the East Pakistan assembly seeking a confederation in April 1957, Suhrawardy was unable or unwilling to prevent the West Pakistan assembly from approving a resolution to dissolve the One Unit in September of the same year, which provoked a sharp rebuke from its chief architect, General Ayub. Under pressure from the general, the prime minister was obliged to issue a joint statement with the president in support of maintaining the federal structure until general elections could be held.[39]

In less than a month, Suhrawardy's government fell after the Republican Party withdrew support from the government (reportedly on Mirza's insistence). When the prime minister tried to seek a vote of confidence from the CAP, the military-backed president threatened him with dismissal and forced him to resign.[40] The Suhrawardy government's demise spelled the effective end of parliamentary government in Pakistan because no parliamentary party could muster a majority to form a stable government. Each government was dependent on fickle coalitions. For instance, the next government, headed by Muslim League prime minister I. I. Chundrigar, fell quickly after the Republican Party withdrew its support for separate electorates. Finally, the head of the Republican Party, Malik Feroze Khan Noon, was able to form a multiparty alliance that included Suhrawardy's Awami League, but it was cut short by the military coup in October 1958.

How are we to interpret the motives behind the coup? Some scholars have described it as defensive military action to repulse threats to its corporate interests. Mazhar Aziz contends that the generals feared that the national elections scheduled for February 1959 would bring a hostile government to power, which would have directly threatened its institutional privileges, including unhindered access to budgetary resources.[41] Corporate grievances have provided powerful triggers of military intervention in other contexts as well.[42]

The victory of a Bengali or Bengali-led coalition in the forthcoming elections might have put the military's resources and even its vision of internal stability and foreign policy in danger. Bengali nationalists' demands for real decentralization of power to East Pakistan, the eradication of economic disparity between the two wings, their more conciliatory attitude toward India, and their preference for nonalignment in the bipolar Cold War stood in direct opposition to the military's firm belief in centralized government, anti-India hostility, and a pro-US foreign policy. In fact, even the Muslim League and other West Pakistani leaders had started to question the utility of the Cold War alliance with the United States because of that country's lack of commitment to resolving the Kashmir and other disputes with India. Therefore, they were advocating a nonaligned foreign policy.[43]

However, considering the military's preemption of an unfavorable national election, a corporate interest stretches the term's meaning. Pakistani officers led by Ayub were not driven simply by the desire to preserve military budgets or corporate autonomy. They wanted to change the structure of government. As would become evident soon after the coup, Ayub and his colleagues desired to establish a new form of democracy in accordance with his 1954 plan. Their reasoning was simple: parliamentary democracy had failed to address the country's political, economic, and social problems, and politicians could not be trusted to solve them because they were too power hungry, corrupt, and selfish. However, these perceptions were not sufficient to cause intervention. Intervention was also predicated on the officer corps's belief in the appropriateness of extraconstitutional change to realize a broader political project of reform of state and society beyond simply safeguarding its borders.[44] If the issue is seen in this way, it becomes clear that an important factor in the Pakistani military's calculus of intervention was the internal organizational legitimacy of "praetorian dreaming in the barracks."[45] In other words, the military had an ideal state in mind that its members believed could be achieved only by the application of military skills and solutions to civilian political problems. In fact, the military high command had been ready for years to step in when necessary to put Pakistan on a proper course as defined by the military. Ayub had declared his intention to intervene as early as 1953.[46] His constitutional scheme and his participation in the cabinet of talents in 1954 left little doubt that he had no qualms about trespassing on civilian turf in what he considered the national interest.

Between January and April 1957, senior officers repeatedly recommended drastic action to Ayub on several occasions to reverse the "country's rapid drift towards chaos."[47] In November of that year, the Ministry of Defence reported to the cabinet the military's discontent stemming from the general feeling in the ranks that political instability was "retard[ing] the pace of progress in the country" and preventing the resolution of fundamental national problems like Kashmir, canal waters, and inflation.[48]

Military accounts of the time show that the armed forces were particularly proud of their impeccable record of national service and disgusted by inept civilian politicians whom they thought would easily sacrifice the country's vital interests for political and personal self-aggrandizement, thus creating the need for a military solution.[49] With the self-image of guardians of the national interest, military officers were highly sensitive to the negative impact of adverse economic and political conditions on the country. As Ayub Khan noted: "The army could not remain unaffected by the conditions around it. Nor was it conceivable that officers and men would not react to all the political chicanery, intrigue, corruption and inefficiency manifest in every sphere of life. They had their relatives. They read newspapers."[50]

Because the officers were "accustomed to good government within the army," many of them believed that they understood and could resolve these problems better than anyone else. Hence they took several initiatives to right perceived civilian wrongs. For instance, the military organized Operation Close Door in December 1957 to stem the loss of revenue in East Pakistan as a result of the smuggling of food and imported goods to West Bengal and Assam by sealing the borders.[51] Concerned about the impact of the operation on Hindu families transferring their capital across the border, Hindu members of the provincial assembly put pressure on the Awami League government to act. Responding to demands from his Awami League coalition partners in the center, Prime Minister Feroze Khan Noon reportedly intervened with the general officer commanding on their behalf, and also agreed to amend the ordinance that had given the army special powers to conduct anti-smuggling operations.[52] The army deeply resented this civilian malfeasance because it undermined its operational activities and threatened "the very concept of coordinated military command."[53] General Ayub promptly warned the prime minister through President Mirza to stop meddling and let the army finish its task.[54] However, the adverse effects of such interference were that even the enlisted ranks developed "an intense hatred of the politicians and the officer class felt thoroughly disgusted."[55]

During the campaign for the first national elections, initially scheduled for November 1958, all the major parties in West Pakistan's smaller former provinces demanded the dissolution of the One Unit, and the Bengalis reiterated their demands for full regional autonomy, thus threatening what the military leadership considered the fundamental institutional pillars of internal cohesion and stability. When reporters asked General Ayub about the army's combat preparedness months before the coup, he bluntly advised them to stop worrying about the army's business and to "attend to your leaders who are wrecking the country."[56] As he explained more vividly in his first speech after the coup:

> This is a drastic and extreme step, taken with great reluctance, but with the fullest conviction that there was no alternative to it except the disintegration and complete ruination of the country. These chaotic conditions as you know have been brought about by self-seekers, who in the garb of political leaders, have ravaged the country. . . . In their thirst for power, they allowed things to drift and discipline to go to pieces. There is no limit to the depth of their baseness, chicanery, deceit and degradation. The country and the people could go to [the] dogs as far as they were concerned. . . . Our ultimate aim is to restore democracy . . . but of the type that people can understand and work.[57]

Ayub's words can easily be dismissed as military clichés or opportunistic self-justifications, an affliction common to most coup makers.[58] But the general's visceral denunciation of politicians also reflected the military's institutional assessment that civilian ineptitude and imported democracy were responsible for Pakistan's arrested political and economic development. By 1958, senior members of the officer corps appear to have concluded that getting rid of a dysfunctional democracy and establishing military rule was the only option left to save Pakistan from its quarreling, corrupt, and unpatriotic politicians, who, they believed, were interested only in acquiring power for power's sake without any regard for national unity and security.[59] In October 1958, when the military finally intervened, the high command had seen all available and acceptable parties and possible coalitions in government.[60] Because none of them had met exacting military standards of proper government, the generals decided to uproot the alien political system, which in their view had already caused enough turmoil.[61]

Domestic Threats and External Influences

According to the military's postcoup assessment, the coup followed a period of economic deterioration evident in rising inflation, food shortages, and high budget deficits.[62] But there was no serious economic crisis at the time, and in almost all economic measures, India was faring no better than Pakistan. "In all cases," wrote Wayne Wilcox, "an objective [India-Pakistan] comparison would favor Pakistan. . . . [But] no one seriously advocated martial law for India."[63] There was also no real threat of internal fragmentation or public tumult before the coup.[64] Questioned by some as fabricated, the main internal threat cited by the military as a rationale for the coup was the declaration of independence by the ruler (khan) of the princely state of Kalat in October 1958.[65]

If the intervention was actually driven by a threat to national unity and public order posed by a volatile political and economic situation, why could the intended objective not have been achieved by military action in aid of civil power rather than a coup? The point is not whether the political crises or other internal threats were imagined or real.[66] To put it in Lewis Coser's words, "If men define a threat as real, although there may be little, or nothing in reality to justify this belief, the threat is real in its consequences."[67] In other words, what mattered in shaping the military's institutional response to these perceived threats was how the military interpreted them.[68] In effect, the officer corps's guardian beliefs meant that they would see only certain options to deal with the situation as the most appropriate, and even seemingly minor political and economic threats would provide magnified cues for institutional action to preserve state cohesion.

The military did perceive an immediate threat to its integrity from a Nasserite-style junior officers' coup, which General Ayub feared was the handiwork of politicians who wanted to divide the military for their petty political gains. Because the military believed that it was the only thing standing between anarchy and order, destroying the army would simply destroy Pakistan.[69] In other words, the generals were not "some capricious ogres whose only interests are destroying democracy and raiding the national treasury. Their intervention, they believe, is always in the national interest—to save their country or protect their institution, which is the very embodiment of nationhood."[70]

But even this apparently grave threat to military cohesion does not explain why the high command upended constitutional government rather than dealing firmly with the alleged coup plotters, something it had done earlier in the Rawalpindi conspiracy. There might be another side to the story. Because the military was not a neutral political actor (and was not seen as one by most civilian politicians), and because there was no guaranteed electoral route to power, some self-interested politicians may have simply tried to exploit an already-politicized military, which in turn reinforced the military's fear that they would even break up the only national institution holding the country together.[71]

One final factor that deserves attention is the alleged role of the US government in fomenting the coup, an argument typically favored by some Marxian scholars. In this view, the "primary reason for the coup was the overriding desire of the U.S. to protect its oil interests in the region, along with the maintenance of the Pakistani military's newly acquired privileges."[72] Why the United States needed just the Pakistani military to secure its oil supply remains unclear. It is quite plausible that the United States did not view favorably the independent, nonaligned foreign policy advocated by the major Bengali and West Pakistani leaders. The military coup in Iraq in July 1958, which displaced the pro-Western King Faisal II and jeopardized the US-led Baghdad Pact alliance, combined with increasing Soviet influence in that country and growing Soviet pressure on Afghanistan and Iran to enhance the importance for Washington of maintaining a friendly government in Pakistan. The country provided "territory within striking distance of the Soviet Union," and US-built airfields and other military installations were considered crucial for "U.S. strategic air operations in the event of hostilities."[73]

That these concerns actually led Washington to forcefully disrupt the political process in Pakistan appears less convincing. There are no primary Pakistani sources on the coup. The main historical source is the declassified record of the US State Department and the National Security Council, which can shed light on the US role. Although it is hard to rule out the possibility that documents pointing to a more overt US role might appear in the future, the existing publicly available official US documents provide no evidence of a direct American role in organizing or sponsoring the military coup (unlike US involvement in the coups in Iran in 1953 and Chile in 1973, for which there is concrete documentary evidence).[74]

There is no doubt that the most important goal of US Cold War foreign policy, not peculiar to Pakistan, was to seek stability, not democracy, in what was known as the third world. In Pakistan, this emphasis translated into clear US support for the moderate, anti-Communist defense establishment, led by General Ayub Khan, in return for the Pakistani military's cooperation with the United States and participation in Cold War regional alliances designed to contain the Soviet Union. The National Security Council summed up US policy: "Support the present government of Pakistan so long as it remains friendly to the United States, and seek to insure that any successor government is not Communist controlled and is friendly to the United States."[75]

Ayub, as well as Mirza, clearly exploited US fears of Soviet expansionism by ratcheting up the Communist threat posed by left-wing politicians, especially in East Pakistan, to the country's pro-West foreign policy. At the same time, they projected the military as the only force ready to fight communist countries,[76] stopping Communist infiltration into Pakistan, and keeping the rowdy mullahs in line. For instance, Mirza loyally informed American diplomatic officials in advance of the central government's allegedly necessary suspension of the UF government and the imposition of governor's rule in East Pakistan in 1954,[77] a decision Washington supported. As then US ambassador to Pakistan Horace Hildreth noted, "Law and order appear to have been restored and the vigorous and imaginative Governor, Major General Iskander Mirza, may be able to do much to improve conditions in the province," and "the postponement of democratic processes with a longer continuation of Governor's rule than at first expected might in the end save the province" from communism.[78] Before the 1958 coup, Mirza and Ayub also made it clear to the US and British ambassadors that they would impose martial law in the country. The US government made no attempt to dissuade Mirza or the military from this planned authoritarian intervention. If nothing else, US acquiescence helped minimize the potential external costs of such actions for the military.

In theory, the US government continued to back civilian rule in Pakistan.[79] One State Department assessment concluded that "prospects for orderly evolution toward more stable constitutional government in Pakistan would be diminished should general elections be postponed or extraordinary executive powers be invoked for anything other than [a] short pre-election period."[80]

But Washington obviously did not walk this democratic talk. Given the Pakistani military's critical dependence on US armaments, the military is unlikely to have moved against civilian rule without a green signal from Washington. In fact, the haste with which Eisenhower endorsed what he called the "extraordinary political measure" and wished the Pakistani president every success is telling.[81] Mirza was delighted to receive the letter, and indicated to then US ambassador James Langley that he would like to release it to the public after consulting Ayub.[82] The Department of State informed the embassy that the White House did not want Eisenhower's letter to be made public.[83] Mirza obliged.

In a letter to Mirza written a week after the coup, Secretary of State John Foster Dulles also backed the coup makers' contention that there was no single route to democracy and that Pakistan was an exception to the democratic rule. Admitting that dictatorships might be dangerous elsewhere, he thought that one would be benign in Pakistan, given its new leadership's "selfless dedication to the welfare of their country." Dulles went on to reassure that leadership that the coup would not alter in any respect the close ties between the two countries, assuring Mirza that "I write this note merely to assure you of my recognition and appreciation of that fact, and also to let you know that my sympathy goes out to you and your associates as you face the heavy task of finding a form of government adapted to the difficult conditions which confront your nation." In other words, coup or not, it would be business as usual.[84] And it was. In March 1959, the two countries signed an agreement of cooperation under which the United States pledged to take "appropriate action, including the use of armed force in case of aggression against Pakistan," a clear assurance to the military government that the United States would come to its aid in case of an Indian attack.[85] The military government leased the United States land for a secret air station in Peshawar, run by the 6937th Communications Group of the United States Air Force Security Service, for intelligence collection and U-2 aerial reconnaissance over the USSR. US officials believed that such facilities had considerable national security importance as critical links in the global network of American electronic intelligence facilities needed to monitor Soviet missile capabilities.[86] In other words, the base "put Pakistan on the frontline of the Cold War."[87]

This brief assessment is not meant to underplay or condone US complicity in the military's political ascendance. But Washington's policies toward the military can be more aptly described as enabling rather than decisive. The US reaction to the coup clearly betrayed American endorsement of the military's action, but there is no evidence to suggest that the CIA or any other US government agency directly aided or abetted the coup. The more compelling factors behind the military putsch were domestic.

In October 1958, the military finally captured state power, citing threats to national security from internal strife, partisan bickering, provincialism, and economic degradation. Objectively speaking, there was no catastrophic danger of internal fragmentation or economic collapse at the time of the coup. However, the military's attitudes regarding its role as the guardian of the national interest and its interpretations of the extant situation as harmful helped produce the military consensus to openly cross the ultimate threshold of political insubordination. In sum, the military instituted a coup against the duly constituted government because its members concluded that the unsuitable political and economic situation in the country was caused by the ineptitude of the politicians and the fundamental flaws of parliamentary democracy, which left the military no choice but to end divisive politics, install a military government (which it believed would be neutral), and create a new, partyless democracy to create stability, foster national unity, and ensure economic development.

3

"REVOLUTION" TO REVOLT

By seizing power in 1958, the military institution moved from a position of political tutelage to that of political control, "cementing many of the political distortions that arose in the first decade."[1] Once the military carried out the coup, it became clear that its action was more than just a temporary measure designed to restore "sanity and stability."[2] Although the military moved quickly to target "the vermin, leeches and sharks"[3] accused of hoarding, smuggling, and disturbing the public peace, General Ayub Khan wished to implement a foundational political and economic project. First, the generals stated their intent to establish a real democracy that catered to local conditions. Second, they resolved to put Pakistan squarely on the path of economic development as an instrument of modernization and East-West integration.[4] The irony of a Punjabi-dominated military government that had effectively blocked the Bengalis' primary means for political representation and participation via elections promising to address their legitimate concerns was obviously lost on the high command.

Military Rule, Civil War, and State Breakup

Because the coup was ostensibly inspired by the military's desire to save Pakistan from disintegration at the hands of ineffectual and self-serving politicians exploiting the parliamentary system, General Ayub established a military-led presidential system, banned political parties, suppressed fundamental rights, and censored the press. The military government disqualified hundreds (if not thousands) of politicians, a majority from East Pakistan, including former prime minister H. S. Suhrawardy, from seeking public office,[5] reflecting its particularly low opinion of Bengali politicians as the primary source of national disunity and political dissent in the country. The high command was initially involved in directly governing the country, with General Ayub as president, commander in chief of the army, and chief martial law administrator and the two commanders in chief of the air force and the navy as deputy chief martial law administrators. In 1959, Ayub elevated himself to the post of field marshal and appointed the loyal General Mohammad Musa commander in chief to manage the administration and operations of the army.

The military government relied heavily on the bureaucracy, especially the elite Civil Service of Pakistan, the legatee of the Colonial Indian Civil Service, for day-to-day administration and kept the military institution largely out of governmental affairs, especially after General Ayub lifted martial law in 1962.[6] Senior bureaucrats played important roles in the military government, including Aziz Ahmed, who was appointed deputy martial law administrator in October 1958. The Civil Service of Pakistan continued to dominate key civilian policy-making positions, including those in the central secretariat and provincial administrations, as well as important public corporations, like the Water and Power Development Authority and the Industrial Development Corporation. Commenting on the structure of the regime, Gerald Heeger noted: "What emerged in Pakistan [under Ayub] was less a military government than an administrative state strengthened by military support. Political roles in the system were eliminated or at least sharply curtailed and replaced by administrative equivalents. Decision making was restricted to the senior military elites around Ayub and to the bureaucracy."[7]

However, it is important not to overstate the civilian character of the regime. The army leadership that took over power in 1958 already had institutional bases of power in the state, and the coup "did not disrupt its chain of command. Instead its unity simplified decision-making."[8] The institutional power of the government lay squarely in the army; it was military in its origins and initial structure. The army ultimately acted as the real force in "carrying out, implementing and propagating Ayub's policies."[9] The civil bureaucracy served at the military president's behest. The high command also had the sword of the Public Offices Disqualification Order, 1959, to keep individual bureaucrats in line. The military could use it to sack or demote civil servants on charges of corruption, misconduct, and subversive activities, and over 500 officers were retired or removed from office.[10]

Democracy by Diktat

As described earlier, Ayub's contempt for parliamentary politics was matched only by his desire to establish a controlled democracy to prepare the people for full democracy in due course. As soon as the exceptional circumstances that had necessitated the drastic military action in the generals' eyes passed, Ayub began implementing its foundational project to make Pakistan as disciplined and organized as its army. Having captured power in an irregular fashion, Ayub also needed to legitimate his rule by creating at least a semblance of democratic representation. In 1959 he introduced the Basic Democracies (BD) scheme to "awaken" and empower the illiterate and innocent people at the local levels through elected councils, because in their "existing state of intellectual development" they could not be expected to elect the right kind of representatives who could protect their interests at the national and international levels.[11] Hence the voter would be asked to "vote for a person he knows—for his local council—and on issues which he understands and which concern his daily life."[12]

Under the BD system, the country was divided into 80,000 wards (single-member constituencies of 1,000 to 1,500 people each) to elect a Basic Democrat on the basis of universal adult franchise.[13] The BDs were equally divided between East and West Pakistan, although the government nominated additional members to the union, *tehsil* in West Pakistan, *thana* in East Pakistan (subdistrict level), district, and divisional councils not to exceed one-half of the elected members.[14] The deputy commissioner was the chairman of his district's council, and the commissioner chaired the divisional council. At the apex of the system was the Provincial Development Council, an advisory and grant-making organization headed by the centrally appointed governor and made up of twenty-four official members and an equal number of nonofficial members, of whom only one-third were elected. The primary function of the BD councils was to promote rural development, such as sanitation, water supply, and public health, as well as to foster progress through village cooperatives, industries, and agriculture and the creation of civic consciousness.[15]

Ayub's revolutionary system earned him laurels from the renowned British historian Arnold Toynbee, who felt that "the Basic Democracy was a bona fide attempt on the present Government's part to help the people of Pakistan to self-train themselves for effective self-government in the future on a national scale."[16] Samuel Huntington described it as the virtually perfect example of "the institutional link between government and countryside which is the prerequisite of political stability in a modernizing country." Because of this magnificent feat of institutional innovation, he thought that Ayub was "a Solon or Lycurgus or Great Legislator on the Platonic or Rousseauian model."[17] The truth was closer to Heeger's assessment: "Even when Ayub sought to provide for some degree of popular participation, he did so within the context of a bureaucratic hierarchy (the Basic Democracies), rather than through the traditional participatory apparatus of parties and interest groups."[18]

In interviews, a number of officers recruited during the 1960s concurred with Toynbee's view that a local-level democracy was essential for an uneducated people who could not understand the complexities of democracy at the national level or properly exercise the right of universal adult franchise.[19] As one of them noted, the BD was a "perfect governance model for an underdeveloped society. But lacking direct army control, it was undermined by the corrupt administrators and the police."[20]

In essence, the BD system was a form of delegated authoritarianism designed to entrench regime control by nurturing a dependent local political base that could undercut political parties, depoliticize governance, and dedemocratize the competition over public resources and power. Hence these local bodies had no real power over the administration or development of their respective jurisdictions.[21] Real authority rested with the bureaucracy, especially the deputy commissioners and the commissioners, who were ultimately answerable to the military government through the provincial governor. It was these mandarins who controlled their respective councils on behalf of the guardian military and gave the BDs "instruction in the art of government and in the problems of development."[22]

Authoritarian Politics

The real political function of the BDs was to give Ayub the title to govern by acting as the presidential electoral college. In February 1960, Ayub validated his presidency by a vote of confidence from the BDs, 95.6 percent of whom voted in his favor.[23] Having demolished all avenues of democratic representation, he also used the referendum as a mandate to give the country a constitution. As recommended by his handpicked constitutional commission, headed by former chief justice Muhammad Shahabuddin and composed of lawyers, industrialists, and people from other spheres of public life, Ayub abandoned the failed parliamentary system and adopted the presidential form of government.[24] His new constitution, promulgated in March 1962, mirrored his 1954 constitutional plan. It was federal in principle but unitary in effect. The constitution affirmed the paternalistic logic of denying the right of universal franchise to the people, and the BD system was retained as the electoral college for the president and the legislative assemblies. Executive powers were vested in the president, who was to be elected for a five-year term. The constitution also provided for a unicameral legislature (that is, an indirectly elected National Assembly) and two provincial assemblies with severely constrained legislative authority.[25] Simply put, the constitution was "drafted in such a way as to perpetuate the present regime and to eliminate the competition of political parties for a long time to come."[26] In fact, it went further than just ensuring regime longevity. Civilian democratic control is, by definition, impossible in a military-led government, but the 1962 constitution formally abolished the concept by decreeing that only an army officer of the rank of lieutenant general (or equivalent from the air force or navy) could become the defense minister of the country for the next twenty years.[27]

The constitution also made the 1962 referendum retrospective; therefore, Ayub could remain president until 1965.[28] In April 1962, the regime organized indirect elections for the National Assembly and formally ended martial law and legalized political parties two months later. But Ayub's centralized authoritarian rule, now formally codified in an authoritarian constitution, engendered bitter opposition, especially from East Pakistan. The constitution had brazenly discounted the opinion of Bengalis, who "strongly favored a parliamentary system, a decentralized federal structure, and direct elections."[29] Bengali politicians from the now-defunct United Front, the National Awami Party, and other parties, led by Suhrawardy, were joined by anti-Ayub Muslim Leaguers in the National Democratic Front to mobilize opposition to the Ayub dictatorship. As demands for a new, democratic constitution gained public resonance, students protested and clashed with the police in both East and West Pakistan. To placate political discontent, the government restored judicial authority to enforce fundamental rights and promised political liberalization.

In August 1962, the government established a Franchise Commission to inquire into the appropriateness of universal franchise and the introduction of direct elections for the office of the president and for national and provincial assemblies, given the circumstances and conditions in the country.[30] The commission unanimously recommended the adoption of universal adult franchise as the prerequisite for democracy and the only meaningful method to ensure democratic representation. It also recommended direct elections for legislators, but a minority of its members dissented from the majority on direct election of the president. Displeased (or perhaps relieved) by this division of opinion, President Ayub ordered the Ministry of Law to review the report. The ministry's expert analysis confirmed the military government's paternalistic thinking on questions of political participation, voting, and democratic rights. It contended that the Franchise Commission had failed to make the necessary distinction between the right of franchise and the method of franchise. Mirroring Ayub's view on the desirability of controlled democracy for Pakistan, it noted that the method of franchise must take into account the special conditions and requirements of a country, adding that universal franchise would be meaningless without universal education[31] because the people would be readily influenced by local, sectarian, and parochial loyalties.[32]

Hence the more able and responsible members of an electoral college should elect the president, as well as the legislatures, because two different methods of election would create conflict and undermine the authority of the president.[33] That would be unacceptable because "in our conditions of mass illiteracy, low standard of living, [and people's] imperfect political understanding," the need for a "stable government must take precedence over all other considerations."[34] Providing further justification for indirect democracy, it cited the 1954 elections in East Pakistan as an example when the "right of direct voting exercised without having an understanding of the issues involved and in an atmosphere charged with emotions had nearly undermined the very basis of the country."[35] It recommended that until the majority of the people became literate and intelligent, direct voting would allow the election of "unpatriotic and hostile elements" who would "create confusion and arrest the progress of the country."[36]

However, legitimacy continued to evade Ayub Khan. At the end of his first presidential term in 1965, Ayub sought reelection, albeit in a contested election open to political parties. The field marshal formally entered politics and was elected president of a supportive Muslim League faction, the ML-Conventional. Emboldened by the legalization of political parties, Ayub's opposition coalesced in an electoral alliance, the Combined Opposition Parties, which put forward Fatima Jinnah, Mohammad Ali Jinnah's sister, as its presidential candidate.

But the election was decidedly stacked against the Combined Opposition Parties. Although Ayub contested the election as the head of his own party, he relied on intelligence agencies to monitor, pressure, and intimidate his opponents. In particular, he expanded the traditional mission of the ISI, collecting military intelligence and conducting covert operations, to domestic counterintelligence, including the surveillance and suppression of politicians, the media, trade unions, and student groups.[37] Ultimately, Ayub won the indirect vote. But despite his authoritarian tactics, Fatima Jinnah managed to get 36 percent of the national vote and 47 percent of the vote from East Pakistan, revealing heightened Bengali frustration with Ayub's authoritarian rule.[38] The election eroded any residual legitimacy that the military government claimed.

On the economic front, aid and technical assistance from the United States helped the military government score impressive growth in the industrial and agricultural sectors. Pakistan's GNP grew at 6 percent for a decade. But Ayub's development miracle was deeply flawed. Maximization of growth without an emphasis on redistribution widened economic inequalities.[39] Economic wealth was largely concentrated in the hands of a few industrial groups in West Pakistan, or, in the stark terms of the Planning Commission's chief economist, Mahbubul Haq, "twenty-two families," which controlled two-thirds of the industrial assets, 80 percent of banking, and 79 percent of insurance.[40] By the mid-1960s, economic disparities along both regional and class lines had begun to exacerbate existing political grievances about the lack of democratic participation.

In East Pakistan, Ayub's military-led government cemented the Bengalis' sense of collective marginality because they had virtually no representation in the upper echelons of the military. The military made some piecemeal efforts to increase Bengali representation in the armed forces, but, as Table 3.1 shows, they constituted no more than 5 percent of the army officer corps even five years after the 1958 coup.[41]

The 1958 coup and subsequent military rule had ended the possibility that the Bengalis could use their demographic majority to gain control over the state democratically. The limited legislative authority of indirectly elected assemblies in a centralized presidential government made parliamentary participation altogether meaningless (both for the Bengalis and for other West Pakistani ethnic groups). Economic disparities in per capita incomes, government development expenditures, foreign aid allocations, and industrial subsidies between the two wings grew steadily, intensifying the widely held Bengali nationalist opinion that they were trapped in a system of internal colonialism.

Waging War, Losing the Peace

In 1965, the Pakistani army initiated a conflict with India in the belief that it ought to exploit the closing window of opportunity presented by India's military defeat in the Sino-Indian War of 1962. The

Table 3.1 East Pakistani officers, 1963

Officers	East Pakistan percentage of total officers	East Pakistan percentage of total population (1964)
Army	5	
Navy	5	54.5
Air Force (General Duty Pilots)	11	

Source: National Assembly of Pakistan Debates 1 (March 8, 1963): 29–30.

military's objective was to "defreeze the Kashmir problem . . . and bring India to the conference table without provoking a general war."[42] Buoyed by their success in repelling Indian advances in the Rann of Kutch earlier in the year, the generals infiltrated some 7,000 guerrillas, trained by the army's Special Services Group, into Indian Kashmir in early August 1965 to destroy or damage military targets in the hope of sabotaging the authority of the so-called occupation power in the state and inciting a rebellion against New Delhi.[43] But the plan, code-named Operation Gibraltar, backfired after Kashmiri herdsmen reported the presence of the Pakistani intruders to the Indian authorities, and India launched attacks across the cease-fire line to seal off the guerrilla bases in Pakistani Kashmir.[44] On September 1, the Pakistani army's Twelfth Division in Murree launched a supplemental offensive in Indian Kashmir, code-named Operation Grandslam, to take the strategically important Akhnur bridge to "sever the only road link between India and Kashmir."[45] Although the Pakistani army failed to take Akhnur, an Indian counterattack on Pakistan's eastern border (mainly in the Lahore, Sialkot, and Kasur sectors) broadened the conflict into a full-fledged war. Ultimately, the war ended in a stalemate, and the UN Security Council secured a cease-fire on September 22. A few months later, in January 1966, Pakistan and India signed the Tashkent Agreement under Soviet auspices, which committed the two sides to the withdrawal of troops to prewar positions and the resumption of diplomatic relations.

However, the military's "ruinous policy of armed confrontation with India . . . had disastrous effects on the viability of Pakistan as a unified country."[46] During the war, the Indian naval blockade of East Pakistan left it to fend for itself against a potential Indian invasion and exposed its deep military vulnerability because the bulk of the country's armed forces were deployed in West Pakistan.[47] The Pakistani military's national defense plan revolved around the strategic concept that the defense of East Pakistan lay in West Pakistan. In this view, it was essential to maintain maximum force levels in the western wing because "even if the hostilities commence in

East Pakistan, strategic factors dictate that major and decisive battles would be fought from West Pakistan."[48]

This neglect of East Pakistan's defense needs exacerbated the deep Bengali alienation fomented by the systematic denial of economic, administrative, and political power and galvanized the Six Points movement for maximum regional autonomy under the Awami League, headed by Sheikh Mujibur Rahman.[49] The military's subsequent arrest of Mujibur along with Bengali civil officials and army officers on trumped-up charges of colluding with India for the secession of East Pakistan (known as the Agartala conspiracy after the Indian town where the conspiracy was supposedly hatched) bolstered the popularity of the Six Points movement.

In West Pakistan, the lack of meaningful institutions for political participation, uneven economic development, the use of coercion to suppress collective claims against the state, and the continued denial of provincial autonomy to the smaller provinces through the One Unit had also bred widespread frustration along subnational and social lines among the Pashtuns, the Sindhi, and the Baloch and the urban middle classes, students, and labor unions, respectively. Ayub's "policy of appeasement of the army by giving them lands, increased pay and pension benefits, and other venues of employment after retirement"[50] increased antiregime sentiments, especially among industrial workers in West Pakistan, whose real wages had fallen by one-third because of inflation.[51] The field marshal's capitulation at Tashkent, which came as a shock to many Pakistanis fed on military propaganda of certain victory against cowardly Hindu India, coupled with the unmitigated failure of his developmental state to dent economic inequalities, gave enough ammunition to political parties, such as Zulfiqar Ali Bhutto's left-of-center Pakistan People's Party (PPP) in West Pakistan, to capitalize on and further energize the antiregime opposition.[52] Bhutto had been a member of the first cabinet established after the 1958 coup and later had risen to the position of foreign minister in General Ayub's military government. After the 1965 war with India, he broke ranks with Ayub over the latter's diplomatic squandering of presumed Pakistani success on the battlefield, a posture that helped catapult him into a major opposition figure.

By early 1969, violent opposition protests and countrywide strikes had crippled Ayub's authority. Students and labor unions were at the forefront of the anti-Ayub agitation. In March 1969, the port city of Karachi, responsible for 40 percent of Pakistan's industrial capacity, was brought to a standstill by a labor strike. Demands for political representation and freedom of expression were combined with workers' demands for the right to strike, minimum wages, and access to social services.[53] In East Pakistan, "with the government's power gone, strikes paralyzed the economy. . . . Arson went unchecked, prices for scarce foodstuffs soared, and administrative services were at a standstill," bringing the eastern wing of the country "to the brink of anarchy."[54]

Ayub, who had seized state power in the name of political stability and national unity, was initially unfazed by this growing, often violent threat to his rule. He even made a last-ditch attempt to gather all political parties and leaders at a roundtable conference to work out a constitutional settlement. But as regime authority all but collapsed, the military high command concluded that "drastic action was in order lest East Pakistan became another Biafra." The generals were also convinced that such decisive action was possible only when the military institution was "not hobbled by an unpopular and repudiated" military government.[55] Abandoned by the military, Ayub was left with no choice but to concede publicly that "the situation is no longer under the control of the government." However, rather than transferring power to the titular National Assembly speaker (who happened to be a Bengali) in accordance with the 1962 constitution, he handed it over to the armed forces because "there [was] no other constitutional and effective way to meet the situation."[56] In essence, the military high command under the commander in chief, General Yahya Khan (1969–1971), simply reasserted itself and formally recaptured the state, a clear indication of an institutional consensus on the necessity of maintaining military control over the state.

Military Government: Round Two

However entrenched its bases of power in the state or antidemocratic its institutional inclinations were, the military could no longer openly deny the democratic aspirations of the people in both West and East Pakistan. Hence, in his first address to the nation on March 26, 1969, Yahya declared that the armed forces "have no political ambition" except the "creation of conditions conducive to the establishment of constitutional government."[57] He pledged to hold elections on the basis of universal adult franchise and to transfer power to the genuine representatives of the people as soon as sanity was restored. As one astute observer noted, "There was no mention of East Pakistan's discontents or of the possible consequences to the nation of this further constitutional breakdown." What was obvious was that "only the armed forces were the best judges of what was sane and what was not, and therefore, on them lay the task of restoring sanity."[58]

The Yahya government's initial structure closely resembled that of Ayub's. However, unlike his predecessor, Yahya continued as commander in chief so he could exercise effective command over the army. But like Ayub, he took charge as the chief martial law administrator and appointed himself president of Pakistan, while the army chief of staff, Lieutenant General Abdul Hamid Khan, the air force commander, Marshal Nur Khan, and the naval chief, Vice Admiral S. M. Ahsan, assumed the offices of deputy chief martial law administrators. These four officers also made up the military cabinet, known as the Council of Administration, headed by Yahya, who was in charge of the Ministries of Defense, Foreign Affairs, Economic Affairs, and Planning, while the rest of the ministries were divided among Hamid Khan, Nur Khan, and Ahsan. The most powerful administrative instrument of the military government was the headquarters chief martial law administrator, headed by Yahya's principal staff officer, Lieutenant General S. G. M. Peerzada, which acted as the gatekeeper to the general-president. In the provinces, local army commanders called the shots as zonal martial law administrators but reported to the headquarters chief martial law administrator on all matters related to martial law.

Yahya's administration was different from Ayub's in at least one more way: he "involved more and more army officers in the civil administration and activities of a political nature."[59] The martial law administration's limited stated objectives were belied by the actions of its members, especially Air Marshal Nur Khan, who embarked on an ambitious program of social and education reforms that raised suspicions about the junta's actual intentions, especially in East Pakistan. Differences between Yahya and Nur Khan over the scope of the junta's responsibilities led the army president to dissolve the council and replace it with a civilian cabinet. Both Nur Khan and the naval chiefs were retired and appointed governors of West and East Pakistan, respectively. Despite this apparent move toward civilian appointments, however, the martial law administrators in each province wielded the ultimate executive authority.[60]

On March 30, 1970, Yahya Khan dissolved the One Unit, an action that revived West Pakistan's four provinces (the North-West Frontier Province, Sindh, Balochistan, and the Punjab). On the same day, he laid out a blueprint for the transition to civilian rule that conflicted sharply with the regime's rhetoric about the restoration of democratic institutions. Known as the Legal Framework Order (LFO), it was clearly designed to maintain military control over the future constitution and the structure and powers of parliament.[61] The order sharply curtailed the soon-to-be-elected parliament's sovereignty by requiring that it enact a new constitution within four months of its election and then seek the (military) president's consent or face dissolution.[62]

Ballots to Bullets

The military government of Yahya Khan organized universally enfranchised elections in 1970, Pakistan's first since independence in

1947. However, it also employed a divide-and-rule strategy to ensure an electoral outcome that would preserve what the military perceived as national integrity. To this end, General Yahya created the National Security Council, under the command of Major General Ghulam Omar, a former head of military intelligence. Superimposed over the ISI and other intelligence agencies, the council's main purpose was to direct an intelligence operation designed to prevent any political party from winning an overall majority in elections.[63] The military government tried "to influence political parties by threats, inducements and even bribes . . . for bringing about a particular kind of result during the elections of 1970."[64] It patronized and financially supported the electoral campaign of Islamist parties and various factions of the Muslim League in order to achieve a diversification of political forces, a thinly veiled plan to fragment the vote among several parties to create a hung parliament in order to deny the Bengalis their numerical majority.[65]

The elections were finally held in December 1970. The results turned the tables on the generals because the voters chose the wrong people. With its support boosted by the military government's callous inefficiency in handling relief operations during a deadly cyclone in East Pakistan a month earlier, the army's bête noir, the Awami League (AL) swept the elections, winning 167 of the 169 provincial assembly seats from East Pakistan and a comfortable majority (167 seats of 313) in the National Assembly, but none from the provinces of West Pakistan. The less distrusted but still unpalatable avowedly socialist PPP secured a majority from the provinces of West Pakistan by bagging 81 of the 138 seats, mostly from the Punjab and Sindh. It did not win a single seat from the eastern wing. The popular vote was thus clearly divided along regional lines and "demonstrated the failure of national integration in Pakistan."[66]

Both the AL and the PPP made their grab for power at the national level. Buoyed by their resounding victory in East Pakistan, Mujib and the AL demanded their right to govern on the basis of majoritarian democracy. The AL wanted the future constitution to be framed in accordance with the Six Points, which called for radical decentralization of central powers, on the basis of which it had fought the elections. Bhutto demanded changes in the AL's Six Points, which he saw as a formula for constitutional secession, and wanted Mujib to share power with the PPP on the basis of its regional majority in West Pakistan.[67]

Their differences allowed the military to act as the main arbitrator.[68] The armed forces (and the West Pakistani or, more precisely, Punjabi bureaucratic and political elite) deeply distrusted the AL, which they perceived as a threat to Pakistan's integrity and, more specifically, to the institutional interests of the military. As one former general noted, "Mujib's victory was not accepted by many in the military hierarchy. . . . The military were afraid that the Awami League, when in power, would adopt a conciliatory attitude towards India, relegate Kashmir to the back burner, and direct funds from defense to economic development in East Pakistan."[69] According to G. W. Choudhury, a constitutional adviser to the government, prominent members of Yahya's "inner [military] cabinet," such as Lieutenant Generals Hamid Khan and Peerzada, the chief of general staff, Lieutenant General Gul Hassan, and a few others, did not intend to transfer power to an elected government, least of all one controlled by the Bengalis. In fact, they were planning to create a Turkish-style civil-military regime to perpetuate institutional army tutelage over the state.[70]

Thus, instead of respecting the AL's electoral mandate and allowing it to assume power, the high command denied the party its legitimate claim to national power through a strategy of delay and divide. It employed the ISI to try to infiltrate and weaken the AL.[71] General Yahya initially agreed to convene the newly elected parliament on March 3, 1971. He then delayed its inaugural session indefinitely on March 1, citing Bhutto's statement that the PPP would not participate in the parliament unless Mujib agreed to the basic features of the future constitution. In fact, Yahya Khan had already created grounds for its postponement by amending the Legal

Framework Order to allow the elected members of the National Assembly to resign before its commencement and "persuading some political parties and [their] elected members . . . to refuse to attend the session."[72]

The postponement devastated the Bengalis, who saw it as yet another attempt by West Pakistani elites to deny them their democratic right to govern the country. Their suspicions were confirmed when the military tightened its control over East Pakistan by replacing the governor of East Pakistan, retired Admiral Ahsan, with Lieutenant General Sahibzada Yaqub Khan, commander of the army's Eastern Command.

Mujib responded to the postponement with a call for a province-wide *hartal* (strike) on March 2 and 3, which shut down much of East Pakistan. The military responded with force and imposed a curfew, resulting in a number of Bengali deaths. On March 6, Yahya made an inflammatory speech in which he announced March 25 as the new date for the inaugural National Assembly session but threatened to use decisive force to preserve the unity of the country. On the same day, the general officer commanding in Dhaka, Major General Raja Khadim Hussain, warned Sheikh Mujib that if he challenged the integrity of Pakistan, the army would gather all its "tanks, artillery and machine guns to kill all the traitors and, if necessary, raze Dacca to the ground. There will be no one to rule, there will be nothing to rule."[73]

The military had already made contingency plans for a military option.[74] The regime's strategy was "to provoke the AL into declaring independence which would provide it with the justification for a crackdown in East Pakistan."[75] Mujib was under immense pressure from radical AL elements and militant student groups to declare independence, which he had so far resisted in the hope of finding a political settlement. On March 7, he publicly announced his decision to attend the National Assembly session, but only if the military abrogated martial law, withdrew troops, investigated the killings on March 2, and immediately transferred power to the people's elected representatives. To mollify hard-liners, he also announced a nonviolent civil disobedience campaign. As a result, there was a complete breakdown of governmental authority in East Pakistan. The Bengalis' successful noncooperation and defiant display of collective resistance to the military authorities confirmed the generals' remaining doubts about the loyalty and sincerity of Mujib and the AL to Pakistan.

With the exception of a few officers, such as Yaqub Khan, who ultimately pleaded for a political resolution,[76] Yahya and the general headquarters were fully prepared to find a final solution to the Bengali problem. The final round of negotiations between Yahya and Mujib between March 16 and 23 ultimately failed to yield an agreement.[77] On March 25, 1971, the generals ordered their troops to crush Bengali resistance "according to plan."[78]

For the military, the logic behind using force was cold and calculated. Notwithstanding some differences of opinion in the senior officer corps on the modalities of military operations, there was a consensus on its objectives and strategy. The objectives were to decapitate the AL and restore government authority by arresting the party's leadership, neutralizing its radical elements (especially students), and disarming the Bengali army and police personnel suspected of mutiny.[79] In fact, a number of senior officers did not think that there was a real problem in East Pakistan in the first place. For instance, in the forcefully expressed opinion of then chief of general staff Gul Hassan, "The people of East Pakistan harbored many grievances against . . . the West Wing," but that these were not genuine, and that "local Hindus and the Indian propaganda had brainwashed the people of the East Wing effectively." Otherwise, there was no reason why they would support "an unreliable and dangerous character . . . a traitor" like Sheikh Mujib.[80] Handing over power to a proved traitor was thus out of the question.[81]

According to the official Pakistani Hamoodur Rehman Commission of Inquiry, Yahya and his generals "brought about a situation in East Pakistan which led to a civil disobedience movement, and armed revolt by the Awami League."[82] They were certain that

Mujib and his supporters would not be able to sustain their opposition and that, if need be, they could be tackled by a determined show of force. This belief was anchored in the colonially inspired stereotype firmly held by the army's martial leadership of the Bengalis as nonmartial, effeminate, and cowardly people who did not have it in them to squarely face the barrel of a gun. Therefore, Yahya and his commanders calculated that "the upsurge of Bengali nationalism and their demands would cool down in a few days after military action. . . . Short and harsh action would bring the situation under control and the politicians would be cowed down. The killing of a few thousand would not be a high price for keeping the country together."[83]

Yahya Khan described the military action, code-named Operation Searchlight, as an attempt to save the solidarity and integrity of Pakistan, which was threatened by its enemies, that is, Mujib and his party.[84] The military's virtually genocidal campaign—fully aided by army-trained and armed, locally recruited Islamist militias (that is, al-Badr and al-Shams),[85] reportedly killed thousands, if not hundreds of thousands, of Bengali civilians.[86] The crackdown sparked a civil war between the army and the Bengali insurrection led by the Mukti Bahini (liberation force), consisting of Bengali officers and personnel of the East Bengal Regiment, the paramilitary East Pakistan Rifles, police, and irregulars. The conflict triggered mass refugee inflows into West Bengal, prompting an Indian military intervention to liberate East Pakistan that ultimately culminated in the Pakistani army's surrender and the creation of the new state of Bangladesh in December 1971.

At the time, the military's precipitous fall from grace, capped by its defeat in the war with India and the loss of half the country on its watch, seemed to spell the end of the military's political role. In fact, according to most accounts, including officers' memoirs, the humiliating surrender in Dhaka shook the military's collective pride, as well as the assiduously constructed public myth of its invincibility as the chief guardian of national security.[87] Apart from the desertion of

Bengali officers and soldiers, the disgraceful reverses on the battle-field against India fomented splits in the Pakistani military between the junta and sections of the officer corps. Holding the ruling generals responsible for the professional debacle, angry and disappointed junior and midranking officers heckled the army chief of staff, Lieutenant General Hamid Khan, during a speech at the general headquarters on December 19 that was ostensibly designed to seek their support for the junta's attempt to stay in power. Brigadier F. B. Ali and several officers based in Gujranwala demanded the resignation of Yahya Khan and other generals and reportedly threatened to march on Rawalpindi if they did not comply. On the same day, officers from the Special Services Group refused to provide protection to Yahya Khan.[88] With military unity at stake, the army chief of general staff, Lieutenant General Gul Hassan, and the air force chief, Air Marshal Rahim Khan, persuaded Yahya to resign. The new high command under Hassan transferred power to Bhutto the next day, December 20, 1971, thus formally extricating the military from power.

The Consolidation of Tutelary Professionalism

The period between the military coup of 1958 and the 1971 war represented the officer corps's first collective experience of military government. Interviews and memoirs indicate that military officers' beliefs about the appropriateness of their role as the sole guardians of state interests gained wider institutional traction during this prolonged period of military rule. The attempts of the high command under Yahya Khan to perpetuate military control even after conceding the right of the people to choose their elected representatives warrants an examination of the internal developments in the military in the years after the 1958 coup.

It was under Ayub Khan's ostensibly stable and prosperous rule that the officer corps experienced its first direct and sustained exposure to national politics and administration, even though the bulk of the military institution remained focused on combat against India.

Comparing the political stability and impressive economic growth under military rule in the 1960s with the perceived instability and laggard growth in the first decade after independence, officers who had undergone their formative professional experiences in the 1950s and 1960s developed the notion that the military had a broader sphere of responsibility, including a governing function. Ayub's long tenure as commander in chief (1951–1959) and then as supreme commander and field marshal (1959–1969) gave him the opportunity to inculcate his forcefully expressed vision of the appropriateness of this role in the officer corps, which left a strong imprint on the succeeding generations of officers.[89] The senior officers under Ayub transmitted these beliefs to their juniors as their staff trainers and field commanders. Over time, these politically expansive notions of professionalism became embodied in the expectations of succeeding generations and thus gave them organizational acceptance and legitimacy.

Army officers recruited or on active duty in the 1960s generally held a positive view of Ayub's military rule and its accomplishments, which provided a conceptual frame of reference for future behavior. According to Lieutenant General Gul Hassan, who had served as director general of military operations in the 1965 war, Ayub was a "national leader . . . who thought of Pakistan as an entity, unlike our politicians whose vision never extended beyond provincial boundaries. . . . Ayub had rendered constructive and demonstrable services to the country despite [civilian] corruption. It was a period of stability and prosperity unknown to Pakistan."[90] Another officer notes: "I entered and graduated from the military academy and became an officer under military rule in the 1960s. That was my main experience. As I began to rise through the officer ranks, it had become commonplace to discuss, in the messes and even during field exercises, and to reflect on the dismal state of the country before the coup, and the drastic changes after it. We naturally looked to Ayub Khan as our role model who had brought political and economic stability."[91]

In the words of a former major general who was serving as a colonel in the early 1960s, "Ayub built roads, dams, industry, and boosted commerce which put Pakistan at par with South Korea. What have the civilians done for this country? Had the army under Ayub continued in power, Pakistan would be a different, more developed and modern country today."[92] Another officer who was recruited in the Ayub era and rose to top command and staff positions, including corps commander and adjutant general in army headquarters, evaluated his experience in these words: "As a young officer, I was not sure about army rule. It was not part of being a soldier. But I was proud of the fact that the army was in control of the country. We were still a highly professional army, engaged in hard training from morning to evening. But mess talk often involved discussions on how civilians bungle up things, and how the tonic of military command had injected a new spirit in the people: hoarding stopped, smuggling was curbed, and corrupt politicians were weeded out."[93]

In the process, political generals became the role models to emulate. For some officers, though, the transition was difficult. One of them was former major general Naseerullah Khan Babar, who had entered the army in 1948 and had become deeply concerned about the political virus that had infected the army after the military coup of 1958.[94] Another officer, recruited in 1951, resented the permissive environment in the messes regarding politics, a "beast banned in the British Indian Army."[95] However, more than a decade of army control over the state lowered any residual internal restraint on military involvement in politics. A former corps commander who graduated from the Pakistan Military Academy in 1962 opined that "our training was focused on military combat and war. But the old tradition of an 'apolitical army' lost all its meaning with the army in power. . . . In the officers' messes, politics was no longer considered taboo."[96]

Besides the seemingly pervasive belief in the positive aspects of military rule under Ayub, military officers also shared a sense of institutional correctness that may have contributed to their political and military conduct. The tendency among officers is to blame all that went wrong in 1971 on a few bad military apples, civilians like Bhutto and Mujib, and of course, the Indians. In interviews, a number of military officers were typically reluctant to admit that the so-called decade of development under Ayub was also the period when the economic exploitation and political exclusion of East Pakistan by West Pakistani elites reached new heights, or that Bengali separatism and rebellion against the state, which ultimately led to civil war and the dismemberment of Pakistan, were the military's fault. Even less acceptable were the suggestions that the 1971 war was an institutional military failure and that the Pakistani military was involved in the systematic murder of Bengalis. Instead, the writings of several senior military officers identify the military government's decision to permit free and fair elections without contingency planning as the culprit and hold that this decision left Pakistan at the mercy of two parochial politicians, "each uncompromising, and selfish to the extent of breaking up the country."[97]

The response of many other officers to questions about responsibility for the debacle at Dhaka was to pin blame on Bhutto for creating a political deadlock by allegedly refusing to share power with the Bengalis and therefore leaving the military no choice but to use force to preserve Pakistan's integrity. In this view, "Surrender was intended to smear the army's image and to shatter its credibility to such an extent that people would clamor for Yahya's removal. By his masterly stroke, Bhutto killed two birds with one stone and sacrificed Pakistan to his ambition [of] becoming the number one man in the country."[98] Bhutto's role in the crisis was controversial, to say the least. He wanted the PPP to wield power at the national level on account of its regional majority, so he opposed the AL's right to craft the constitution and to form a government independently. This intransigent attitude widened the gulf between the PPP and the AL, which may have strengthened the military's hand in dealing with the AL. However, Bhutto had no executive power. He did not control the state. He did not make the crucial decisions to postpone the National Assembly session or order a military crackdown. The general headquarters did. And the buck on East Pakistan stopped with the army high command, not Bhutto or the PPP.

Ultimately, the institutional narrative pins the blame on India. In this view, Pakistan was embroiled in a well-planned war of attrition by India to damage Pakistan militarily and economically. Both the Bengali insurgents with their bases in India and the regular Indian troops were "systematically weakening the Pakistan forces and the economic life of the province." Besides, had the crisis been solved by political means, India would have lost the opportunity to defeat the Pakistani armed forces, and the "real victors would have been the people of East Pakistan." In sum, had India not aided the Bengali secessionists and invaded East Pakistan, the military would have resolved the problem through dialogue and the threat of force if necessary.[99] To put it more harshly, the military would have taught those Bengali traitors a lesson. No doubt India trained, armed, and gave sanctuary to the Mukti Bahini and invaded East Pakistan, and its actions decisively tilted the scales against the Pakistani army. But by the time India became a decisive actor in the conflict, the Bengalis had already exhausted their voice and had decided on exit from the Pakistani state. However, the Pakistani army still considers Indian treachery the primary reason for its professional debacle in former East Pakistan:

> Quick reaction by the Pakistani authorities restored 80% normalcy in the eastern wing of the country. Covert operations having failed, India concentrated about 400,000 regular army personnel in 12 divisions supported by five tank regiments, seven air force squadrons and Indian Navy. These forces, further strengthened by about 1,00,000 [sic] guerillas (Mukti Bahini) attacked from all directions on 20 fronts across the international border on 21 November, without a formal declaration of war. Intense fighting raged till 16 December in both Pakistan's wings; no town or battalion

position could be overrun, till a ceasefire accepted by Pakistan was perfidiously changed into surrender by Indian-Soviet machinations.[100]

In sum, the permissive institutional conditions for military politicization, the particular military interpretations of political events and regional history, the lack of a tradition of political subordination, and officers' belief in the appropriateness of the military as a broader vocation must form part of the explanation of the military's behavior during and after the East Pakistan crisis. These habits of the mind were evident in the army's refusal to unconditionally accept civilian supremacy over the state even after it was severely discredited, denounced, and rejected by the people as a governing formula.

4

RECAPTURING THE STATE

Defeated and disgraced, the military yielded power to Zulfiqar Ali Bhutto's Pakistan People's Party (PPP), which had won the 1970 elections in West Pakistan (what remained of Pakistan). Decisive defeats in war can erode a military's professional cohesion, undermine its morale, and badly tarnish its professional reputation. Thus they can mortally weaken the political influence of authoritarian militaries and open the way for their depoliticization.

The Pakistani military's political and professional defeat presented the PPP leadership with a similar opportunity to establish authority over the armed forces and reduce its political clout. Stephen Cohen observed at the time, "Conditions for civilian control in Pakistan are probably better now than they ever have been."[1] A Pakistani writer noted the "total eclipse of the army," arguing with optimism that the "only contingency in which it would reacquire political control would be the total breakdown of civilian control and a law and order situation verging on anarchy. Short of that, the political role of the army has been effectively neutralized for a long time to come."[2]

Bhutto had the mass legitimacy and public mandate to challenge the political power of the discredited military officer corps.

He instituted a series of political, administrative, and institutional reforms in the military, including formally proscribing military interference in politics, confining its role to external defense, and changing the army command structure. However, these measures proved insufficient to deter military intervention. When Bhutto's opposition, the Pakistan National Alliance (PNA), contested the results of the March 1977 elections and took violently to the streets, the military seized power in July 1977, established Pakistan's longest authoritarian regime to date, and hanged Bhutto on dubious murder charges two years later.

The task here is to understand why and how the military rebounded so quickly to recapture the state. Defeat and humiliation in war in 1971 had led to regime collapse and had pushed the military out of power. However, the dictatorships of Ayub Khan and Yahya Khan had inculcated in the officer corps a belief in the appropriateness of an expansive professional role, including governing the country if needed. Schooled in this authoritarian tradition, the senior officers who took the reins of the military immediately after 1971 were not genuinely reconciled to a subordinate role in the state and continued to hold tutelary beliefs that were in conflict with the norm of democratic civilian supremacy.

The generals who carried out the 1977 coup had been recruited into the army during World War II, but they had had their decisive staff and command experiences during military government between 1958 and 1971. In the view of these guardians of national security and social order, the boundaries between politics and the military were thus ephemeral and permeable and could be breached when necessary. Crucially, the military institution also escaped accountability for prior military coups, the defeat in the 1971 war, which was clearly linked to its active political role, and its members' human rights excesses in East Pakistan. This avoidance of accountability reinforced the generals' belief that they could do no wrong.

Despite continuing belief in the legitimacy of its political role, the military remained detached from direct politics between 1972 and 1976 and focused on recovering from its losses and rebuilding its tarnished professional image. But the presence of these tutelary attitudes meant that it could assume a more active political role if it was provided the opportunity. The military's direct and prolonged involvement in civilian administration during counterinsurgency operations in Balochistan between 1973 and 1977 renewed officers' belief in their ability to run the affairs of government better than civilians. Civil disorder during the 1977 crisis severely tested the military's conditional allegiance to the democratic government. The military's judgments of the government's declining legitimacy, its doubts about the efficacy of the 1973 constitution's ability to resolve conflict with military officiency, and perceived threats to military unity ultimately led the military to take over the reins of government once again.

Military Politics, 1971–1972

The attitude and actions of the first postwar commander in chief, Lieutenant General Gul Hassan, provide a clear example that the military had not reconciled itself to the norm of political subordination. Despite being severely discredited, the army under Gul Hassan made its support for the government conditional on its respect for military institutional autonomy and the protection of its interests, for instance, by securing the release of the Pakistani prisoners of the 1971 war.[3]

While he was in office, Hassan displayed thinly veiled contempt for Bhutto and his cabinet ministers[4] and routinely resisted or defied the civilian government's orders. His actions demonstrated that institutional norms can "blind its members to changed environmental circumstances" and lead them to "behave not as the situation requires," but as they deem appropriate.[5] The general rejected a civilian request to brief the national cabinet on the army's combat readiness,[6] refused to fulfill his obligation to assist the government in aid of the civil power[7] unless he thought it was in the supreme interest of Pakistan,[8] sent junior-level officers to ministerial meetings on defense,[9] and allegedly kept tabs on the president and other

PPP leaders.[10] In fact, as chief of general staff under Yahya Khan, the general, as well as some of his colleagues, remained stubbornly attached to an "active political role for the armed forces" similar to the Turkish model of guardianship of the political system.[11]

Not surprisingly, the most serious threats to the government's survival emerged from the military commanders less than two months after the war. According to Mubashir Hassan, PPP secretary general and Bhutto's finance minister, there were increasing reports of the disparaging remarks made by Gul Hassan and the air force chief, Air Marshal Rahim Khan, against the government.[12] Ghulam Mustafa Khar, governor of Punjab and a Bhutto confidante, claims that the Intelligence Bureau tipped off the government about coup talk between the two.[13] Although it is hard to verify this claim independently, Bhutto had an acute fear of military coups.[14] He later acknowledged, "Their behavior pattern was unfortunately too conditioned by the past. It was unacceptable because I want the services to be accountable to political authority. I want to emphasize civilian control."[15]

To forestall this alleged putsch, Bhutto and his close aides, including Khar, organized a countercoup, inviting the two military chiefs to the president's house under false pretenses and obtaining their resignations. Bhutto then placed them under detention to prevent retaliation while he appointed their successors.[16] Having secured his flanks, Bhutto took the unprecedented step of publicly announcing their sacking and denouncing the military's "Bonapartist tendencies" in a televised speech.[17] The two were sent out of the country as ambassadors, ostensibly to keep them away from Pakistan.[18] Bhutto also purged the military of some thirty other senior officers for their involvement in the Yahya government or the conduct of the 1971 war.[19] He replaced Gul Hassan with Lieutenant General Tikka Khan (1972–1976), who had been passed over for promotion but had continued on active duty in disregard of military tradition. Hence Bhutto brought him in from the cold, resurrected his career, and expected loyalty in return. In March 1973,

Tikka proved his reliability when the ISI foiled what came to be known as the Attock conspiracy case, a coup plot hatched by mid-ranking army and air force officers against the Bhutto government and senior army leaders for their role in the 1971 debacle.[20]

Bhutto also retained the portfolio of defense minister and closely monitored military promotions (above the level of brigadier) with assistance from his military secretary, Brigadier (later Major General) Imtiaz Ahmed, and Tikka, delaying or denying promotion to those he suspected of Bonapartism while promoting others he considered loyal to the government. The Intelligence Bureau, the main civilian intelligence agency reporting to the prime minister, was reportedly tasked with the surveillance of officers with alleged political leanings or connections.[21] Although the Pakistani army was unlikely to carry out an institutional coup so soon after its resounding rout on the battlefield, Gul Hassan's unceremonious exit and the purge of senior officers loudly signaled to the military that Bhutto would not tolerate insubordination.

Crafting Control

The Bhutto government used a series of constitutional, administrative, and institutional mechanisms to curtail the political power of the military. The legal-institutional framework for civilian supremacy was provided by Pakistan's first democratically crafted constitution, which clearly demarcated narrow military jurisdictions and formally prohibited military intervention in politics.

The constitution, which came into effect on August 14, 1973, established a federal parliamentary form of government. It unequivocally subordinated the armed forces to the federal government and specified a narrow mission for them, namely, "to defend Pakistan against external aggression or threat of war, and, subject to law, act in aid of civil power when called upon to do so."[22] Constitutional subversion was declared a crime against the state,[23] and later, an act of parliament made it punishable by death.[24] The military officers' oath of service, included in the constitution, explicitly forbade them to engage in any kind of involvement in politics.[25] The titular president was made the civilian commander in chief of the armed forces, but the federal cabinet, led by the prime minister, acquired de facto authority over the military and national defense policy.

Besides constitutional injunctions, the Defense Committee of the Cabinet was revived to serve as the country's highest policy-making body in matters related to national defense.[26] The committee, chaired by the prime minister, was made responsible for the conversion of defense policy into military policy.[27] Under the rules of business (1973), which were to govern the operations and responsibilities of all government ministries, the Ministry of Defense was made "responsible for policy and administrative matters pertaining to the Defense of the Federation and the three Armed Forces."[28] The Bhutto government also created a separate Ministry of Defense Production to spur an indigenous arms industry.

Following the example of India, Bhutto abolished the colonial-era post of the commander in chief, designated the three military service chiefs as chiefs of staff, and initially fixed their tenures at four years (later reduced to three).[29] The government also adopted a firm policy of not extending their tours of duty, ostensibly to prevent the ascendancy of another officer like Ayub Khan, who had presumably used his long tenure to build a support base in the military. Bhutto also targeted the military's civilian partner in crime, the Civil Service of Pakistan. Because the bureaucracy was the main point of contact between the government and the people, it had also become synonymous with the excesses of military rule. Bhutto capitalized on public discontent to tame the "steel frame"[30] and abolished the service in 1973. He also introduced a scheme of lateral entry to induct political appointees directly into the civil service.[31]

The Hamoodur Rehman Commission of Inquiry into the 1971 war, established to determine the causes of the military's defeat and surrender to the Indian military in 1971, had strongly recommended the creation of a Joint Staff because of the dismal lack of coordination among the three armed forces during the 1971 war.[32]

In 1976, the PPP government issued the *White Paper on Higher De-fense Organization*, ostensibly to establish civilian control by intro-ducing changes in the military's command structure.[33] The white paper's rationale was that "national defense policy is no longer a military affair alone"; instead, it required "effective political control at the top" and "a number of institutions and agencies at the base to produce the necessary data and appreciations on which political decisions can be based." Accordingly, it made the prime minister the principal locus of national authority on defense: "The Prime Minister determines the national aims in the field of defense and directs their national efforts towards their achievement." The prime minister was the "sole authority for deciding the allocation of resources to defense within the state capacity, establishing, expand-ing and/or reorganizing institutions to ensure the coordinated ap-plication of such resources, and the raising and development of the armed forces."[34]

The white paper reorganized the military high command by creating a Joint Staff, a decision that some observers claim was pri-marily aimed at diluting the overwhelming power of the army chief.[35] Under the command of a Chairman Joint Chiefs of Staff Committee, the Joint Staff was allotted functional authority over integrated planning and coordination of war, but no direct opera-tional control over the three military services. The chairman was to act as the principal military adviser to the government and was to be separate from the regular chain of command of the three armed forces.[36]

The army chief of staff, Lieutenant General Tikka Khan, remained generally loyal to the government and focused his time and energy on rebuilding the army's prestige and firepower during his four-year tenure from 1972 to 1976. After Tikka's retirement in March 1976, Bhutto rewarded him for his loyalty with a cabinet-level position as adviser on defense and national security. To replace Tikka, Bhutto chose an obsequious and devout three-star general, Lieutenant General Ziaul Haq, then commander of the army corps stationed in Multan. Zia was junior to half a dozen general officers and, according to then military secretary Lieutenant General Faiz Ali Chishti, lacked the requisite experience to be considered for the position of the chief of the army staff.[37] Shahid Javed Burki has argued that Zia was an obvious choice for Bhutto because he was a migrant from India who was unlikely to form alliances with the Rajputs or the Pashtuns, the two martial races that dominated the army. His meek manner and "reputation of serving his superiors with unquestioning loyalty"[38] made him a safe bet for a prime minister haunted by the specter of military intervention.

Even as Bhutto removed senior military officers and instituted changes in command structures, he appeased the institution of the military to win its support. Although Pakistan's military expenditures had historically been high since 1947, they rose by over 200 percent between 1971 and 1977.[39] In 1973–1974, Pakistan was spending 6.6 percent of its GNP on the military, compared with an average of 5 percent between 1968 and 1971.[40] Just two weeks before the 1977 coup, Bhutto's wife and Member of National Assembly Begum Nusrat Bhutto described the PPP government's annual budget as the "budget of a government whose primary concerns have been the defense of our country." That year alone, the government raised military allocations by 14.5 percent to assure the military of the importance it gave to national defense.[41]

In order to recover from the military's losses in the 1971 war, including the internment of some 93,000 military and civilian personnel by India, the PPP government approved the raising of two additional army divisions, increased military salaries and benefits, procured urgently needed military supplies and weapons from abroad despite severe financial constraints, helped kick-start a domestic arms-manufacturing industry to reduce Pakistan's dependence on expensive imported weaponry, shielded Pakistani prisoners of war from prosecution for war crimes as demanded by the new state of Bangladesh under Sheikh Mujibur Rahman,[42] and eventually secured their release from India in 1974.

Some observers have argued that Bhutto strengthened the military because he shared the military's antipathy toward India, which he cynically exploited during his intensive 1970 election campaign in the martial heartland of the Punjab by offering its residents what he said would be a thousand-year war with India.[43] Bhutto was no dove, nor did he seem averse to using the India card to his political advantage. But a more balanced assessment is that he could not afford to antagonize the military permanently by attacking its basic corporate requirements,[44] which could have given the army justification for a rebellion.

Bhutto also tried to appease the military in other ways. Initially, he strongly criticized the senior military leadership in public for the 1971 debacle. (The Pakistani army's surrender to Indian forces was telecast on Pakistan Television, much to the chagrin of the senior officers, who saw it as Bhutto's attempt to rub salt into their wounds.) However, Bhutto was politically savvy enough not to wage a systematic propaganda campaign against the institution of the army or to carry out a wholesale purge of the officer corps.[45] He did appoint the Hamoodur Rehman Commission, which submitted its report in July 1972.[46] It offered a scathing indictment of the senior officer corps and detailed the rot that can afflict the professional competence of politicized armies. In fact, the commission found sufficient evidence to hold "all senior officers" deployed in East Pakistan "collectively responsible for the [military] defeat"[47] and urged the government to properly try to punish them for bringing "disgrace and defeat to Pakistan by their professional incompetence, culpable negligence and willful neglect in the performance of their duties . . . to ensure against any future recurrence of this kind of shameful conduct . . . and serve to emphasize the concept of professional accountability which appears to have been forgotten by senior army officers since their involvement in politics, civil administration and Martial Law duties."[48]

Quite reasonably, the commission recommended a revision of military training syllabi to firmly instill respect for democratic institutions in the officer corps.[49] However, Bhutto reportedly shelved the report on the insistence of the military or, as he described it from death row, "to save its honor."[50] It is reasonable to speculate that Bhutto did not make the report public, let alone act on its recommendations, because of its potentially adverse effects on the military's already-low institutional morale and the fear of a backlash. Many in the army considered the report a whitewash because its terms of reference excluded examining the role of Bhutto and Tikka Khan in the 1971 disaster.[51] Bhutto's decision to oblige the army rather than hold its senior members answerable for their incompetence and culpable negligence when they were shamed and degraded was perhaps one of his more consequential miscalculations. Letting the institution of the military off the hook at a time when there was direct public support for holding the generals accountable[52] reinforced officers' presumptions of impunity.

What Went Wrong?

Why did civilian appeasement and seemingly far-reaching institutional reforms, especially changes in the command structure of the army, not inhibit military intervention? Scholars have attributed this failure both to Bhutto's patrimonial politics and authoritarian tendencies[53] and to continuing imbalances between the nonelected and elected institutions of the state.[54] Still others have singled out PPP factionalism;[55] the government's socioeconomic policies, including labor reforms that hurt small-scale enterprises; the nationalization of industry, which alienated big business; and income transfers to low-income groups and the nationalization of educational institutions, which aggrieved the urban middle classes—all of whom backed the PNA in the 1977 elections.[56] In addition, the PPP lost the support of middle-class urban leftists and students, who had played a crucial role in the rise of the PPP during the anti-Ayub agitations, because of Bhutto's purge of the party's Left, the party's landlordization in the mid-1970s,[57] and his use of authoritarian devices to stifle opposition, including the continuation of the state of emergency imposed during the 1971 war, police coercion, national security statutes, such as the Defense of Pakistan Ordinance (1965) and the Prevention of Anti-national Activities Act (1974),[58] and the suppression of media freedoms through the Ayub-era Press and Publications Ordinance (1963).[59] Still other factors include creation of the Federal Security Force, which challenged the military's monopoly over violence; the perceived external threat environment in post-1971 Pakistan, which continued to impose high defense expenditures; and, less convincingly, rumors of an American conspiracy to oust Bhutto to prevent Pakistan from acquiring an atomic bomb.[60]

These mostly nonmilitary factors, whether separately or in combination, could at best have created the opening for military intervention by eroding the public support of the PPP government. However, they did not make the coup inevitable. In order to understand the process of the breakdown of civilian rule more fully, we must also contend with the military institution itself, which had been socialized into the norm of a legitimate professional role in resolving political problems. Even though the military had disengaged from power, it had not fully internalized the principle of unreserved political subordination and thus posed a latent threat to the existence of democracy. The officer corps perceived Bhutto's attempts to exert civilian control over the army not as the government's democratic prerogative but as undue interference in its corporate affairs. For instance, the prime minister's appointment of Zia as chief of the army staff was seen as a political decision that violated the professional principles of seniority and competence,[61] even though Zia met the technical qualifications for the post: any officer who had reached the rank of lieutenant general and had commanded a corps was technically fit to become army chief.

Nor had the military abdicated its role as the permanent guardian of the national interest. Even under the outwardly subordinate Tikka Khan, the management of national security and foreign policy was subject to military advice and consent. The army's strong positions on such issues as negotiations with India over troop disengagement, the recognition of Bangladesh, and the return of the prisoners of war were tantamount to "offering the terms of surrender to a defeated enemy."[62]

Throwing money at the army, modifying its command structure, and legally prohibiting military interference in politics did not directly affect the military's authoritarian beliefs and inclinations. Additionally, the lack of prosecution for its past misdeeds and crimes meant that the Pakistani military institution never accepted responsibility for its actions. Although the army commissioned an internal study on the 1971 war, it was not circulated widely and was restricted to the purely military aspects of the war on the western front.[63] No systematic attention was paid to examining the deleterious effects of military rule on the military's professional fighting capacity or organizational integrity, or to the role of the military in the secession of East Pakistan. These bitter truths were simply swept under the carpet. In fact, topics such as the emergence of Bangladesh were considered taboo for discussion and analysis in the professional training of senior armed forces' officers up until the early years of the twenty-first century.[64] As noted earlier, the disaster of losing half the nation on the military's watch was internally attributed to the top members of the military government of Yahya Khan; this attribution helped the military institution qua institution avoid responsibility for its failures.

Rival Armed Force

Armed rivals foment military interventions because they challenge the military's monopoly over violence, especially when they pose an existential threat to the regular armed forces of a country.[65] In October 1972, Bhutto created a special civilian armed organization, the Federal Security Force (FSF), to serve as a "first class reserve force" that could compensate for the weaknesses of the police in maintaining order, and reduce the government's dependence on a capricious military and prevent its involvement in civil administration.[66]

The FSF was armed with light modern weaponry. Hence it was no match for the army's firepower and did not pose a direct threat to

its existence, nor did it jeopardize officers' careers, military allocations, or force size.[67] Saeed Shafqat has argued that the military
feared loss of status to the FSF, and that this fear influenced its relationship with the civilian regime and increased its motivation to
intervene.[68] Resentment of the FSF ran high among the officer
corps.[69] In fact, the military disbanded the organization immediately after the 1977 coup.[70] However, as Claude Welch contends,
such civilian infringements are insufficient for military intervention
unless they combine with a military tradition of political insubordination and conditional acceptance of democratically elected governments.[71] A military that positively identifies with the norm of civilian supremacy is unlikely to see a civil armed force as a rival unless
that force seeks to replace the professional army.[72] India is an example of a country where both the union and state governments have
raised a large number of paramilitary forces for internal security.
Prime Minister Indira Gandhi (1966–1977, 1980–1984) used these
forces extensively to curtail dissent and opposition, especially during
the Emergency (1975–1977), without provoking military intervention.

External Security Environment

If the Indian threat was the primary driver of military clout in politics, then, as some analysts contend, the loss of East Pakistan ought
to have reduced military insecurity and permanently rolled the military back to the barracks. In this view, India gained only a slight
edge in qualitative and quantitative military terms from victory in
East Pakistan, not an overwhelming superiority.[73] In fact, it "consolidated Pakistan's military assets" on the western front,[74] which
should have eased Pakistan's security dilemma vis-à-vis India because it is easier to defend a smaller population concentrated in a
smaller territory than a country divided into two noncontiguous
wings.

Pakistan also signed the Simla Agreement with India in July
1972, which committed both sides to "settle their differences by
peaceful means through bilateral negotiations," to respect each

other's territorial integrity, and, pending a final settlement of all bilateral issues, to desist from unilaterally altering the status quo.[75] India agreed to give back some 5,000 square kilometers of West Pakistani territory that it had acquired in the 1971 war and pledged not to conduct war-crimes trials of Pakistani prisoners. In sum, the loss of the eastern wing and the Simla Agreement should have been "a reasonable enough pretext to prune the state's debilitating requirements" and for "recasting the regional defense imperative."[76]

The problem is that objective threat analyses discount the powerful effects of the military's assessments of enemy intentions. The army's self-image as the sole guardian of national security was based on the perception of India as a permanently hostile enemy unreconciled to Pakistan's existence, which became an all-too-glaring reality in 1971. This provided a powerful barrier to any reevaluation of the state's security posture after 1971. Rather than abating the threat of war, the decisive defeat and state dismemberment at the hands of its mortal enemy presumably engendered a desire in the military to rebuild and to avenge its humiliation.[77] Military planners saw India's continued procurement of sophisticated weaponry and military modernization as evidence that India wanted to lock in its new military preponderance and use it to impose its hegemonic preferences in disputes with Pakistan.[78] India's explosion of a nuclear weapon in 1974, allegedly for peaceful purposes, only deepened Pakistan's insecurity and spurred its search for a nuclear deterrent.

However, external threat perceptions failed to produce the rally-around-the-flag effect, which is believed to increase the likelihood of civilian control by reorienting the military outward, because Pakistan was not a shared political community even after the exit of the Bengalis. Although the insurgency in Balochistan was triggered by governmental policy, it testified to the continued absence of national cohesion. In other words, threat perceptions of India were not universally shared in Pakistan. Similarly, even though the military had its work cut out for it in preparing for war, it was still tempted to intervene in politics, primarily because its underlying assumptions and beliefs about its guardian role in the state survived the shock of defeat in war.

In fact, external threats were compounded by perceived internal security problems that made the military more, not less, relevant to national security. The military had lost half the country, but in the view of many officers, this was in good measure due to the external abetment of internal rebellion in East Pakistan. Pakistan's civilian government and the military were also alarmed by the actions of the new Afghan government of President Sardar Mohammad Daud (1973–1975), which renewed its irredentist claims on the North-West Frontier Province and allegedly provided material support to Baloch nationalists. To counter Kabul's meddling, Islamabad adopted a forward policy in Afghanistan centered around recruiting, training, and organizing support for dissident Islamists, such as Gulbadin Hekmetyar and Ahmed Shah Massoud, who were fleeing the Daud government's repression.[79]

Parliamentary Elections and Political Crisis

In contrast to the military defeat of 1971, which had politically weakened the military relative to civilian politicians, the political crisis of 1977 opened the way for a reassertion of military power over the civilian government. It is important to examine this crisis to understand the military's role in the demise of civilian rule.

The crisis was triggered by parliamentary elections held on March 7, 1977. Buoyed by his government's good overall economic performance, as well as optimistic intelligence estimates of a comfortable PPP victory, Bhutto called an early election in March 1977.[80] Bhutto was quite confident of his party's reelection, not least because the PPP's opposition was hopelessly fragmented among Islamists, ethnic nationalists, and centrists. Although some of the opposition parties had earlier come together in the United Democratic Front, this disparate group formed a broader electoral alliance, named the Pakistan National Alliance (PNA), within a week of the election announcement.[81] Dominated by the Islamist Jamaate Islami (JI), the coalition was essentially tied together by the animus of several of the party leaders toward Bhutto and their desire to pool the opposition vote against the PPP.[82] The PNA campaigned on a platform of ending un-Islamic practices, bureaucratic abuse, inflation, and unemployment.

Although the PPP was generally expected to win the election, it won an absolute majority, 155 of the 200 National Assembly seats, and the PNA could win only 36.The alliance immediately rejected the results, boycotted the provincial ballot, and demanded Bhutto's resignation and the appointment of a caretaker government to hold new elections under the supervision of the army.[83] Even though Bhutto did not immediately agree to new elections, he offered the PNA a dialogue to resolve their differences and directed the election commission to hold summary inquiries and annul election results if it found grave illegalities.[84]

But this compromise did not satisfy the PNA's leaders. Instead, the alliance decided to step up the pressure on Bhutto and staged a nationwide strike on March 11. The success of the PNA's first strike in major cities emboldened the alliance to organize more protests in the belief that sustained disorder was the only way to goad the army into removing the government and holding new elections.[85] The agitation started in the southern port city of Karachi, a JI stronghold, and quickly spread to other cities, including Lahore. The government responded with force, detaining PNA leaders and thousands of its workers.[86] Protests and demonstrations organized by the JI and its militant student wing, the Islami Jamiat Talaba, against the government turned violent, which aggravated their mutual distrust. On April 9, the police and the FSF opened fire on a demonstration in Lahore, killing eighteen people and injuring over a hundred.[87] The government's use of excessive force galvanized the PNA and its supporters and increased clashes between the government and the opposition, resulting in more violence and economic disruption across the country. Although the PNA's focus and energies were initially devoted to demanding new elections, the Islamists within the alliance, sensing a historic opportunity for political success, were able to shift the campaign's main goal to the implementation of Nizam e Mustafa (literally, System of the Prophet), or an Islamic sociopolitical order.

On April 17, Bhutto opted for a tactical compromise to defuse the crisis by promising to enforce sharia law within six months, shutting down bars, and banning alcohol and gambling; a month later, he declared Friday a public holiday.[88] The PNA was not impressed by this belated capitulation and continued its agitation. By mid-April, the death toll from the violence had reached over 200, with hundreds more injured. Unable to effectively contain the violence, the government sought the army's assistance. Arguing that calling out the army under existing "aid of civil power" provisions would not work, General Zia reportedly gave the government prior assurance that it would swiftly stem the violence as long as it was given complete autonomy and control over its operations.[89] Bhutto conceded, and the newly elected parliament hurriedly amended the constitution to authorize a constitutional martial law. On April 21, a curfew was imposed in the three major cities, Karachi, Hyderabad, and Lahore, which were placed under the jurisdiction of the army.[90] Three weeks later, the army's actions were exempted from the writ jurisdiction of the provincial high courts to give military authorities even more latitude in the execution of their task and to prevent them from judicial scrutiny that could bring "humiliation to the integrity and to the patriotism of the armed forces."[91]

Amid the political deadlock, Bhutto tried to discredit his opposition by claiming that the PNA agitation was not *desi* (indigenous) but part of a massive international conspiracy designed to unseat his government because it was pursuing nuclear capability for the Islamic state of Pakistan.[92] Concerned with a potential nuclear arms race in South Asia, Washington had applied intense pressure on Bhutto to abandon the search for nuclear technology. In 1976, US secretary of state Henry Kissinger had reportedly told the Pakistani ambassador in Washington that "if the Democrats won [the elections], they would want to make a horrible example out of your country" unless Islamabad abandoned its pursuit of nuclear-reprocessing technology.[93] It was during the PNA-government deadlock a year later that Bhutto apparently discovered what he considered smoking-gun evidence of American plans to oust him. He deduced this from a conversation intercepted by Pakistani intelligence in which Robert Moore, the American consul general in Karachi, was heard telling the US embassy's political counselor, Howard B. Schaffer, that the "man is gone, the party is over."[94] Bhutto also publicly displayed a letter from the US secretary of state, Cyrus Vance, offering quiet diplomacy to discuss Pakistan's grievances as further indication of US guilt.[95]

To add fuel to the conspiracy fires, the US State Department canceled the export of a consignment of $68,000 worth of tear-gas canisters to Pakistan at the height of the PNA protests because supporting a repressive regime would conflict with the Carter administration's human rights policy.[96] In June 1977, Washington also called off an earlier offer to sell A-7 aircraft to Pakistan,[97] a move seen by Bhutto as evidence of American disapproval of his government at a time when it was mired in a political crisis.[98]

Notwithstanding PPP allegations against foreign powers, Bhutto sought the help of Saudi Arabia to break the deadlock. The Saudis were able to broker talks between the government and the PNA,[99] which began on June 3.[100] Several rounds of talks yielded an agreement on June 15.[101] The government agreed to hold a fresh round of parliamentary elections in October, and the PNA dropped its insistence on Bhutto's resignation.[102] However, before the agreement could be signed, the military under General Zia intervened on July 5, 1977, overthrowing the PPP government and imposing martial law. Zia blamed the PPP and the PNA for failing to reach a political settlement and claimed that their deadlock "would throw the country into serious chaos and crisis. That risk could not be taken in view of the larger interest of the country. The Army, therefore, had to act."

Zia declared that "his sole aim was to organize free and fair elections which would be held in October this year."[103]

Scholars have argued that during political crises, civilians can push an otherwise reluctant military into intervention by jumping on its bandwagon.[104] Did civilians similarly drag the Pakistani military into politics in 1977? Pakistan's experience warrants a reexamination of the argument that civilian prompting shapes military decisions to intervene. When the army is seen as an alternative game in town, there are compelling incentives for politicians to court the men in uniform. The Pakistani military had preempted elections in 1958 by a coup and had denied the Awami League its electorally acquired democratic mandate by using naked repression in 1971. The military held the ultimate power to decide the fate of any government; hence both the government and the opposition tried to co-opt the generals to their side.

The JI leadership had appealed to the army to overthrow Bhutto as early as 1973, but that incitement had fallen on deaf ears because it came too soon after the 1971 debacle. In May 1977, one of the PNA leaders, Asghar Khan, knocked on the garrison's doors, urging the military to disobey the unlawful commands of an illegal regime or risk being seen as "a degenerate police force, fit for killing unnamed civilians." He also appealed to its patriotism: "There comes a time in the lives of nations when each man has to ask himself whether he is doing the right thing. For you the time has come. Answer this call honestly and save Pakistan. God be with you."[105] Khan and other PNA hard-liners apparently tried to block the conciliatory efforts of opposition moderates through an ironclad guarantee from army headquarters that the generals would hold free and fair elections within three months of ousting Bhutto. The JI's Ghafoor Ahmed, who was also the PNA's secretary general and its key negotiator, has admitted that "we were under constant pressure from the hawks to abort the negotiations. It could not have been just a bluff. Asghar Khan could not have claimed to speak on behalf of the army without the high command's nod."[106]

Rafi Raza, a close Bhutto adviser and former minister, has also claimed that "there were several indications that the army was in contact with some PNA leaders. . . . [There were] persistent rumors that some [intelligence] agencies had a hand in the troubles. Plainly, there was merit in the argument that the army leadership had not reconciled itself to a secondary role in a civilian setup."[107] Another senior PNA leader, Nawabzada Nasrullah Khan, claims that the ISI was playing each side against the other, sowing mistrust in the minds of the PNA regarding Bhutto and vice versa.[108]

Because the army was not perceived as a neutral actor, Bhutto too tried to enlist it on his side.[109] For instance, the government obliged the military by giving it a pay hike.[110] Bhutto also secured from the military a public pronouncement of its support of the government. The military service chiefs and the Chairman Joint Chiefs of Staff Committee issued this unusual statement: "While the military code prohibits the soldiers, the sailors, and airmen to have anything do with politics, the Armed Forces who belong to the nation have to remain on call to safeguard the country's integrity when threatened on account of external aggression or internal subversion. . . . We wish to make it absolutely clear that the Pakistan Army, Navy and Air Force are totally united to discharge their constitutional obligation in support of the present legally constituted government."[111]

It is not clear why the army had to reiterate its democratic intent publicly if the military code prohibited any political meddling. According to General Zia, this was done "voluntarily to strengthen the hands of the government and to make the PNA believe that the armed forces were with the government."[112] However, the statement also made it clear that this apparent oath of fealty to the constitution and government was conditional and was linked to the absence of internal and external threats. From there, the leap to intervention required only that the military come to the conclusion that the civilian deadlock was a threat to internal stability or a fillip to foreign aggression.

Scholars have argued that civilian dependence on the military to provide internal security had already "enabled the men in uniform to renew their taste for power and drew them back into politics."[113] Of particular importance in this regard was military deployment for counterinsurgency operations in Balochistan from 1973 to 1977, which has been described as "Bhutto's waterloo" because it allowed the army to carry out its field operations autonomously of the government, which helped the generals regain their foothold in national politics.[114]

Although the military had previously suppressed Baloch rebellions against the central government in 1948 and 1953 and during the 1960s, this latest insurgency was sparked by the PPP government's decision to dismiss the National Awami Party–Jamiat Ulema-e-Islam (NAP-JUI) provincial government and impose presidential rule in the province in February 1972 after receiving reports of civil disturbance from the province. The provincial government was dismissed on the grounds that it had failed to maintain law and order, which posed a "grave menace to the peace and tranquillity of the province."[115] The NAP-JUI government in the North-West Frontier Province resigned in protest.

Bhutto and some PPP leaders claimed that his decision was motivated by the ISI's discovery of arms in the Iraqi embassy in February 1973, which it alleged were to be supplied to the NAP for subversive activities in Pakistan.[116] Whatever the real reason, the counterinsurgency operation in the province "re-established the military's credentials as the saviour of Pakistan's unity," which had been badly marred in 1971.[117] More specifically, it reaffirmed and reinforced the officer corps's traditional belief in the incompetence of civilians and their own superior ability to perform civilian tasks. In fact, Bhutto's top security advisers had eerily cautioned him in July 1976 about the potential contagiousness of a budding political infection in the officer corps: "For all intents and purposes, it appears in Balochistan that the army has taken over even the field of development and in formulating all policies. It is time that the experiment of gradual withdrawal of the army from law enforcement is given a trial because the impression amongst junior army officers that the army is a panacea for all ills . . . is again gaining ground. It can be very infectious and cannot remain confined to one province. This infection may not be allowed to spread."[118] In a year's time, this infection would develop into the full-blown disease of military intervention.

Military Perceptions and the 1977 Crisis

An accurate description of the institutional military's role in a coup requires "a portrayal of the interaction between officers' beliefs and the political events that preceded their decision to intervene."[119] When the Pakistani military took over the administrative control of three major cities in April 1977, it became directly involved in running governmental affairs, including such tasks as the control of basic commodity prices and prosecuting civilians in military courts, without any oversight.[120] By early May, the army corps commanders gained direct access to Bhutto, who reportedly invited them to special meetings with his cabinet ministers to solicit their views on political and security conditions and dealing with the PNA agitation.[121] From that vantage point, the generals could see at close quarters the regime's weakness and dependence on them to manage a political crisis.[122] The more the PPP government relied on the generals to suppress the opposition, the more it confirmed their view that the politicians, especially Bhutto and his cabinet ministers, could not be trusted to govern the country honorably and wisely because they cared only about their selfish interest in power, even if that meant using the most important national institution, the military, to settle scores with the opposition or, worse, to wage civil war.[123] Many officers endorsed the view of a former chief of general staff that the "politicians could not care less if the country slipped into chaos," and that those who had "taken an oath to protect the country could not idly stand by while Pakistan went to the dogs."[124] Once the senior army officers made this political judgment about

140

the government's intentions, it became the primary motive for the coup.[125]

It was difficult for military officers to understand why Bhutto would not immediately compromise. Some blamed his refusal on his authoritarian personality, describing him as arrogant, conniving, and a clever trickster always concerned with increasing his personal control and power (a view shared by many in the PNA).[126] In this view, Bhutto called an early election to achieve the two-thirds majority needed to amend the constitution to create a strong presidential system.[127] "If Bhutto had had political sagacity to share rather than monopolize power," observed then commander of the army's X Corps, Lieutenant General Faiz Ali Chishti, "he would have come to an agreement with the PNA and there would have been no need for the coup."[128] For the coup makers, it was thus a necessary institutional step to restore sanity and order, which had been marred by the political avarice of Bhutto.

Officers who participated in the 1977 coup claim that the military wanted a negotiated solution to the crisis. However, once the crisis unfolded, unrest spread to several major cities, the government lost its standing with the people, and the military's low tolerance for disorder and strife was severely tested. Zia and his corps commanders decided to act because negotiations could drag on, and there was a risk of renewed violence, so the army had to prepare for the worst. Says Chishti, "The economy was in tatters. The country was threatened by political violence. There was no end in sight. The PPP was not going to honor its commitments. The PPP and the PNA were like two children. They could start fighting and bloodying their noses again . . . leaving us no option but to intervene and save both from each other," implying that the military was the guardian that had to chasten these errant children. Chishti claims that the high command was deeply disturbed by the possibility of a street confrontation between the PPP and the PNA after Bhutto told Zia on July 4 that the PNA was "not coming on the correct path" through talks, and that he would "have to deal with them differently."[129] The army later claimed that the PPP workers were arming themselves for a showdown,[130] and it feared a bloodbath.[131]

Hence, in the opinion of members of the military, the politicians created the conditions for the coup. To quote Chishti again, "Bhutto wanted power at all costs. The PNA wanted to throw him out of power. The army was caught in the middle." Hence "we were forced to take over power to separate the warring parties for the nation's sake and to create a level playing field for free and fair elections."[132] Therefore the coup was code-named Operation Fairplay. Lieutenant General Chishti and then major general Khalid Mahmud Arif, military secretary in the general headquarters in 1977, chief of staff to Chief Martial Law Administrator Zia (1977–1984), and later vice chief of army staff (1984–1987), both assert that the coup could have been avoided if Bhutto had allowed free and fair elections under the supervision of a neutral government agency like the army rather than prolonging the talks. They thus reveal the military's expansive conception of its professional role, including a legitimate role in organizing elections.

However, in a democracy, the right to act as a political mediator is not the military's to exercise in the first place. Unlike constitutions in many Latin American states, which entrusted the military with the special mission to safeguard the constitutional order,[133] or Turkey's 1980 constitution, which gave it the duty to protect the basic secular structure of the republic, Pakistan's constitution at the time had no such role for the military. In fact, as mentioned earlier, it confined the military to defense against external aggression and aid to civil power under the direction of the civilian government.[134] However, the Pakistani military was not accustomed to political subordination and continued to harbor tutelary notions.

Evidence from the time does not fully support the coup makers' contention that Pakistan was on the brink of collapse. According to PPP sources, the general law-and-order situation in the country had remained calm since at least May 26, and there was no immediate necessity for action on July 5, 1977. After the initial wave of heightened protest and violence between March and April, the levels of violence had gone down, and curfews in the main cities had been relaxed. In fact, as noted earlier, the opposition and the government had initiated parleys early in June, four weeks before the coup. By the middle of June, they had reportedly finalized an accord on the basic issue of holding new elections. Some PPP and opposition leaders later claimed that had the military waited one more day, the lingering question whether a final agreement was to be signed on July 5 would have been resolved once and for all.[135]

At the time, the PNA "neither maintained that an agreement had been reached, nor condemned General Zia for acting precipitately."[136] In fact, a number of PNA leaders joined the military's postcoup advisory council and later, in August 1978, the cabinet Zia created.

Some politicians and observers assert that the army played the role of a spoiler during the talks. For instance, the generals raised serious objections to two key opposition demands: the withdrawal of the army from counterinsurgency operations in Balochistan and the dissolution of a special tribunal (in the southern city of Hyderabad) that was trying opposition leaders for antistate activities.[137] However, the army accepted both PNA demands after the coup. It remains unclear whether the army deliberately impeded the final resolution of the deadlock, or whether Bhutto used military objections to stall the PNA.[138]

Members of General Ziaul Haq's junta, such as K. M. Arif, concede that the army had reservations about troop withdrawal from Balochistan and the Hyderabad tribunal, but Arif refutes the claim that the army sabotaged the agreement.[139] Instead, the army high command believed that Bhutto himself delayed the agreement. According to Chishti, there were triumphant announcements of successful talks on June 15 and then in early July, but they were all false starts because of the lack of trust between the two sides. Chishti and Arif claim that until the end, there was no agreement on paper. Like many in the PNA, the military believed that Bhutto had ulterior motives in prolonging the negotiations and never really wanted to concede power. According to Ghafoor Ahmed, some in the PNA suspected that Bhutto was exploiting divisions in the alliance between those like Maulana Mufti Mehmud and himself, who wanted the talks to succeed, and the hard-liners like Asghar Khan and Sherbaz Mazari, who wanted a brief period of martial law followed by elections.[140]

Chishti noted with bitterness that when the two sides announced that they had all but finalized an accord that resolved all the basic disagreements on June 15, Bhutto suddenly departed on a tour of five Muslim countries for almost a week, thus leaving everything up in the air.[141] In sum, senior military officers believed that the politicians, or more specifically Bhutto, lacked the sincerity and serious will needed to overcome their political differences for the sake of the country. Extrapolating from the protests and opposition to Bhutto and their own assessment of his intentions, observed at close quarters, the generals concluded that there was no chance of improvement in the way things were going and no prospects for compromise simply because the wrong people were running the affairs of the government. According to Chishti, "The period between 7 March and July 4 was a long one. It was just a series of inconclusive talks with no end in sight."[142]

Once senior members of the officer corps developed this generalized perception of the government, any further delay in the signing of the agreement strained their conditional support for the government. In fact, the high command had clearly informed the prime minister in June that "time was not on the government's side . . . and that if the deadlock continued, the army would have to exercise a military option."[143] Chishti claims that the army had planned to carry out the coup on July 3, but that Zia delayed it in the hope that the government and the PNA would conclude a final agreement. When rumors started to circulate that Bhutto was going to make changes in the high command, and the generals feared that the coup plan might be leaked,[144] the military struck shortly after midnight on July 5.

Legitimacy of the Government

Although different regimes have different levels of legitimacy, whether the military accepts a regime as legitimate can be crucial in its decision to intervene.[145] In fact, legitimacy deflations have provided the military an opportunity to intervene in many countries, including Brazil (1964), Chile (1973), and Turkey (1980).[146] The military's willingness to fight unarmed protestors, especially on behalf of a weakened and insecure government that is dependent on soldiers to maintain basic order, can vary depending on the degree of legitimacy it accords that government. It is reasonable to conclude that the allegations of electoral fraud, the consequent violence and instability, the PPP government's repressive reaction, and its dependence on the military to contain the violence crucially eroded its legitimacy in the eyes of the military.[147] As one retired brigadier remarked, "The Bhutto government's credibility was eroded both by rigging the election, and then using state repression to silence the opposition."[148] Junior and midranking officers resented being ordered to shoot at people in defense of "cheats and election riggers," and many viewed the PNA mass movement as clear evidence that the Bhutto regime had lost its right to rule.[149]

Whether the military respects and abides by the constitution is also important to whether it will continue to play by the rules of the game during a crisis.[150] The Pakistani military had had a negative opinion of the parliamentary system since the 1950s, but its members viewed the unbridled powers of the prime minister in the 1973 constitution as a recipe for instability.[151] The deadlock in 1977 confirmed their view that the constitution lacked the checks and balances needed to restrain the prime minister and resolve political conflict. Typical of this adverse evaluation of the constitution was K. M. Arif's view that even though "the country was in turmoil[,] . . . President

Chaudhry Fazal Elahi remained a silent spectator and virtually twiddled his thumbs. The Constitution did not permit the Head of the State to act except on the advice of the Prime Minister. The President's helplessness during the national crisis disclosed a lacuna in the Constitution. The division of power between the President and the Prime Minister was unrealistic."[152]

Ultimately, though, military perceptions of the government's declining legitimacy or lack of respect for the constitution provide insufficient grounds for military intervention. Also crucial is whether the military considers intervention a legitimate method of changing the government.[153] Whether this is so is particularly revealed during periods of crisis. Under such uncertain conditions, actors will interpret their environment according to the learning they have undergone, and the institutions or norms that have arisen as a result will act as ready-made sources for guiding behavior.[154] Interviews with military officials, as well as officers' memoirs, suggest that the imprinting of the past in the form of the precedent of the successful coup in 1958 not only played an important role in reducing coup makers' uncertainty about "what if" but also helped narrow the range of appropriate options.[155] In the revealing words of the corps commander, Lieutenant General Chishti: "We thought to ourselves: what would Ayub Khan have done in such a situation? The answer was clear. He would have done the same. This example strengthened our resolve that it was the army's duty to take over if the government is not performing effectively or worse, taking the country to ruin, as Mr. Bhutto's government seemed to be doing."[156]

The military's fears of general anarchy were exacerbated by more profound institutional worries about preserving its own unity. The high command feared that institutional discipline could be severely eroded by the direct involvement of army troops in protecting an unpopular government's position in office.[157] Self-preservation is a first-order concern for any organization. When that organization is endowed with what Samuel Finer calls a "manifest destiny" to save the nation from external and internal enemies, it is almost natural for its members to equate threats to its integrity with the demise of the state itself.[158] Urging Bhutto to find a quick negotiated solution to the political impasse, the high command reportedly issued a warning at a meeting in early May: "It was explained to the PM that the generals were with him. It was the lower echelon of the Army which was not with him and was reluctant to fire. . . . That situation if allowed to persist would hit the very fiber of the army . . . risking the end of Pakistan."[159]

A number of army officers expressed identical concerns in interviews. "Any splits in the army," one former army divisional commander argued, "would have not just been the end of the army, but the end of Pakistan."[160] Echoing this conclusion, a retired major general who had carried out martial law duties as a captain in Karachi feared that Pakistan's "breakup along ethnic or regional lines was imminent and had to be prevented."[161] Some military commanders believed that Bhutto had selfishly endangered the country's internal stability, thereby creating the opportunity for the external enemies of Pakistan to subvert it from within. With less-than-pleasant memories of the 1971 war and India's direct role in splitting Pakistan fresh on their minds, the high command interpreted the real or exaggerated danger of fragmentation of the officer corps as a golden opportunity for the "Indians to cross into Lahore and over-run Pakistan."[162] In fact, the corps commanders reportedly warned the government on June 14 that the negotiations must succeed, or, as the corps commander of Lahore, Lieutenant General Iqbal Khan, pointed out, the PNA could start agitating again, which would not only threaten the army's integrity but also weaken its defense capability because troops would be deployed in the cities.[163]

Whether or not the 1977 coup was a response to a real threat of the army's disintegration, the important thing is that the army commanders believed that it was. This collective agreement on the nature of the threat enhanced internal unity and the will to act against the government. By the time the negotiations started in June, the high command was at best equivocal about Bhutto's right to stay in office and more concerned about maintaining its cohesion. Two weeks before the coup, General Zia had reportedly warned Bhutto that the army could crack unless the government found a swift political solution to the crisis.[164]

In fact, senior officers were apprehensive that by pitching the military against unarmed Pakistanis in the Punjabi heartland, continued army deployment under the mini-martial law could transfer the anti-Bhutto sentiment to the army itself. The PNA protesters' provocative actions, including taunting the troops for their shameful surrender in Dhaka, served to reignite the humiliation the military had suffered in the former East Pakistan.[165] Moreover, part of the junior officers' anger was directed at their commanders for supporting a government that had no problems in using the army to shoot at unarmed civilians.[166] "The mass agitation reached a stage," asserts Chishti, "when the army had to decide whether it should continue to be a barrier against the masses and get destroyed in the clashes or to remove Bhutto."[167] The generals were profoundly disturbed by the refusal of three brigadiers from the army's IV Corps in Lahore to fire on unarmed civilians.[168]

Bhutto's postcoup contention that this episode of spectacular defiance was prearranged by the military aside,[169] these officers had crossed the institutional red lines of disobedience and dereliction of duty. Their willful act of indiscipline presumably stemmed from their professional assessment of shooting unarmed civilians as conduct unbecoming a soldier. But, surprisingly, few, if any, military officers resigned in protest or refused to take part in the July 1977 coup out of respect for the sanctity of the constitution, which they had sworn to protect with their lives. The firm absence of even a much less dazzling act of soldierly insubordination against the coup makes sense when it is seen as an institutionally framed response to saving the national army by subverting the constitution, or, in the military's oft-used surgical metaphor, severing the limb to save the body.

In other words, the military might have responded differently to the apparently corrosive effects of internal security duties if it had

148

internalized the norm that subordination to the civilian authorities was an inviolable principle of military professionalism. In that case, it would have simply recused itself from meddling in a political dispute because of the potential ramifications for military cohesion. After all, if the army could organize a successful coup against an elected government, it was powerful enough to avoid internal missions that eroded its unity.

The experience of Pakistan under Bhutto shows that the military's nondemocratic tendencies can survive severe external shocks, such as humiliation and defeat in war. Formal civilian institutional constraints on the military, such as constitutions upholding civilian supremacy or even changes in army command structures, also may not be sufficient to confine the generals to the barracks for long because these do not seem to affect its tutelary norms and inclinations. The PPP government's unwillingness or inability to hold the military institution accountable for the disaster in East Pakistan, especially when the military was severely disgraced, saved the military from facing the consequences of its actions or realizing the risk of repeating them. Despite putative reductions in the threat from India, there was no significant change in military threat perceptions, which made the task of permanently reversing its political role quite difficult. Military deployment in Balochistan renewed officers' beliefs in their ability to perform civilian security and governance functions better than civilians. The postelection crisis in 1977 proved to be the decisive turning point that activated the military's interventionist resolve. The military seized power when it decided that politicians, especially Bhutto and the PPP, were not sagacious enough to put aside their selfish political interests and swiftly resolve the deadlock, which had caused political disorder and threatened to erode military integrity.

5

FROM ZIA TO MUSHARRAF

The influence of institutional factors on the military's interest and involvement in politics stands out even more clearly in the period from 1977 to 1999. During this time, the military ruled for eleven years under General Ziaul Haq (1977–1988) and then permitted a transition to democracy that was marked by the alternation of power among four short-lived civilian governments (1988–1999), only to recapture state power in October 1999 under General Pervez Musharraf. On the one hand, the authoritarian legacies of Zia's military government created structural conditions vulnerable to political crises and instability. On the other hand, the generals' belief that politicians could not be trusted to preserve national security or to govern properly led them to impose limits on the exercise of authority by the political leadership. These constraints caused civil-military conflicts that, in turn, prompted military meddling in civilian affairs, thus confirming the military's view of politicians as incompetent and corrupt. Over time, the military (and many civilians) began to develop grave doubts about the suitableness of continuing with what they thought was the sham of democracy in Pakistan. By 1999, when differences over the Kargil war with India strained relations between the military and the government of the day, the military swiftly switched from its guardian role to its governing role.

The Pakistani military has been opposed to the dispersal and dilution of authority that it has considered inherent in the parliamentary system since the early 1950s. After the 1958 coup, General Ayub Khan abrogated the decentralizing 1956 constitution, replacing it with a centralized presidential constitution in 1962. Although that constitution did not survive its sponsor's political demise, Yahya Khan's Legal Framework Order left little doubt that the military high command had intended to retain its tutelary powers through the presidential veto of any future constitution if it did not continue to rule the country directly.

Insofar as the military found the 1973 constitution a recipe for instability and the primary cause of the prolonged political crisis of 1977, the coup heralded a foundational program of political restructuring implemented with "the iron fist of military rule, hidden inside the Islamic glove."[1] That restructuring entailed military revision of the rules of the game through what the high command believed was a proper division of powers between the president and the prime minister, which the military's senior members thought would prevent the recurrence of such political crises in the future.[2] Hence the military government drastically rewrote the 1973 constitution to ensure checks and balances on future civilian governments through a strong president armed with the constitutional power to dissolve parliament arbitrarily and made an unsuccessful attempt to back it up with a National Security Council (NSC) in which the military had a dominant role. The military has since internalized and articulated the efficacy of these two institutional safety valves and has tried to implement them to make parliamentary democracy safe for Pakistan.

The Military Government of General Ziaul Haq

From 1977 to 1985, the military government of General Ziaul Haq ruled Pakistan without any serious threat to its hold on power. Having accepted the challenge of governing Pakistan as a "true soldier of Islam,"[3] Zia promised to transform Pakistan's "socioeconomic and political structure in accordance with the principles of Islam."[4] In Zia's view, Pakistani society lacked cohesion because the people had adhered to a secular system of politics and development for three decades rather than observing the fundamental tenets of Islam. Therefore, Islamizing Pakistani society was the only way to ensure genuine national integration.[5]

Zia introduced significant Islamic changes in the criminal laws, the judicial system, and the economy, including the imposition of the *hudood* (singular *hud,* meaning limit) punishments defined in the Quran and the Sunna for certain crimes, such as drinking, theft, and adultery *(zina);* the establishment of the Federal Shariat Court to examine whether specific laws were repugnant to Islam; and the imposition of *zakat* (a compulsory religious wealth tax) and *ushr* (land tax).[6] However, Zia did not extend his claimed foundational project to the structure of the military. Zia knew that the support of the military institution, especially the higher echelons of the officer corps, was crucial to his government's survival. Members of the army high command had removed both Ayub Khan and Yahya Khan from power when they threatened the military's perceived corporate interests and reputation. According to Shahid Javed Burki, a World Bank official who developed a close personal association with Zia, the general had learned a crucial lesson from their experience: do not relinquish control of the army to another officer.[7] When General Ayub headed the military government, he delegated authority over military affairs to his commander in chief, General Muhammad Musa. However, when he desperately needed the military's backing during the popular mobilization against his government in 1969, the high command under the then commander in chief, General Yahya Khan, abandoned him at that crucial moment. Although Zia also deputized several senior officers to manage the military institution, first appointing a deputy chief of the army staff and then replacing the position with an army vice chief of staff, he remained the chief of army staff throughout his stay in power, even after the purported move toward greater civilian participation in his regime in 1985.[8]

After the 1977 coup, the reins of government lay formally in the hands of the Military Council, which mainly consisted of the army chief and chief martial law administrator (CMLA) General Zia; the chairman of the Joint Chiefs of Staff Committee (CJCSC); and the chiefs of staff of the air force and the navy. However, important domestic and foreign policy decisions were made by Zia and his *rufaqaa* (colleagues), including Lieutenant Generals Faiz Ali Chishti (X Corps, Rawalpindi), Iqbal Khan, (IV Corps, Lahore, V Corps, Karachi, and from 1978 to 1980 deputy chief of the army staff), and Sawar Khan (XI Corps, Peshawar, IV Corps, and from 1980 to 1984 vice chief of the army staff).[9] With the exception of Chishti, who was made an adviser and cabinet minister in charge of the Establishment ministry, Kashmir affairs, and the Federal Inspection Commission (1977–1978),[10] the corps commanders also doubled as zonal martial law administrators and later as provincial governors (until 1980).[11]

Another important institution welding the military government with the military institution was the Martial Law Administrators' Conference, headed by the CMLA and attended by the four zonal/provincial martial law administrators, the CJCSC, and the deputy chief or vice chief of the army staff, which dealt exclusively with martial law affairs.[12] The military also introduced its own parallel court system, comprising both summary and regular courts and ultimately presided over by Zia as the CMLA.[13] After 1980, the offices of the governor and the corps commanders were separated, but Zia continued to appoint lieutenant generals as provincial governors. For these important posts, he chose officers he had either previously served with in the army or could trust because of their professional or personal reputations. In effect, the military institution was fused with the military government, and Zia acted as a bridge connecting the two in his dual capacity as CMLA and army chief of staff.

The Zia government's stability was rooted in the institutionalization of the army high command as the principal body for governing the country, which, at least in part, indicated a strong internal consensus on the legitimacy of the military's governing role.

With the exception of Chishti, Zia did not fire or retire his corps commanders, including core members of the coup group, such as Sawar Khan and Iqbal Khan. Instead, he circulated them among top posts until their retirement. Zia even retained Chishti for three years after the coup. However, he retired Chishti when he "got too big for his boots."[14]

The Zia government exceeded both previous military dictatorships in Pakistan in the extent to which the institution of the military infiltrated the civil administration, society, and the economy. This militarization brought material rewards to officers, but its pervasiveness stemmed partly from officers' belief that they were well qualified to perform expansive nation-building tasks. Zia appointed an unprecedented number of senior officers as ambassadors, secretaries, and heads of autonomous public corporations.[15] In 1980, the military reserved for itself a statutory quota of 10 percent in the three important civil services (the District Management Group, the police, and the foreign services), thus starting a process of the formal militarization of the bureaucracy that has since continued.

As Ayesha Siddiqa's book *Military Inc.* describes in rich detail, the military's interventions into the economy also assumed a new scope and scale. General Zia institutionalized the previous practice of allotting agricultural and urban residential and commercial land to military officers, and the military's subsidiaries, like the National Logistics Cell, specializing in cargo transportation, became monopolies that crowded out civilian competition. Protected by their association with the military, military welfare foundations, such as the Fauji Foundation, expanded from small-scale welfare enterprises to industrial conglomerates, investing in such businesses as real estate, fertilizers, oil and gas, and cement. Even divisional and unit-level commanders were permitted to invest in business cooperatives to raise funds, which have often been used for the personal enrichment of army officers. In defense of this military economy, the standard military argument is essentially that these ventures provide welfare to officers and their families, and that this benefits the overall health of the economy. Often in stark contrast to the facts, military officers exhibit a strong tendency to contrast allegedly successful military enterprises with corrupt and inefficient civilian public-sector corporations and to argue that the army is able to manage these enterprises successfully because of its managerial prowess, discipline, and efficiency.[16]

Less recognized is the military's educational expansion into civil society, which stemmed from the belief that the officer corps had to enhance its civilian capacity, given the comprehensive nature of national security. Under Zia, military officers were sent to civilian universities for postgraduate education in the social sciences, history, and strategic studies. Many were also sent abroad for advanced nonmilitary education.[17] Although the number of these officers is unknown, interviews for this book showed that higher levels of nonmilitary education have reinforced officers' beliefs in their superiority to civilians, especially the "uneducated" and "feudal" politicians.

The Army and America

The military's on-again, off-again alliance with the United States peaked in the 1980s. US financial and diplomatic support played a pivotal role in augmenting the Zia government. It also reinforced the military's sense of impunity for its unconstitutional actions and allowed it to commit gross human rights violations without any serious repercussions. To assuage domestic and congressional concerns about democracy and human rights, senior US officials typically pledged that Washington would seriously apply the American policy of supporting democratic governments in Pakistan, only to ignore the military nature of the government and its worst excesses because of the country's "limited tradition of representative government."[18]

When Zia assumed power, ties between the two countries were strained by Pakistan's pursuit of nuclear weapons technology. As the sole protector of Pakistan's integrity, the military continued to develop a nuclear deterrent despite US pressure. The Carter administration (1977–1981) used both sticks and carrots to prevent Pakistan from developing nuclear weapons. For instance, it successfully persuaded France to halt the sale of a nuclear reprocessing plant to Pakistan. In April 1979, the United States enforced the Symington Amendment, which prohibited US economic and military aid to countries seeking nuclear enrichment technology.[19] However, fearing that sanctions could be counterproductive, Carter followed up the aid cutoff with an offer of fighter planes and technical assistance with nuclear energy under international safeguards.[20]

The Soviet invasion of Afghanistan in December 1979 drastically shifted US foreign policy goals in the region and catapulted Pakistan from a virtual pariah state to a frontline American ally. It was also a boon for Zia's internationally isolated military government. The Carter administration readily abandoned its nuclear-proliferation concerns and instead offered Pakistan's generals $400 million in economic and military assistance to help them counter the threat posed by the Soviet intervention. Confident that the United States would not have even "an inch of soil" of influence in the region without Pakistan's help," Zia famously spurned the aid as "peanuts."[21] When the Reagan administration came into office in January 1981, the United States was again able to court and co-opt Pakistan's military for its strategic objectives and provided it with military and economic aid worth $3.2 billion over six years in return for assistance in the US-led effort to wage an anti-Soviet jihad on Pakistan's western border.[22] Despite tangible evidence of Pakistan's continuing efforts to acquire nuclear materials for its weapons program,[23] the administration set aside US nonproliferation concerns because of the even higher priority of fighting Soviet forces in Afghanistan, for which it needed the Pakistani military's cooperation.[24]

The presence of Soviet troops on Pakistan's western flank raised the Pakistani military's fear of encirclement from two fronts.[25] Before the Soviet incursion, Afghanistan did not pose a substantial military threat, even though it periodically revived its irredentist claims on Pakistan's North-West Frontier Province. Pakistan's forward policy in Afghanistan had started under the Bhutto government, but it was intensified under Zia. Even before the Soviets entered Afghanistan, the military had started backing Afghan Islamist opposition groups, especially after the Afghan Marxist regime assumed power in Kabul in 1978. The generals perceived that regime's rule as a security threat because it could facilitate a future Soviet intervention in Pakistan and the region. The military provided the resistance groups sanctuary, training, and logistical support.[26]

Although the military had collaborated with the Jamaate Islami (JI) in the 1971 war, the relationship between the army and Islamists also changed dramatically under Zia. Given the regime's emphasis on Islamization and its antagonism toward the Pakistan People's Party (PPP), the Islamist parties were its natural allies. The JI, which was a major Pakistan National Alliance component party, joined Zia's cabinet in 1978 and became its "staunchest ally, almost a surrogate political party domestically and its closest partner in the U.S.-sponsored jihad in Afghanistan."[27] Zia also co-opted another important member of the Pakistan National Alliance, the revivalist Deobandi Jamiat Ulema-e-Islam (JUI). With government backing and financial aid from Arab countries, the JUI rapidly expanded its existing chain of madrassas in the North-West Frontier Province and Balochistan, which indoctrinated students for the jihad in Afghanistan.[28]

Because the Americans wanted plausible deniability, the CIA franchised the Afghan jihad to the Pakistan military and, more specifically, to the ISI. Until then, the ISI had still primarily focused on external intelligence. However, the Soviet invasion gave it a strong impetus to expand its spectrum of activities toward internal security and guerrilla warfare.[29] The ISI virtually controlled the Afghan resistance by selectively channeling CIA (and Saudi) money and arms (an estimated $6–12 billion) to the seven Peshawar-based mujahideen groups, including the Hizbe Islami of Gulbaddin Hekmatyar and the Jamiat e Islami of Burhanuddin Rabbani.[30]

In the process, military officers delegated to the ISI developed extensive skills and experience in organizing guerrilla warfare, as well as ties to radical extremists, many of whom were later deployed in Indian Kashmir and post-Soviet Afghanistan. ISI officers also conceived grandiose notions of their strategic capabilities during this time, and after the fall of the Soviet Union, this created an organizational creed of superiority rooted in their claim of single-handedly tearing down a superpower.

The ISI also significantly increased its capacity for domestic surveillance and political repression under Zia, a development that would ultimately threaten and undermine democratic civilian rule after the military's exit from government in 1988. Worried about both potential Soviet collusion with the Pakistani Left and the stability of his own government, Zia used the agency's dreaded Internal Security Wing to counter the propaganda and allegedly antinational activities of labor and trade unions, Sindhi nationalists, and other opposition groups.[31] Zia also employed the ISI to patronize and arm the JI's militant student wing, the Islami Jamiat Talaba (commonly known as Jamiat), which carried out a violent ideological purge of public universities, targeting leftist student organizations, including the PPP's People's Student Federation, and secular/leftist faculty members. The Jamiat also collaborated with the ISI in mobilizing public support for the Afghan war.[32]

Domestic Political Restructuring

The generals under Zia had ostensibly captured state power in 1977 with the goal of creating the right conditions for holding fair and free elections. Hence Zia's military government did not initially ban political parties, although it proscribed their political activities. It lifted the ban on partisan politicking in the run-up to the scheduled October 1977 elections and allowed proregime political parties, like the JI, to organize election campaigns.

Like Ayub and Yahya before them, Zia and his senior military colleagues shared the military's institutional contempt for uncontrolled politics, which was reinforced by the 1977 crisis. Soon after assuming power, Zia qualified his initial promise of holding elections by arguing that "elections for the sake of elections is not the answer"; instead, "the election results must bring a positive change in the form of a somewhat stable political government."[33]

Fearing Bhutto's' continued popularity, the generals repeatedly postponed the elections. Zia decided that elections would bring a stable government only under the right conditions, namely, the accountability of the previous prime minister and his family and associates. Toward this end, the military government issued four white papers implicating Bhutto and his government in electoral rigging, the abuse of state institutions, and financial wrongdoing.[34] It also incarcerated Bhutto's wife, Nusrat, and daughter, Benazir, for prolonged periods.

Like Ayub, Zia created nonpartisan local governments to seek legitimacy and to undermine the PPP's political support base. In September 1979, the military government organized elections to local councils. Candidates associated with the PPP scored impressive gains at the polls, after which the government decided to postpone national parliamentary elections once again. Unable to eliminate the PPP's popular support, Zia ultimately banned political activities and imposed harsh controls on party activities and finances.[35]

The Movement for the Restoration of Democracy (MRD) posed the most potent challenge to the Zia regime. In 1981, the PPP and seven other banned opposition parties organized the MRD to demand the end of martial law, the holding of impartial elections under the 1973 constitution, and the restoration of democracy. The movement was fueled by Sindhi alienation from the military-controlled state amid the broader denial of democratic participation. The movement peaked between August and October 1983, especially in the PPP stronghold of the interior parts of Sindh, including Bhutto's hometown of Larkana. The immediate impetus was Zia's August 12 announcement of legislative elections in which political parties would not be allowed to participate. The second round of nonparty local elections in September–October 1983 stoked further violence.[36] Ultimately, the military ruthlessly crushed the MRD, reportedly laying siege to entire villages and allegedly using gunships against unarmed civilians. Government forces killed over one hundred people and arrested thousands, and military courts sentenced over a hundred to imprisonment and flogging.[37]

Although the MRD was not strong enough to dislodge Zia, the movement effectively questioned the military government's legitimacy and compelled the general to liberalize his regime by holding parliamentary elections. Before taking that calculated risk, Zia got himself elected president for five years in a fraudulent referendum in 1984 in which he claimed to have received 97.7 percent of the votes.[38] Having formally secured his presidency, Zia exploited festering ethnic tensions between Muhajirs (Urdu-speaking migrants from India) and Sindhis as a counterpoise to the PPP.[39] This divide-and-rule policy helped the emergence of the Muhajir Qaumi Movement (MQM), a neofascistic party claiming to represent the rights of the Urdu-speaking migrant community, with far-reaching consequences for politics in urban Sindh.[40]

As indicated earlier, the generals regarded the 1973 constitution as a source of deadlock and instability because it had no built-in mechanism to balance the power of the prime minister. To achieve the desired balance, Zia authorized himself to amend the constitution in 1980. Faced with judicial challenges to his authority, he first purged and subordinated the judiciary.[41] He then drastically reconfigured the 1973 constitution, assigning the prime minister's important executive powers to the president, including the power to appoint key state officials, such as military service chiefs, provincial governors, the chief election commissioner, and even Supreme Court judges, who were supposed to interpret the legality of presidential powers. Second, in a throwback to the viceregal system, Zia granted the president constitutional coup powers to dissolve the national assembly arbitrarily.[42] Zia also created a National Security Council (NSC) to make "recommendations relating to the proclamation of emergency under article 232, the security of Pakistan," and other important national matters. The NSC was to consist of the president, the prime minister, the Senate chairman, the CJCSC, the service chiefs, and provincial chief ministers. The composition of the NSC clearly indicated that it was designed to give the president (who was also the army chief) and the military service chiefs a "constitutional role in supervising the functioning of government rather than evolving a coherent national security policy."[43]

The military government organized parliamentary elections in March 1985. As a price for lifting martial law in December of that year, Zia had the resulting parliament legalize all martial law regulations and ratify his far-reaching constitutional amendments except the NSC, which the parliament rejected. He also appointed a civilian government under his handpicked prime minister, Mohammad Khan Junejo (1985–1988), a veteran Muslim League politician elected from Sindh. However, Zia was loath to share power and frequently used his presidential bully pulpit to criticize the government and encourage his Islamist allies "to dispute the legitimacy of the democratic and electoral processes."[44] Although Junejo was broadly compliant, he alarmed the high command by criticizing the generals' perks and vowing to introduce austerity measures in the armed forces. The prime minister irked the generals further when he trespassed on foreign policy issues, for instance, when he invited all political parties to build a broad political consensus on the 1988 Geneva Accords dealing with the timetable for Soviet troop withdrawal from Afghanistan. The last straw was the prime minister's decision to order an inquiry into the mysterious explosion of an army ammunition depot located at the Ojhri Camp in Rawalpindi on April 10, 1988, which killed or injured over a hundred people in both Islamabad and Rawalpindi.[45] The depot was used to store weapons to be supplied to the Afghan mujahideen. On May 29, before the results of the inquiry could be made public, Zia dissolved the parliament and sacked Junejo and his cabinet after less than three years in office. Three months later, Zia was killed in a mysterious plane crash along with key senior military officers.[46] The dictator's death paved the way for a transition to democracy in 1988.

An Islamist or Professional Army?

Before analyzing the transition from Zia's authoritarian rule, it is important to examine the impact of the Zia years on the military's professional values and beliefs, with particular attention to the often exaggerated fears about the Islamization of the Pakistani officer corps during the 1980s as a prelude to an Islamist coup. This nightmare scenario continues to reverberate almost three decades later in the context of the Pakistani army's participation in the US-led War on Terror.

The Pakistani army has traditionally deployed religious imagery, rhetoric, and myth as devices for motivational purposes. After independence, military officers stressed that the "Islamic character of Pakistan was reflected in the Islamic character of the military." Military publications traced the history of Pakistan to the history of "Muslim dominance in South Asia." These beliefs ultimately fed into the grossly inflated self-image of the army as a martial army superior to the army of "Hindu India . . . contaminated by non-martial groups" and its institutional rejection of the Bengalis as cowardly, downtrodden, and poor officer material.[47]

Islam began to permeate the army's institutional symbols, structures, and socialization processes more deeply under Zia. Stephen P. Cohen has documented the introduction of Islamic themes in military curricula, especially in the Command and Staff College at Quetta.[48] Cohen shows that this Muslimization of military education and social life was an important factor in shaping the social attitudes and outlook of the officer corps. Under the influence of at least one professional officer, Colonel Abdul Quyuum, officer students were taught to integrate Western and Islamic strategic thought while using the Quran as the basis of finding strategic and historical truth.[49] Brigadier S. K. Malik's book *The Quranic Concept of War*, which was widely distributed in the military, represented the most comprehensive application of Quranic thought to the art of modern warfare.[50] Drawing on scripture and the example of historic Muslim battles, such as the Battle of Badr in 624 CE, the book suggested that the only justifiable war was one waged in the name of God, which had one primary purpose: "to fight the [infidel forces] of tyranny and oppression."[51] In his foreword to this polemical treatise on the Islamic theory of war, Zia defined the duty of a Muslim soldier and citizen: "The professional soldier in a Muslim army, pursuing the goals of a Muslim state, cannot become 'professional' if in all his activities he does not take on the color of Allah. The non-military citizen of a Muslim state must likewise be aware of the kind of soldier that his country must produce and the only pattern of war that his country's armed forces may wage."[52]

Although many officers heeded Zia's advice and took on the color of Allah in their personal and professional lives, Cohen rightly notes that the pedagogical emphasis on Islam did not foment any broad shift toward the collective Islamization of the officer corps. Cohen also argues that after 1971, the military's collective political and military failures undermined the more relaxed attitude toward Islam adopted by the British and American generations of Westernized, upper-class officers. That attitude, combined with enhanced recruitment of the lower middle classes from small towns and rural areas,[53] or the so-called Zia generation, increased the army's conservatism. For instance, individual displays of piety and devoutness, such as the keeping of beards and the offering of prayers in units and messes, became normal. Zia also extended the Bhutto-era prohibition on the consumption of alcohol to officers' messes and encouraged and facilitated the proselytizing activities of the Tablighi Jamaat, an influential Islamic missionary movement, in the army.

The growing pietization of sections of the officer corps under Zia was reinforced by the expansion of the military's professional mission from protecting Pakistan's physical frontiers to safeguarding its ideological boundaries, as well as extensive deployments in Gulf and Arab countries.[54] However, it is unclear how these seemingly significant religious changes in the officer corps have affected the nature and scope of the military's institutional involvement in politics. Historically, both liberal and conservative officers and both Westernized and Pakistani ones have intervened in politics in defense of the military's national security perspectives, policies, and prerogatives.

Beyond introducing Islamic thought into professional military training, however, Zia consolidated a parallel process of using Islamist militancy as an instrument of national security policy. Emboldened by the presumed success of jihad in evicting the Soviets from Afghanistan, the ISI has continued that policy, deploying militants to fight an asymmetric war against Indian forces in Kashmir and to gain control over Kabul. In the 1990s, the military also used these extremist groups to destabilize noncompliant elected governments in Pakistan.[55]

However, the policy of using militants as strategic tools of foreign and domestic policy exerted feedback effects on the military. By creating a more permissive institutional environment for the permeation of radical ideologies among the officer corps, especially during the Afghan jihad, it radicalized the political views and behavior of a number of officers of the Zia generation. This link between Islamist militants and military personnel was most clearly demonstrated when a group of army officers conspired to overthrow the PPP government and establish a caliphate in 1995. Led by Major General Zaheerul Islam Abbassi, with the collusion of Qari Saifullah, leader of the Pakistani militant group Harkatul Jihadul Islami, the conspirators had also planned to neutralize the military high command by seizing army headquarters during a corps commanders' meeting. However, Military Intelligence (MI), acting on a tip from Customs Intelligence officials who had intercepted a military vehicle laden with arms and ammunition, detained the conspirators and foiled the coup plot. The successful suppression of the plot not only suggests that noninstitutional coups tend to fail but also provides evidence against any wholesale radicalization of the officer corps.

The point is that military men may come from different ethnic and social backgrounds and may subscribe to different ideologies. Exceptions aside, professional army officers consider the survival and integrity of their institution, which is inextricably linked in their minds to national integrity, more important than anything else.[56] In interpreting the military's political propensity and relationship to civilian authorities, the important effects of secular military socialization cannot be underestimated. By its very nature, professional military training is designed to erase individual affiliations to religious, cultural, or ethnic groups and to produce a uniform worldview and intense loyalty to the country and the institution. Like any other professional military, the Pakistani military's institutional creed is nationalism, not Islamism, despite the Muslimness of Pakistan's hegemonic national identity. Although the concept of jihad as military strategy still has currency among the officer corps, an examination of the training curriculum and professional writings of members of the higher officer corps trained at the National Defence College (which was renamed the National Defence University in 2007) since 2000 indicates strong socialization into a dominant organizational narrative about the army's politically expansive professional role in safeguarding internal order and external security, not creating an Islamist state. Before turning to that examination in the next two chapters, I will discuss the transition to political democracy in 1989 and its breakdown in 1999.

Transition to Curtailed Democracy

The military's decision to allow a transition to democracy rather than continue its rule was shaped by a combination of domestic, international, and institutional factors. The immediate trigger was the death of the dictator. The inherent lack of legitimacy of military rule, compounded by popular demands for political participation led by the PPP under Benazir Bhutto, who had been greeted by mammoth crowds on her triumphant return to Pakistan in 1986 after several years in exile in London, was another reason. The pressure for formal democratic compliance in a post–Cold War international environment, made all the more urgent by reported American disapproval of continued military government, possibly played an important role.[57] However, the primary motivation was institutional.

Zia's repressive military government had tarnished the public reputation of the military institution. Hence it seems that "the cost of repression exceeded the costs of toleration," which provided a powerful impetus.[58] Within hours of Zia's death, his successor, Chief of the Army Staff (COAS) General Mirza Aslam Beg (1988–1991), held a meeting with the naval and air force chiefs. They decided to appoint the chairman of the Senate, Ghulam Ishaq Khan, acting president in accordance with the constitution, signaling their intent to permit the transition to political democracy.[59] Beg declared that the army was committed to a free and fair election and wished to stay out of politics.[60]

However, the officers' beliefs about the legitimacy of the army's guardian role in the polity shaped their calculations. As stated earlier, the Pakistani army lacks a tradition emphasizing the appropriateness of permanent military government, which would, in any case, interfere with its primary professional vocation of combat preparedness. When asked why the army had decided to permit a democratic transition, one senior officer expressed the widely shared view that "there was no need to block the transfer of power to a civil government, even though it was not a popular decision in the army. Many of us were afraid that the PPP might come to power and settle the scores for eleven years of harsh policies towards their leaders."[61]

However, the military saw no reason to abdicate its role as the exclusive watchdog of the national interest or wholeheartedly embrace the norm of political subordination. It was, in fact, the military's belief that civilian parties and politicians were incapable of governing prudently and, especially in the case of the PPP, could not be trusted to handle sensitive national security issues properly. This belief led it to impose a series of institutional constraints on the autonomy and authority of democratically elected governments. "There were enough safeguards to guide the transfer of power," says one former lieutenant general; "if the civilians misgoverned, or otherwise crossed the lines of political propriety, the president could reset the system."[62] The reset function was the president's constitutional prerogative to dismiss civilian governments arbitrarily, carried over from the Zia era. Even after imposing this confining condition on civilian governments, the military kept them on a short leash. According to Husain Haqqani, a former adviser to two prime ministers in the 1990s, "The level of military support for elected civilian leaders corresponded with their willingness to support the military's internal autonomy and veto over India policy."[63]

The military feared that the PPP, which was poised to win the elections, might seek retribution for what it claimed was Bhutto's judicial murder and might interfere in Afghanistan, Kashmir, and nuclear policies.[64] As one former ISI official described it, the high command's aim was to "control a PPP landslide which would have tilted the political balance away from the right."[65] Hence the election rules were rigged. For instance, the president issued a decree that barred those without national identification cards from voting, which disproportionately affected the PPP's voter base of the rural and urban poor, especially women.[66]

The army's main means for neutralizing the PPP's potential electoral victory was the ISI.[67] It brokered and funded a right-wing alliance, the Islami Jamhoori Ittehad (Islamic Democratic Alliance, IJI), mainly consisting of a Pakistan Muslim League faction headed by former Punjab chief minister Nawaz Sharif (PML-N) and the JI.[68] Aided by the PPP's organizational weaknesses and the military establishment's support, the IJI was able to contain the PPP's success in the election held in November 1988, winning 55 of the 217 national assembly seats to the PPP's 94, a mere plurality. No less important, the IJI was able to form a government in the Punjab, the largest, most populous, and politically most important province.

Given its narrow victory, the PPP was forced to form coalition governments with the MQM at the center and in Sindh. It also formed a government in alliance with the Pashtun nationalist Awami National Party in the North-West Frontier Province.

Bhutto's clearly weak position allowed the military to delay the transfer of power to her until she agreed not to encroach on vital military interests. The military is believed to have made three main demands: government support for the retention of key state personnel, including the military's candidate, Ghulam Ishaq Khan, as president for a five-year term and Sahibzada Yaqub Khan as foreign minister; continuity in foreign policy, especially with regard to India and Afghanistan; and a pledge that military internal affairs (including budgetary allocations) would not be subject to civilian scrutiny and cutbacks. These constraints on the civilian government clearly undermined its power to exercise authority over key state personnel and policies, thus weakening democratic institutions before they could find a foothold. As Bhutto described it a year later, her government's freedom of action was "curtailed, institutionally, economically, politically [and] structurally," and it had to tread "cautiously so as not to ruffle feathers."[69]

In August 1990, after less than two years in power, the president dismissed the Bhutto government on charges of corruption. However, the decision to sack Bhutto was actually taken in an army corps commanders' meeting held days before the presidential dismissal.[70] The dismissal was executed in a couplike manner in which the military took over key government installations and kept Bhutto and several members of her cabinet under house arrest. Bhutto later told a press conference that President Ishaq Khan's hand had been forced, and that the dissolution order was actually drafted by the general headquarters' Judge Advocate General branch.[71]

Allegations of corruption, often planted and publicized in the media by the ISI, had undermined the government's credibility.[72] Lacking a sound parliamentary majority and facing a hostile military establishment, Bhutto had promised something to everyone,[73] first to forge a ruling coalition and then to maintain it.[74] Unable to get its demands satisfied, the MQM defected from the coalition in October 1989, and this led to a violent confrontation between the MQM and the PPP in urban Sindh. As negotiations failed and violence escalated, the government sought the army's assistance in maintaining law and order. Unaccustomed to taking direction from civilians, the army took matters into its own hands. MI officials sternly warned all belligerents to desist from violence, or the army would step in to restore peace.[75] The most blatant example of army interference in civilian politics came when the Corps Headquarters at Karachi arranged an exchange of prisoners between the two parties' student wings, the All Pakistan Muhajir Students Organization and the Peoples' Students Federation, without the consent of the provincial government.[76] Then the corps commander, Lieutenant General Asif Nawaz Janjua, contemptuously told the PPP members, "You people are totally immature and therefore, incapable of running a government."[77]

In May 1990, the provincial PPP government launched a cleanup operation against MQM activists. A police raid on the Muhajir locality, Pucca Qilla, in Hyderabad turned bloody and resulted in the killing of many Muhajirs. The army intervened unilaterally and forced the police to withdraw. The incident strained the government's relationship with the military, and Bhutto accused it of supplying weapons to the MQM.[78]

The underlying source of conflict was, however, what the army saw as the government's backtracking on its transitional guarantees. Already distrustful of the PPP leadership, the army labeled Bhutto a security risk, initially keeping her in the dark about Pakistan's nuclear program, and resented her for her public criticism of the army's "crossing the red line" of enriching uranium to weapons-grade.[79] The army leadership was also deeply apprehensive of Bhutto's friendly overtures to India, which seemingly proved her willingness to jeopardize the national interest.[80] The army reportedly conducted large-scale exercises without informing the prime minister or her government.[81]

According to Lieutenant General Hamid Gul, the rationale of at least one major exercise, Zarbe Momin (the strike of the faithful), conducted in 1989, was to "block the prime minister's design to undermine our defense."[82]

Bhutto had also irked the army by appointing a committee under former air force chief Zulfiqar Ali Khan to review and recommend reforms in the state's intelligence apparatus.[83] But the final straw was Bhutto's interference in the army's internal affairs and command structure. For instance, Bhutto removed key ISI officials she suspected of destabilizing her government, including the additional director general of the ISI's Internal Security Wing, Brigadier Imtiaz Ahmed, and the Zia-era director general of the ISI (DGISI), Lieutenant General Gul.[84] She replaced Gul with retired Lieutenant General Shamsur Rehman Kallu in order to undercut the domestic political influence of the high command under Beg. Although the government could legally appoint a civilian official or a retired army officer to the position under the Rules of Business (1973), the army had always maintained that an active-duty officer should hold the position.[85] The appointment of Kallu did not enhance civilian government control over the ISI. Instead, it increased frictions with the army. As one general noted, "The ISI was an extension of the army," and "decoupling the ISI from the army" by appointing a retired army official "sent a signal" to the military leadership that "this action could be a prelude to something bigger."[86] General Beg reportedly transferred the ISI's political duties to MI, and active-duty military personnel in the ISI ostracized Kallu.[87] In August 1989, Bhutto tried to prematurely retire the CJCSC, Admiral Iftikhar Sirohey, a move that Ishaq Khan repulsed.[88] However, her action raised Beg's suspicion that she would remove him as well.[89]

Exploiting the split in the ruling coalition, General Beg brokered an agreement between the MQM and the IJI, creating the Combined Opposition Party. The military then backed this party's attempt to unseat Bhutto through a no-confidence vote in parliament in November 1989. Following Beg's orders, Brigadier Imtiaz

Ahmed and ISI officer Major Amir tried to coax some PPP members of the National Assembly to secure their support for the motion because, they claimed, Bhutto was working for India, destroying the Afghan cause, and undermining the military.[90] Much to the high command's disappointment, Bhutto survived the vote. But winning the people's confidence through an election was insufficient to keep her in power because she had lost the confidence of the army.[91] The final blow that reportedly triggered the military's decision to remove Bhutto from power was her unsuccessful attempt to extend the services of the commander of V Corps, Lahore, Lieutenant General Alam Jan Mehsud, ostensibly to appoint him deputy chief of army staff so that he could replace Beg after his scheduled retirement in 1991.[92]

Prelude to a Military Coup

After dismissing the PPP government, President Ishaq Khan appointed an interim cabinet under Prime Minister Mustafa Jatoi (founder and president of the IJI) to hold elections within the constitutionally mandated ninety days. The ISI initiated a vicious media campaign to discredit Bhutto and her husband, Asif Ali Zardari, accusing them of corruption and abuse of power. They were both put behind bars, and special accountability tribunals were set up for their trials.[93] The ISI also funneled money from a special fund financed by the private Mehran Bank (headed by Younis Habib, banker to the military establishment) to IJI politicians to boost their electoral campaigns. As a result, the PPP fared poorly at the national assembly polls in the 1990 elections, securing 44 seats as part of an electoral alliance, while the IJI won 106. Although Jatoi wished to become prime minister, Beg and his corps commanders picked Nawaz Sharif over him because of the IJI's electoral performance in the Punjab.[94]

But even the ostensibly promilitary IJI government under Prime Minister Sharif (1990–1993) developed serious differences with the military over external and internal security affairs. Soon after Sharif assumed power, COAS Beg began to flex his military muscles. The government's support for the US-led invasion of Iraq in 1990 provoked a strong reaction from the military, and Beg openly called for "strategic defiance" of the United States.[95] In fact, suspicions of Beg ran so high in the government that Sharif feared that the general might orchestrate a nondemocratic change in government.

Beg's retirement in August 1991 brought a temporary civil-military truce. However, the army under his successor, General Asif Nawaz Janjua (1991–1993), proved no less assertive and violated democratic norms by willfully working at cross-purposes with the elected government. Civil-military tensions arose when Sharif appointed the Islamist Lieutenant General Javed Nasir DGISI, ostensibly in disregard of Janjua's preference. In June–July 1992, friction between the government and the army intensified over an operation in aid to the civil power in Sindh. In May, the government had requested the army's assistance under Article 245 of the constitution in curbing antisocial elements in rural Sindh. However, the army widened the operation to the urban areas of Karachi to target the allegedly antistate MQM, a coalition partner of the Sharif government.[96] Despite the government's objections, the army continued its crackdown on the MQM, exploited divisions within the party, and co-opted dissidents into a new faction, the MQM-Haqiqi. Ultimately, the army's actions frayed the ruling coalition, and the MQM parted ways with the IJI government. Sharif's interior minister later claimed that the army had kept the federal government in the dark about the scope of its operation.[97]

Seeking to wrest prime-ministerial powers from the president, Sharif challenged President Ishaq Khan (and, by default, the military) when he decided to curtail the president's powers by appointing a parliamentary subcommittee to review Article 58(2)b.[98] The conflict between the two over the appointment of the army chief of staff after Janjua's untimely death in January 1993 widened their differences.[99] The president ignored Sharif's choice for the COAS post and instead appointed the ostensibly nonpolitical commander of the army corps stationed in Quetta, Lieutenant General Waheed Kakar, without even consulting the prime minister. Kakar continued his predecessor's policy of using force against the MQM, which further estranged the IJI government from the army.[100]

With their mutual antagonisms intensifying, Ishaq Khan reached out to the PPP-led opposition to seek its support for his reelection, scheduled for December 1993. Once he had secured his flanks, Khan sought and received clearance from the new COAS to dissolve the national assembly and sack Sharif, which he did in April 1993. The president leveled allegations of corruption, economic mismanagement, and "subversion of the authority of the armed forces" against Sharif.[101] But the prime minister challenged his dismissal in the Supreme Court, which declared the presidential action unconstitutional and restored Sharif to office in May 1993. However, tensions between Sharif and Ishaq continued to escalate in the Punjab, where the PML-N chief minister, Ghulam Haider Wyne, lost a vote of confidence and was replaced by Mian Manzoor Wattoo, a leader from a rival faction of the Muslim League.

Even though Sharif received a fresh vote of confidence from parliament after his reinstatement, Kakar and his corps commanders decided that the only way out of the deadlock would be for both Sharif and Ishaq to resign and for the army to organize new elections. In the meanwhile, sensing an opportunity to weaken her rival, Bhutto announced a long march on Islamabad to force fresh elections. With the deadlock deepening, Kakar persuaded Bhutto to call off the march and presented Ishaq and Sharif with the fait accompli, and they relented. He then entrusted the DGISI, Lieutenant General Javed Ashraf Qazi, with the job of finding the right candidate for the job of caretaker prime minister and getting the approval of all sides. The ISI was also involved in checking and clearing the names of cabinet ministers and provincial chief ministers.[102] In the 1993 elections, the army, led by its nonpolitical chief, was conspicuous by its ubiquitous presence. To ensure a free and fair poll, which, according to Lieutenant General Naseer Akhtar, then the corps commander in Karachi, was the army's national duty,[103] the army deployed over 150,000 troops and created election cells at the general headquarters.[104] The generals practically "set up a hierarchy running parallel to the one put in place by the Election Commission of Pakistan with two to three army personnel deputed to each polling station."[105]

The PPP won the elections held in October 1993.[106] Having been bitten once, Benazir Bhutto tried to tread more carefully, especially in national security matters, in her second tenure (1993–1996). Ironically, the moderate, liberal prime minister of the PPP fully backed the military's new Afghanistan policy involving the rise of the Taliban in Afghanistan. According to Pakistani journalist and author Ahmed Rashid, the ISI and Bhutto's interior minister, retired Major General Naseerullah Babar, wanted to break the stalemate in Afghanistan and install a Pashtun-led government in Kabul.[107] The Bhutto government was also keen to open trade routes to Central Asia, blocked by the internecine warfare among different mujahideen warlords.[108] It was in this context that the ISI shifted its support from Hekmatyar to the Taliban (students, who were mostly schooled in JUI madrassas) and facilitated its capture of Kandahar in 1994 and, ultimately, Kabul through military, financial, and logistical support.

Despite this apparent strategic convergence between the military and the civilian government on Afghanistan, Bhutto's tenure was again cut short when Ishaq Khan's successor, President Farooq Leghari (a senior member of the PPP who was elected president on the party's nomination but had grown wary of Bhutto), dismissed her in November 1996 on familiar charges of corruption, nepotism, and economic mismanagement. Leghari reportedly made his decision after the army warned him of growing unrest in its ranks over the government's performance and provided him with evidence of corruption involving Bhutto's spouse, Asif Ali Zardari. In classic coup fashion, army troops closed down all major airports and surrounded the prime minister's house, parliament, and radio and television stations in key cities.[109]

President Leghari appointed an army-vetted cabinet to hold elections and pursue corruption charges against Bhutto and Zardari. Electoral laws were amended to disqualify politicians who had defaulted on bank loans or had unpaid electricity bills; these provisions mainly targeted the PPP and the PML-N.[110] By 1996, the unsettling pattern of government by musical chairs between the same two parties had confirmed the military's doubts about the political leadership's capabilities to govern and tackle difficult structural reforms.[111] At the time, the army, led by the COAS, General Jehangir Karamat (1996–1998), was reportedly in favor of postponing the elections to allow more time for accountability.[112] Leghari claims that there was widespread public support for the "extension of the caretaker government for two years to allow time for accountability and reforms." In the end, he claims, he decided to "hold the elections in accordance with the constitution."[113] Just a month before the elections, however, Leghari also set up the Council for Defense and National Security at the military's behest. Headed by the president,[114] the council was a supraconstitutional entity designed to give the military a formal role in decision making at the highest level so it could stabilize national politics.[115]

However, Sharif's PML-N won a two-thirds parliamentary majority in the elections held in February 1997.[116] The government abolished the council.[117] With a clear mandate to restructure state power, it also moved quickly in parliament to disempower the president with the cooperation of the opposition PPP through the Thirteenth Amendment to the constitution in April 1997, repealing the president's constitutional coup prerogatives and reinstating prime-ministerial control over the appointment of military service chiefs and provincial governors and the approval of the appointment of superior-court judges. Given the instability inherent in this constrained democracy, Sharif and Leghari were soon embroiled in a power struggle. The conflict started after Sharif refused to approve the appointments of several Supreme Court judges recommended by Chief Justice Sajjad Ali Shah. Justice Shah, in turn, sought the president's help against the prime minister, initiated contempt and corruption charges against the prime minister, and ultimately annulled the Thirteenth Amendment so the president could sack Sharif. But the court itself was split after several judges revolted against the chief justice and reversed his decision. As the final arbiter of any government's fate, the army under COAS Karamat intervened in the crisis. Although it would not allow Sharif to impeach Leghari,[118] the army considered it wise to withdraw support from an ineffectual president (and a beleaguered chief justice) rather than destabilize or remove a government elected with a two-thirds majority.[119]

India's nuclear tests on May 11, 1998, created another point of civil-military disagreement. The Indian tests created strong domestic pressure on the government to respond in kind. The Bharatiya Janata Party government's hostile statements on Kashmir only upped the pressure on Sharif. For example, Indian home minister L. K. Advani publicly warned Pakistan to "roll back its anti-India policy," adding that India's nuclear tests had "brought about a qualitative new state in India-Pakistan relations, particularly in finding a lasting solution to the Kashmir problem. It signifies India's resolve to deal firmly and strongly with Pakistan's hostile designs and activities in Kashmir."[120] Still, the Pakistani prime minister was initially reluctant to order nuclear tests because of their potential implications for Pakistan's fragile economy.[121] Several members of his cabinet also were not in favor of reciprocating the tests and wanted to accept US economic and military assistance offered by President Bill Clinton to dissuade Pakistan from testing.[122] But both the opposition PPP and Islamist parties pushed for a test. Ultimately, Sharif relented in the face of pressure from the military, which wanted to demonstrate the credibility of Pakistan's nuclear deterrent.

However, Sharif shocked the military when he fired COAS Karamat in October 1998, just three months before his scheduled retirement. Sharif replaced him with Lieutenant General Pervez Musharraf, corps commander of the army's I Strike Corps at Mangla, bypassing two senior generals, including the chief of general staff, Lieutenant General Ali Kuli Khan. Sharif reportedly chose Musharraf over Ali Kuli Khan (a Pashtun) because he was a Muhajir and, therefore, was perceived as lacking a constituency in the army that he could mobilize against the government.[123]

The prime minister's decision to sack Karamat was prompted by the general's blunt public criticism of the government. In a speech at the Naval War College in Lahore on October 5, 1998, Karamat described the quick turnover of civilian governments in the 1990s as "a permanent election campaign environment" and warned the government that "the country could not afford the destabilizing effects of polarization, vendettas and insecurity-driven expedient policies."[124] As a way out of growing misgovernance and political polarization, the general recommended the institutional integration of the military into the government through the creation of a National Security Council.

Karamat's speech reflected an institutional consensus, carried over from the Zia years, that the army ought to have a formal role in policy making to ensure balance and stability. In this case, the army was particularly concerned about what it considered to be the damaging effects of Sharif's brute majority, including the decline in the economy after the nuclear tests, growing law-and-order problems, and the government's alleged corruption.[125] Karamat's response to a question about the rationale behind his speech and subsequent exit is worth reproducing: "I left because of a difference of opinion. My suggestion was meant to help the government regain credibility. I offered the inherent strength of my institution to the government— they could have evolved any methodology for interaction. . . . Why do most countries of the world have a National Security Council or some such body?"[126]

Several points deserve comment. First, the NSC as it is constituted in democratic countries is led and dominated by political leaders.[127] However, there was no provision in Pakistan's 1973 constitution for an NSC or some other mechanism for military participation in state policy making and governance.[128] Second, and related to the first point, the army leadership obviously believed that it reserved the right to publicly indict the government's ability to govern and evidently viewed the application of its "inherent strength" and skills to civilian affairs as legitimate. Third, the speech was significant not just for the articulation of the military's institutional concerns but also for its silences. In my correspondence with him, Karamat admitted that he had "stepped out of line to say what needs to be said," but noticeably absent was any serious acknowledgment that the military is legally subordinate to the elected government, and therefore, has no right to claim a stake in policy making.[129]

To the disappointment of some of his colleagues, including Chief of General Staff (CGS) Ali Kuli Khan, who had allegedly advised him to stand his ground,[130] General Karamat accepted the prime minister's decision.[131] In conjunction with Sharif's successful clipping of presidential coup powers and the resignation of President Leghari and the chief justice, analysts described Sharif's unprecedented move as a sign that the balance of political power had shifted from the army to the civilians.[132] The army considered the prime minister's action a provocative demonstration of his growing dictatorial tendency.

One former corps commander accurately summed up this sentiment: "This is just not done. The army is not just any other department of the government that politicians can take for a ride. All parties have to keep in mind that there has to be a proper balance between the civil side of government and the army. Or the ship of state will be in danger."[133]

Others, including the former adjutant general and corps commander of Lahore, Lieutenant General Moinuddin Haider, claimed that Sharif's decision endangered the proper alignment of civil-military relations.[134] On hearing that Karamat had supposedly resigned, General Musharraf claims that he was shocked by "the meek manner" in which his predecessor had capitulated to the prime minister, and that "it caused great resentment in the army, as soldiers and the officer corps alike felt humiliated."[135]

According to one corps commander, Sharif's "unwarranted" assertion of power had a "strong rallying-around-the-[army]-chief effect."[136] In fact, after Karamat's retirement, there was a tacit consensus in the army high command that the removal of another chief would be unacceptable. As Musharraf described it, he "told them to stop brooding over the forced resignation of General Karamat and get on with our jobs. We would not allow another humiliation to befall us in case the prime minister tried something like this again."[137]

Crossing swords with the military by firing its top commander may have aroused military antagonism against Sharif. However, it was the prime minister's activism in foreign policy, especially his efforts to change Pakistan's India policy, that ultimately strained civil-military relations to the breaking point.[138] Pakistan's nuclear tests in May 1998 had triggered sanctions by the United States, Japan, and the European Union. With the country in dire economic straits and internationally isolated, Sharif tried to revive peace negotiations with India, which he had first initiated in 1997. He met with Indian prime minister Atal Behari Vajpayee on the sidelines of the UN General Assembly Session in September 1998, and the two sides decided to initiate high-level talks to seek a peaceful resolution of all outstanding problems. To further the process, Sharif took the unprecedented step of inviting Vajpayee to Pakistan. Vajpayee accepted the invitation, and Pakistan and India signed the Lahore Declaration in February 1999, committing both sides to accelerate their dialogue to solve bilateral conflicts, including Kashmir, peacefully, "refrain from intervention in each other's internal affairs," and reduce the "risks of accident or unauthorized use of nuclear weapons."[139]

The military resented what it considered this sellout on Kashmir.[140] Unknown to the government at the time, the military had already thrown a spanner in the works. Starting in December 1998, Musharraf and three other general officers, the CGS, Lieutenant General Mohammad Aziz Khan, the commander of X Corps, Lieutenant General Mahmud Ahmed, who had direct operational responsibility for Kashmir, and his subordinate, the general officer commanding of the Force Command Northern Areas, Major General Javed Hassan, carried out a covert plan to infiltrate troops into the northern Kargil sector of Indian-administered Kashmir, yet another of the Pakistani army's attempts to resolve the Kashmir dispute by asymmetric warfare.[141] The operation's main military goal was ostensibly to capture strategic peaks and give the army the ability to cut off the Indian army's main supply route into Siachin.[142] The planners' calculation was that India would not escalate the conflict, and the danger of full-scale war between two nuclear-armed powers would force the international community to intervene to bring about the cessation of hostilities, thus leaving Pakistan in a dominant position on the ground and putting the Kashmir conflict back in the global diplomatic spotlight.[143]

There is controversy about whether the civilian government approved the military operation. Musharraf claims in his autobiography that it was a defensive maneuver to capture "unoccupied gaps along the Line of Control" that was within the "purview of the local commander." Still, Musharraf says the army briefed Sharif twice to explain its actions, first on January 29 and then on February 5, 1999.[144] The prime minister and his cabinet colleagues deny that they had any prior information. Sharif has said that "as Prime Minister, I was not taken into confidence about Kargil," and that "four months after the operation when [the army] revealed some details, they assured me that it would not lead to complications, there would be no major casualties, and the army will not take part in the operation."[145] Then Foreign Minister Sartaj Aziz claims that the army informed Sharif about increased mujahideen activity along the Dras-Kargil sector in a briefing in March 1999 after Pakistani troops had already captured several heights, a fact that was unknown to the government at the time, but that "there was no mention of the involvement of the Pakistan army or paramilitary personnel, or of any plans to cross the LoC [Line of Control] to occupy positions previously occupied by India."[146] It was not until May 17, when media reports of clashes between Pakistani and Indian troops surfaced, that the high command decided to disclose to the political leadership that the army had "crossed the LoC and occupied several Indian posts."[147] The most damning evidence that bears out the civilian government's version is a telephone conversation between Musharraf and Lieutenant General Muhammad Aziz Khan, then the CGS, that was reportedly intercepted by Indian intelligence and shared with Sharif by the Vajpayee government.[148] On May 26, Aziz told Musharraf, "We told him [Nawaz Sharif] there is no reason for alarm and panic. Then he said that I came to know seven days back, when Corps Commanders were told."[149]

India's detection of Pakistani intruders not only buried the prospects of regional peace but also sparked the first ground war between two nuclear-armed adversaries. India mounted an effective counterattack to evict the Pakistani raiders, and Pakistan came under intense international and US pressure to withdraw its forces.[150] As Pakistani casualties and diplomatic isolation mounted, Prime Minister Vajpayee threatened to launch a full-scale counterattack across the international border.[151]

On July 4, 1999, Sharif rushed to meet Clinton in Washington and agreed to a formal retreat of Pakistani troops to its side of the LoC. As a face-saving gesture for Pakistan, the US president issued a statement that he would take a personal interest in encouraging the resumption of dialogue between Pakistan and India.[152] According to Bruce Riedel, then director of Near East and South Asian Affairs at the US NSC, who attended the meetings between Clinton and Sharif, "The Pakistani prime minister was worried about his own hold on power and the threat from his military chiefs who were pressing for a tough stand. . . . The PM knew he had done the right thing . . . but he was not sure his army would see it that way."[153]

Admiral Fasih Bokhari, then the chief of naval staff, claims that Sharif was considering prosecuting Musharraf and others responsible for the debacle, and that this motivated the military coup against him.[154] In the words of a senior air force officer, the outcome of Kargil would be either "a Court Martial or Martial Law."[155] Sharif blamed the army for the debacle and claimed that he had been kept in the dark. There was disquiet in the army over the embarrassing withdrawal from Kargil, even though Musharraf had reportedly asked the prime minister to find a way out.[156] Musharraf visited various army corps headquarters and formations throughout August, where he faced tough questions from his officers. The general reportedly put the onus of the total surrender at Kargil on Sharif, who had chickened out under pressure.[157] According to him, the army had no choice but to carry out the government's orders.[158]

By September, the prime minister and the army were at daggers drawn. There were rumors that Sharif would sack Musharraf, and the latter had reason to suspect the prime minister's motives after Kargil. To defuse the tension and allay the general's suspicions, Sharif confirmed Musharraf's joint appointment to the post of CJCSC on September 29,[159] which Musharraf later speculated was part of the prime minister's strategy to "lull him into false security."[160] It is unclear whether Sharif was actually going to take legal action against Musharraf, although he had decided to sack him from the position of COAS at an opportune time.[161] On October 12, after the prime minister had ostensibly become convinced that the military had decided to oust him,[162] Sharif tried to remove Musharraf while the latter was on a commercial flight returning from an official trip to Sri Lanka and replaced him with a more reliable general, Lieutenant General Khawaja Ziauddin, the DGISI. Within a couple of hours, the army overthrew Sharif in a coup.

Interviews with officers who either participated in the coup or were directly involved in its planning suggest that Musharraf and at least two top generals, Lieutenant Generals Ahmed and Aziz, had first worked out a contingency plan in late August or early September to forestall any attempt by Sharif to fire a second army chief.[163] In a meeting in mid-September, Musharraf secured the formal approval of the corps commanders for the coup in case Sharif tried to fire him. However, one of Sharif's few allies in the high command, Lieutenant General Tariq Pervez, commander of the army's XII Corps in Quetta, tipped him off.[164] Pervez had reportedly fallen out with Musharraf after he criticized the Kargil operation in a corps commanders' meeting. Musharraf swiftly retired him for undermining military discipline.[165] A few days before his departure for Sri Lanka, Musharraf held a meeting with Ahmed, Aziz, Lieutenant General Ehsanul Haq (the director general of Military Intelligence), and Major General Shahid Aziz (the director general of military operations) in which the coup decision was finalized.[166]

One of the main motives Musharraf cited for the coup was a threat to the integrity of the military institution. In a postcoup speech, he explained, "It is unbelievable and indeed unfortunate that the few at the helm of affairs in the last government were intriguing to destroy the last institution of stability left in Pakistan by creating dissension in the ranks of the armed forces of Pakistan."[167] Other officers directly involved in the coup also believed strongly that the government "was politicizing the army by firing a second army chief to subdue it and make it compliant on the political plain." In their view, politicization of the army would lead to its disintegration.[168]

The other most commonly cited rationale for the coup was that, as the military and many civilians saw it, democracy in Pakistan had become a sham behind which Sharif was establishing his dictatorship.[169] In this view, as the permanent guardian of the state and the guarantor of the right balance among national institutions, the army could not be expected to remain a silent spectator. As retired Lieutenant General Asad Durrani, former DGISI, described it, the coup was a necessary response to "save the army from a prime minister who was out to browbeat all institutions, the judiciary, the presidency, parliament, the bureaucracy and the military."[170]

Musharraf described the army coup as a countercoup and praised the army for its unity: "How the army reacted to defend its honor is a study in the presence of mind."[171] However, the reality was slightly more complicated. After Sharif appointed Ziauddin COAS, the new army chief's first order of business was to consolidate his position in the army. He appointed Lieutenant Generals Mohammad

Akram and Saleem Haider as CGS and commander of X Corps, respectively, the two most important positions for carrying out a coup, which were then occupied by Lieutenant Generals Aziz and Ahmed, members of Musharraf's core group. He also contacted the army corps commanders to inform them that he had taken over as COAS.[172] Although they assured him of their support, a number of them were sitting on the fence.

However, Lieutenant Generals Aziz and Ahmed reacted quickly after the government broadcast Musharraf's retirement on television. Mahmud Ahmed reportedly ordered the commander of the 111th Brigade, Brigadier Salahuddin Satti, to secure the prime minister's house. Aziz and Ahmed called the corps commanders from the general headquarters to inform them that the coup was in motion, thus tilting the balance in favor of Musharraf. The army completed the coup after taking over the main television station and confining the prime minister, Ziauddin, and Akram to the prime minister's house. Ultimately, "Everyone worked together towards the common goals of stopping the prime minister's coup."[173]

At the least, the institutional cohesion displayed by the institution of the army during and after the coup suggests that the general officer corps considers irregular change of governments legitimate. The corps commanders overcame their temporary uncertainty once it became clear that Musharraf would stay as COAS. However, their hesitation had little, if anything, to do with their constitutional obligation of loyalty to the democratically elected government. Instead, as then commander of the I Corps at Mangla, Lieutenant General Tauqir Zia, explained, "It was a difficult situation. Foremost on our minds was the institution and its integrity. If any of us had made a rash decision by standing up for this or that side, the consequence would have been the weakening and destruction of the army."[174]

In fact, Sharif's decision to remove Musharraf was seen as a "gross misuse and misapplication of the law" because "you cannot summarily dismiss the army chief, a constitutional appointee, without giving him just cause and affording him due process."[175] But sacking the prime minister, who had the constitutional authority to appoint and fire the COAS, did not seem illegal or unconstitutional to the Pakistani army. When Ziauddin was asked why the army had not followed his orders even though the prime minister had appointed him COAS, he noted that "we train our officers to be highly professional soldiers. But our training is deeply flawed in at least one respect: we do not teach our men to disregard an illegal command, especially as it concerns the constitutional structure of government."[176]

In sum, the two major parties' courting of the military to weaken each other strengthened the military's hand and contributed to the ultimate breakdown of democracy. However, more important was the army's belief that civilian governments could not be trusted to govern effectively, which posed a constant threat to the quality and sustainability of democracy in the 1990s. Distrust of the politicians prompted the military to curtail their authority, thus reducing their ability to govern. This led to charges of civilian incompetence and failure against successive civilian governments, which confirmed the military's self-fulfilling diagnoses, which then led it to depose elected governments by presidential decree. This cycle of reactions and counterreactions created an unstable civil-military equilibrium that broke down within ten years of the transition from Zia's authoritarian rule. When the second PML-N–elected government (1997–1999) used its parliamentary majority to reverse the presidential powers to dissolve the national assembly and clashed with the military over decisions of war and peace, the generals dashed democracy once again through a blunt military coup in October 1999.

6

MUSHARRAF AND MILITARY PROFESSIONALISM

After seizing power on October 12, 1999, General Pervez Musharraf declared a state of emergency and appointed himself the chief executive (CE) of the country. He placed the constitution in abeyance, suspended the national and provincial assemblies, and sacked the prime minister, his cabinet, and all four provincial governments. The Emergency, which brought the "whole of Pakistan under the control of the armed forces," was the result of the "collective deliberation and decisions" of Musharraf, the nine army corps commanders, and the chiefs of the navy and the air force.[1]

Musharraf created a National Accountability Bureau to initiate a politically motivated accountability drive to target his government's opponents, especially the Pakistan Muslim League (Nawaz) (PML-N). In August 2000, Sharif was sentenced to life imprisonment for hijacking the plane carrying Musharraf from Sri Lanka on the day of the coup.[2] In December 2000, Musharraf agreed to exile the former prime minister and his family to Saudi Arabia for ten years in a deal brokered by the Saudi royal family.[3]

Like his military predecessors, Musharraf had his coup legitimized by the Supreme Court in 2000 under the doctrine of state necessity, although the validation required that elections be held within three years. It gave the CE the authority to make necessary constitutional amendments to achieve his declared objectives as long as they did not affect the basic structure of the constitution, including the federal system, the parliamentary form of government, and judicial independence.[4]

The military government increased Pakistan's international isolation. The country's relations with the United States were already strained by Pakistani sponsorship of the Taliban regime in Afghanistan (which had provided sanctuary to al-Qaeda leader Osama bin Laden) and militancy in Indian Kashmir. The May 1998 nuclear tests had triggered US and international sanctions. The coup led to further US sanctions under a provision of the Foreign Assistance Act of 1961 that bans all forms of US assistance to "any country whose duly elected head of government is deposed by military coup or decree."[5] At the time, military officers were aware that the international community no longer considered coups an acceptable means of regime change. According to one corps commander, "We were acutely conscious of the fact that the military takeover would not be welcomed with open arms and could lead to further diplomatic and economic difficulties." Another general stated that "we knew that the world will reject 'martial law,' and it would lead to further isolation for Pakistan in the community of nations."[6]

Although Musharraf's main audience was domestic, the structure and rhetoric of the military government also targeted the international community. Therefore, it was decidedly less militaristic than previous ones, especially Zia's. Instead of following his predecessors, Musharraf chose not to impose martial law and took on the corporate-political title of chief executive. He explained, "The Constitution has only been temporarily held in abeyance. This is not martial law, only another path towards democracy. The armed forces have no intention to stay in charge any longer than is absolutely necessary to pave the way for true democracy to flourish in Pakistan."[7]

Even though Musharraf made important domestic and foreign policy decisions with the advice and consent of the corps commanders, the military institution stayed out of formally governing the state. Just five days after the coup, Musharraf announced a seven-point plan for national reconstruction. The plan was the result of army deliberations and Musharraf's consultation with retired army and civilian advisers. The seven points were as follows: (1) rebuild national confidence and morale; (2) strengthen the federation, remove interprovincial disharmony, and restore national cohesion; (3) revive the economy and restore investor confidence; (4) ensure law and order and dispense speedy justice; (5) depoliticize state institutions; (6) devolve power to the grassroots level; and (7) ensure swift and across-the-board accountability.[8]

On October 30, 1999, Musharraf also created a military-dominated National Security Council (NSC), headed by the CE, with six additional members: the chiefs of the air force and navy and appointed civilians with expertise in legal, finance, foreign policy, and national affairs. The NSC was to advise the CE on a broad range of matters, including "national security, foreign affairs, law and order, corruption, accountability, recovery of bank loans and public debt from defaulters, finance, economic and social welfare, health, education, Islamic ideology, human rights, protection of minorities and women development so as to achieve the aims and objectives enshrined in the Objective Resolution of 1949."[9]

Working under the NSC's guidance was a civilian cabinet. Musharraf appointed prominent nongovernmental organization leaders and social activists as cabinet ministers to signal his reformist agenda to international donors and to the development sector of civil society in Pakistan.[10] Rather than applying blanket press censorship, he also promised to respect the freedom of the press and to liberalize private television and radio channels.

To allay US and international concerns about the potential for conflict with India in the wake of the Kargil war, he assured the world that there would be no change in Pakistan's foreign policy, and that his government would strive for peace and stability in the region. Musharraf also pledged that Pakistan would continue to pursue a "policy of nuclear and missile restraint and sensitivity to global non-proliferation and disarmament objectives."[11]

Despite these overtures, the military government's isolation continued for almost two years, until the al-Qaeda terrorist attacks on the United States on September 11, 2001. Just as the Soviet invasion of Afghanistan had been a boon for Zia, the events of 9/11 were a blessing in disguise for the military because it once again became a critical frontline ally in the US fight against al-Qaeda. The Bush administration presented Pakistan with the ultimatum to choose whether it wanted to be with the United States or against it. The administration demanded Pakistani cooperation in the interception of al-Qaeda leaders, landing and overflight rights, use of naval and air bases, intelligence sharing, condemnation of the terrorist attacks, and a cutoff of material assistance to the Taliban.[12] Under US pressure and desperate to ease its isolation, the military high command decided to formally withdraw support from the Taliban regime in Afghanistan after that regime refused to hand over Osama bin Laden to the United States despite the Musharraf government's and the ISI's hectic last-minute efforts to persuade its leadership to give him up.[13]

In return for Pakistan's cooperation, Washington lifted both nuclear- and democracy-related sanctions.[14] The administration also declared Pakistan a major non-NATO ally and pledged $5 billion in military and economic aid. US support clearly bolstered Musharraf and the Pakistan military's coffers. Restoring democracy in Pakistan had not been high on the US foreign policy agenda before 9/11, but the administration put even its residual concerns about the restoration of democratic rule in cold storage because of the Pakistani dictator's resolve to "wholeheartedly support the war on terrorism despite considerable domestic costs. . . . [Even with] the entire gamut of Pakistani religious parties against him, Musharraf has held firm . . . [and] acted against domestic extremists."[15] Unconditional US backing drastically reduced the external costs to the military of its domestic actions.

Political Restructuring and the Unity of Command

Although the real motive for the 1999 coup might have been the preservation of both institutional autonomy and control over national security policy, once the military took power, the goals of the intervention were radically broadened to include a program of political restructuring. The military's negative evaluation of the PML-N government's performance and capabilities formed part of the narrative of civilian dysfunction that made the coup acceptable to its members. Military concerns about political instability, corruption, economic mismanagement, and ethnic conflict in urban Sindh were perceived as justifying the military takeover of government. Moreover, there was a widely shared belief that democracy had gone off the rails because it lacked unity of command. Hence, according to one corps commander, the military decided to restore the balanced political system first put in place by Zia to avoid another Sharif with a "heavy mandate gone to his head."[16]

Within two months of the coup, Musharraf created the National Reconstruction Bureau (NRB) under retired Lieutenant General Tanvir Naqvi to conceptualize and formulate political and administrative reforms. In July 2002, the NRB produced a package of proposed constitutional reforms to restructure the parliamentary system. The reforms were implemented through the Legal Framework Order (LFO) of August 21, 2002. The LFO validated the actions, acts, and decrees of the military government, including the five-year extension of Musharraf's presidential term and his position as chief of army staff. The president was reauthorized to dissolve the national assembly at his discretion, to appoint military service chiefs and governors, and to approve the appointments of judges of the superior courts. The LFO also formalized the NSC and thereby gave the military a legal-institutional role in government. According to Musharraf, these steps "were essential to introduce real democracy in Pakistan," which was moving "from democratic dictatorship to the elected essence of democracy."[17] Responding to critics that his amendments had violated the essence of parliamentary democracy by empowering a uniformed president to dissolve the national assembly arbitrarily, General Musharraf noted, "Unless there is unity of command, unless there is only one man in charge on top, it [the system] will never function."[18]

However, facing the inevitable domestic legitimacy problems of authoritarian rule, Musharraf initiated a process of political liberalization by opening up private broadcast media and allowing limited political pluralism. In April 2002, he organized a referendum to be elected as president for five years. The referendum asked voters to vote for Musharraf so that he could consolidate his reforms for "the reconstruction of institutions of state for the establishment of genuine and sustainable democracy, including the entrenchment of the local government systems, to ensure continued good governance for the welfare of the people, and to combat extremism and sectarianism."[19] Musharraf received 97.5 of the vote, which independent observers and opposition parties declared fraudulent.[20]

Meanwhile, the ISI created a new right-wing political party, the Pakistan Muslim League (Quaid-e-Azam) (PML-Q), to act as the civilian face of the military government. The agency did this by exploiting disaffection with Sharif within the PML-N and by coercing, bribing, or blackmailing some party leaders to join the PML-Q. Even though Musharraf projected himself as a moderate and secular leader, his military government supported the Mutahida Majlise Amal (United Action Front, MMA), an alliance of six Islamist parties of different theological and sectarian persuasions, to further squeeze the PML-N's right-of-center vote.[21] For instance, it decreed a bachelor's degree as the minimum educational qualification for holding electoral office, which disqualified many PML-N and PPP politicians from contesting elections, while extending equivalence to madrassa degrees, which clearly benefited the MMA (especially the predominantly madrassa-trained leadership of Jamiat Ulema-e-Islam). The government also instituted electoral rules to marginalize the opposition leadership, such as the Sharif- and Bhutto-specific clause barring anyone from holding the office of prime minister more than twice.

The government finally held a parliamentary election in October 2002, which brought the PML-Q to power at the center and in the Punjab, the largest province, thereby allowing the military government to cloak itself in a veneer of democracy.[22] The military's helping hand facilitated the MMA's impressive electoral victories, allowing it to form a government in the strategically crucial North-West Frontier Province and a coalition government with the PML-Q in Balochistan. The rise of the MMA also allowed Musharraf to exploit Western fears of an Islamist takeover of Pakistan and to project himself as the sole bulwark against Islamist extremism and terrorism.[23] At the same time, Musharraf got the support of the MMA to ratify his LFO through the Seventeenth Amendment to the constitution in December 2003, except for the clause establishing the NSC, which was ratified through an act of parliament in 2004.

Even as Musharraf flirted with Pakistani Islamist parties for domestic gain, the military's cooperation with the United States against al-Qaeda led to reprisals, including assassination attempts on Musharraf in December 2003. Under US pressure to stem the flow of cross-border attacks by Taliban militants on the United States, NATO's International Security Assistance Force, and Afghan security officials, the army carried out search-and-destroy operations in South Waziristan, starting in March 2004. Militants inflicted heavy costs on the army, both in casualties and declining morale, which led the high command to strike three peace deals with the militants in South and North Waziristan between 2004 and 2006.[24] These agreements mostly backfired by giving the militants the time and opportunity to regroup, recruit, and rearm to carryout cross-border attacks, and to increase and spread their extremist influence from the tribal areas to the rest of the North-West Frontier Province.

Devolving Despotism

Pakistani army officers have long harbored a disdain for unfettered parliamentary democracy. For many officers who joined the army in the 1970s and 1980s, this legacy was cemented by their formative experience under the Zia dictatorship. In interviews and in their writings, military officers questioned the wisdom of counting on the gullible and uneducated masses to elect the right leadership for the country. In fact, senior officers (and many urban middle-class civilians) see illiteracy as a key factor in Pakistan's inability to develop a democratic culture.[25] According to one brigadier posted to the National Defence University, "Political structure based on democratic norms is best served by educated masses, which is [*sic*] lacking in Pakistan."[26] In the language of a former director general of the ISI, Lieutenant General Ahmed Shuja Pasha (2007–2012), who was a brigadier at the time of the 1999 coup, lack of education results in lack of "awareness of rights and duties as citizens," and "the electorate finds it easy to be manipulated and identifies itself more with representatives from their own ill-educated stock."[27] Rooted in both the military officers' paternalistic view of society and their contempt for the "sham" democracy of the 1990s, the new military government's national reconstruction agenda was politically centered on establishing genuine democracy, which had to "evolve from the bottom up, not be thrust from the top down."[28]

General Ayub Khan had similarly implemented his grassroots vision of democracy in the Basic Democracy scheme. After abolishing democracy in a military coup, General Musharraf predictably set about re-creating it through the devolution of power from the top directly to the local levels. In his words, devolution was "the beginning of a constructive, democratic, dynamic revolution—whose sole objective is to place in the hands of the people the power to shape their own destiny. . . . An unprecedented transfer of power will take place from the elites to the vast majority."[29]

No doubt the concept and scope of Musharraf's devolution project were qualitatively different from those of his predecessors. Like Ayub's Basic Democracy and Zia's local bodies, the plan called for the reestablishment of a three-tiered system of elected councils established at the union, *tehsil* (subdistrict), and district levels. But unlike previous systems, the NRB's proposed devolution plan ostensibly vested real administrative authority in district and subdistrict governments and provided matching budgetary resources to fulfill these new responsibilities. Each level was to have an elected *nazim* and *naib nazim* (mayor and deputy mayor), council, and administration.

For the first time in Pakistan's history, elected officials were formally placed at the apex of the district government with executive powers and responsibilities for law and order to create one coherent structure in which the Deputy Commissioner and the police would be answerable to the elected chief executive of the district.[30] Reflecting the military's distrust of party politics, Musharraf made it clear that he would continue the previous practice of holding local bodies' elections on a nonparty basis to discourage "petty political rivalries" at the district level.[31]

The plan was criticized by independent observers and rejected by opposition parties.[32] By devolving power from the federal government directly to the local levels, the plan undermined federalism because it completely bypassed the provinces. According to the independent Human Rights Commission of Pakistan, local bodies directly created by the generals in the absence of provincial and national assemblies led to a symbiotic partnership between the two that had proved baneful in the past. It rejected the plan as an attempt to "depoliticize governance and to earn a lease of life for the government behind a sort of democratic façade."[33] In effect, the plan was no different from Ayub's or Zia's because the military-controlled state selectively distributed resources and authority to create dependable nonparty local elites, severed from formal links to political parties, which could be used to create a support base for sustaining military rule.

Despite these criticisms, military officers' assessments of the plan corresponded closely with those of the Musharraf government, demonstrating the powerful effects of assimilation into institutional thinking. Expressing an opinion shared by other officers, one officer claimed that devolution to the local levels was imperative because of the mistrust between the federation and the provinces, which had prevented effective governance in the past. According to another, democratic practice at the grassroots level should be allowed so that true democracy and civil society could flourish. Although "inefficient and incapable politicians would continue to seek power," the people would "learn to better understand" democratic values and ultimately reject traditional politicians when they were allowed the right to choose their leaders at the local level, which they could understand.[34] The paternalistic implication, like that of Ayub's Basic Democracy, was that the people were unable to make informed choices at the provincial and national levels because of their limited education and horizons.

A fundamental characteristic of devolution, said one officer, was "to challenge political and administrative decadence and bring forth revolutionary but controlled political change."[35] Despite expected problems of implementation and inertia, the merit of the plan was to "place the people at the center of development and governance through empowerment, participation and representation." The plan could succeed "with sincere efforts to empower local representatives, politically, economically and socially."[36] Other officers expressed the fear that local government could work, but only if it was implemented properly and saved from hijacking by vested interests, including the caricatured feudal politicians.

Institutionalizing Military Checks and Balances

It is not surprising that one of Musharraf's first steps after seizing state power was to establish the NSC. The precedent dated back to

Zia, who had unsuccessfully tried to create the NSC before ending martial law. The army has periodically revived the idea since then. As discussed in Chapter 5, the primary cause of Chief of Army Staff Jehangir Karamat's falling out with the Sharif government in October 1998 was his public advocacy of formally incorporating the military into the governmental decision-making process. Hence Musharraf was realizing the military's preferred route to establishing an institutional role for itself at the highest level of government, where it could apply authoritarian checks and balances on the prime minister. In Musharraf's view, it was also essential to block future military interventions because the army chief would have "an institution to voice his concerns (and the concerns of the worried public)" to the prime minister or the president. Or, as he pithily put it, "If you want to keep them [the military] out, bring them in."[37]

Musharraf tried to institutionalize the NSC by turning it into a constitutional body through the LFO. However, in the negotiations over parliamentary ratification of his constitutional changes between Musharraf's PML-Q and the MMA, he had to give up this constitutional cover. Instead, the NSC was created as a statutory body in 2004. Its members were the president, the prime minister, the Senate chairman, the National Assembly speaker, the leader of the opposition in the National Assembly, the chief ministers of provinces, the chairman Joint Chiefs of Staff Committee, and the three service chiefs. The NSC was to serve as a "forum for consultation on strategic matters pertaining to the sovereignty, integrity and security of the state, and matters relating to democracy, governance and interprovincial harmony."[38]

Many in the military strongly supported the idea. Writing in the official *Pakistan Army Green Book*, one officer stated that nation building could be achieved "provided the military does not interfere in politics, halfheartedly." Hence the army's multifaceted role in nation building should be redefined, institutionalized, and given legal cover through legislation so that it could perform these tasks without political pressure.[39] Another officer described the NSC as the most effective national mechanism for ensuring interprovincial harmony through the equal distribution of resources among the provinces.[40] A number of senior officers, including those who did not particularly like Musharraf either as a soldier or as a politician, supported the urgent need to give the army a formal role in government.[41] Reflecting Musharraf's view, one former chief of general staff argued that the NSC not only could stabilize governance but also democratize defense policy making by bringing all major civil-military stakeholders to the same table.[42]

Policing, Dividing, and
Militarizing the Bureaucracy

General Ayub Khan and his government had relied mainly on the Civil Service of Pakistan for day-to-day governance. He continued the practice of appointing civil service officers to important policy positions at the highest levels of government and public-sector corporations. Protected by constitutional security of tenure, members of the service maintained control over the selection, training, and posting of its members and were therefore able to retain its institutional autonomy. Under Zia, the District Management Group (DMG), the service's successor, was at best a junior partner in the military government even though its higher echelons continued to dominate top civilian secretariat positions. But Musharraf's military government had a decidedly antagonistic view of the bureaucracy, especially the DMG.

When Musharraf began to justify the continuation of military government on the basis of a reform agenda, he and his advisers knew well that relying on a politicized and discredited bureaucratic machinery associated with sham democracy would be a difficult sell both domestically and externally. Foreign aid organizations and influential sections of civil society in Pakistan, including the media and nongovernmental organizations, have long blamed bureaucratic corruption and centralization for Pakistan's political and administrative malaise. Musharraf echoed these concerns: "The entire administration system has been distorted and interference by the Federal Government in local affairs has been extreme."[43]

The first phase of the military government's assault on the civilian bureaucracy came in the form of monitoring. The army assigned junior and midlevel army officers the task of ensuring the efficiency and effectiveness of public services. Army monitoring teams, consisting of active-duty army officers, including staff from Military Intelligence and ISI field units, were deployed at the provincial and district levels to identify "all the organizations, institutions . . . that need resuscitation by the army,"[44] gauge "the impact of governance on public perception," and provide "input to the Chief Executive and National Security Council" for "evolving policies" and restructuring government machinery.[45] Thus they performed two functions: policing the bureaucracy and intelligence gathering.

In interviews, a dozen captains and majors who participated in monitoring teams acknowledged that it was not their job to watch and reform the civil government. However, their stated reluctance to accept broader civilian roles was motivated more by their concern about the lack of proper training than by any inherent inappropriateness of the military's tutelary role. In fact, all but two of these officers considered the process an extension of their nation-building role rather than an intrusion into civilian affairs, and concerns about adverse effects on professionalism, such as the disruption of training cycles, were trumped by positive evaluation of their contribution to bringing accountability and transparency to governance in the country. Human Rights Watch and other rights organizations accused the monitoring teams of abuse of authority and excessive exercise of police powers. Although several of these officers acknowledged rare lapses in the judgment by some members of the monitoring teams, they were quick to dismiss these allegations as creations of disgruntled and negative elements.

Army monitoring teams were the prelude to the military government's planned restructuring of the government machinery. Funded by international donors (such as the United Nations Development Programme and the UK Department for International Development) that fully accepted the military's mantra of devolution as revolution, the NRB spearheaded the military government's effort to establish its dominance over the administrative structure of the state by diluting the influence and autonomy of the DMG. The NRB's rationale for weakening the DMG was simple: "over-concentration of authority, particularly in the office of the Deputy Commissioner which creates the potential for abuse of authority, diffuses operational focus and results in the expedient handling of routine functions through crisis management."[46] The Musharraf government's divide-and-rule strategy also targeted the group by exploiting inter-group rivalries in the civil service between the DMG and other services, such as the police and the income tax. In its "Structural Analysis of National Reconstruction," the NRB laid out the logic: "The civil service is effectively controlled by the DMG. The group has close relations with international donors. . . . Other groups in the public administration chafe under the control of one group and would welcome a democratisation of civil service structure as a basic element of civil service reform. The end of the domination of the bureaucracy by one group is a necessary pre-condition for the attainment of administrative power by the Army and the creation of conditions for national reconstruction."[47]

Besides diluting the powers of the Deputy Commissioner through the devolution plan, the Musharraf government also deepened the military's penetration of the civil service even further than Zia had. In addition to the military's existing statutory 10 percent quota, over 1,000 active-duty or retired officers were appointed to manage major public-sector organizations, universities, foreign missions, anticorruption bureaus, and even sports federations for cricket and hockey.[48]

Shuja Nawaz argues that this large-scale induction of military officers into the public sector was a means of patronage that "ensured the continued loyalty of the military" to Musharraf.[49] But it was about more than just distributing goodies among the old boys.

In fact, in addition to this lateral reform of state institutions, the military government also considered it necessary to stem the rot in its roots. Hence the process of reconstruction was extended to the civil service induction and training process with the aim of instilling an ethos of public probity, service, and sound administration (defined by the military as discipline, punctuality, patriotism, and dedication to the national interest). The result was almost complete domination by the military of the structure of recruitment, training, and professional development in the civil services. In 2005, the chairman and three members of the Federal Public Service Commission, the agency in charge of recruitment, were former military officers. The commission's chairman is also ex officio the head of the Central Selection Board, which approves the promotion of the top three tiers of civil officers (grade 19 to grade 20 and above). The head of the Civil Services Academy, which trains entry-level civil service officials, was a two-star major general. The Pakistan Administrative Staff College for senior officials was run by a former lieutenant general. Military officers also headed three out of the four National Institutes of Public Administration for midlevel officers. Former military officers were appointed as master trainers in the college and the institutes.

Training for Tutelage

The high command under Musharraf rationalized and reinforced a politically expansive conception of military professionalism. Its formal institutional rationale was both external and local. The editorial of the *Pakistan Army Green Book 2000* noted, "Gone are the days when the sole role of an army was limited, either to invade or beat back the invaders. . . . Geopolitical and geo-strategic regional compulsions of South Asia have made the revision and redefinition of Pakistan Army's role a necessity."[50] Explaining the more urgent domestic basis of this calibrated professionalism, Musharraf noted, "It remains an incontrovertible reality that Pakistan Army has always stood out as the last bastion of strength for the nation during times of emergency. Presently, the nation is confronted with grave problems like economic strangulation, ethnic strife, sub-nationalism and sectarian bigotry. . . . Being the most well-organized and focused national institution, Pakistan Army has accepted the challenge to assist the nation in these trying and uncertain conditions."[51]

The army's higher professional training and staff discourse after the coup drew on the fairly wide acceptance in the officer corps of the army's unique mission as the final savior of the country, which had been ravaged by the politicians. One of the most important institutional sources of imprinting and reinforcing this tutelary mentality is the National Defence University (NDU), the military's highest war college.[52] Formerly known as the National Defence College (NDC), it trains officers of the rank of colonel and brigadier for promotion to the next stage of their careers. Between 1972 and 2009, its program comprised two courses: the War Course for colonels, which focused on purely military strategy, and the broader National Defence Course for officers of the rank of one-star brigadier.[53] Held annually, the forty-four-week National Defence Course acted as a ladder for promotion to the rank of two-star major general. Each year, a cohort of about seventy students entered the course; some 40 percent were brigadiers, 20 percent were Pakistani civil servants, and the rest were military officers from allied countries like Jordan, Egypt, Bangladesh, Sri Lanka, and Malaysia. The course's syllabus encapsulates what the military views as its apposite role in the polity, derived from a comprehensive view of national security.[54] The college selects qualified officers and trains them for "assignments at the national policy planning level."[55]

An examination of the syllabus, students' individual research papers, and the university's journal between 2000 and 2007 reveals at least two important findings. First, and expectedly, the materials show strong socialization effects. Students choose topics for research from a list of preapproved subjects. Their understanding of the military's role and functions, prognoses of national political, economic, and security problems, and the policy conclusions derived from them were remarkably similar and were regularly replicated every year.

Second, these texts advocated and legitimized a broad military role in governmental affairs. This was evident in the regular attention officer-students paid to civilian issues, both in their research and in lectures and discussions with civilian experts, including "the inadequacy of the constitution in forging national integration,"[56] "elimination of corruption,"[57] "health care sector reforms," and strategies for greater national harmony integration through building the educational system,[58] macroeconomics (fiscal and monetary policy), agricultural development, industrialization, privatization, and poverty reduction, as well as the "development of civil society without compromising national security."[59] It is clear from these texts that during the Musharraf years, the primary focus of instruction, research, and debate at the NOU was a more direct, activist, governing role in national reconstruction. One component of this training was the study of the Turkish NSC model, both as a possible template for higher defense organization and for "configuring civil-military relations."[60] Officers also evaluated and debated other models of army-led nation building, such as Indonesia or Burma, to explore their applicability to the task of national reconstruction that had been thrust on the army in Pakistan. The research papers written between 2000 and 2006 provide a glimpse of the wide latitude given to officers to deliberate on the policy-formulation process in aid of what the Musharraf government considered to be its revolutionary reform agenda.

Underlying the process of professional socialization in nonmilitary affairs was the belief that the military is the ultimate watchdog of the national interest and has the right to take any steps necessary to preserve that interest. Even a cursory look at military professional texts produced during Musharraf's authoritarian rule reveals the percolation of a savior mentality throughout the general staff. This is how Musharraf explained his choice to subvert the constitution in October 1999: "The choice was between saving the body—that is the nation, at the cost of losing a limb—which is the Constitution, or saving the limb and losing the whole body. The Constitution is but a part of the nation, therefore I chose to save the nation."[61] It is clear from Musharraf's statement that only the army is the essence and the protector of the whole nation, whereas all other institutions, including the constitution, are fragments of this whole.

The surgical metaphor employed by Musharraf informed the army's postcoup discourse. For instance, the official *Pakistan Army Green Book 2000*, which contains articles on the role of the army in nation building written by seventeen active-duty officers of the rank of brigadier or above, as well as junior officers, is striking because of the almost universal belief in the army's messianic mission to resuscitate the nation (the patient). As one major general noted: "A focal point of the Army's role in nation building must be that of a surgeon, who has to make hard decisions on behalf of the patient for saving his life, including amputation if required. Those decisions will bother some who have vested interests . . . but the condition of the patient warrants such bold actions."[62]

Imaginatively comparing the military's tutelary role to that of a gardener, a major general explained that the "mere love of flowers does not make a good gardener. To develop a garden, the gardener must also be wary of weeds and must use all possible means to uproot them." The obvious target, the weeds in this case, are all those civilians who are skeptical of the therapeutic effects of the army's surgical prowess and consider military participation in governance as an "incursion on their domain" or, worse, give it a "political color for their vested interests."[63] Deriding political partisanship as inherently antistate, a lieutenant general writes in the editorial that this misguided interpretation of the military's commitment to the national interest is the product of "judgment . . . beclouded by . . . biased partisanship in matters of true national interest."[64]

Because officers believe the military has the rightful monopoly over the definition of national interest, those who question it cannot be considered true patriots. Branding civilians who oppose the military as "with us or against us" also made it easier to deal with dissent as a danger to national security. As an extension of their belief in their righteousness, many military officers assumed that their patriotic zeal for nation building was widely accepted, understood, and appreciated by the masses because the army was the only stable and efficient institution that could properly do the job. As one major general described it, the army was generally considered "an efficient organization, capable of delivering the goods. The majority of the people and the intelligentsia view it as an anchor of stability amidst chaotic conditions, and an island of excellence in an incompetent sea of civilian politicians and bureaucrats."[65]

Disciplining Democracy

Because democracy had gone terribly wrong in the military's assessment, the Musharraf government took it up on itself to diagnose and right its systemic wrongs. In their writings, officers typically attributed Pakistan's political underdevelopment at the national level to a "leadership crisis" fomented by "inept," "fickle-minded," "decadent," "irresponsible," and "corrupt" politicians who lacked the "vision" and "acumen" of statesmen and were obsessed with "non-issues." In the opinion of one colonel from the Armed Forces War Course, which purportedly deals with purely military strategy, Pakistan lacked "strong and able leadership" as well as institutions, and this lack had led to political disharmony, as well as economic mismanagement, since independence. Others admitted that elections were still considered a legitimate mechanism for deciding who rules. However, the people had become increasingly cynical about the democratic process over time and had developed the perception that civilian governments were inefficient and wasteful because elections basically circulated power among the same discredited politicians. Hence, in this view, the people felt that the ballot was not a sufficient condition for establishing the legitimacy of governments. Because of poor leadership and the general lack of education, most officers considered democracy in its original form unfeasible in Pakistan. As the last bastion of national strength and character, the army therefore had the duty to correct these structural flaws.

Some officers did acknowledge that previous military interventions had not been an all-out blessing for Pakistan, but their diagnosis of the problem was that military intervention was the product of endemic instability, corruption, and politicians' inability to govern honestly and effectively. In the words of one officer, the "civilians mess up, and then the army is obligated to take over." Even though some disgruntled elements considered military rule an unmitigated failure and blamed the army for intervening in politics for selfish motives, the army had taken "many landmark and bold initiatives" with "ever lasting impression and development of the national political scene and matters of governance."

Reflecting a view that has become a staple of the military's institutional view of politics since the late 1970s, military officers generally perceived parliamentary democracy as particularly inappropriate for Pakistan and its weaknesses and failures as responsible for instability and military intervention. A number of officers were ambivalent about the choice between presidential and parliamentary forms of government, but they firmly believed that the political "system selected has to be tailored to the domestic environment of Pakistan," thus reflecting General Ayub's strong imprint on the political preferences of the succeeding generations of officers.

NDU officer-students identified the main problem with parliamentary government as the concentration of power in one individual, the prime minister, without sufficient checks and balances. Hence officers almost universally recommended nondemocratic safeguards to keep the prime minister under control, thus subverting the norm of civilian control of the armed forces, at least in theory. Not surprisingly, many of them considered the creation of the NSC and presidential checks on the prime minister the ultimate panacea to correct democracy. In line with this institutional consensus, Musharraf instituted both these so-called safeguards during his eight-year rule.

Another problem considered endemic in parliamentary democracy was federalism, which appeared to many officers as a recipe for fanning what they called "fissiparous tendencies." One brigadier, for instance, recommended that in order to rationalize the political system, the Senate should have direct elections; another thought that the Senate should be abolished because it gave undue importance and voice to unsavory autonomy-seeking elements.[66] Trained in the supremacy of the unity of command as the most efficient and effective principle of organization, other officers cautioned that a multiplicity of parties caused political fragmentation. Hence regional ethnic parties should not be allowed to contest national-level elections. Instead, the government ought to decree that only three or four national parties would have the legal right to operate.

But many officers thought that even the existing parties needed major restructuring and reforms because landlords dominated them, and members of the educated middle classes were excluded. Some officers compared parties to family mafias and feudal fiefdoms. In order to break the stranglehold of families and feudal elements, these officers were convinced that parties needed internal democracy. In a statement typical of this view, strongly held by many officers even after the democratic transition in 2007–2008, one active-duty brigadier noted, "Political parties are not democratic themselves as no party elections are held, nor debate/difference of opinion is allowed within party affairs."[67] Preferred solutions included applying the army's strength to democratize parties through internal elections, strict party laws, accountability for party finances, and declaration of assets by elected officials.

One frequent recommendation was a code of ethics for politicians (similar to the military code of honor) and standardized educational qualifications for public office as a prerequisite for creating modern and honest leaders. General Musharraf's regime appeared to have acted on these recommendations when it decreed in 2002 that contesting parliamentary elections would require at minimum a bachelor's degree and instituted strict party laws requiring internal polls, account audits, and asset declaration.

There is no denying the importance of political party reforms, including elections for party officeholders, for deepening democracy. The point, therefore, is not that these reforms are misguided per se.

It is simply that the military has neither the right nor the capability to reform political parties. Forcing parties to reform by employing the gun barrel lacks legitimacy and is unlikely to offer a substitute for reforms initiated as part of the larger democratic process, whether its impetus comes from inside political parties or from civil society. It also overlooks the fact that the leaders of these political parties see their survival as linked to concentrating and centralizing power in their own hands, given the hostile environment under which parties have traditionally had to operate in Pakistan. This includes blanket party bans under military dictatorships in the past, as well as military-ISI efforts to subdue opposition to military governments through divide-and-rule polices.

Fearing, Loathing, and Tackling India

The external threat from India has long been central to the military's justification of its enlarged institutional role in the polity. The military teaches its officers that India does not accept Pakistan as a sovereign equal and that its primary foreign policy objective is to achieve regional hegemony, which requires a weak and unstable Pakistan. Hence there is a deeply ingrained fear in the officer corps that in addition to using traditional foreign policy tools of warfare and diplomacy, India is committed to destabilizing Pakistan through the use of covert means designed to foment and exploit the country's internal divisions. In the blunt words of one recently retired major general, "Since an all-out war is no longer a viable option in the nuclear environment, India is likely to use other means of weakening Pakistan: backing secessionists, terrorists and miscreants wherever it can find them. These internal threats can only be handled effectively if the Army employs its institutional strength."[68] Echoing this politically broad professional ideology, which rationalizes military role expansion into nonmilitary spheres, another major general asserts:

> Although the primary orientation of the army remains safeguarding national integrity against external aggression,

nowadays, the threat to national integrity from within is becoming more pronounced. The internal dynamics and centrifugal forces of a developing country, whether indigenous or with foreign patronage, can be subverted to damage/destroy the country's polity. To guard against such a threat, apart from maintenance of law and order which is absolutely essential for political stability and economic growth, the Army by virtue of its inherent organizational ability to operate efficiently in times of crises has the capacity to expand its conventional role to contributing towards overall improvement in the country, by remarkable managerial skills and technical expertise.[69]

One senior officer noted that externally abetted strife could have a "domino effect creating political instability followed by an economic collapse," eventually resulting in a "two-front war" for the army, which would impair its ability to revive Pakistan from the civilian-induced governance paralysis. On the external front, the military's capability to take "proxy wars to enemy territory and a likely fillip to already activated fissiparous tendencies, nuclear deterrence and strong diplomatic efforts are needed to secure Pakistan."[70] Internally, in his opinion, the only effective way to respond was proactive army involvement in nation building to block enemy efforts to foment social, political, and economic unrest.

One such involvement was in Balochistan, which strained an already ethnically fragile Pakistan. Military rule, in general, is seen as a cover for Punjabi domination by political leaders, lawyers, and human rights activists in Pakistan's smaller provinces, especially Balochistan. Musharraf's military government deepened the sense of Baloch alienation, especially after it supported the Islamist MMA in Balochistan in the 2002 elections, undertook what was locally interpreted as the Punjabi occupation of the Gwadar seaport through military and civilian land grabs, and awarded port-development contracts to Chinese firms that hired non-Baloch labor. The military government denied that there was a problem in Balochistan and instead blamed the tribal chiefs (sardars), especially Akbar Khan Bugti, for keeping the province underdeveloped by blocking economic progress.[71] Rather than addressing Baloch political and economic grievances, the military chose to use intimidation and coercion, illegally detaining, torturing, and killing hundreds of Baloch nationalists to suppress resistance.[72] At the same time, the Musharraf government offered development aid for infrastructure projects, apparently to circumvent the antidevelopment sardars, but these projects included the building of new army cantonments in three sensitive districts: Sui, Gwadar, and Kohlu. Sui has the primary natural gas reserves, Gwadar is a strategic deep sea port, and Kohlu is home to the diehard nationalist Marri tribe. The cantonments were bitterly opposed in the province, including by the Balochistan provincial assembly, because they were widely seen as furthering Punjabi military occupation. However, it was the military's cold-blooded murder of Bugti in August 2006 that further inflamed an already-volatile situation and fueled the nationalist insurgency, for which the military blamed India.[73] The Musharraf government did not produce any evidence of Indian involvement, and India denied these accusations.[74]

Paradoxically, the same institutional norms that legitimize military intervention, including the military's role as a guardian, act as a brake on permanent military rule. Just like security threat from India coheres the Pakistan military and gives it its professional essence, an internal political threat to the military's organizational integrity can act as a unifying force, an "absorber of uncertainty" especially during periods of crisis or flux. Threats help organizations and social groups overcome internal differences. But it is much easier to create a consensus around a coup than, for example, social policy.[75] Hence, like other militaries, the Pakistani armed forces are not immune to consensus erosion and internal disagreement over institutional policies and actions, including prolonged participation in military government. For instance, some officers in Musharraf's army did think that without a deeper role of the army, the opportunity to perform urgent tasks of improving governance would be lost. As part of this total mission, one officer recommended a repeal of the army's constitutionally limited charter of aid to civil power and constitutional coverage for autonomous action so the army could intervene in internal law-and-order crises without waiting for requisition from the civilian administration.[76] It is important to note that these differences of opinion should not be construed as a threat to military cohesion. In fact, the institutional military has proved itself quite adept at suppressing internal fissures and differences by separating itself from the military government to protect its integrity, prestige, and status when authoritarian rule stumbles because of public opposition or the inevitable loss of the right to rule.

Overall, though, enduring army rule is outside the realm of possibilities for most officers, especially at the junior and midranking levels. The military's main security mission is combat against India, and by definition the institutional imperatives of war fighting conflict with anything but an interim military intervention designed to resolve perceived national political or security problems or crises. Even senior members of the officer corps tend to view military coups and rule as "temporary bypasses created when a bridge collapses on democracy's highway"; "after the bridge is repaired, then there's no longer any need for the detour."[77] As one senior officer described it, one of the most recognizable threats to the army's reconstruction agenda was the temptation to prolong military rule. The army has the capacity to jump-start the process, but the "system must gain its own momentum, failing which a protracted military involvement in civilian affairs will ensue," which will adversely affect both economic recovery and the country's external image.[78]

Many officers remained wary of the potentially deleterious effects of participation in civilian affairs on military morale, training, and operational readiness, including a decline in discipline, the development of social ills like corruption, and a poor work ethic.[79] In this view, corroborated in interviews, "military deployment and resource allocation should reflect the threat environment," which must be balanced against the need for any urgent or temporary army intervention in public life to address internal threats, such as "rampant corruption, inefficiency and poor delivery by the public sector."[80] For many officers, the answer to this dilemma was short-term, precise, goal-directed intervention to preserve military professional efficiency and integrity while performing important nation-building tasks.

However, if history is any guide, these temporary interventions rarely remain temporary and typically turn into decades of military rule. The generals often try to maintain influence and oversight of civilian government after leaving power by enacting legal-institutional arrangements, such as the NSC, but they are unable to sustain these structures because they tend to lack broader legitimacy and constitutional sanction in the postauthoritarian context. However, the military's tutelary norms and beliefs tend to survive the eclipse of authoritarian structures because the institutional processes that produce them remain unaffected by military disengagement from government. Even after the military withdraws to the cantonments, it conditions its support for the government on the latter's performance or polices and reserves the right to act autonomously of the government's wishes to preserve its national security interests. At the least, such contingent military loyalty can erode the "authenticity of democratic regimes and indirectly contribute to their breakdown."[81]

As a way of creating a broader consensus on what the military considers the proper way to approach national security problems, the NDU sought to indoctrinate important civilian stakeholders, including politicians, journalists, and lawyers. According to an NDU faculty member, "Educating civilians in the national security aspects through programs in the military universities and the corresponding exposure of military professionals to higher civilian education" is key to "straightening the ideological and perceptual angularities" between the military and society.[82] According to another officer, civilian "leaders should be properly trained at various tiers so that they can effectively manage state affairs," and the NDU could play a crucial role in that project.[83]

Although military officers have been attending civilian universities since at least the 1980s, the NDU expanded the reverse process of civilian immersion in the comprehensive national security paradigm beyond the annual training of selected members of the bureaucracy. In 2003, the NDU initiated an intensive five-week National Security Workshop. Its curriculum mirrored the NDU's regular training program in condensed form, and it was geared mainly toward parliamentarians, but it also included district *nazims* (mayors), ambassadors, senior bureaucrats, journalists, industrialists, and lawyers.

In the opinion of Naqvi, the former NRB chairman, it was essential to train and educate parliamentarians so they could properly exercise oversight of the military:

> During my association with NRB, I met as many people and institutions as possible to learn from best practices, including German foundations. They told me that these foundations, belonging to political parties, have institutionalized training and education of Parliament and Parliamentarians. Every MP [member of parliament] goes through a course. I come back to it that probably the cause of it all is the fact that those who want to be and ought to be in control are not necessarily equipped to be in control and therefore they are unable to assert themselves morally and intellectually to acquire control. The more we invest into that [training of MPs] in direct proportion will be our pace for civilian supremacy and oversight of Armed Forces.[84]

Although it is important to build parliament's capacity to oversee the defense establishment, the views of Naqvi (which are shared by many other officers) point to a broader problem with how the military sees the question of civilian control of the armed forces and how it evaluates the competence of civilian politicians. Naqvi reduces the lack of civilian supremacy to the technical question of training (which lends itself to a quick military solution, such as training at the NDU), in the absence of which MPs are supposedly unable to exercise their moral and intellectual authority over the military.

Even if Pakistani MPs were as well trained as their German counterparts whom Naqvi cites, this would still leave out the fact that MPs in Germany face a very different type of military institution, one that has internalized the norm of political subordination. The point is that parliamentary oversight is not simply a capacity-building issue. It also requires a military that has accepted unconditionally the principle of civilian democratic supremacy. The Pakistani military is distrustful of politicians' role in national security, of which officers consider themselves the only rightful custodians. In fact, when Pakistani MPs raise questions about the army in parliament, they are dubbed security risks. According to PPP senator Farhatullah Babar, the military has to understand that when MPs "comment on a security sector issue, it does not make them less patriotic. We are as patriotic as any general and we don't need a certificate of patriotism from a military general." For instance, when Senator Babar asked in parliament whether there had been any inquiry into the Kargil episode, the reply was that this was "a security question which could not be answered." He says that his other inquiries, such as whether military officers declare their assets and what laws govern the operations of intelligence agencies, were declared impermissible because they "infringe upon our national security."[85] As long as the military has not accepted that parliament, and civilians in general, have the right to hold them accountable, and that military officers are subject to the law, parliamentary oversight of the armed forces will remain stillborn even if every MP is formally trained in apposite parliamentary procedures and committee work.

To recapitulate, the Musharraf dictatorship reinforced officers' beliefs in the rightness of a broad notion of military professionalism that included active control over the state as a legitimate military mission. The *NDU Journal*, the sample of individual research papers, and the *Pakistan Army Green Book* do not systematically represent the views of the army as an institution. However, given that the military is a hierarchical institution that powerfully shapes officers' views of the world through assimilation and socialization, they provide an important window into the officer corps' mind-set, or at least that of the nucleus of the current and future leadership of the military. For example, of the brigadiers writing in the *NDC Journal*, the sample of papers (2000–2006), and the *Pakistan Army Green Book 2000*, at least nine served in top military command and staff positions, including the last director general of the ISI, Lieutenant General Ahmed Shuja Pasha, two corps commanders, and a chief of army logistics. Many more have held important field and staff appointments.

Ideas change slowly. Many of these officers are still on active duty, and their beliefs about the military's guardian mission are unlikely to have changed drastically even though the larger political context changed after 2007. The next time there is a political crisis that the military considers a serious danger to national security, or it perceives a direct threat to military institutional integrity, these beliefs are likely to guide its behavior.

7

THE MILITARY AND DEMOCRACY

The military government of General Pervez Musharraf yielded power to civilians in 2007–2008 in the wake of severe legitimacy problems triggered and amplified by contentious opposition to his rule. Prompted by Musharraf's fateful decision to fire the Supreme Court chief justice in March 2007, lawyers, other members of civil society, and political parties mobilized against the dictator, ultimately eroding his hold on power by persuading the military institution to launch an extrication coup in 2007.

Musharraf had earlier tried to bolster his domestic position by striking a US-brokered power-sharing deal with Bhutto. He sealed his own fate on November 3, 2007, however, when he suspended the constitution and imposed a state of emergency rule to avert a legal challenge to his "uniformed" presidency. As domestic and international pressure mounted on the general to relinquish his army post and to hold elections, Musharraf finally retired from the army in late November, after having secured a second presidential term from the outgoing parliament. He organized a parliamentary ballot in February 2008, which resulted in a narrow victory for the Pakistan People's Party (PPP). The party formed a short-lived coalition government with the Pakistan Muslim League (Nawaz) (PML-N) in the center and in the Punjab. In August 2008, Musharraf was forced to resign from the presidency under threat of impeachment from the coalition government.

The End of the Military Government

Within two years of seizing power, Musharraf had initiated a process of gradual political liberalization: relaxing curbs on civil liberties, opening up private broadcast media, and allowing limited political pluralism. But liberalization turned out, as it often does, to be a dangerous gamble. As Guillermo O'Donnell and Philippe C. Schmitter have argued, once an authoritarian regime permits even limited contestation, it sends out the signal to society that the costs of collective action are no longer high.[1] As a result, previously barricaded arenas of opposition become available for contestation, especially if "exemplary individuals" are willing to probe the boundaries of the regime's tolerance. In Pakistan, the strategic choices and symbolic leadership provided by the chief justice of the Supreme Court, Muhammad Iftikhar Chaudhry, helped mobilize and unite opposition in both civil and political society.[2]

As noted previously, Pakistan's courts have typically condoned military interventions in the past. Judicial sanction has performed an important function for military governments, bestowing legitimacy on them and thereby perpetuating a warped civil-military relationship. Chaudhry himself was part of the twelve-member bench of the Supreme Court that legalized Musharraf's coup in December 1999, and he supported the president on several other occasions that validated Musharraf's extraconstitutional actions, including his 2002 presidential referendum, his 2003 constitutional amendments, and his retention of the post of army chief during his first presidential term.[3] However, this judicial accommodation of the authoritarian regime began to unravel when Justice Chaudhry was appointed to the country's top judicial post in 2005. Buoyed by support from the newly independent media, the Chaudhry court began to challenge the government through public-interest litigation, intervening to regulate commodity prices, canceling corrupt public sector privatization contracts, and pursuing the cases of hundreds of "disappeared" persons, mostly terror suspects illegally detained by military intelligence agencies since Pakistan joined the US-led War on Terror in 2001.

In October 2007, Musharraf's five-year presidential term was set to expire.[4] No longer certain that the Supreme Court would rubber-stamp his presidency,[5] Musharraf and his intelligence chiefs made an ill-fated attempt to fire Justice Chaudhry for alleged misuse of authority on March 7, 2007. When Chaudhry refused, he was held against his will while the directors general of the ISI and Military Intelligence tried to press him to quit.[6] Unsuccessful, the military government then declared him "dysfunctional" and put him under house arrest. The regime's firing and maltreatment of Chaudhry, symbolized by media footage of a police officer roughing him up, sparked lawyers' protests across the country.[7] Led by the Supreme Court Bar Association, prominent lawyers, jurists, and human rights activists strongly condemned the regime for its frontal "assault on the independence of the judiciary."[8] Subsequent media coverage of Justice Chaudhry's strategic speaking tours to bar associations across the country, epitomized by large crowds thronging his vehicle, helped morph these sporadic protests into the "lawyers' movement." The movement was focused on the narrow goal of restoring the chief justice, but it also tapped into latent political resentment against military rule, mobilizing broader opposition from the media, rights organizations, and political parties.[9] To the chagrin of General Musharraf, the Supreme Court rejected the charges against Chaudhry and restored him to office in July 2007.

Facing judicial activism and pressure from civil society, Musharraf realized the urgency of striking a transitional bargain with the political opposition. Since he could not readily mend fences with Nawaz Sharif, he reached out to the self-exiled former prime minister and PPP leader, Benazir Bhutto. As the most popular moderate politician of the country, Bhutto also received backing from the United States, which sought to salvage Musharraf's position in power by broadening the popular base of his regime.[10] Bhutto's main motivation for engaging the regime was to end her decade-long self-exile and return to power. She placed several key preconditions on the table: Musharraf's retirement as army chief, free and fair elections, the lifting of the ban directed specifically at Bhutto (and, by default, Sharif) on seeking a third term as prime minister, and most important, the removal of "politically motivated" corruption charges against her and her spouse, Asif Ali Zardari.

Several rounds of preliminary talks between the two sides held in 2005 were inconclusive. Several direct meetings between Bhutto and Musharraf took place, followed by a series of talks between their aides. The two key interlocutors for the military government were Musharraf's national security advisor, Tariq Aziz, and then director general of the ISI, Lieutenant General Ashfaq Pervez Kayani. These talks reportedly resulted in a power-sharing "deal" in August–September 2007. Under its terms, the PPP agreed to support Musharraf's reelection as president in return for a retraction of the corruption cases and the removal of the third-term ban on Bhutto's election as prime minister.[11] Although he did not remove the reelection bar, citing opposition from the Pakistan Muslim League (Quaid Azam) (PML-Q), Musharraf agreed to rescind the corruption charges and enacted an amnesty law, the National Reconciliation Ordinance (NRO), on October 5, which paved the way for Bhutto's return.[12] He then moved to secure a second presidential term by a controversial parliamentary vote with the PPP's help.[13]

But the NRO was immediately challenged in the Supreme Court, which suspended its operation pending a review of its constitutionality. Acting on a petition challenging Musharraf's presidential eligibility, the court also stayed the election results until it could make a final decision. Expecting to be disqualified, Musharraf suspended the constitution and declared an emergency on November 3, 2007.

Fully backed by the military's top commanders,[14] the general armed himself with a new authoritarian constitution, the Provisional Constitutional Order, in order to purge the courts.[15] He then packed the Supreme Court with loyalist judges and had them legalize his reelection.

Musharraf's "second coup" hastened the regime's demise by galvanizing a broader and more vocal civilian opposition in both political and civil society, comprising lawyers, students, academics, journalists, activists, opposition parties, and ordinary citizens. In response, the government arrested thousands of protesters and gagged the media. The regime's actions made it politically difficult for Bhutto to openly continue her cooperation with Musharraf, and she was obliged to demand his resignation, a step that coalesced the democratic opposition by bringing the PPP and the PML-N closer together.[16]

Although the general staff had formally supported the emergency, another five years of Musharraf's "military" presidency did not have a strong constituency among members of the officer corps, demoralized at least in part by fighting what many of them saw as Washington's War on Terror on their own soil. Ultimately, the military institution withdrew active support from Musharraf to preserve its institutional esteem. Although the antiregime protest movement did not constitute a "people's power" insurrection that could have forced the military's hand, the uniformed military deliberately avoided direct involvement in repression. According to an active-duty major general, there was a growing sense of anxiety in the officer corps about the army's continued association with Musharraf. Hence, the corps commanders ultimately decided that they could "no longer stand by Musharraf and provide him institutional cover," especially when he had become the main target of collective rage in political and civil society.[17]

The Bush administration also insisted that Musharraf relinquish his uniform and hold elections.[18] Having lost the crucial backing of his commanders and reeling under domestic and external pressure, the general finally relinquished his army post on November 28, 2007, after which he was sworn in as a civilian president. Musharraf also promised to end emergency rule before holding elections in January 2008. Parliamentary elections were finally held in February 2008. After Bhutto was murdered during the election campaign, the PPP, led by her widower, Asif Ali Zardari, won a plurality of seats in the National Assembly and formed a coalition government with the PML-N and the Pashtun nationalist Awami National Party in the center and provinces.[19] The PML-N left the federal government in May 2008, after the expiration of a mutually agreed deadline to restore the judges. However, Sharif continued to support the government in parliament, and on August 7, they reached another agreement to restore the judges and to impeach Musharraf. Subsequently, the four provincial assemblies passed resolutions demanding that Musharraf seek a vote of confidence, resign, or face impeachment. As political support for his impeachment gathered momentum, there were rumors that he would preempt the move by dissolving the national assembly and dismissing the government under Article 58(2)b. The army reportedly dissuaded him from taking any action that would jeopardize the political system, however. Once the government and its coalition partners decided to initiate impeachment proceedings against Musharraf, Kayani and his army corps commanders decided in meetings on August 7 and 8 that they would not support the presidential decree to oust the government, in light of its negative consequences for political stability and public opinion.[20] At the same time, the army leadership was decidedly against Musharraf's impeachment because it would humiliate the institution.[21] Thus, Musharraf was persuaded to resign. The government gave him de facto immunity from prosecution and allowed him to leave the country. Along with the army, external powers, especially the United States and the United Kingdom, reportedly played an instrumental role in securing him a "safe passage" abroad.[22]

After exiting power, the army high command under the chief of the army staff (COAS), General Kayani, took several steps that signaled its intent to disengage from politics to "recover lost ground in the eyes of the public."[23] The success of opposition parties in the February 2008 elections showed that the military refrained from systematically manipulating the ballot[24] and remained relatively neutral during and immediately after the elections. Once the coalition government led by the PPP assumed power, General Kayani prohibited officers from meeting politicians and announced the recall of several hundred active-duty officers assigned to the civilian bureaucracy by Musharraf. Press reports indicated that the high command also shut down the notorious political wing of the ISI, which had been implicated in rigging elections,[25] blackmailing, and bribing politicians in the past. These steps led some observers to contrast Musharraf's lack of professional restraint with General Kayani's professional dedication to keeping the military out of politics.[26]

However, as we have seen, the extent to which the military is willing to meddle in politics is shaped by military beliefs and norms. To examine the role of these institutional norms in shaping the Pakistani military's behavior since the transition from authoritarian rule in 2007–2008, it is important to make a distinction between the military's unconditional commitment to democratic government and its tactical acceptance of democratic institutions based on the political and economic performance of a civilian government.[27] Put differently, has the military absorbed the norm that civilian supremacy and political subordination are inherently legitimate, or is its exit from government contingent on how civilians behave?

The military has obviously not seized power. Its immediate postwithdrawal behavior broadly conformed to democratic norms. Nevertheless, its institutional behavior between 2008 and 2013 reveals that it reserves the right to abandon its declared political aloofness and intervene in governmental affairs whenever the high command determines that the civilian government is not acting properly, and that its actions or performance are undermining political stability, military institutional autonomy, and national security. The military's tutelary mentality has since reasserted itself in its efforts to arbitrate political conflict, exercise oversight of the government, preserve its corporate autonomy, and skirt the rule of law.

Tutelary Interventions

Whether a military has actually internalized the norm of political neutrality or adheres to it only conditionally is particularly revealed during political crises. During such periods of uncertainty, precedent and the learning political actors have undergone shape their behavior by providing ready-made cues or templates for action. One such crisis was the political deadlock over deposed judges in February–March 2009. Although the PPP government had released the judges from house arrest immediately after assuming power, it was reluctant to reinstate Chief Justice Chaudhry because of his known opposition to the NRO. Still, President Asif Ali Zardari had assured his main coalition partner, the PML-N, which had made restoration of the judges a key plank of its 2008 election campaign, that his government would restore the judges. However, Zardari reneged, first in May 2008 and again in August 2008, fearing that the Chaudhry-led court would repeal the corruption amnesty.

In August 2008, the PML-N formally left the coalition government.[28] Because the government continued to stall on the issue of the judges, the leadership of the lawyers' movement decided to march on Islamabad and hold a *dharna* (sit-in) before parliament on the second anniversary of the sacking of Justice Chaudhry (March 9, 2007). The PML-N joined hands with the lawyers, as did other parties, including the Jamaate Islami and the Pakistan Tehreek-e-Insaaf (Pakistan Movement for Justice).[29] In a preemptive strike, Zardari used a court ruling disqualifying Nawaz Sharif's brother, Shahbaz Sharif, the chief minister of Punjab, from holding electoral office to dismiss his government and impose governor's rule in the province.[30] To repair this seeming breach of the "bridge of democracy,"[31]

General Kayani intervened and reportedly threatened to implement the minus-one formula, that is, the ouster of President Zardari while keeping the rest of the government intact.[32] Under army and opposition pressure, the PPP government finally relented and reinstated the Chaudhry court on March 16, 2009.

The military has also sought to exercise its role as watchdog of the government. In October 2010, a news report suggested that General Kayani had conveyed the high command's disapproval of the PPP-led cabinet's performance to President Zardari and demanded the sacking of several corrupt ministers.[33] Similarly, the corps commanders openly signaled their displeasure with the government when they expressed their concern over increasing violence in Pakistan's commercial capital, Karachi.[34] In fact, General Kayani all but blurred even the formal civil-military boundaries when he chaired a meeting of the secretaries (top civilian officials) of several government ministries at army headquarters in 2010, ostensibly to create a consensus on the strategic dialogue with the United States, thereby revealing the army's desire to dominate the country's important foreign relations to the point of micromanagement.[35] Concerned with its short-term interests, the United States has only enabled and encouraged this dominance by preferring to deal with the generals directly, exclusively, and, if need be, covertly.[36] For instance, besides funneling untraceable monies through under-the-table deals to the ISI as bounty for capturing al-Qaeda militants, which undercuts civilian authority,[37] the CIA has operated its unmanned drones targeting al-Qaeda and Taliban militants in the Federally Administered Tribal Areas (FATA) through a secret political understanding with the military on using Pakistani airbases.[38] In 2010, the Obama administration worked behind the scenes to press the Pakistani government to extend Kayani's tenure as COAS to ensure continuity in the fight against terrorism.[39] The PPP government obliged both the United States and Kayani by giving him an unparalleled three-year extension, clearly revealing its political need to accommodate both the army and America.[40]

Managing National Security

As a corporate organization, the military seeks to enhance internal control and limit external interference. However, the Pakistani military's prerogatives over its internal structure and functions clearly limit the scope for the establishment of civilian supremacy over the armed forces. Since the transition, the military has sought to maintain and in some cases even increase control over military promotions and appointments. For instance, General Kayani has awarded service extensions to several general officers beyond the age of retirement without even seeking the requisite formal approval of the government.[41]

The military has made nominal concessions on budgetary allocations since 2008 by allowing the disclosure of an itemized annual budget before parliament.[42] But it has evaded any real accountability because it believes that the disclosure of sensitive budgetary matters would undermine national security by exposing critical information to enemy agents. It has also advised the government to streamline wasteful civilian expenditures rather than question the military budget.[43]

Whenever the PPP government has threatened its institutional autonomy, the military has shown itself capable of vetoing government decisions. In July 2008, Prime Minister Yousaf Raza Gillani decided to place the ISI under the operational, financial, and administrative control of the Ministry of Interior, both to rationalize the country's intelligence structure and to create civilian oversight over the ISI. The high command perceived the ISI's formal subordination to the ministry as a damaging political encroachment on core institutions of the country. Hence it virtually forced the government to backtrack within hours of the official notification, clearly indicating the limits it can impose on the exercise of civilian democratic authority.[44]

The military's reaction reflected entrenched norms that hold that military institutional autonomy is necessary for fulfilling its national security mission and consider civilian leaders, officials, and agencies incapable and corrupt. Testifying before the Abbottabad Inquiry Commission set up by the PPP government in June 2011 to inquire into the circumstances of Osama bin Laden's death,[45] the former director general of the ISI, Lieutenant General Ahmed Shuja Pasha, observed that putting the ISI under the Ministry of Interior would have been a disaster because the agency had no business with the ministry, which in any case was incapable of properly discharging its basic responsibilities, like the other civilian institutions of the state.[46]

Instead of accepting subordination to the government, the military, acting in accordance with its self-image as the last bastion of national strength and guardianship, has usurped civilian functions. The ISI, for instance, has no authority over counterterrorism and has admitted that the PPP government never entrusted it with that responsibility. However, the agency, in Pasha's opinion, had no choice but to step in because other nonmilitary intelligence and law-enforcement departments had failed to "realign their focus on the primary threat of terrorism" since 9/11 on account of their ineffectiveness and the broader "dysfunctionality of the prevailing system."[47] Although civilian government departments are hardly paragons of effectiveness, this view ignores the fact that the military, including the ISI, often hinders them from doing their assigned jobs and denies them the space and resources they need to perform their functions.[48] The military disagrees. According to the army's adjutant general, "Neither the army nor the ISI had overstepped its responsibilities. However, they were often forced to fill the vacuum left by the failure of civil departments."[49] Expressing a view shared by a number of officers, one retired officer noted, "It is just fashionable to say the army doesn't let civilians work. Question is, do they want to work?"[50]

In the past, civilian governments of both the PPP and the PML-N have traditionally sought to ease tensions and normalize trade relations with India, if only to reduce the military's domestic power and monopoly over national security. In November 2011, the PPP-led cabinet decided in principle to grant India the status of most favored nation after a series of talks between the commerce ministers of the two countries. However, the military reportedly pressured the government to slow the process because its trade policy was uncoordinated with security policy.[51]

The military has traditionally espoused a first-use nuclear policy against India to offset the latter's superiority in conventional war. In 2008, President Asif Ali Zardari publicly overturned this policy by endorsing a no-first-use policy, telling an Indian audience that "Pakistan would not be the first to use nuclear weapons against India."[52] Zardari might be the military's commander in chief, but Pakistan's nondemocratically inclined generals effectively killed his proposed policy shift by not endorsing it.[53] Similarly, after the ISI-backed Haqqani network (an Islamist Afghan insurgent group based in North Waziristan operating against US and coalition troops in eastern Afghanistan under the leadership of the former mujahideen commander Jalaluddin Haqqani) allegedly attacked the US embassy in Kabul in September 2011 and the Obama administration stepped up pressure on Pakistan to eliminate the group's sanctuaries on its soil,[54] Zardari pledged to take action against the Haqqanis.[55] However, the army stalled and demurred on the grounds that its troops were stretched thin by existing deployments in FATA.

Manufacturing Public Opinion

The absence of a military norm of political subordination is also evident in the way the military remonstrates through the management and manipulation of the media and public opinion. Although the military retains its ultimate capability to destabilize or seize the government by force, brute coercion is less effective for protecting its interests in a posttransitional context defined by the empowerment of new institutional centers of power and persuasion, such as the higher judiciary and the broadcast media. Hence the military has adapted itself to these changing civil-military dynamics by articulating its opposition to threatening government initiatives through mobilizing the support of judges and journalists.

The military has long had a dedicated media wing, Inter-Services Public Relations (ISPR), which constructs and maintains a glorified public image of the armed forces.[56] For instance, amid public and media criticism of the PPP government's poor response to devastating floods in 2009, the ISPR vigorously publicized the army's more efficient and effective flood-relief efforts.

The stated primary goal of the military's media policy is to harness its role as an "element of national power" to "mold public opinion and develop a consensus . . . on national security."[57] Adapting to the growing power of information in a globalizing world and wary of domestic and external concerns about the restriction of civil liberties under authoritarianism, the Musharraf government extensively liberalized the broadcast news media. At the same time, the military expanded the ISPR to increase its institutional capacity to police both the electronic and print media more effectively.[58] In 2007, the National Defence University (NDU) initiated a special media workshop to enable journalists and media managers to understand the crucial role of the media in pursuing the "national interest."[59]

One example of using the media to control perceived threats to national security posed by civilian government policy was the military's reaction to the Kerry-Lugar-Berman Bill, signed into law by President Barack Obama as the Enhanced Partnership Act of 2009, which offered Pakistan $1.5 billion annually in nonmilitary, developmental US aid for five years. But the bill had strings attached, mainly the requirement of an annual certification by the US secretary of state of Pakistan's support of US counterterrorism efforts, civilian control over the armed forces, and nonproliferation efforts. Although the PPP government welcomed the aid, the military joined opposition parties in publicly expressing its "serious concern over clauses impacting on National Security."[60] The military high command was offended by the bill's "critical provisions that were almost entirely directed against the army," especially its required assessment of civilian control over military promotions and military abstinence from interference in political and judicial processes.[61] Any military that was unequivocally committed to democratic norms would have quietly aired its objections to the civilian government through proper official channels. Instead, the Pakistani army chose to undermine and embarrass the civilian government by openly rejecting the aid bill and branding it a threat to Pakistan's sovereignty. The ISI manufactured public opinion against the law by encouraging the media to present it as a blatant example of US interference in Pakistan's internal affairs in order to gain more leverage with the Americans by citing public opposition.[62] Thus cable news channels concocted conspiracy theories, painting the bill as part of the United States' sinister design to weaken the country's security institutions.[63]

As an institution with a monopoly over sensitive defense information, the military can use its expert knowledge to manipulate the media. In fact, the ISI runs its own Information Management Wing. Headed by a military officer of the rank of major general or the equivalent from the air force or navy, it metes out both punishments and rewards. In recent years, the agency has been widely accused of intimidating and blackmailing errant journalists while cajoling others through both monetary incentives and exclusive scoops to sway public opinion against designated internal and external threats. For instance, after the American CIA contractor Raymond Davis was arrested in Lahore for killing two Pakistanis in January 2011, the ISI summoned selected journalists to spread the word that the PPP government's lax visa policy had made it possible for the CIA to expand its spy network within Pakistan. It also leaked the names of over fifty other alleged American spies to expose the extent of American espionage activities[64] as well as the CIA station chief in Pakistan to settle scores with the Americans for the humiliation they had caused by the undetected Special Forces raid on May 2 that killed Osama bin Laden.[65]

That highly embarrassing aerial intrusion strained the patron-client relationship between the military and the media. Even prominent friendly journalists launched unprecedented criticism of the military for its disastrous policies of nurturing militants and its transparent incompetence despite receiving a large share of the national budget.[66] In turn, the military publicly warned its critics to stop "trying to deliberately run down the Armed Forces and the Army in particular" and threatened to put an end to "any effort to create divisions between important institutions of the country."[67] At least in one case, the generals seem to have lived up to their words. On May 29, the ISI reportedly abducted, tortured, and brutally murdered the Pakistani journalist Saleem Shehzad,[68] just one day after he exposed links between al-Qaeda and navy personnel involved in a deadly attack on a naval base in Karachi.[69]

Judging the Judges

The main goal of the contentious antiregime mobilization that facilitated Musharraf's demise was the restoration of the sacked judges of the superior judiciary. The Chaudhry-led court's triumphant return has endowed it with the moral and legal authority to assert its autonomy and power. In addition to media manipulation, the military has sought to harness judicial activism to protect what it considers national security from threats posed by the political leadership. This strategy was exemplified by the so-called memogate affair, in which Mansoor Ijaz, a US businessman of Pakistani origin, alleged in a *Financial Times* op-ed that the PPP government had sought his assistance in seeking US help to avert a military coup in the wake of the killing of bin Laden.[70] The alleged memorandum requesting American intervention was ostensibly written by Pakistan's then ambassador to the United States and Zardari confidante, Hussain Haqqani, who had played an instrumental role in the Kerry-Lugar aid. In return, the government pledged to appoint a new US-friendly national security team, abolish the ISI's external operations or S wing to stop the agency's support of Islamist militants, and place Pakistan's nuclear program under international safeguards. After allegedly establishing the authenticity of the memo, the military pressured the government to investigate the matter and hold the ambassador to account.[71]

Denying involvement, the government recalled and fired Haqqani and tasked the Parliamentary Committee on National Security with determining the truth behind the allegations. But the parliamentary inquiry was prematurely undermined when, sensing an opportunity for political gain, the opposition PML-N filed a petition in the Supreme Court seeking a judicial investigation. Heeding the advice of the army and ISI chiefs who defiantly broke ranks with the civilian government by declaring the memo a national security threat,[72] the court readily agreed to constitute a judicial inquiry commission.[73] Deeply embarrassed by the army's "unconstitutional" and "illegal" court statements, Prime Minister Gillani responded with a firm warning to the generals that his government would not tolerate a state within a state.[74] He then fired the secretary of the Ministry of Defense, a former general loyal to Kayani, and appointed a trusted civil servant to the post. The army retaliated by reminding the prime minister that his accusations could have "potentially grievous consequences for the country."[75] As coup rumors began circulating in the media, General Kayani signaled the army's intent to instigate a coup by calling an emergency corps commanders' meeting and replacing the commander of the 111th Brigade.[76] Before the two sides could reach the brink, the civilian government reportedly backed down.

Memogate serves as a potent recent example of the military's ability to achieve its objectives by adapting its methods to changed political conditions. In the past, the memo might have been sufficient to persuade the military to destabilize the government or launch a coup. But because its public reputation has been badly tarnished by both a long decade of military rule and its more recent professional failures in a context defined by new centers of power, the military has learned to exercise its influence by other means. Despite the military's apparent political weaknesses, however, the civilian government was either unable or unwilling to press its advantage, in part because of the very real fear of a coup, as well as judicial challenges to its authority.[77] Amid media reports that the government was planning to sack the army and ISI chiefs for their illegal actions, the Supreme Court admitted a petition seeking to restrain the civilian government from using its constitutional prerogative to remove the two.[78]

But the judiciary's relationship with the military is not clear-cut. Although it has aligned itself with the military on national security, the judges have also questioned the military's human rights violations. The Chaudhry court's aggressive pursuit of the so-called missing persons was one of the reasons that Musharraf tried to sack him in 2007. However, since its restoration in 2009, the court has continued to investigate these cases. In at least one harrowing case involving eleven illegally detained terror suspects, four of whom died in ISI custody, the court ordered the agency to produce the remaining seven in court, allow them proper medical care, and explain the legal basis of their detention.[79] The judges have also reprimanded the military for its alleged human rights violations in Balochistan and have even specifically demanded an end to all military operations (including the paramilitary Frontier Corps's kill-and-dump operations) and abolishment of the death squads run by the ISI and Military Intelligence (MI).[80] However, ISI and MI officials continue to impede judicial inquiries by denying involvement, blaming the disappearances on foreign intelligence agencies, and delaying action on court directives by claiming immunity under the cloak of national security.[81] In May 2012, the military openly defied the court's orders to produce two missing Baloch activists by allegedly dumping their dead bodies on the roadside.[82] In at least one case in which an ISI brigadier was charged with kidnapping, the Supreme Court itself restrained the police from executing his arrest orders because "it was a matter of respect of an institution."[83] These toothless inquiries only reinforce the military's presumption of impunity. Hence the military has paid little heed, and senior military officers, including the chiefs of the ISI and MI and the inspector general of the Frontier Corps, continue to evade judicial authorities.

Under mounting public criticism of the Supreme Court for selectively targeting civilians, the judges dug up the sixteen-year-old Mehran Bank scandal (discussed in Chapter 5), which embarrassed the military. Ultimately, it held the former army chief, General Aslam Beg (retired), and the former director general of the ISI, Lieutenant General Asad Durrani (retired), responsible for violating the constitution. However, rather than risk antagonizing the generals, it vaguely instructed the government to take necessary legal action against them while issuing specific instructions that politicians who took bribes should be interrogated by the Federal Investigation Agency. The military has not taken this judicial trespassing lightly because "judicial activism is seen as questioning the role of state functionaries. This earns a bad name for the security forces in general, and Army and ISI in particular."[84] Kayani issued a thinly veiled warning:

> No one should become a party in weakening institutions. . . . Such allegations should not be done because it demotivates the soldiers who are sacrificing their lives every day. They are defending the country on the highest altitude and places like Parachinar where the temperature is 20 degrees below freezing point. I am visiting my troops to boost their morale but the baseless criticism proves counterproductive and is harming my efforts. Let the army and Inter-Services Intelligence (ISI) work within their mandate and domain. No uncalled-for interference should be done in their work.[85]

Avoiding Accountability

In a democracy, the military (or other state institutions) cannot be above the rule of law. However, the Pakistani military operates outside the purview of the civilian legal system with impunity because it considers itself above the law and views its internal accountability system as far more effective than civilian ones. For instance, General Kayani initially stalled the efforts of the UN Commission of Inquiry into the assassination of Benazir Bhutto by blocking access to senior military officers because of their alleged involvement in the Musharraf regime's cover-up of her murder.[86] The commission's final report claims that the then director general of MI, Major General Mian Nadeem Ijaz Ahmed, ordered local police officials to hose down the crime scene within two hours of the suicide attack that killed Bhutto, and that this resulted in the loss of crucial forensic evidence.[87] Instead of investigating the allegations, the military rejected the report as a "bid to malign the national institution" and persuaded the foreign ministry to lodge a protest with the United Nations and seek a reopening of the inquiry.[88]

Similarly, the military refuses to subject its members to civilian prosecution for corruption. For instance, in 2009, two lieutenant generals, one major general, and two civilians stood accused of causing a loss of almost 2 billion rupees (US $200 million) to the National Logistics Cell by investing public funds in the stock market in violation of government rules.[89] However, General Kayani repeatedly stonewalled civilian investigations by claiming that he was initiating an internal inquiry. In July 2011, the National Assembly's Public Accounts Committee ultimately referred the case to the National Accountability Bureau, the government's primary anticorruption agency. But Kayani protected the three former army officers from civilian scrutiny by reinstating them in the army so that they could be tried under the Army Act of 1952.[90]

The military has also expanded its legal powers over civilians, ostensibly to counter terrorism and militancy. For instance, during the Emergency in 2007, Musharraf amended the Army Act of 1952 to empower the military to try civilians in military courts for offenses considered prejudicial to the security and defense of Pakistan.[91] After the transition, the army pressured President Zardari to promulgate the Actions in Aid of Civil Power Regulation, 2011, which authorizes the military to detain terror suspects indefinitely during its operations in the FATA and the provincially administered tribal areas.[92] Although the ISI and MI have no legal powers of arrest, they have allegedly detained, tortured, and even killed suspected Islamic militants with American and British complicity.[93] In Balochistan, they have resorted to classic dirty-war tactics against nationalist leaders and human rights activists.[94] One military intelligence official reportedly told Bashir Azeem Baloch, the seventy-six-year-old secretary general of the Baloch Republican Party, during his unacknowledged detention, "Even if the president or chief justice tells us to release you, we won't. We can torture you, or kill you, or keep you for years at our will. It is only the Army chief and the intelligence chief that we obey."[95]

Civilian Political Loyalty

Insofar as democracy is contingent on the unconditional acceptance of democratic norms by all politically significant actors, it is important to assess the loyalty to democracy of civilian political elites since 2008. In the early stages of the democratic transition, some politicians and parties continued to flirt with the idea of a democracy guided by the military.[96] However, the leaders of the two major political parties, the PPP and the PML-N, have emerged from the experience of their zero-sum political rivalry in the 1990s committed to not repeating their past mistake of knocking on the garrisons' doors against each other. Leaders from both parties acknowledged that their mutual antipathy and disrespect of democratic norms and procedures left them vulnerable to military manipulation and eventually opened the door for the direct military seizure of power in 1999.[97] Hence the two parties agreed to a set of reforms designed to strengthen democratic institutions and civilian democratic control over the military. In May 2006, Nawaz Sharif and Benazir Bhutto signed the Charter of Democracy, in which they pledged not to "join a military regime or any military sponsored government [or] solicit the support of military to come into power or to dislodge a democratic government"; to make the military and its intelligence services accountable to the elected government, create a civilian-controlled nuclear command and control structure under the Defence Committee of the Cabinet, scrutinize military budgets, abolish both the National Security Council (NSC) and presidential powers to dissolve the national assembly, and desist from using extraconstitutional means against each other.[98]

Although there has not been any meaningful progress toward civilian control of military intelligence agencies, the military budget, and nuclear weapons, the two parties have cooperated in instituting a number of constitutional reforms designed to strengthen the prime minister and the parliament in relation to the president. The most significant of these is the Eighteenth Amendment to the constitution, which was the result of more than a year of deliberations and compromises among political parties of all persuasions represented in parliament. Passed into law in April 2010, the amendment restored the 1973 constitution as it existed before Musharraf's coup, reducing the president to a titular head of state bound by the advice of the prime minister and the cabinet. It reassigned the presidential authority to appoint military service chiefs to the prime minister. It also excised the presidential coup powers enshrined in Article 58(2)b, thereby depriving the military of an important constitutional tool for securing its interests vis-à-vis an elected government.[99] The amendment enhanced the scope of the constitution's Article 6, which designates the subversion of the constitution as high treason, by barring the judiciary from legalizing the overthrow of democratic governments.[100] Similarly, it abolished the presidential prerogative of appointing the chief election commissioner and entrusted that responsibility to a bipartisan parliamentary committee that chooses the commissioner from a list of candidates provided by the prime minister and the leader of the opposition in the outgoing National Assembly. In February 2012, the parliament also passed the Twentieth Amendment bill, which governs the process of appointing a caretaker prime minister through a bipartisan consensus.[101] That appointment also was a presidential prerogative in the past.

Although the exact impact of these statutory changes on civil-military relations is unclear, they might help consolidate civilian supremacy in at least three ways. First, short of a military coup, democratically elected governments will no longer be subject to a sudden loss of power by presidential decree. Second, the democratically elected prime minister will retain the power to exercise democratic control over the military by choosing the service chiefs.[102] Third, the more autonomous election commission and a less politically biased caretaker government will, at least in theory, lend credibility to the electoral process and reduce the scope for fraud and malpractice which can be used by the losers to discredit the winners.

The real test of both these reforms and politicians' loyalty to the democratic process was the May 11, 2013, elections, which marked the first transition in Pakistan from one democratically elected government that completed its tenure to another. It is true that an orchestrated campaign of violence by the Taliban in the run-up to the elections against what they see as pro-American, secular parties, such as the Awami National Party, the Muttahida Qaumi Movement (known as the Mujahir Quami Movement until 1997), and the PPP, tilted the playing field in favor of more conservative parties, like the PML-N. Allegations of localized voter fraud on polling day also marred the balloting process. Despite these problems, the election commission was able to hold an election generally considered free and fair by international observers.[103] The PML-N won a simple majority of seats in the national assembly and a two-thirds majority in the Punjab assembly and thereby formed governments in the center and the Punjab. Unlike the past, when parties in control of the federal government would typically prevent the opposition from forming provincial governments, the PML-N allowed the Pakistan

Tehreek-e-Insaaf and Baloch nationalist parties to form their own governments in Khyber Pakhtunkhwa and Balochistan.

Military Loyalty

As this book has stressed, successful democratization also requires a military committed to democratic norms.[104] One indication that the military continues to harbor an institutional commitment to its tutelary role is the NDU's curriculum. In fact, in what appears to be a step toward furthering the institutional unity of thought, the military merged the strictly military War Course with the National Defense Course in 2010. The new consolidated version has been named National Security and War Course. This integration of the two distinct streams of officer training will ensure that almost all officers above the rank of colonel (or the equivalent in the air force and navy) will be formally socialized into the same expansive narrative of national security.

The gap between the democratic rhetoric of the military leadership and the actual depth of the military's adherence to democracy and the constitutional order is poignantly revealed in the NDU's 2012–2013 curriculum. Out of the total 987 contact hours, students attend just one two-hour lecture on the constitution of Pakistan by a civilian legal expert. The lecture has four components: the constitution's "suitability and inadequacies in forging national integration," the impact of the Objectives Resolution (discussed in Chapter 1), the role of the armed forces, and recommendations for constitutional reform.[105] If the lecture time is divided equally, the students probably spend no more than half an hour on the constitutional duties of the army. Leaving aside the principle of civilian democratic supremacy, the course has no dedicated instruction or discussion of the subordinate role of the army in a democracy, especially in a parliamentary system. Even though students make a customary call on the speaker of the national assembly as part of their inland study tour, there is no explicit lecture or panel discussion on the role and functions of parliament or, for that matter, on the army's proper relationship and responsibilities to the elected representatives of the people. To place things in perspective, it might be instructive to look at Bangladesh, which has also experienced recurrent military interventions like those in Pakistan and is undergoing the process of completing a transition from authoritarian rule that began in 2009. The Bangladesh National Defence College devotes several sessions to ensuring the democratic socialization of the armed forces, including panel discussions on the democratic nature of politics in Bangladesh and the constitution, and lectures on the electoral system and the role, functions, and practice of parliament in the context of a parliamentary democracy.[106]

To be meaningful, the military's outward compliance with democratic norms should also be accompanied by internal change. Although military professional discourse generally shows less emphasis on the army's direct activist role in nation building than was evident during the military government of Musharraf, the army continues to define its role in a politically permissive manner. Despite Kayani's repeated claims of the army's firm commitment to the democratic process and the constitution, he continues to project the institution as the sole guardian of national security, a role that naturally gives it a monopoly over both defining threats and defending against them.[107] However, the military's broad conception of national security means that it can claim prerogatives over spheres of public policy that lie outside its constitutional purview of external defense and aid to the civil power. As one officer described it, the objective of national security is not just to preserve "national interests and integrity," but also "economic growth to raise the living and social standards of the people."[108]

The military's perception of itself as guardian extraordinaire will adversely affect the future working of democracy insofar as it uses its far-reaching definition of national security to evaluate democratically elected governments' policies and performance. If an elected government is unable to provide social development or raise living standards, the military can easily conclude that it is jeopardizing national security, and that the army should do something about it.

In interviews and in their writings, a number of active-duty and recently retired military officers concede that Pakistan's future economic and social progress is linked to democracy. Many see military coups and rule as harmful to Pakistan's global image and internal cohesion. As one officer observed, "Our political institutions have not matured prima facie due to the lack of continuity."[109] However, for military officers, every silver lining has a dark cloud. According to one brigadier, democratic systems require "the integrity of both purpose and person" and a democratic culture in which political parties are internally democratic and the people are educated enough to understand what democracy means more than just voting.[110] In the opinion of another brigadier, only by building a democratic culture at the "grass-roots level . . . would we have a culture, wherein people should vote in a democracy and not for democracy."[111]

Officers continue to hold negative opinions of politicians, especially on issues related to national security. Former ISI director general Pasha believes that the political leadership lacks adequate knowledge, the aptitude to read basic defense policy documents, and even the ability to think, which is why "they cannot formulate any policy."[112] An active-duty brigadier observed that the "low caliber of the leadership means that the army will have to bear the brunt, even though the army may not be in full control of security policy under a democratic dispensation."[113]

Some officers believe that politicians may get the votes but lack the vision. In this view, politicians exploit gullible voters by inflaming parochial ethnic, linguistic, or other identities, and their actions undermine national cohesion and, therefore, pose a direct threat to national security.[114] Others hold that vested elite interests, who deny the middle class their representation, have created a vacuum between the state and society and have hijacked politics for their selfish gains. These elite politicians and the parties they lead are seen as unable or unwilling to make "coherent efforts . . . to reach a consensus on different contentious issues."[115]

These military perceptions of politicians and their acumen and intentions are clearly in conflict with the prospects of deepening democracy, especially if and when they combine with adverse assessments of civilian governments' political and economic performance. These views and attitudes also mean that the military has not yet reconciled itself unequivocally to the legitimacy of elections as a mechanism for determining who should rightly govern Pakistan. In fact, many officers believe that merit, honesty, moral resolve, and dedication to the nation should be given equal, if not more, weight as qualifying criteria for public office.[116] For instance, one officer recommends that the presumably Chinese principle of "the right person for the right job" should be adopted in Pakistan. He writes further: "Legislation in this regard needs to be done in order to ensure implementation at ministerial level as well, as political leadership is not equipped with such skills and mostly do not have requisite education level. There is a need to increase percentage of technocrats in National Assembly and Senate up to 50%. This will help in correct management and planning of available resources for development of country."[117]

In defense of this approach, officers pointed to the broad public disappointment with the last PPP government's alleged corruption and inability to resolve major problems, like the energy crisis.[118] However, their doubts were not restricted to the PPP but extended to the entire political leadership. Many believed that the 2013 elections held "scant possibility of substantial change" from perverse patterns of the past, defined by the absence of "right, honest and reliable leaders."[119] Although the concept of political subordination typically brought out adverse reactions in interviews, even officers' political neutrality remains linked to the ability of democracy to deliver the goods and the politicians' willingness to put "Pakistan first," a phrase drilled into the army's vocabulary by Musharraf. It would be tempting to dismiss these views as those of individual officers. However,

General Kayani, the military's chief spokesman, articulated this contingent democratic commitment before the elections:

> Awareness and participation of the masses . . . can truly end this game of hide and seek between democracy and dictatorship. If we succeed in rising above all ethnic, linguistic and sectarian biases to vote solely on the basis of honesty, sincerity, merit and competence, there would be no reason to fear dictatorship or to grudge the inadequacies of our present democratic system.
>
> Our salvation resides in transforming the government into a true platform of public representation . . . [by giving] primacy and precedence to the larger public interest over personal interests. Otherwise, may it be democracy or dictatorship, governance would continue to remain a means of self-aggrandizement and that of plundering national wealth and resources. . . . We must never forget the success of . . . democracy is intimately linked with the wellbeing and prosperity of the nation.[120]

One former officer reaffirmed the general's populist vision of democracy when he wrote that "General Kayani's speech was more of a charge sheet that conveyed the Army's displeasure to the political elite. He certainly had in mind the 'sham democracy' and mis-governance witnessed in the last five years, when he stated that success of democracy is intimately linked with the well being and prosperity of the nation."[121]

In the absence of sustained political unrest or perceived grievous threats to the military, a blunt military coup will likely be a hard sell in the army, domestically unpopular, and externally unwelcome.[122] Also, the army high command would rather not take direct responsibility for resolving Pakistan's complex political, economic, and security challenges. But the military has little confidence in the capacity or will of politicians to address these problems. Hence, as a reserve option, officers (as well as prominent civilians) advocate a soft coup, that is, a military-sponsored technocratic government that can effect institutional and economic reforms along the lines of Bangladesh.[123] In 2007, the Bangladeshi military declared a state of emergency and installed a technocratic front government in the wake of intense preelection violence. However, the military largely failed to achieve its objective of cleansing politics of corrupt elites, such as the leaders of the two main political parties (the Awami League and the Bangladesh National Party), and had to yield power to them. This makes the Bangladesh example a cautionary tale, not a model to be emulated.

But no such lessons have been drawn in Pakistan. The peddlers of the idea, in and outside the military, would like to create a broad national government because Pakistan's underlying problems are monumental and therefore defy solutions by a particular political party government. Backed by the institutional will and strength of the army, such a government could be composed of technocrats, as well as representatives from all major parties and provinces, to create a consensus among all stakeholders on evolving coordinated policies and seeking comprehensive solutions for domestic problems, such as poverty, and external problems, such as Kashmir.[124]

Observers have accused the military of sponsoring the large rallies of a Muslim cleric, Allama Tahirul Qadri. On January 14, 2013, Qadri marched into Islamabad with tens of thousands of supporters and camped out in front of parliament for several days. He threatened to use any means necessary to implement his demands, which included the removal of the corrupt PPP-led government, the disbandment of the current parliament, the creation of a technocratic government backed by the army and the judiciary, and the implementation of Zia-era constitutional clauses (Articles 62 and 63) that lay down strict financial, religious, and moral qualifications for election to parliament. Although Qadri called off his protest after the government assured him of cooperation, strict implementation of Articles 62 and 63 in the scrutiny of the 2013 election candidates' nomination papers led some observers to argue that this was the outcome of the military's "new coup playbook" or its desire to cleanse politics.[125]

Short of a full-blown military-backed authoritarian government, many officers see the "institutional approach" as the most sensible solution to the connected problems of governance and national security. First, deeply concerned about perceived misgovernance and maladministration, especially since the end of Musharraf's military rule, officers consider drastic reforms imperative to ensure political stability and security. In this view, state institutions have withered because of political interference, malfeasance, and the lack of proper skills. What is needed is a course correction to reinvigorate and modernize state institutions, which are all imprints of the past.[126] As a way to compensate for these weaknesses, some officers recommend the appointment of competent and sincere technocrats and military officers to top bureaucratic positions.[127]

More specifically, military officers blame deteriorating internal security and incidents of terrorism on the inefficiency and ineffectiveness of the police. Senior officers want the police, the Intelligence Bureau, and the Federal Investigation Agency depoliticized, given proper training and equipment, and restructured in the image of the military and the ISI. According to former ISI director general Pasha, civilian intelligence agencies like the Intelligence Bureau do not work because they are run by police officers who lack basic knowledge of intelligence work.[128] The answer, according to one active-duty brigadier, is to re-create the police in the image of the army. In the context of police reforms, he notes:

> It is useful to study the army's own organization model, which can be emulated to ensure the adoption of a uniform pattern of change throughout the entire police force, independent of political manipulation. Specifically, the police force could reorganize in line with the arms and services

structure of the army (i.e., categorized into fighting and supporting arms and services). In doing so, the police force would have all of the necessary branches to support the task of law enforcement, as the threat dictates. Apart from the main police force, the organization would also have intelligence, investigation, forensics, logistics, and training branches—which would include police training schools, staff colleges (for middle-tier and senior leaders), and the capacity for research and analysis within the fields of policing and law enforcement.[129]

In the interim, he recommends inducting army officers into the police on an enhanced scale and training senior police officers at the NDU, junior officers at the Pakistan Military Academy, and police intelligence officials in the School of Military Intelligence.[130] In addition to poor capacity, there is the issue of confidence in civilian officials. Military intelligence officers say that they do not share information with the police and prefer to operate on their own because the police cannot be trusted with sensitive information. Instead, they have demanded arrest powers for the ISI so that they can legally avoid relying on the police.[131]

Second, the so-called institutional approach is also seen as the panacea for fixing higher organizations of national defense. This not-so-new logic is forcefully expressed in the NDU's *National Strategy Paper, 2012*, written by midranking military officers and civilian officials under the supervision of a chief instructor of the rank of major general. According to this paper, civilian politicians and institutions lack the capability to lead and to anticipate threats; hence Pakistan requires institutionalized arrangements for defense policy management.[132]

Many other officers share the preference for the "institutional approach." One active-duty brigadier recommends that the government "consider revisiting the concept of the NSC, which could be modified into a truly functional body which might become a source of stability as all stakeholders would be on-board."[133] According to a retired major general, "The NSC is still needed for developing a broad consensus on all important national issues, as a hedge against military-civil conflict. While there is no constitutional provision for such a body, that does not eliminate its urgency."[134] As a brigadier writes in the section of the *Army Green Book 2011* dedicated to "hard core professional issues": "Modern leadership structures are not averse to inclusion of the military stream at the highest level of national decisionmaking forums." This is important because the country's "political leadership has not been able to develop as other streams [of leaderhip have]. . . . The reason for the short earnings of political leadership has been the absence within the present political framework of any institutionalised system of checks and balances."[135] This continued emphasis on the NSC to manage national security despite the PPP government's decision to abolish the NSC in 2009 attests to the resilience of institutional norms, which have survived the democratic transition without changing. To quote Adam Przeworski, removing the military from politics is not the same thing as "removing politics from the military."[136]

Complex Threat Environment

In 2011, General Kayani wrote:

> Pakistan is going through an unusually complex security situation for the last decade or so. The full spectrum of threat has caused us to re-visit and analyze our conception of response to the extent of reviewing the very connotation of national interest and the viability of strategy based thereupon. The convergence of hostile sub-national, regional and international interests threaten the country at a time when the security forces are locked in a defining struggle against terrorism. As the main repository of national security, therefore, the Army will have to bear the brunt and lead the national response options.[137]

In his statement, Kayani identified three overlapping threats to Pakistan's security: subnational, regional, and international interests. The army's threat calculus has traditionally focused on external threats from India and internal threats aided and abetted by India. For example, the Joint Strategic Directive of 2007, which is considered the fundamental text for the armed forces on defense policy, identifies India as the primary security threat and further identifies an indirect threat posed by extraregional forces (ERFs) (a euphemism for the United States) on Pakistan's western border.[138] As one major general articulated it in the *Pakistan Army Green Book 2008*, "Direct external threat primarily originates from India. Pakistan Armed Forces' credibility is directly linked to response to these threats. ERF may also exert itself against Pakistan in connivance with India."[139]

Even though the United States has fully committed to withdrawing its military troops from Afghanistan in 2014, military officers see ERFs as part of the United States' greater game plan to isolate and denuclearize Pakistan and support India as a counter to China, which would require a continued US presence with Indian cooperation.[140] Some officers believe that democracy in Pakistan can survive only if it stands up to this new challenge by mobilizing the people. Another way of countering the threat is to eliminate internal fault lines, such as "institutional turf wars," "overly personalized political discourse," and "inter-institution disharmony."[141] These specific fault lines refer primarily to the inability of civilians, especially the judiciary and the political leadership, to recognize the threat.

According to the 2007–2008 NDU National Strategy Paper, another core area of weakness is FATA. Officers see India's sponsorship of militants in FATA, along with the lack of an ethnically balanced (read compliant with Pakistani policies) government, as the primary causes of militancy and instability in the region.[142] Another factor contributing to unrest is that the United States may be seeking to create an autonomous region between Pakistan and Afghanistan comprising the Pashtun areas on both sides.[143] While the military has consistently upheld the status quo in FATA and sought to increase its legal and administrative powers since its deployment in the area, the Strategy Paper reveals a belated recognition amongst some officers that the people of FATA are alienated from the Pakistani state in part because the latter continues to administer the area with the draconian colonial-era Frontier Crimes Regulation (1901).[144] In this view, the writ of the state has also weakened in part because of militancy, although there is little acknowledgment that the army's peace deals with Taliban militants between 2004 and 2009 allowed them to consolidate their positions in North and South Waziristan. The authors of the National Security Strategy Paper 2007–2008 believe that the answer to both these presumed external machinations and domestic structural problems is internal political reforms, including amendments in the Frontier Crimes Regulation and ultimately the integration of FATA into the North-West Frontier Province, to mainstream the population and reduce their marginalization.[145]

Officers acknowledge the serious nature of the threat of militancy and terrorism, as well as the limits of military solutions to these problems, including the potentially deleterious effect of internal deployments on the army's preparedness for conventional fighting.[146] But many also believe that despite the success of military operations in some areas, intense foreign involvement means that these threats are likely to persist in the long term.[147] Ironically, the growth of militancy is also seen as linked to inadequate US troop levels on the Pakistan-Afghanistan border, which allows militants to find refuge in Pakistan, as well as American-Afghan connivance in harboring Taliban militants wanted by the army. But, in the officers' opinion, the Americans needlessly blame Pakistan for not doing enough to stop cross-border infiltration into Afghanistan.[148]

Many officers see this duplicity as indicative of broader US malicious intent, which is even more sharply revealed in the perceived US tilt toward India. In this view, one particular demonstration of the betrayal felt is the US civil nuclear agreement with India in violation of Non-Proliferation Treaty conditions, while similar opportunities are not provided to Pakistan,[149] thus upsetting the balance of power in South Asia.[150]

Others see a broader US plan to actively destabilize Pakistan. According to a major general, "All out efforts are in hand to create environments to disintegrate Pakistan" by fanning subnational conflict.[151] Hence the insurgency in Balochistan is viewed as inspired and organized by "foreign hands," who have allegedly organized the main insurgent group, the Balochistan Liberation Army on the pattern of the Irish Republic Army and the Sri Lankan Liberation Tigers of the Tamil Ealam as evidenced in the BLA's "headquarters/branches, recruitment/training centers and terrorist activities."[152] More specifically, the conflict in Balochistan is part of a US strategy to redraw Pakistan's boundaries by carving out an independent state in the area.[153] Such a docile independent Balochistan would apparently be much easier to control than a defiant Pakistan, so the United States could "attain control of the region for subsequent exploitation of Central Asian energy reserves, and the local mineral resources," while denying China access to the region.[154]

In this great game, the United States is not alone. Instead, it is seen as colluding with not just Pakistan's archenemy India, but also Afghanistan, Israel, and a host of nonstate actors, to weaken the writ of the army and to scare Pakistan with the ultimate aim of taking away its nuclear weapons.[155] According to the NDU's *National Strategy Paper, 2012*, this nexus is waging a systematic campaign to turn Pakistan's internal fault lines into major security vulnerabilities, not just because of nuclear weapons but also to undermine Pakistan's principled stand on Kashmir and the end game in Afghanistan. The analysis concludes that this new kind of nonkinetic war is being waged on different fronts, especially through the application of such means as diplomacy, economics, and information management. These include the use of aid and conditionality (for example, the Kerry-Lugar-Berman Bill), espionage through covert operatives and contractors like Raymond Davis, and effect-based operations such as the Osama bin Laden raid to challenge Pakistani sovereignty and weaken national resolve.[156] No less important, this alleged campaign involves perception management by shaping a global narrative about Pakistan as a terrorist hot spot, maligning the country (especially the army and the ISI) for playing a double game in Afghanistan, depicting it as an unreliable ally with a record of nuclear proliferation, branding the Kashmir freedom struggle as terrorism and linking Kashmiri militant groups like the Lashkare Tayyaba to global terrorism, and putting Pakistan in the same league as failed states.[157] Pakistani academics and journalists critical of the military are seen as part of this campaign, as Indian or American agents, to malign the armed forces at the behest of their patrons.

Particularly worrisome for the military is New Delhi's political and military involvement in Afghanistan, such as its training of the Afghan National Army under the Strategic Partnership Agreement signed by the two sides in October 2011. In the context of the American troop withdrawal from Afghanistan in 2014, Indian military involvement in that country is perceived as a sinister plan to knock the traditionally unthreatened western border off balance. The paper also reflects the broader belief in the military that Indian "intelligence centers disguised as consulates" along the Afghan border, and Zahidan in Iran, which indicate Iranian and Afghan collaboration with New Delhi, have given India the "opportunity for sponsoring militant activities inside Pakistan."[158] In this view, India is trying to "level the score of insurgency it is facing at the hands of Kashmiris," or else to compel Pakistan to "submit to its hegemonic designs" in the region.[159] Moreover, expressing an opinion shared by many officers, one major general believes that the likely future presence of Indian forces in Kandahar and Jalalabad would directly threaten the western border and thus strain existing defense capabilities by engaging Pakistan on two fronts.[160]

Given the multiplicity of perceived threats facing Pakistan and its material weaknesses, many officers reluctantly admit that Islamabad's traditional India policy—namely, unconditional support of the Kashmiri right of self-determination in line with UN resolutions—may not be yielding the desired dividends and needs to be carefully reevaluated. Hence some advocate giving dialogue a chance and approaching all issues with an open mind.[161] Several officers see dialogue with India as an opportunity to engage in the management of regional conflicts to enhance Pakistani security without compromising the basic stance on Kashmir.[162] Despite disagreement on the best way to proceed, there is a consensus that protecting the national interest on Kashmir will require negotiating from a position of strength that can be achieved only by putting Pakistan's internal house in order. In the meantime, deescalating post-Mumbai 2008 tensions with India over New Delhi's accusation that elements of the Pakistani state were involved in the planning of the attack, revitalizing the South Asian Association for Regional Cooperation, strengthening conflict-avoidance and other confidence-building measures, and committing to the bilateral composite dialogue will act as force multipliers.[163] In this view, the resulting breathing space would enable Pakistan to allocate greater resources and manpower to create internal cohesion, which is threatened by sectarian, religious, ethnic, and ideological cleavages combined with weak governance and socioeconomic disparities, and thus afford the internal strength needed to succeed.[164] But many other officers prefer a decidedly more aggressive approach given that the Indians are "true followers of Chanakya, who "advocates continuous hostility towards neighbors."[165] This includes the use of asymmetric jihad warfare in addition to diplomacy and conventional military means.[166] It seems that military-institutional policy has co-opted both approaches. As one major general put it, "We should give talking to India a chance, but retain all options, including sub-conventional warfare, to deal with India."[167]

However, the NDU's 2012 strategy paper warns that Pakistan must urgently take action against the multidimensional threats and their applications, including creating chaos aimed at changing state structures, or risk becoming a Libya or an Iraq.[168] It argues that Pakistan is ill equipped to fight this new threat because its traditional system of national security management, mainly the Defense Committee of the Cabinet and the parliamentary committees, is outdated and unable to formulate timely and coherent responses to evolving threats. Instead, what Pakistan needs is a "Comprehensive National Security Paradigm," implemented through "an efficient and well articulated National Security Management System." Given the "multiplicity in the control and management of institutions and policies" and the lack of proper planning and execution mechanisms in these institutions, the answer is a central umbrella structure that can "coordinate, synergize and develop the capacity for national security."[169]

Evidence that the high command wants senior officers to appreciate these threats is the fact that the 2012–2013 syllabus of the NDU's National Security and War Course has an entire module dedicated to nonkinetic warfare that is spread over forty-four contact hours, compared with just thirty hours for defense planning and nuclear studies. This module is dedicated to information warfare, developing nonkinetic capabilities, media management, and the role of nonkinetic means in the entire spectrum of conflict.[170]

This emerging national security narrative, steeped as it is in conspiracy and paranoia, sheds light on three issues that could complicate the task of democratization in Pakistan. First, the military's doubt about civilian capabilities and its cognizance of its mission as dealing with a full spectrum of threats rather than just answering external security threats by conventional means suggest that internal weaknesses, such as state fragility, ethnic conflict, and sectarian violence, could, in the eyes of the military, justify meddling in civilian affairs in order to foil enemy exploitation. Therefore, instead of allowing future civilian governments to set the direction of security policy and focusing on implementing it, the military will, in Kayani's words, seek to "take the lead and formulate national response options." Second, to borrow Frederick Nunn's description of the Chilean army, Pakistani "officers see no end to the need for the armed forces' talents and expertise to [be] put to domestic use."[171] Officers' belief in the legitimacy of their extensive roles means that they continue to regard themselves as superior to and more qualified than civilians in managing nonmilitary affairs. The combination of this self-image and the right circumstances could provoke one or another form of intervention. Third, the Pakistani military's policy of asymmetric warfare has pushed India to develop offensive military doctrines, and the Pakistani army will be motivated to upgrade and modernize its forces in response.[172] Hence Pakistan's military allocations are unlikely to be reduced in the short to medium term. Perceptions of security threats and high military budgets will ensure the military's disproportionate institutional influence in the state.

Military officers' interviews, training curricula, and research studies show that officers consider politically expansive professional roles to be fundamentally appropriate and conditionally accept formal subordination to civilian authorities as long as those authorities do not impinge on the army's corporate autonomy, privileges, and security missions. This tutelary professionalism is at once rooted in and rationalized by threat perceptions of India and its many alleged internal and external collaborators. This concern with the full spectrum of threats, combined with a formally inculcated belief in its role as the guardian of the national interest, leads the military to assess Pakistan's internal weaknesses as security vulnerabilities that necessitate a military response or role. Not surprisingly, the military's extrication from government has not meant its removal from politics. Although the military does not seem interested in direct rule, its noninterference in governmental affairs is likely to remain conditional on behavior by the elected government that does not undermine national security in the military's view.

To the extent that the military high command believes that tutelage is justified because civilian leaders cannot properly govern, or that it has the right to contest or veto civilian policy initiatives or decisions because civilians cannot be trusted with national security, or that it stands above the rule of law, given its special status as the sole repository of national wisdom and patriotism, these beliefs will continue to affect the quality of democracy independently of other factors. Although the military allowed the democratic transition to take place and has since stayed in the barracks for institutional, domestic, and external reasons, it continues to evade democratic accountability and enjoys institutional autonomy, unimpeded access to budgetary resources, and veto over national security policy. These restrictions on the exercise of democratic authority by the political leadership are fundamentally incompatible with the ultimate normative goal of democratic consolidation. In the past, such roadblocks have led to civil-military antagonisms or political crises, which reinforced the military's negative opinion of civilian capabilities and intentions. During such crises, tutelary beliefs became especially salient and, depending on the threat perceived by the military to the national interest, can provide a strong justification for a military solution to governmental or political problems, which may or may not lead to a direct seizure of power by the generals. As one officer explained, when "politicians have crossed the limits of political propriety," the army has a duty to "step in to temporize till such time as a new political order sets in to make a new beginning."[173]

CONCLUSION

This study began with the central paradox of the modern state, namely, who guards the guardians? It concludes with a related question: How shall we guard the guardians? This question has urgent significance in a new or transitional democracy like Pakistan. In view of the military's authoritarian inclinations, its availability as a potential alternative to democracy, and its monopoly over coercive resources, controlling this institution is one of the most difficult tasks confronting any democratically elected government in a post-authoritarian context.[1]

In Pakistan, the historically shaped combination of domestic and external factors—a strong perceived threat from India and weak national integration—defined the military's formative experience in the early years after independence and critically shaped its institutional propensity to exercise independent political power grossly disproportionate to its appropriate position in the state.

But as I argued in the Introduction, despite restrictive colonial legacies, such as severe ethnic imbalances in military recruitment, and the enormous administrative, political, and economic difficulties surrounding the birth of Pakistan, there was no inevitable reason for the country to embark on a decidedly authoritarian path with a dominant military. Certainly, colonial legacies decreased the founding Muslim League elite's room to maneuver. But a close examination of those early years also reveals that independence provided the earliest possible chance for major decisions and initiatives because political and institutional arrangements were still in relative flux and fundamental reforms were possible. However, Mohammad Ali Jinnah and his successors made fateful initial choices, such as the adoption of the viceregal political system and the establishment of Urdu as the sole national language in order to create a singular, hegemonic Muslim nation-state in a multiethnic society defined by its opposition to "Hindu" India. Such actions empowered a Janowitzian civil-military bureaucratic coalition vested in the status quo ante.[2] The foundering of nation-state building on the rocks of strong subnational identities, especially in East Pakistan, created further incentives for repressive centralization, which diminished provincial autonomy. That, in turn, alienated the Bengalis and other ethnic minorities in West Pakistan and thwarted the chances of the peaceful accommodation of sociopolitical differences through an early constitutional bargain.

The perceived insecurity vis-à-vis India led Pakistan's founding civilian elites to subordinate the needs of society to that of security, which fostered rapid military institutional development. Jinnah and his lieutenants, most familiar with the Westminster parliamentary form of government as well as the colonial tradition of an apolitical military, did not anticipate the military's involvement in politics and abdicated their right to control the military under conditions of imminent warfare. The government's decision to co-opt junior Pakistani military officers in violation of the military chain of command for the war in Kashmir (1947–1948) and military resentment over the civilian leadership's subsequent decision to seek a cease-fire with India sowed the seeds of military insubordination and rebellion. This was most vividly revealed in the 1951 Rawalpindi conspiracy, hatched by a group of officers led by then chief of general staff major general

Akbar Khan. At the time, the military institution remained outwardly loyal to the civilian government, but not for long.

The threat from India gave the army a distinct sense of its corporate identity as the only force standing between a hostile Hindu India and the Muslim homeland of Pakistan. However, geopolitical danger did not rally society around the national flag and direct the military away from politics, as expected by some scholars.[3] Instead, Pakistan's experience suggests that the level of prior national unity may condition the effect of external threats on domestic politics. Without a national consensus on the nation, it is much more difficult to achieve a consensus on who its real enemies are. While an external threat may lead to unity within the military institution, it can divide civilians.

Not all social or ethnic groups will perceive the threat as existential enough to accept the state's heavy investment in the military as legitimate. In Pakistan, the military's predominantly Punjabi composition worsened the Bengali sense of exclusion from and resentment against the state. And the more the state invested in an ethnically exclusive military at the expense of democratically inclusive political institutions, the more it undermined the prospects of forging national cohesion, or the "we" feeling that provides a necessary background condition for building a democracy.[4]

Because domestic extraction was insufficient to balance the threat from India, the military forged an alliance of convenience with the United States, which bolstered its fighting capability and self-assuredness. The military's relatively quicker institutional modernization sharpened the contrast between its professional success and the perceived failure of politicians to forge what the army considered a cohesive nation and stable institutions. The military was initially content with securing its corporate needs while playing second fiddle to the civilian viceregal executive. However, professionalization stimulated its interest in politics and motivated it to assume responsibility for directly governing the state in October 1958 to save it from "chaos" and "disruption." In other words, contra Samuel

Huntington, Pakistan's coup makers were "professional soldiers, the graduates of the military academies, whose life career was the army."[5]

Led by the military's first Pakistani commander in chief, Ayub Khan, who had inherited a strong scorn for politicians from colonial officials and developed an equally strong belief in the military's capacity to reconstruct Pakistan through a controlled democracy, officers, trained and socialized in an organization with strong pressures for conformity and assimilation, internalized the norm that military skills and solutions were applicable to sociopolitical problems that politicians neither had the capacity nor the willingness to resolve. The thirteen-year period of military rule, first under Ayub and then Yahya, that followed the coup cemented and ingrained in the officer corps this broad conception of military professionalism that included a role in governing or guiding the state.

The civil war between Bengalis and the army in East Pakistan and the army's catastrophic subsequent defeat in the 1971 war with India led to the collapse of General Yahya Khan's military junta. The divided and disgraced military institution extricated itself from power and handed over the reins of government to the Pakistan People's Party (PPP) under Zulfiqar Ali Bhutto. The military's political weakness created an opportunity to depoliticize the officer corps. The PPP government crafted a democratic constitution that formally subordinated the military to the federal government, placed clear limits on its domestic role, and outlawed military intervention in politics. It also reconfigured the military's higher command structure by formally reducing the stature of the service chiefs, fixing their tenures, and creating a Joint Staff. But these civilian constraints proved insufficient to tame the generals. When a postelection political crisis in 1977 led to street agitation by the opposition Pakistan National Alliance that turned violent, eroded the government's credibility, and involved the military in keeping public order, the generals under Chief of Army Staff Ziaul Haq carried out a coup.

Civilian institutional measures to keep the military at bay failed in part because military organizational choices are more decisively shaped by the extent to which the military believes in the legitimacy of democratic institutions, including the constitution. Presumptions of impunity reinforced by the absence of accountability for professional and political failures in 1971, entrenched military norms of guardianship, and the lack of a tradition of political subordination meant that military officers would see only a military coup as the most feasible resolution even though Bhutto and the Pakistan National Alliance were reportedly close to a deal. Interviews with officers and their writings show that they believed the crisis threatened the integrity of their institution, and by default, the integrity of Pakistan, by dragging the military into politics and asking it to shoot at unarmed civilians.

The military under General Ziaul Haq ruled Pakistan with an iron hand for eleven years. This government represented a new phase of military intervention in that Zia sought to gain legitimacy for his dictatorship by Islamizing political, economic, and judicial structures. No less important, the military sought to permanently restructure the political system to institutionalize its tutelage and keep civilian governments in line through the introduction of several reserve domains, such as the presidential prerogative to sack elected governments arbitrarily. While the Pakistan military had always perceived itself as the armed defender of the territorial borders of an imagined Muslim nation, Zia expanded the military's mission to the protection of its ideological frontiers.

Zia's dictatorship ended in 1988 after his death, which paved the way for a transition to electoral democracy. Lacking legitimacy, the military retreated to the barracks to preserve its public prestige. Hence its acceptance of democracy was tactical rather than the result of any commitment to democratic norms. Apart from jealously guarding its corporate autonomy, the military retained Zia-era reserve domains in the constitution, domestic politics, and national security policy that enabled it to exercise tight tutelage of government. These severe constraints on the democratically elected political leadership's authority sparked civil-military conflicts that confirmed the military's skepticism about the ability of politicians to govern efficiently and effectively. These conflicts ultimately prompted a shift in the attitudes of military officers (and many in civil society) from the considered appropriateness of the military's behind-the-scenes guardianship to governorship. In October 1999, the military executed yet another coup after then prime minister Nawaz Sharif tried to assert greater control over it, notably by firing army chief General Pervez Musharraf for initiating a military conflict with India. Musharraf's dictatorship, which remained in power for eight years, reinforced officers' beliefs in a politically expansive conception of professionalism that involved a direct military role in nation building on the grounds that civilian governments in the 1990s had reduced democracy to a sham, politicized the bureaucracy, and undermined the state's capacity. What many in the military saw as parliamentary democracy's inherent weaknesses, including the absence of "proper" checks and counterchecks on the authority of the prime minister, led the military government to reinstate reserve presidential coup powers and to establish a military-dominated National Security Council. The higher officer corps' professional socialization, spearheaded by the National Defence University, stressed an activist, governing role for the military during the Musharraf years as the only option for reconstructing the body politic to establish a "true" democracy defined by the so-called devolution of powers and good governance.

However, acknowledging the sticky nature of military interventionist attitudes should not be read as a counsel of despair. In fact, the arguments in defense of the military's expansive tutelary role are quite similar to those of authoritarian militaries in Latin America and East Asia. But experience from those regions also indicates that real changes in such attitudes are possible under the right circumstances, though perhaps not likely in the near term in Pakistan.[6] In fact, a more optimistic view would hold that Pakistan too may be departing from its long and tortuous authoritarian path. In 2007–2008, the military extricated itself from power in the face of antiregime protests that had deepened officers' anxieties about, and badly eroded, the institution's public standing and prestige. Since 2008, the generals have tolerated political democracy because direct military rule has been seen as antithetical to the military's image and interests. Not surprisingly, the military's retreat to the barracks has, once again, masked deeper authoritarian inclinations, including the right to veto the policies and initiatives of democratically elected governments. In almost pendulum-like fashion, it appears the military has gone from governorship back to guardianship. For instance, military behavior and public statements revealed that it had accepted political subordination only conditionally, and it continued to consider itself the ultimate definer and defender of national security. The military intervened to preserve its institutional autonomy, maintain control over national security, and resolve perceived political crises, typically of its own making, such as the March 2009 deadlock over the restoration of the Chaudhry-led court that Musharraf had sacked by employing the threat of force. During civil-military conflicts, the military mostly prevailed over the PPP leadership (for example, the deadlock over the sacked judges in 2009 or the memogate episode in 2011–2012), and the latter accepted the military's preferred outcomes to avoid losing power.

In May 2013, Pakistan reached the important democratic benchmark of the first transfer of power from one democratically elected government that completed its tenure to another. Constitutional reforms, including the Eighteenth Amendment, which eradicated the authoritarian legacy of presidential powers to dissolve the National Assembly and reflected a broad political consensus on the rules of the game, provided a firm basis for the completion of the transition, as did the mostly democratically loyal behavior of the two major parties, the PPP and the Pakistan Muslim League (Nawaz) (PML-N), despite their political differences.

The elections were relatively free and fair (although more so for right-of-center parties like the PML-N and the Pakistan Tehreeke Insaaf than for the PPP and the Awami National Party, whose election campaigns were marred by targeted violence because of their opposition to the Taliban). No less significant, the ruling party accepted its defeat, and the opposition PML-N was sworn into office, thus lifting Pakistan's curse of zero democratic alternation in power.

Although civilian governments will have to perform well to strengthen democracy, the long-term prospects of democratization will also hinge on whether the military will accept the process. The Pakistani army is unaccustomed to the norm of civilian supremacy and has yet to unconditionally consider democracy the only game in town. Democracy cannot be safe in the long run if the military continues to hold nondemocratic attitudes and beliefs. In a break from the Musharraf era, military professional training no longer instills the appropriateness of a direct governing role for the military. However, it continues to inculcate the norm among senior officers that the military has a broader professional vocation, including its role as the ultimate guardian of an expandable realm of national security pivoted on India and, to a lesser degree, Afghanistan. The military's policy of intervention in that country's internal affairs is either threatened, or perhaps legitimized, by the perceived US collusion with New Delhi and Kabul. Domestically, this self-image leads the military to make political judgments and pronouncements about the performance and integrity of democratically elected governments as security threats, a practice that is ill suited to the prospects of democratic deepening. Externally, the military continues to see merit in retaining the jihadi option despite the clear feedback effects of that policy in the form of violence and terrorism, including increased Sunni sectarian violence against minorities, especially the Shias.

Lessons from Old and New Democracies

Beyond its democratic necessity, subordinating Pakistan's armed forces to civilian authorities has important international security implications. According to a well-established statistical observation known as the democratic peace, two democratic states rarely wage war on each other, in part because those who are accountable to the electorate have to make costly decisions about war and peace.[7] It is reasonable to argue that South Asia might have experienced fewer interstate wars had Pakistan's military not exclusively controlled national security decision making and thus blocked feedback from

multiple civilian channels, including the foreign ministry.⁸ India
and Pakistan did fight each other in Kargil in 1999, even though
both had democratically elected governments.⁹ But the Kargil war is
not so much a repudiation of the democratic peace than a demonstration that democracy is more likely to act as a brake on militarized
conflict when civilian leaders and institutions have firm control over
the military. The Pakistan military was able and willing to initiate
the Kargil war precisely because it is autonomous of civilian oversight and believes civilians to be either incompetent or untrustworthy,
especially in sensitive matters of war and peace, which it considers to
be its sole prerogative. Hence several military officers in strategic
posts led by army chief Musharraf decided to ratchet up the ante in
Kashmir without much regard for its diplomatic and even military
fallout, including the possibility of a full-scale conventional attack
by India across the international border.

The military's institutional biases and beliefs also help explain
why it continues to nurture extremist militant groups like the Lashkare Tayyaba and the Haqqani network despite the disastrous consequences of this policy. The dangerous presence of both lethal terrorist
groups and atomic weapons on Pakistani territory has raised the catastrophic possibility that Pakistan could become the world's first
failed nuclear-armed state. But the military continues to believe that
the short-term costs of these policies are lower than their long-term
benefits in achieving Pakistan's security against India.

The basic purpose of democratic reforms of civil-military relations is to make, in Richard Kohn's words, "security subordinate
to the larger purposes of the nation, not the other way around."¹⁰
There is no magic bullet here for postauthoritarian contexts. In
South America, the democratic reform of the armed forces during the third wave worked in part because democratically elected
leaders consciously adopted a cautious approach so as not to antagonize the military too much. In Argentina, the Raul Alfonsin
administration's harsh budgetary cuts, trials of military personnel
for human rights violations committed during the "Dirty War,"

and legislation to extend civilian oversight sparked military rebellions in 1987, 1988, and 1990.[11] Similarly, in Egypt, President Morsi's direct challenges to the Supreme Council of the Armed Forces (SCAF) (including the reduction of military prerogatives in legislation and constitution making and the sacking of the defense minister and armed forces chief of staff in 2012) too seem to have backfired.[12] However, Pakistan's experience suggests that civilian governments' default strategy of sweeping the reform of civil-military relations under the carpet for political expediency and survival has hardly worked either. Vexing issues relating to the enforcement of civilian authority over the military inevitably resurface with a vengeance, often leading to civil-military crises in which the military prevails, thus undermining the authority and autonomy of elected governments.

Then how should they guard the guardians? The distinguished former Spanish defense minister and scholar Narcís Serra, who spearheaded successful democratic reforms in his country's armed forces after the *ruptura* (break or breach) of the late 1970s, has usefully outlined a comprehensive sequence of the processes by which a country's political leadership can reform the armed forces in postauthoritarian settings.

According to Serra, the process of reform can be divided into two phases: transition and consolidation. In the first phase, the primary task of democratizers is to reduce the military's capacity to intervene in politics and keep the democratic process functioning. The second phase involves consolidating democratic supremacy through strengthening the administrative capacity of the MoD, parliamentary oversight, the removal of prerogatives in nonmilitary spheres, and the redefinition of military missions and professionalism to make them compatible with democracy.[13] The example of Spain may not be directly replicable in Pakistan and other new democracies, given differences in historical and political contexts. While the timing and scope of the democratic reform of the armed forces may differ across different countries, Serra does offer useful lessons on managing what he calls the military transition.

Many of the reforms suggested in the pages below might seem to some as too ambitious or impractical in the case of Pakistan. But it is important to point to a set of policies, benchmarks, and goals of democratic control of the armed forces so that one can judge the achievements, the setbacks, and the required progress for attaining those goals in the future. Serra puts it quite clearly when he says "the fact that the criteria [for reforms] are beyond reach at a given time does not mean that they are unfair and that they must be redefined [or relaxed] so that some day they can be achieved. That is why it is essential to undertake a description of the whole process."[14]

Domestic Factors

MAKING DEMOCRACY WORK. To state the obvious, reforming civil-military relations is closely linked to the broader process of democratization. Only when that process moves forward does controlling the military become possible. Even then there are no fireproof guarantees that democracy or civilian control will not backslide, as the experience of Pakistan in the 1990s clearly shows. However, it must be readily admitted that progress in institutionalizing democratic institutions may also be contingent on military influence embedded in its interventionist attitudes.

Be that as it may, in the near to medium term, one of the necessary, if not sufficient, conditions for moving the democratic process forward and reducing the chances of military intervention is at least two peaceful turnovers of power following relatively free and fair elections. The first turnover is significant in a symbolic sense. Pakistan achieved it in May 2013. The second one shows that two major political leaders and parties are "sufficiently committed to democracy to surrender office and power after losing an election," and that when the people are dissatisfied, they change the leaders of a government, not democracy itself.[15] Pakistan must meet the test with another turnover.[16]

As the experience of other third-wave democracies shows, political armies can be restricted to the barracks when democratic institutions start to take hold. By lengthening the time horizons of

264

politicians, the certainty of electoral competition helped pave the way for democratically elected leaders to transform the institutions inherited from authoritarian rule in Indonesia, Turkey, Brazil, Argentina, and Chile. Elections do not equal democracy. But regular elections signify a vital shift in the rules of the game for political parties, the military, and civil society. When electoral competition becomes widely taken for granted in society, the costs of both conceiving and carrying out at least direct military interventions are likely to rise.[17] Besides, a generation of army officers who grow up and live under democratic regimes may be less inclined to view their professional skills as both superior to those of civilians and readily transferable to political and governmental affairs.

On the civilian front, the more united the politicians are on the basic rules of the game, the better the prospects of advancing democratization. The post-2008 constitutional reforms in Pakistan, most notably the Eighteenth Amendment, which eliminated significant authoritarian legacies, augur well for the prospects of sustained democratization. So does the evolving consensus among mainstream political parties to refrain from knocking on the military's doors, which would deprive the military of an oft-used rationalization for intervention in politics. However, politicians also need to keep democracy working to keep the military at bay.[18] The allegations of widespread corruption against the last PPP government and its perceived inability to improve the economic and social well-being of the people—constrained though it may have been by perverse legacies of the Musharraf era and resource shortages—put a question mark on its performance legitimacy. Pakistan also continues to face a number of crippling problems that could reinforce the pathologies of civil-military relations, including a faltering economy, a severe energy crisis, growing religious extremism, and continued terrorism, all of which could further dent public faith in the ability of democratically elected governments to provide basic public goods like security. Unfulfilled expectations can spiral into the politics of system blame, which can be exploited by the military. As hard as it may seem, performing governments supported by the public facilitate the reform of civil military relations by endowing "broad and un-questioned [performance] legitimacy" on democratic regimes.[19]

MINISTERIAL REGULATION. Strong institutions of supervision, primarily a civilian-controlled MoD, are widely considered by schol-ars and practitioners as the most effective way to ensure checks and balances on the military.[20] Admittedly, establishing civilian institu-tions with the capacity to regulate the defense establishment is a long-term project, more likely to be effective when democracy itself finds a more solid footing.

Regulatory institutions do exist on paper in Pakistan. However, because of repeated military interventions and a deep-seated tradi-tion of military tutelage of civilian government, these institutions have never had a real chance to develop. The MoD is formally re-sponsible for policy and administrative matters relating to the three armed forces.[21] This formal ministerial authority over the military is technically exercised through a defense minister, assisted by a fed-eral secretary who is the chief administrative and accounting officer of the ministry.[22] However, defense ministers have not wielded the political, administrative, or institutional authority to perform the key functions of a MoD, inter alia, to direct defense policy, define mili-tary missions, oversee budgets, and regulate personnel policy. Since the early 1950s, the prime minister has typically retained the defense portfolio. Prime Minister Nawaz Sharif has continued this tradi-tion, which allows the military direct access to the chief executive and enables it to assert autonomy from any ministerial supervision. In fact, even when appointed, the minister is generally kept out of the loop. According to a former defense minister, files pertaining to the military are dealt with by the secretary (typically, a retired lieutenant general) and returned to the army without ministerial input. The military considers the MoD as its administrative arm when, in principle, the military is an attached/subordinate depart-ment of the MoD.[23]

As pragmatic as it may be, the answer to ineffective defense ministers is not for the prime minister to concentrate defense matters in his or her own hands. Rather, it is to appoint an influential and competent politician to the post who enjoys the confidence of the prime minister and who interacts with the military establishment mainly through the minister and, when needed, through the Defence Committee of the Cabinet. While the military may find it hard to believe that such politicians exist in Pakistan, within the broader context of democratic governance, this would, at least in theory, help convince the generals that the minister derives his or her authority directly from the head of the government and is respected within the ruling party and the cabinet.[24]

Beyond the minister, the core of the MoD is its bureaucratic staff. As a general rule, senior bureaucratic positions in the MoD are also controlled by the military. The defense secretary is typically a retired lieutenant general, and active-duty military officers also occupy the next level of additional secretaries. The militarization of the MoD reflects not only the military's institutional assumption that civilian administrators do not have the requisite capacity to manage military affairs but also that they cannot be trusted with sensitive matters of national security.[25]

The demilitarization of the MoD would, at least technically, reduce the undue influence of military service headquarters on policy matters, such as arms acquisition and personnel management. The government has the authority to do this, and it would not require any legal or administrative changes. Civilian bureaucrats posted for fixed tenures, who should no doubt be under firm democratic control, can develop familiarity with military affairs and develop the institutional competence and capacity of the MoD.

DEMILITARIZING CIVILIAN ADMINISTRATION AND SECURITY FORCES. In Pakistan, successive periods of military rule have resulted in the systematic insertion of the military into civilian administrative posts. Democratically elected governments will sooner or later need to consider demilitarizing the civil bureaucracy as part of broader democratic reforms. This includes abolishing the Zia-era military quotas in the District Management Group, the Foreign Service, and the Police Service of Pakistan.[26] This prerogative not only is unfair to those civilians who have to undergo competitive examinations for entry into the civil service but also reinforces military officers' assumption that their military training and skills qualify them to perform civilian tasks.

An essential institutional condition for democratic civil-military relations is a "sharp organizational separation between internal and external violence forces."[27] In Latin America and Southern Europe, police forces were typically under the control of the military during the authoritarian period. Turning them into civilian organizations was a key part of the democratization process. Pakistan does not face that problem, as the police are a civil force. Since law and order is a provincial subject in Pakistan's 1973 constitution, Pakistan's police are under the control of provincial administrations. However, the Pakistani army has established institutional bases of power in paramilitary forces dealing with internal security, such as the Frontier Corps and the Rangers, which are essentially responsible for border protection, and are therefore outside the military's professional ambit of external combat. Like civil armed forces (mainly, the Central Police Organizations) in India, these forces fall under the authority of the Pakistani government's Ministry of Interior, the equivalent of the Indian Home Ministry. But in India, civil armed forces (such as the Indian Border Security Force and the Central Industrial Security Force) are usually headed by police officers and other civil servants ultimately accountable to the civilian political leadership. In Pakistan, they are officered by active-duty army personnel who are part of the regular military chain of command. This strategic prerogative over internal security provides the military with an additional layer of control over the domestic use of force that is outside the control of democratically elected leaders and prevents the development of civilian capacity for handling internal security, thereby reinforcing military assumptions about civilian incompetence. Pakistan's police are notoriously incompetent and corrupt, and civilian governments have been unwilling or incapable of wresting back internal security missions from the army and its paramilitary arms, as in Balochistan. But the answer to ineffective police forces is not to entrust the military with policing tasks. Instead, it is to reform the broader security sector, especially the police and other civilian law enforcement institutions, to make them compatible with democratic norms, including the respect for human security and citizens' rights.[28] Effective and accountable policing is also central to maintaining the rule of law, which is the sine qua non of democracy.[29] Besides, the literature on counterinsurgency shows that police forces are more successful than military ones in curbing insurgencies and terrorism. One reason is that the police have extensive on-the-ground presence, which gives them a distinct advantage in collecting intelligence on insurgents and terrorists hiding among civilian populations.[30]

The Taliban insurgency in Pakistan has in fact allowed the military to position itself as the principal agency for deciding "the quantum, composition and positioning of military efforts" against militancy.[31] With American assistance provided through the Pentagon's Counterinsurgency Capability Fund, the army-controlled paramilitary Frontier Corps has trained for counterinsurgency (COIN), including the ability to conduct "hold and build," which require civic action and community development skills. The army has been less accepting of American training for political reasons. However, it has introduced changes in the training of its officers at the PMA, the School of Infantry and Tactics, and the Command and Staff College to better prepare them for COIN, including "clearing operations," and law enforcement in conflict areas.[32] As discussed in Chapter 7, the NDU has also directed part of its training focus to dealing with low intensity conflict (LIC). Army units deployed in the FATAs (mainly South and North Waziristan) receive four weeks training in LIC.[33] This institutional focus on developing counterinsurgency capabilities is crucial for combating militancy in the northwestern tribal areas. However, because COIN inevitably involves developing nonmilitary skills, exclusive military control over internal security missions often encourages military role expansion, as the Latin American experience shows. All else equal, the more extensively and more autonomously the military manages internal security missions, the less likely it is to cede ground to civilians.

PARLIAMENTARY SCRUTINY. Parliamentary oversight of military budgets and defense policy is an established principle for exercising democratic control over the armed forces. In Pakistan, parliamentary standing committees on defense are technically empowered to examine the budgets, administration, and policies of the MoD and its associated departments, including the military.[34] But given the history of military dominance, military resistance to civilian control, and a strictly enforced tradition of official secrecy surrounding national security, the standing committees on defense exercise no more than token oversight of the military budget and focus instead on nonsensitive defense issues, such as civil aviation, defense housing, and military lands. Between 2008 and 2011, for instance, the Senate Committee on Defense and Defense Production spent most of its time reviewing the performance of the national carrier, Pakistan International Airlines, which fell under the administrative control of the MoD[35] until June 2013, when it was placed under a newly created aviation division by the PML-N government as part of reforms in the moribund aviation sector.

In the past, senior army officers typically avoided appearing before parliamentary committees. Instead, the army would assert its autonomy by holding briefings for parliamentarians at the general headquarters.[36] The US Special Forces raid in May 2011 in Abbottabad that killed Osama bin Laden badly tarnished the military institution's public reputation. Media criticism and parliamentary demands for accountability put the military under pressure and offered a rare opportunity to affirm civilian control, for instance, by holding the top military leadership accountable. However, the military deftly deflected responsibility by taking its case to parliament. Senior military officials, including the ISI's director general, Lieutenant General Ahmed

Shuja Pasha, and the deputy chief of the air force, appeared before a special joint parliamentary session in camera, thus affirming the principle that national security is too important to be discussed at regular parliamentary forums. Pasha admitted that the agency's failure to detect bin Laden's presence in Pakistan was an intelligence lapse. Nevertheless, he rallied parliament behind the military by blaming the United States for carrying out a sting operation on an ally.[37]

In contrast to the ineffective standing committees, Pakistani legislators have tried to reduce military prerogatives over the country's defense policy by creating a special Parliamentary Committee on National Security (PCNS) to provide them with guidelines and periodic reviews on important security policies, especially counterterrorism.[38] The committee set a good precedent when its chairman refused to attend a military briefing on foreign policy at army headquarters in October 2011 and publicly reminded the army that it is subservient to parliament, not vice versa.[39]

After a US helicopter attack on Salala, Mohmand Agency, killed twenty-four Pakistani soldiers in November 2011 and prompted Pakistan to bar NATO and US access to ground lines of communication linking Afghanistan to the Arabian Sea, the committee took a proactive stance in drafting new rules of engagement with the United States, recommending greater transparency in military dealings between the two states, the parliamentary approval of all foreign military agreements, an end to US drone strikes against al Qaeda and Taliban militants because of civilian casualties, and the denial of Pakistani territory to such militants. With minor changes, a joint sitting of the parliament approved these policies in March 2011.[40] The PPP government hailed the resolution as a significant victory in the struggle for parliamentary sovereignty over national security matters. The lines of communication were reopened in July 2012. However, none of the measures suggested in the parliamentary resolution became policy, which shows the continued weakness of institutional frameworks designed to exercise oversight of the military.

MILITARY INTELLIGENCE SECTOR. A key democratic challenge, especially during a transition from military authoritarian rule, is to transform state intelligence agencies from being tools of authoritarian regimes to organizations subordinate to democratically elected regimes. This often involves reducing military control and influence over nonmilitary intelligence gathering. Militaries with independent access to internal political information and the capacity and willingness to monitor and influence domestic politics are a new democracy's Achilles' heel. Pakistan's ISI and MI allow the military to do just that.

In third-wave democracies, civilianizing the intelligence organizations of authoritarian regimes was an arduous and uncertain process. The notorious Brazilian National Information Service (Serviço Nacional de Informações, or SNI) comes the closest to the ISI. Like the ISI, the SNI was both the top domestic and external agency with responsibility for internal security, special operations, and strategic intelligence. Much the same as the ISI, it also coordinated intelligence operations of the three armed forces. Still, it was not until 1999, a full fourteen years after the transition to democracy, that Henrique Cordoso, then president of Brazil, appointed a civilian to head the defense ministry and created the civilian-controlled Brazilian Intelligence Agency, or Agência Brasileira de Inteligência (ABIN). Only after the creation of this agency did democratically elected officials begin to assert a degree of control over intelligence functions.[41]

There are also some key differences between the ISI and the SNI (and other authoritarian intelligence organizations in South America). The SNI became relatively autonomous of the military hierarchy in the context of fighting armed leftist groups between 1968 and 1974. In the process, the military institution lost control over the intelligence sector, which posed a direct threat to military unity, split the authoritarian regime, and forced leaders of the military government to start a process of political liberalization by reaching out to civil society.

However, there is little if any evidence that the ISI has defied the overall direction and control of the high command despite its relative operational autonomy in the field. In fact, the ISI has long been the military's primary tool for securing its institutional interests in politics. The leaders of the PPP and the PML-N should know well, since they have been largely at the receiving end of both the ISI's and MI's machinations. In the 2006 Charter of Democracy, the leadership of the two parties categorically affirmed their commitment to reforming the military's intelligence apparatus, for instance, by placing the ISI under the control of the cabinet and ending its political interference.

Legal reform is the first step in that direction. Pakistan's intelligence sector operates in a legal vacuum, for there is no legislation governing their operations. For instance, the federal government has no authority over the ISI. As the Abbottabad Inquiry Commission report makes clear, the ISI has appropriated the functions of civilian law enforcement and intelligence agencies.[42] This is in part because there is no legal framework delineating its operational jurisdictions.

Former president Zardari made a positive, if short-lived, effort to introduce legislation for civilian control of the ISI in 2012. Introduced as a Private Member's bill by Farhatullah Babar, a senator and presidential spokesperson, the rationale behind the proposed Inter-Services Intelligence Agency (Functions, Powers and Regulation) Act of 2012 was that "the absence of appropriate legislation regulating functioning, duties, powers and responsibilities of the agency is not consistent with the principles of the natural justice and accountability of authority and power, and has given rise to resentment against the premier national agency." Significantly, the bill envisaged the creation of an "Intelligence and Security Committee" comprising nine members from both the National Assembly and the Senate for oversight of the expenditure, administration, and policies of the ISI. It also formally placed the agency under the control of the prime minister, who was "required to present a copy of the annual report of the committee before parliament together with a statement explaining the reason for the exclusion of sensitive matters." The bill recommended the appointment of an independent ombudsman to address the complaints of misuse of authority against ISI officials. However, the bill was quickly withdrawn without any explanation.[43]

Previous efforts to establish civilian control of the ISI have not met with much success. In 2009, the PPP government's decision to put the agency under the control of the Ministry of Interior clearly backfired. But that is no reason why the two major parties and other parties cannot work together in parliament to introduce legislation for the reform of the ISI. A lack of interest or resignation to the status quo, which usually passes in the name of policy, is unlikely to take the problem away.

After Pakistan joined the War on Terror in 2001, the ISI assumed the role of the lead intelligence agency responsible for counterterrorism, including the execution of joint operations with the CIA against al-Qaeda. The agency established a separate cell for counterterrorism and cooperation with the United States that evolved into a dedicated Counterterrorism Wing in 2007. Given the serious threat of terrorism and militancy in Pakistan, this would be a positive development had the ISI been a civilian agency under the control of the democratically elected leadership. But given that the ISI is controlled by the military, the more power and capacity it accumulates, the more likely it is that it would continue to marginalize civilian intelligence, such as the federal Intelligence Bureau, which is responsible for internal security, including counterterrorism.

The ISI and MI are also involved in suppressing the insurgency in Balochistan, where they have committed gross human rights violations. Both the PPP government and the present PML-N government have appeared helpless (or uninterested) in seriously addressing the issue of enforced disappearances and extrajudicial killings. The Abbottabad Inquiry Commission noted wryly that there is no accountability of the military's intelligence agencies for their repeated failures, which only reinforces military presumptions of impunity.[44] As discussed in Chapter 7, the Supreme Court has sought to hold the military's intelligence agencies accountable for illegal detentions, but has yet to take any concrete legal action against them.

CONTROLLING MILITARY APPOINTMENTS. Given that the army has largely remained outside civilian control, the main democratic instrument for exercising political authority over the military has been the prime minister's prerogative of appointing army chiefs from a list provided by the general headquarters.

Regardless, successive prime ministers have miscalculated by selecting officers to the post of chief of the army staff on the basis of their perceived political or ethnic affiliations and preferences. The main assumption behind such decisions appears to be that officers from ethnically underrepresented groups, such as an Urdu-speaking General Pervez Musharraf or a less influential Arain Punjabi migrant from India, General Ziaul Haq, will find it hard to plot against a civilian government because of their inability to forge and mobilize internal support networks. An army chief's social or ethnic background or personal political views are not inconsequential for the military's involvement in politics. But in any bureaucratic organization, where one stands depends primarily on where one sits. When the organization at hand is a disciplined army, focusing on individual officer characteristics detracts from the organizational drivers of military behavior. From the standpoint of military politics, it does not necessarily matter whether an officer is a Punjabi or a Muhajir, socially liberal or conservative, secular or Islamic, an infantryman or a gunner. The institution often matters more. Pakistan's past military rulers—Generals Ayub Khan, Yahya Khan, Zia, and Musharraf—were quite different from one another in their personalities, military careers, and social backgrounds. But when they subverted constitutions, stole elections, silenced dissidents, and, in Yahya's case, presided over horrific atrocities inflicted on Bengalis in East Pakistan, they were all acting in their capacity as chief of the army as an institution.

To succeed in establishing democratic control of the military's command structure, civilian politicians will need more than just executive discretion. In India, a special cabinet Appointments Committee approves senior military appointments at the level of army commanders. This procedure helps reduce any military concerns about the politicization of routine military matters. To lend democratic strength and legitimacy to civilian oversight of military appointments, the appointment of service chiefs should be delegated to the cabinet or a designated committee of the cabinet. In addition, parliament can constitute a special committee to vet and approve the appointment of the army chief of staff and the chiefs of the navy and the air force.

DEMOCRATIC RESOCIALIZATION OF THE ARMY. Ultimately, even when effective, civilian institutions and oversight can at best place constraints on the military. If Pakistan's history is any guide, these will not sufficiently determine whether the military will unconditionally obey civilian authorities. How the military interprets civilian reforms and whether it considers political subordination inherently legitimate are crucial ingredients in the success of civilian democratic regulation of the armed forces. In other words, the long-term success of democracy is intrinsically linked to changing the military's tutelary beliefs.

In consolidated democracies, citizens are socialized into democratic norms through civic education at an early age. In Pakistan, the education system can teach students the proper division of labor between the civilian and military arms of the state in a democracy, and stress the inviolable supremacy of the democratically elected leadership. Students can also be taught about clearly defined military missions and roles, such as external defense, aid to the civil power, and international peacekeeping operations.[45] It is clear that the democratic resocialization of the officer corps would require changes in military curricula to emphasize the study of democratic institutions and to instill respect for constitutionalism, including the inviolability of the military officers' oath of service, which prohibits any involvement in politics. As it is presently configured, the

National Defence University's training program pays virtually no serious attention to the proper role of the armed forces in a parliamentary democracy. Pakistani officers share a professional disdain for the politician's vocation and consider politicians incompetent and inferior to the men in military uniform, especially with regard to defense affairs. They are also socialized into the legitimacy of the military's politically broad professionalism, which includes their role as guardians of national security. In fact, the National Defence University considers itself the nation's foremost think tank.[46] In a blatant disregard for democratic norms, the ministry of defense, in fact, tasked the university with creating Pakistan's national security policy in 2011–2012.[47]

As Zoltan Barany rightly suggests, professional military education at each stage of an officer's career should clearly stress respect for democratic norms, and that the soldiers' only political role is their right to cast votes.[48] There is also a strong need for curriculum reform if the military is to abandon the jihadi enterprise. Attempts to reform military habits of the mind that have congealed in its institutional memory and practice are unlikely in the short to medium term because the Pakistan military considers its officers' training its own prerogative.

From Asia to Latin America, many militaries have learned that their political involvement came with high costs, and ultimately endangered and eroded their organizational discipline and effectiveness. However, such self-learning is less likely to happen in the absence of accountability for the military's professional and political lapses. Besides, most of these militaries did not operate in an external security environment matching that of Pakistan. The Pakistani military's privileged and virtually permanent security mission against India has traditionally shielded it from any meaningful accountability, as well as provided it with a high degree of organizational cohesion that facilitates its hierarchical interventions in politics. Thus the institutional costs of military involvement in politics have been relatively low in Pakistan. Changing the beliefs of the military about the appropriateness of its role as the ultimate custodian of national security, its relative superiority to civilians, and its entrenched presumptions of impunity will require at the least a reckoning with the past. The Pakistan military has never had to accept responsibility for its past actions. The PML-N government in November 2013 initiated treason charges against General Musharraf (who returned to Pakistan to contest the May 2013 elections) in response to a Supreme Court injunction. If it is able to prosecute and punish Musharraf for his crimes against the constitution (even if they are restricted to the November 3, 2007, Emergency, as is the case), it could set a positive precedent to help deter military interventions in the future. However, the principle of accountability will remain less effective unless it is applied to the military as an institution. The most significant thing that the government could do to achieve that goal is to establish a high-powered committee to conduct an inquiry into the Kargil war (as Sharif has often pledged), publish its findings, and bring the culprits to justice. There are no indications, however, that the government is seriously contemplating such an action.

ALTERNATIVE POWER. Alternative centers of power and persuasion, including the judiciary and the media, can be critical to puncturing the military's presumptions of impunity. When judges and journalists unequivocally back the democratically elected authorities in consolidating their political gains, especially in relation to the military, they can act as significant defenders of civilian supremacy.

Although the military retains its ultimate capability to use coercion, protecting its interests in a posttransitional context defined by a broad consensus in political and civil society about the continuation of democracy and the emergence of these new poles of power requires a strategic adjustment. So far, the military has rather successfully responded to these evolving civil-military dynamics by co-opting journalists and judges to varying degrees.

The military's ability to exercise inappropriate influence over politics is linked to its ability to shape a dominant national security narrative, which has become all the more important since the proliferation of private television news channels in the past decade. The military takes the adage "Information is power" quite seriously. Apart from manipulating the media, the military (or more precisely, the ISI acting on behalf of the high command) tries to ensure its monopoly over the public discourse on national security by supporting select defense think tanks, intimidating independent-minded scholars, and providing resources and privileged information to sponsored experts. Despite the personal and professional costs of dissent, many individual academics and journalists have challenged the military's lopsided national security narrative through both the popular media and scholarship. Beyond individual initiative, Pakistan's political parties, media, and civil society organizations will have to seriously consider building expertise on defense-related issues so that they can parry the military's well-known argument that civilians have neither the capacity nor the intellect to understand and preserve national security.[49] This is easier said than done given the military's information monopoly in national security matters. Hence, side by side with gradually enhancing civilian capabilities in defense matters, there is a strong need to clip the wings of Inter-Services Public Relations by bringing it under the control of a reformed MoD. This is important if the military is to be deprived of autonomy in its manipulation of public opinion, the dissemination of institutional propaganda as well as its institutional ability to talk back to other institutions of the state.

The 2007 movement for the restoration of the judiciary, which turned into a movement for the removal of Musharraf's military government, has had the unintended effect of broadly delegitimizing direct military rule as a solution to Pakistan's political and economic problems. The military's successive professional failures, including its inability to protect strategic military installations, have fostered rare public and media scrutiny of its professional performance. The anti-Musharraf movement also endowed the judiciary with unprecedented moral and legal authority. The Supreme Court has pledged not to derail the political system or provide legal cover for military interventions in the future. It has also vigorously questioned the military's intelligence agencies about their illegal detention of terror suspects and Baloch nationalists. But even when the military has stalled and defied court orders, the judges have so far exercised restraint and treated the high command with deference. In contrast, the Chaudhry-led court zealously interfered in executive functions and doggedly pursued decades-old corruption cases against the PPP leadership, including President Asif Ali Zardari. This apparent bias brought the judiciary's fairness into question, weakened the PPP government, and provided the military a respite from any serious legal scrutiny. In July 2012, the court removed Prime Minister Gillani from office by declaring him ineligible to hold office because of contempt charges arising from his refusal to request that Swiss authorities reopen an old graft case against President Zardari. This thinly veiled "judicial coup" gave legal sanction to yet another nondemocratic route to regime change.[50] With regard to government-military relations, the Supreme Court's hasty inquiry into the 2011–2012 memogate controversy at the behest of the army chief and its tolerance of the high command's regular contempt in the missing persons' cases demonstrate that the judges accept the military's national security perspectives and prerogatives as appropriate or at least broadly inviolable.

External Factors

PAKISTAN AND THE UNITED STATES. There is no consensus in the democratization literature on the impact of external influences on civilian control of the military.[51] The European Union has generally exerted a strong democratic effect on its members, and even candidate countries such as Turkey, helping to consolidate democracy by strict conditionality requiring the diminution of military autonomy and prerogatives in civilian governance. The US record on democracy promotion is decidedly mixed. The net democratic effect of US policy appears to be negative. From Asia to the Middle East and Latin America, it has aided and abetted some of the most egregious military dictatorships for its own strategic interests, especially during the Cold War, and even in post-Mubarak Egypt.

The impact of decades of US policies toward Pakistan has been corrosive for democratization and civilian supremacy. As in other countries where it had security interests, the United States has typically set aside concerns about human rights and democracy in favor of short-term strategic goals in Pakistan and has shielded successive allied military governments from the diplomatic, financial, and political costs associated with overthrowing constitutional governments. The war on terror is only the most recent reprise of this military-centered US engagement in Pakistan. By aiding and relying covertly and exclusively on the military and the ISI to disrupt and dismantle al-Qaeda, Washington has reinforced the military's control over national security, beefed up its sense of geostrategic importance and impunity, and contributed to the process of military displacement of civilian intelligence and law-enforcement functions.

The Obama administration belatedly recognized the counterproductive effects on US policy of American reliance on the army general headquarters when it enacted the Enhanced Partnership with Pakistan Act in 2009. This act linked the continuation of US security assistance to antiterrorism cooperation and military abstinence from interference in the democratic process. However, the United States has since undermined the efficacy of its conditionality. For instance, despite claiming to have clear evidence of ISI collusion with the Haqqani network, the Obama administration certified to Congress in August 2012 that Pakistan fulfilled conditionality with respect to counterterrorism.[52]

As the US State Department's 2010 regional strategy for "Af-Pak" makes clear,[53] the primary goal of American foreign policy remains the stabilization of nuclear-armed Pakistan rather than its democratization.[54] And if the Obama administration's virtual silence on the Egyptian military's cold and calculated slaughter of Islamist supporters of ousted President Mohammad Morsi is any indication, US strategic interests will continue to trump its rhetorical commitment to democratization in the Muslim world. Secretary of State John Kerry's remark on Pakistan's Geo TV after the Egyptian coup of July 2013 that the army was "restoring democracy" says it all.[55] The statement was all the more surprising for many Pakistanis since Kerry was an ardent supporter of democracy in their country when he was a senator and one of the sponsors of the Enhanced Partnership Act. The bottom line is that given its primary interest in a safe exit from Afghanistan and counterterrorism, the United States is likely to continue to work through the army in Pakistan in the foreseeable future. In fact, Kerry held direct meetings with General Kayani in April 2013 to revive stalled talks with the Taliban in Afghanistan.[56] This may reflect Washington's need to pursue its interests by dealing with the reality of the army's control over Pakistan's national security policies, but it directly contributes to the marginalization of the country's civilian leadership.

As difficult as it might be to conceive of a long-term US engagement with Pakistan, given the increasing divergence in their mutual perceptions, goals, and interests in the region, Islamic extremists are less likely to find easy sanctuary in a globally integrated, democratic, and prosperous Pakistan. Moreover, the stronger Pakistan's civilian governments and institutions become, the less room the Pakistani military and the ISI will have to foster extremism in order to execute national security policies that endanger regional and international security. If the United States desires to see a democratic Pakistan, as almost every American administration claims, Washington should provide Pakistanis with more economic and trade-related opportunities and help strengthen Pakistan's civilian political institutions by meaningfully engaging them rather than ignoring them at the altar of strategic expediency.

EXTERNAL SHOCKS. External shocks, such as a defeat in war, can help disrupt rigid military institutional attitudes and behavior. Failure on the battlefield can shatter military unity and challenge institutional assumptions about the legitimacy of military government. A well-known example is Argentina's military defeat in the 1982

Malvinas/Falklands War with Britain. That particular humiliation, combined with the junta's economic failures and human rights violations, fragmented the officer corps by exposing the fundamental contradiction between ruling and fighting and thereby opened the door for the eventual depoliticization of the military.[57]

The Pakistani military's defeat in the 1971 Bangladesh war with India did induce splits in the officer corps, primarily between the military government and midranking and junior officers who ascribed military failure to the corruption and malfeasance of junta leaders. However, the 1971 shock did not signify the end of military political meddling and interventions because it did not alter and may even have reinforced and enhanced military threat perceptions of a hostile India. Because the Kashmir conflict, which is the primary justification for the military's influence in the state, as well as an important source of its organizational coherence, survived the generals' disgraceful surrender at Dhaka, the military quickly recovered from internal organizational problems to stage an institutional coup in 1977, ostensibly in response to the political crisis created by an allegedly stolen election.

Whether another defeat in war will permanently dissuade and detach the military from politics is unclear. In any case, the nuclearization of the India-Pakistan rivalry makes war too catastrophic even to contemplate. In fact, wars like the 1999 conflict over the Kargil sector of Kashmir may create civil-military conflicts which are conducive for military intervention. Besides, defeat on the battlefield could still have the opposite effect of increasing military organizational unity as a hedge against public accountability and civilian interference in its corporate affairs.

In sum, the Argentine model might be less useful for Pakistan. In fact, most other countries (for example, Indonesia, Thailand, Chile, and Brazil) that experienced successful transitions from military governments during or after the third wave did not face a threatening external environment. For instance, in addition to changed US policy, one thing working in favor of democracy in Brazil after the transition in 1985 was that the country faced no internal enemy and zero external threat, which helped democratically elected governments slowly but surely wean off the military and intelligence from politics and reduce their prerogatives. Even then it was a long, arduous, and uncertain process. In addition to changed US policy, a more viable path to achieve civilian supremacy in Pakistan would entail a lasting resolution of the enduring Kashmir conflict, largely sustained by the military despite a broad political consensus on peace with India. Although the end of the territorial rivalry with India might not be sufficient to depoliticize the military, it would help reorient the geo-strategic priorities of the state and thus deprive the military of its paramount role in determining state policies. Despite increased tensions along the Line of Control in Kashmir in July and August, Prime Minister Sharif, who has long been committed to regional conflict reduction, called for a bold foreign policy review in August 2013 focused on Pakistan's eastern neighbor, as a way of freeing up resources for economic development.[58] If the past is any guide, it seems unlikely that the government can succeed in actually brokering a meaningful peace with India without the blessings of the military. Finance Minister Ishaq Dar's categorical statement that the government had no immediate plan to grant India most-favored-nation status indicates that appearing tough on national security to appease vested domestic audiences is likely to trump economic considerations in the foreseeable future.[59]

The military's prominent and long-lasting role in politics has dealt major blows to the process of democratization in Pakistan. The military has either directly intervened to overthrow governments or has limited the authority and autonomy of elected governments. Military coups and rule have deepened the country's structural problems—from weak state capacity to economic underdevelopment—by preventing solutions through the political process. In other words, the military has repeatedly intervened to arrest the normal development of Pakistan's democracy. Until 2013, Pakistan seemed stuck in a permanent authoritarian trap, briefly interrupted by formally elected governments. The first democratic transfer of power in May 2013 could well hold the key to a more democratic future. Although the challenges, including a domineering military and resource constraints, are many and complex, democracy might have a better chance of consolidation if elected governments can deliver on public expectations, solidly move toward resolving Pakistan's urgent problems, and, together with the opposition, respect democratic and constitutional norms in both rhetoric and practice. In this way they can continue to maintain both democratic and performance legitimacy and thereby deny the military the opportunity to exploit political divisions and assume responsibility for the direct or indirect conduct of civilian affairs.

Since assuming power in June 2013, the Sharif government has formally sought to exercise greater control over the nature and scope of national security policy. However, its rhetoric of civilian supremacy is only matched by its pragmatic accommodation of military demands and interests. In 1998, Sharif had fired Army Chief of Staff General Jehangir Karamat for advocating the military's institutionalized participation in government through a National Security Council. Yet in August 2013, that is precisely what the PML-N government did when it reconstituted the Defence Committee of the Cabinet[60] into the Cabinet Committee on National Security (CCNS), which is little more than an unreconstructed National Security Council. The CCNS has a much broader ambit, ostensibly to facilitate civil-military coordination in light of Pakistan's complex internal and external security environment. According to an official press release, the committee "will formulate a national security policy that will become the guiding framework for its subsidiary policies—defence policy, foreign policy, internal security policy, and other policies affecting national security."[61]

Although creating a formal national security apparatus is the norm in many democratic states, including the United States and India, the composition of the CCNS puts its democratic credentials in question. Chaired by the prime minister, it will include the ministers of foreign affairs, defense, interior, and finance. But unlike the Defence Committee of the Cabinet to which the military chiefs were invited when needed, the CCNS will have the chairman joint chiefs and the three service chiefs as permanent members.

Sharif's advisor on national security and foreign affairs, Sartaj Aziz, the principal civilian architect of the new committee, suggests that this formal integration of the military into national defense policy making will help enhance coordination and reduce misperceptions between the civilians and the military.[62] In reality, though, Sharif's government has fulfilled the military's long-standing desire to formalize its de facto dominance in national security affairs by making the military service chiefs members of a committee of the cabinet.

It is too early to say with any degree of certainty whether this new formalized pattern of civil-military interaction will lastingly impair the democratization process. But it could be reasonably speculated that Pakistan might be heading toward a new civil-military arrangement in which civilian supremacy becomes a euphemism for the military's formal and active participation in matters of war and peace. In other words, this would constitute a situation in which the military does not seize direct power but formally insinuates its nondemocratic privileges into the functioning of democracy.

The limits a guardian military can place on the autonomy and authority of elected governments extend beyond Pakistan. Despite the erosion of military political power and prerogatives from southern Europe to South America, the military's role in shaping the nature and direction of democratic transitions has become crucial once again as militarized authoritarian regimes have either liberalized (Burma in 2012) or collapsed and then rebounded (Egypt in 2011–2013). Similarly, militaries that enjoy vast political and institutional privileges in civilian-controlled authoritarian governments, such as in Iran and China, will likely play significant roles in potential future transitions.

The Egyptian coup of July 2013 testified to the fact that the phenomenon of military intervention in politics is far from over, even though its global frequency may have declined drastically since the end of the Cold War. The Egyptian military's rationalization of the coup sounded eerily familiar to the postcoup pronouncements of militaries in Pakistan and elsewhere that their intervention was a response to the aspirations of the people, was intended to be temporary, and was designed to restore genuine democracy, and that the army will stay out of politics. Pakistan's experience is instructive in part because it reinforces the harsh lesson from other regions that militaries unaccustomed to the norm of civilian control can constrain, and when needed displace, new democratic regimes even when they formally accept a subordinate role. However, studying military professional beliefs and the concrete ways in which the military influences civil-military relations in Pakistan can be instructive about the institutional choices, norms, and rules needed to overcome their influence in other contexts. There are no strict timelines or end states here. And some of the reforms outlined in this chapter may even look far-fetched given the current state of politics in militarized regimes like Egypt. But laying out benchmarks for democratizing civil-military relations can be illustrative of both the reform challenges and opportunities for countries stuck in the gray zone between autocracy and full democracy, especially when the opportunity and circumstances permit movement in the direction of a meaningful democratic transition.

NOTES

1. There are other exceptions as well, including single-party regimes in China, North Korea, and Cuba and the less easily classified authoritarian regime in Iran. These regimes exhibit varying degrees of military involvement in government. But in none of them does the military institution intervene in politics or control the government. Instead, soldiers are subordinate to the civilian party leadership.

2. Larry Diamond, "Is Pakistan the (Reverse) Wave of the Future?," *Journal of Democracy* 11, no. 3 (2000): 91–106.

3. Throughout this book, I use the terms "army" and "military" interchangeably except when making distinctions between the army and the two other armed forces, the air force and the navy, is necessary.

4. Initial conditions, events, and policy choices can create enduring political power relations, institutions, and norms by setting in motion processes that increase the likelihood of their continuity, either by socializing important social and political actors to certain roles or by creating interests vested in their continued existence. Social scientists call this phenomenon "path dependence," a historical process in which, according to Paul David, "one damn thing follows another." See Paul David, "Clio and the Economics of QWERTY," *American Economic Review* 75, no. 2 (May 1985): 332–337. See also Stephen D. Krasner, "Approaches to the State: Alternative Conceptions and Historical Dynamics," *Comparative Politics* 16, no. 2 (January 1984): 223–246; Paul Pierson, "Increasing Returns, Path Dependence and the Study of Politics," *American Political Science Review* 98, no. 4 (2000): 251–267; Kathleen Thelen, "Historical Institutionalism in Comparative Politics," *Annual Review*

of Political Science 2 (1999): 369–404; and James Mahoney, "Path Dependence in Historical Sociology," *Theory and Society* 29, no. 4 (August 2000): 507–548.

5. There is a convergence in the scholarship on Pakistan on the role of the security threat from India as one of the primary drivers of early military dominance in Pakistan. See, for instance, Ayesha Jalal, *The State of Martial Rule: The Political Economy of Defense in Pakistan* (New York: Cambridge University Press, 1991), 43–51; Hasan-Askari Rizvi, *The Military and Politics in Pakistan, 1947–1997* (Lahore: Sang-e-Meel, 2000), 5–8, 54–56; Keith Callard, *Pakistan: A Political Study* (London: Allen and Unwin, 1957), 15–18; and Wayne Ayres Wilcox, "The Pakistan Coup d'Etat of 1958," *Pacific Affairs* 38, no. 2 (1965): 145–147.

6. On the failure of nation building in Pakistan with particular reference to East Pakistan, see Rounaq Jahan's seminal study, *Pakistan: Failure in National Integration* (New York: Columbia University Press, 1972). A thoughtful interpretive work on Pakistan's national identity problems in relation to Islam is Farzana Sheikh, *Making Sense of Pakistan* (New York: Columbia University Press, 2009). However, Sheikh underplays the role of the geopolitical imperative of balancing India that shaped the Pakistani state's identity, interests, and behavior, and arguably exacerbated its identity deficit. See also Yunas Samad, *A Nation in Turmoil: Nationalism and Ethnicity in Pakistan, 1937–1958* (New Delhi: Sage, 1995); Adeel Khan, *Politics of Identity: Ethnic Nationalism and the State in Pakistan* (New Delhi: Sage, 2005).

7. For instance, Hamza Alavi has argued that postcolonial societies in South Asia inherited an overdeveloped bureaucratic-military structure from the British that subdued and prevailed over indigenous social classes. See Hamza Alavi, "The State in Post-colonial Societies: Pakistan and Bangladesh," *New Left Review* 74 (1972): 61. See also Alavi, "The Military and Bureaucracy in Pakistan," *International Socialist Journal* 3, no. 14 (1966): 149–188. See also Ishtiaq Ahmed, *Pakistan: The Garrison State: Origins, Evolution and Consequences* (Karachi: Oxford University Press, 2012), which makes a valuable contribution to the literature on civil-military relations in Pakistan by wedding Alavi's "postcolonial" state with Harold Lasswell's concept of the "garrison state." See Lasswell, "The Garrison State," *American Journal of Sociology* 46, no. 4 (January 1941): 455–468. Lasswell had predicted the role expansion of the armed forces in industrialized democracies by virtue of the contingent mixing of modern technology and the pervasive fear of war. However, by tying up the emergence of the garrison state with Alavi's struc-

tural determinism, Ahmed underplays the significance of the formative decade of independence in shaping Pakistan's political development.

8. Just as Pakistan was not preordained to become an autocracy, the
emergence and consolidation of democracy in India was far from inevitable.
As Sunil Khilnani notes, at independence "the circumstances were ones of
uncertainty and crisis . . . it was far from inevitable that the Indian state
would emerge from this flux as a parliamentary democracy." See Khilnani,
The Idea of India (New York: Farrar, Straus and Giroux, 1999), 29. See also
Ram Chandra Guha, *India after Gandhi: The History of the World's Largest
Democracy* (New York: HarperCollins, 2007), 137–144; and Ashutosh Varshney, "Why Democracy Survives in India," *Journal of Democracy* 9, no. 3
(1998): 36–50.

9. Ayesha Jalal, Philip Oldenburg, and others have argued that India
inherited the colonial state, its seat of government, its international per-
sona, and a more experienced civil service. This administrative continuity
made the transition to independence relatively smoother for India than for
Pakistan, which inherited little in the way of infrastructure or personnel,
and had to create everything from scratch. Jalal, *Democracy and Authoritarianism in South Asia* (Lahore: Sang-e-Meel, 1995), 18. Oldenburg, *India,
Pakistan, and Democracy: Solving the Puzzle of Divergent Paths* (London:
Routledge, 2010), 18–20, 36. Surely the different structural inheritances of
the two states contributed to their postindependence trajectories. But colonial legacy arguments in general, and the administrative continuity the-
sis in particular, emphasize structure. Nonstructural factors, including
agency and contingency, also matter in political development. A close look
at the official correspondence, files, and decisions of the Pakistani government in the archives shows that by 1948–1949 Pakistan had a functioning
central state apparatus. And even if Pakistan had inherited a ready-made
governmental structure, it is not clear how its civil-military relations would
have been radically different. For instance, the war in Kashmir in 1947,
which created the opening for military influence in national politics, had
relatively little to do with the absence of a strong state and more to do with
nationalism, especially the founding nationalist elite's desire to cement
Pakistan's "Muslim" identity by incorporating Kashmir. Pakistan's bifur-
cated geography notwithstanding, India was also much larger in terms of
its population and size, which means that even if it inherited a relatively
more organized or experienced administration, the sheer scale and scope
of administering India at least partly offset the relative advantage of structural continuity.

10. Sudipta Kaviraj, "A Critique of the Passive Revolution," in *State and Politics in India*, ed. Partha Chatterjee (New Delhi: Oxford University Press, 1997), 56.

11. The most compelling historical work on the early militarization of the Pakistani state is Jalal, *State of Martial Rule*. Throughout the book, I generally follow Andrew L. Ross in using the word "militarization" to mean increases in military size, spending, and armaments, which tend to increase both the military's demands on society and its political influence. But when used in the context of civilian politics or administration, "militarization" is meant to indicate the involvement of military personnel in these areas. See Ross, "Dimensions of Militarization in the Third World," *Armed Forces and Society* 13, no. 4 (1987): 561–578.

12. The concept of viceregalism is elaborated in Khalid Bin Sayeed's magisterial work *Pakistan: The Formative Phase* (London: Oxford University Press, 1968), 259–260, 279–300. For a moticulous account of the viceregal executive's role in undermining the prospects of constitutional democracy in Pakistan in the early 1950s, see Allen McGrath, *The Destruction of Pakistan's Democracy* (Karachi: Oxford University Press, 1996).

13. Donald Horowitz, *Coup Theories and Officers' Motives: Sri Lanka in Comparative Perspective* (Princeton, NJ: Princeton University Press, 1980), 160. See also Iftikhar H. Malik, *State and Civil Society in Pakistan: Politics of Authority, Ideology, and Ethnicity* (London: Macmillan, 1997), 60–61.

14. Stephen P. Cohen, "Arms and Politics in India, Pakistan and Bangladesh" (Special Studies no. 49, Council on International Studies, State University of New York, 1974), 16.

15. Guillermo O'Donnell, "Modernization and Military Coups: Theory, Comparisons, and the Argentine Case," in *Armies and Politics in Latin America*, ed. Abraham F. Lowenthal and J. Samuel Fitch (New York: Holmes and Meier, 1986), 102–106.

16. Huntington called this "objective civilian control" in contrast to "subjective civilian control," where civilian groups try to "civilianize" the military by involving it in institutional, class, or constitutional politics to maximize their power. Hence, for Huntington, military professionalism is, by definition, the antithesis of subjective control or military participation in politics. See Huntington's classic study *The Soldier and the State: The Theory and Politics of Civil-Military Relations* (Cambridge, MA: Belknap Press of Harvard University Press, 1957), esp. 80–86.

17. Samuel E. Finer, *The Man on Horseback: The Role of the Military in Politics*, 5th ed. (London: Transaction Press, 2002), 24–26, 32–36. The profes-

sionalization of militaries in South American states in the 1960s and 1970s similarly facilitated their political intrusions. See, for instance, Alfred Stepan, "The New Professionalism of Internal Warfare and Role Expansion," in *Arguing Comparative Politics* (New York: Oxford University Press, 2001), 23–38. Military professionalism has also served to enhance the military's overt and behind-the-scenes political influence in several Middle Eastern states. See Mehran Kamrava, "Military Professionalization and Civil-Military Relations in the Middle East," *Political Science Quarterly* 115, no. 1 (Spring 2000): 67–92.

18. See, for instance, Memo of Conversation between General Ayub Khan, Commander in Chief, Pakistan Army, and Charles D. Withers, First Secretary, American Embassy, Foreign Service Dispatch no. 851, February 28, 1953, http://www.icdc.com/~paulwolf/pakistan/ayub28feb1953.htm (accessed May 6, 2009).

19. "General Ayub Khan's First Broadcast to the Nation," October 8, 1958, in Rizvi, *Military and Politics*, 292–293. The martial law was actually proclaimed by then-president Iskander Mirza, who appointed Ayub Khan as the chief martial law administrator. But the army deposed Mirza in less than a month. For details, see Chapter 2.

20. Wilcox, "Pakistan Coup d'Etat," 142.

21. Zoltan Barany, *The Soldier and the Changing State: Building Democratic Armies in Africa, Asia, Europe, and the Americas* (Princeton, NJ: Princeton University Press, 2012), 25–26.

22. Terry Moe, "Political Institutions: The Neglected Side of the Story," special issue, *Journal of Law, Economics, and Organization* 6 (1990): 213–214.

23. Martha Finnemore, *National Interests in International Society* (Ithaca, NY: Cornell University Press, 1996), 22.

24. James G. March and Johan P. Olsen, *Rediscovering Institutions: The Organizational Basis of Politics* (New York: Free Press, 1989), 21; March and Olsen, "The New Institutionalism: Organizational Factors in Political Life," *American Political Science Review* 78 (1985): 734–749.

25. A total institution is a "place of residence and work where a large number of like-situated individuals, cut off from the wider society for an appreciable period of time, together lead an enclosed, formally administered round of life." In such a context, behavior is regulated, predictable, and repeated, and designated roles and functions are institutionalized. See Erving Goffman, *Asylums: Essays on the Social Situation of Mental Patients and Other Inmates* (Anchor Books, 1961), 11.

26. Morris Janowitz, *Military Institutions and Coercion in the Developing Nations* (Chicago: University of Chicago Press, 1977), 146.

27. Created for the specialized management of violence under highly unpredictable battlefield conditions, professional militaries have to instill and enforce strict discipline and uniformity of views as a professional necessity. This explains why most recruit their members at the ages of sixteen to eighteen (and in some cases even younger) to imprint a definitive military ethos or worldview on them.

28. Elizabeth Kier, "Culture and Military Doctrine: France between the Wars," *International Security* 19, no. 4 (Spring 1995): 69.

29. Eric Nordlinger, *Soldiers in Politics: Military Coups and Governments* (Englewood Cliffs, NJ: Prentice Hall, 1977), 61.

30. See, for instance, editorial, "The Military Mindset," *Dawn* (Karachi), October 7, 2012. At least for analytical purposes, it is important to differentiate between mind-sets and norms. Individuals have mind-sets. But norms are intersubjective, or shared, expectations or obligations about appropriate behavior among the members of a group.

31. These include various editions of the *Pakistan Army Green Book*, the flagship publication of the Inspector General Training and Evaluation Branch of the Pakistan Army. It is published every few years and contains articles written by senior and junior officers. Each issue typically covers specific national security themes, such as nation building, future conflict environment, and information warfare. Although the *Green Book* is not systematically representative of military opinion, officers' views are products of an organizational environment that exerts strong pressures to conform with the institutional zeitgeist.

32. The only other scholarly analysis of military politics in Pakistan that draws on a similar source is Mazhar Aziz, *Military Control in Pakistan: The Parallel State* (London: Routledge, 2008), 83–88, 93–96. However, Aziz sees the corporate interests of the military as primary drivers of military intervention, and although the main focus of his analysis of the "perceptions of the armed forces" is the then National Defence College, the main military publication he uses is the *Pakistan Army Green Book* for 2000. I have extended his analysis to include multiple NDU sources and newer editions of the *Green Book* (e.g., 2008 and 2011), to trace continuity and change in military institutional thinking after its withdrawal from government in 2007.

33. Aziz, *Military Control in Pakistan*, 66.

34. Pervez Musharraf, *In the Line of Fire: A Memoir* (New York: Free Press, 2006), 67.

35. Although the NDU course includes civil service officers of equivalent rank (at present, about 10 to 11 percent of the yearly cohort), these officers

are primarily trained at the civilian National School of Public Policy (formerly known as the Pakistan Administrative Staff College).

36. Stephen P. Cohen, *The Pakistan Army*, 2nd ed. (Karachi: Oxford University Press, 1998), deals extensively with officer training at the Pakistan Military Academy and the Staff College, but not at the NDU, and he focuses mainly on doctrinal and strategic issues, not the military's role in politics per se.

37. The "logic of appropriateness" is a perspective that sees human behavior as driven by "rules of appropriate or exemplary behavior, organized into institutions." Actors follow rules not because of their costs or benefits, but because "they are seen as natural, rightful, expected, and legitimate." Actors do what they believe is appropriate or expected of them in a situation as members of a political community, group, or institution. See James March and Johan Olsen, "Logics of Appropriateness," in *Oxford Handbook of Public Policy*, ed. Michael Moran, Martin Rein, and Robert E. Goodin (New York: Oxford University Press, 2008), 689.

38. Harold D. Lasswell, "The Sino-Japanese Crisis: The Garrison State versus the Civilian State," *China Quarterly* 11 (1937): 649. Lasswell made his seminal theoretical statement in "The Garrison State." See also Lasswell, *Essays on the Garrison State*, ed. Jay Stanley (New Brunswick, NJ: Transaction Publishers, 1998).

39. In Andreski's words, "The devil finds work for the idle hands: the soldiers who have no war to fight or prepare for will be tempted to intervene in politics." *Military Organization and Society*, 2nd ed. (New York: Routledge, 1968), 202.

40. Samuel Huntington, *The Third Wave: Democratization in the Late Twentieth Century* (Norman: University of Oklahoma Press, 1993), 234.

41. See Michael C. Desch, *Civilian Control of the Military: The Changing Security Environment* (Baltimore: Johns Hopkins University Press, 1997), esp. 14–17.

42. Here I draw on the classic sociology literature on the integrative functions of social conflict, such as Georg Simmel, *Conflict*, trans. Kurt H. Wolf (Glencoe, IL: Free Press, 1955); and Lewis A. Coser, *The Functions of Social Conflict* (Glencoe, IL: Free Press, 1956).

43. Adam Przeworski's comment on the dust jacket of Barany, *Soldier and the Changing State*.

44. On the diminishing returns from this policy, see Paul Kapur and Sumit Ganguly, "The Jihad Paradox: Pakistan and Islamist Militancy in South Asia," *International Security* 37, no. 1 (2012): 111–141.

45. "War on Terror Toll Put at 49,000," *Express Tribune*, March 27, 2013; "Terrorists Killed 40,000 Civilians, 2,250 Security Personnel," *Nation*, January 19, 2010.

46. An asymmetric war is one in which one side is stronger than the other. The asymmetry typically refers to disparity in material assets. Hence the weaker side tries to compensate for the conventional imbalance by using subconventional or asymmetric means, such as guerrilla warfare. The classic work on the subject is Andrew Mack, "Why Big Nations Lose Small Wars: The Politics of Asymmetric Conflict," *World Politics* 27, no. 2 (January 1975): 175–200. See also Ivan Arreguin-Toft, *How the Weak Win Wars: A Theory of Asymmetric Conflict* (New York: Cambridge University Press, 2005).

47. See, for example, Major General Shaukat Iqbal, "Security Politics of the Region: Indo-U.S. Nexus and Security Challenges of Pakistan," in *Pakistan Army Green Book* (Rawalpindi: General Headquarters, 2011), 107–113; Major General Shafqaat Ahmed, "Multi-dimensional Threat to the Security of Pakistan," in *Pakistan Army Green Book: The Future Conflict Environment* (Rawalpindi: General Headquarters, 2008), 1–10; Major General Muhammad Ahsan Mahmood, "Future Conflict Environment: Challenges and Responses," ibid., 17–24; and Brigadier Shaukat Iqbal, "Future Conflict Environment: Challenges for Pakistan Army and the Way Forward," ibid., 43–50.

48. The classic statement of the rationale for the subordination of the soldier to the political leadership is Carl von Clausewitz, *On War*, ed. and trans. Michael Eliot Howard and Peter Paret (Princeton, NJ: Princeton University Press, 1989), esp. bk. 8, chap. 6. See also Huntington, *Soldier and the State*, 56–58.

49. Richard Kohn, "An Essay on Civilian Control of the Military," *American Diplomacy*, March 1997, http://www.unc.edu/depts/diplomat/AD_Issues/amdipl_3/kohn.html (accessed February 9, 2011).

50. Morris Janowitz, *On Social Organization and Social Control*, ed. James Burke (Chicago: University of Chicago Press, 1991), 101.

51. Richard Kohn, "How Democracies Control the Military," *Journal of Democracy* 8, no. 4 (1997): 144.

52. An alternative perspective offered by Rebecca L. Schiff holds that civilian control based on the separation of civil-military institutions is an American-Western construction. In her view, the best defense against military intervention in politics is a culturally specific consensus or "concordance" between the political leadership, the military and the public on the proper role and composition of the military. See Schiff, "Civil-Military Re-

NOTES TO PAGES 12–13

lations Reconsidered: A Theory of Concordance," *Armed Forces and Society* 22, no. 1 (Fall 1995): 7–24. Empirically speaking, civilian control of the military is a necessary condition of democracy regardless of whether a country is Western (e.g., India, South Korea). And as Peter Feaver points out, Schiff's theory is based on the very distinction between the military and the politicians that she rejects as empirically and theoretically defective. See Feaver, "The Civil-Military Problematique: Huntington, Janowitz, and the Question of Civilian Control," *Armed Forces and Society* 23, no. 2 (Winter 1996): 149–177.

53. Eliot Cohen, *Supreme Command: Soldiers, Statesmen, and Leadership in Wartime* (New York: Free Press, 2002), 256.

54. For a good discussion of this difficult trade-off between military effectiveness and civilian supremacy, see Peter Feaver, "Civil-Military Relations," *Annual Review of Political Science* 2 (June 1999): 211–241.

55. See Robert Dahl, *Polyarchy: Participation and Opposition* (New Haven, CT: Yale University Press, 1971), 50; and Dahl, *Democracy and Its Critics* (New Haven, CT: Yale University Press, 1991), 245–247. In his classic book *The Man on Horseback,* Samuel E. Finer also emphasized the internalization of the "norm of civilian supremacy" by the military as "the most potent check" on military intervention in politics. See *Man on Horseback,* 22–30.

56. Barany, *Soldier and the Changing State,* 4.

57. Kohn, "Essay on Civilian Control."

58. Barany, *Soldier and the Changing State,* 40.

59. Kohn, "How Democracies Control the Military," 147.

60. Chaudhri Muhammad Ali, *The Emergence of Pakistan* (Lahore: Research Society of Pakistan, University of the Punjab, 2001), 175.

61. Pakistan's Pashtun majority North-West Frontier Province (presently known as Khyber Pakhtunkhwa) was part of Afghanistan until the British annexed it in the nineteenth century.

62. Callard, *Pakistan,* 15; Rizvi, *Military and Politics in Pakistan,* 56.

63. Jalal, *State of Martial Rule,* 49–51.

64. Tilly's original formulation "war made the state, state made war" referred to the state-building efforts, especially the expansion of the state's fiscal base and military forces, spurred by the needs of warfare in eighteenth-century western Europe. See Charles Tilly, "Reflections on the History of European Statemaking," in *The Formation of National States in Western Europe,* eds. Charles Tilly and Gabriel Ardant (Princeton, NJ: Princeton University Press, 1975), 42. T. V. Paul applies Tilly's argument to explain Pakistan's political development, but he suggests an important qualification.

297

He argues that contra western Europe, overinvestment in war has led to state weakness and underdevelopment in Pakistan. However, Paul attributes the origins of Pakistan's maladies mainly to the irrational (or as he puts it, "devoid of prudence and pragmatism"), hyper-realpolitik worldview of Pakistani elites, and argues that the security threat from India was merely a contributing factor. However, a closer analysis underscores the fact that the Hobbesian ideas and beliefs that Paul ascribes to Pakistani elites were not independent of the external threat environment in which they found themselves. Once the state adopted a war-making strategy, these narrow realist national security beliefs (and their associated notions of military professionalism justifying domestic role expansion) developed a life of their own, especially when the military institution subsequently internalized them. See Paul, *The Warrior State: Pakistan in the Contemporary World* (New York: Oxford University Press, 2014).

65. Dunkart Rustow, "Transitions to Democracy: Toward a Dynamic Model," *Comparative Politics* 2, no. 3 (April 1970): 350.

66. Christophe Jaffrelot, ed., *Pakistan: Nationalism without a Nation* (New Delhi: Manohar, 2002).

67. For instance, only 1 of the 133 Indian Civil Service/Indian Political Service officers who opted for Pakistan was a Bengali. Moreover, Bengalis made up less than 3 percent of the strength of the military officer corps, a legacy of the institutionalized colonial policy of military recruitment from the martial races of North India, such as the Punjabis and the Pashtuns. While the Pakistan government broadened civil service recruitment by establishing a special quota for East Pakistan, the colonial policy of military recruitment was left untouched in Pakistan at least in the decade following independence. Ralph Braibanti, *Research on the Bureaucracy of Pakistan* (Durham, NC: Duke University Press, 1966), 49; Stephen P. Cohen, *Pakistan Army*, 44.

68. Jahan, *Pakistan*, 20.

69. Samad, *Nation in Turmoil*, 90.

70. Georg Simmel observed that "a state of conflict . . . pulls [group] members so tightly together and subjects them to such uniform impulse that they either must get completely along with, or repel, one another." See Simmel, *Conflict*, 17–18, 82.

71. Coser, *Functions of Social Conflict*, 89.

72. I am grateful to Zoltan Barany for pushing me on this point.

73. See *Building Democratic Institutions: Party Systems in Latin America*, ed. Scott Mainwaring and Timothy R. Scully (Stanford, CA: Stanford University Press, 1995), 1. The linkage between institutions, especially political parties, and political stability is the central theme of Samuel Huntington's

seminal *Political Order in Changing Societies* (New Haven, CT: Yale University Press, 1968).

74. The demand for a separate state of Pakistan was primarily articulated by elites from Muslim-minority areas who feared the economic, political, and cultural domination of the Hindus in a united India. The Muslim League was formed primarily to preserve the interests of this privileged minority. See D. A. Low, "Provincial Histories," in *The Political Inheritance of Pakistan*, ed. D. A. Low (London: Macmillan, 1991), 7–8. On the class composition and coalitions of the Muslim League, see Maya Tudor, *The Promise of Power: The Origins of Democracy in India and Autocracy in Pakistan* (New York: Cambridge University Press, 2013), esp. 56–64, 123–149.

75. Jahan, *Pakistan*, 24.

76. For an excellent discussion of the conflicting logics of the nation-state and politically salient sociocultural differences and how to reconcile them by crafting state nations, see Juan Linz, Alfred Stepan, and Yogendra Yadav, *Crafting State-Nations: India and Other Multinational Democracies* (Baltimore: Johns Hopkins University Press, 2010), 1–38.

77. Jaffrelot, *Pakistan*, 18.

78. Stephen P. Cohen, "State Building in Pakistan," in *The State, Religion, and Ethnic Politics in Afghanistan, Iran, and Pakistan*, ed. Ali Banuazizi and Myron Wiener (Syracuse, NY: Syracuse University Press, 1986), 318.

79. Ibid., 317.

80. Mohammad Ayub Khan, *Friends Not Masters: A Political Autobiography* (Islamabad: Mr. Books, 2006), 229. See also Ayub's biography by his staff officer and later private secretary, Colonel Mohammad Ahmed, *My Chief* (Lahore: Longmans, Green, 1960); and Major General Sher Ali Pataudi (retd.), *The Story of Soldiering and Politics in India and Pakistan* (Lahore: Wajidalis, 1978), esp. 146–161.

81. Major General Fazal Muqeem Khan, *The Story of the Pakistan Army* (Karachi: Oxford University Press, 1963), 159.

82. Ayub Khan, *Friends Not Masters*, 36.

83. The preeminent American military sociologist Morris Janowitz defined a civil-military coalition as one in which the military "expands its political activity and becomes an active political bloc," and civilian executives or parties can "remain in power only because of the passive assent or active assistance" of the armed forces. See Janowitz, *Military Institutions and Coercion*, 83.

84. Jahan, *Pakistan*, 53.

85. K. J. Newman, "Pakistan's Preventive Autocracy and Its Causes," *Pacific Affairs* 32, no. 1 (March 1959): 18–33.

86. Lieutenant General Abdul Majeed Malik (retd.), former chief of general staff, interview by the author, Islamabad, May 2011.

87. Muhammad Azfar Anwar, Zain Rafique, and Salman Azam Joiya, "Defense Spending–Economic Growth Nexus: A Case Study of Pakistan," *Pakistan Economic and Social Review* 50, no. 2 (Winter 2012): 164.

88. Ayesha Siddiqa, *Military Inc.: Inside Pakistan's Military Economy* (London: Pluto Press, 2007).

89. The ISI was set up by Major General R. Cawthome, then deputy chief of army staff, in 1948 to coordinate intelligence operations of the three armed forces (army, air force, and navy).

90. See former ISI officer Lieutenant General Jahan Dad Khan (retd.), *Pakistan: Leadership Challenges* (Karachi: Oxford University Press, 1999), 31; and President Ayub's close aide and information secretary Altaf Gauhar, "How Intelligence Agencies Run Our Politics," *Nation* (Lahore), August 17, 1997.

91. *Report of the United Nations Commission of Inquiry into the Facts and Circumstances of the Assassination of Former Pakistani Prime Minister Mohtarma Benazir Bhutto*, 60, http://www.un.org/News/dh/infocus/Pakistan/UN_Bhutto_Report_15April2010.pdf (accessed September 2, 2011).

92. The Pinochet government disbanded the directorate and replaced it with the National Information Center (Central Nacional de Informaciones) in 1977 after the former's involvement in the murder of a former Chilean diplomat, socialist politician, and leading critic of the Pinochet regime, Orlando Letelier (along with an American colleague, Ronni Muffet, from the Washington, D.C.–based Institute for Policy Studies, where Letelier was a senior fellow), in Washington, D.C.

93. Zahid Hussain, *Frontline Pakistan: The Struggle with Militant Islam* (New York: Columbia University Press, 2007), 13.

94. Induction into the officer corps can be granted only by the Inter-Services Selection Board. The ISSB selects cadets for the entry-level two-year course at the Pakistan Military Academy (PMA), Kakul, followed by commission into the officer corps as second lieutenants, with the exception of officers in the technical branches, such as medical or education, who are trained separately in specialized colleges and then commissioned as captains after completing a shorter six-month course at the PMA. Once they graduate from the PMA, the lieutenants undergo on-the-job training in units; they also take various professional courses and two promotion examinations each in order to reach the rank of captain and then major. This process is followed by the yearlong staff course at the Command and Staff College, Quetta (for majors), which requires a minimum service of eight

years, and ultimately the NDC/NDU courses (for colonels and brigadiers). According to a former adjutant general of the army, some 55–60 percent of the commissioned officers make it to the level of lieutenant colonel, 20 percent become brigadiers, but only 2–3 percent become general officers. Interview of Lieutenant General Moinuddin Haider (retd.) by author, Lahore, December 2008.

95. Alfred Stepan, *The Military in Politics: Changing Patterns in Brazil* (Princeton, NJ: Princeton University Press, 1971), 235.

96. John Samuel Fitch, *The Military Coup d'État as a Political Process: Ecuador, 1948–1966* (Baltimore: Johns Hopkins University Press, 1977), 7.

97. See, for example, *Pakistan Army Green Book* (2008), 4–5, 223–226, 241–242; *Pakistan Army Green Book* (2011), 95.

98. Interviews, Islamabad, December 2012. See also *Pakistan Army Green Book* (2008), 37, 43–47, 52–54.

99. Ibid., 46.

100. On ideological indoctrination in the Indonesian military, see Jun Honna, "Military Ideology in Response to Democratic Pressure during the Late Suharto Era: Political and Institutional Contexts," *Indonesia* 67 (1999): esp. 79–87.

101. See, for example, *Pakistan Army Green Book: Nation Building* (Rawalpindi: General Headquarters, 2000).

102. This observation is based on the author's analysis of the declassified military officers' individual research papers from 2000 to 2006. Military officers write these papers in partial fulfillment of their training courses at the NDU. Access to the materials of the NDU requires clearance from the ISI, a cumbersome gatekeeping process designed to discourage civilian research on "sensitive" national security issues. I was able to access research papers as a temporary "guest visitor" and had to take extensive notes, since restricted materials cannot be photocopied. I was explicitly prohibited from publishing any information that could identify individual officers.

103. *National Strategy Paper, 2012: Non-kinetic Challenges to the State of Pakistan* (Islamabad: National Defence University, 2012), 25–32; *Pakistan Army Green Book* (2008), 7, 131, 134.

104. Stephen P. Cohen, *The Idea of Pakistan* (Washington, DC: Brookings Institution Press, 2004), 99.

105. Brigadier Sikander Shami, "Targeting the Middle Leadership," in *Pakistan Army Green Book* (Rawalpindi: General Headquarters, 1991), 27.

106. Guy Peters, *Institutional Theory* (New York: Continuum, 2005), 26. See also Ronald Jepperson, "Institutions, Institutional Effects and Institutionalism," in *The New Institutionalism in Organizational Analysis*, ed. Walter

W. Powell and Paul J. Di Maggio (Chicago: University of Chicago Press, 1991), 149.

107. James G. March and Herbert A. Simon, *Organizations* (New York: John Wiley and Sons, 1958), 65.

108. Wilson, *Bureaucracy,* 109.

109. Fitch, *Military Coup d'État,* 9.

110. "Egypt's Army Chief Defends Ousting Morsi," July 14, 2013, http://www.aljazeera.com/news/middleeast/2013/07/2013714225910747466.html (accessed July 17, 2013).

111. Countrywide interviews by the author, 2008–2013.

112. Husain Haqqani, *Pakistan: Between Mosque and Military* (Washington, DC: Carnegie Endowment for International Peace, 2005).

113. Hassan Abbas, *Pakistan's Drift into Extremism: Allah, the Army, and America's War on Terror* (London: M. E. Sharpe, 2005).

114. Shuja Nawaz, *Crossed Swords: Pakistan, Its Army, and the Wars Within* (Karachi: Oxford University Press, 2008).

115. Anatol Lieven, *Pakistan: A Hard Country* (New York: Public Affairs, 2011).

116. For an informative, albeit sympathetic, journalistic account of the army's inner workings and its role in the War on Terror, see Carey Schofield, *Inside the Pakistan Army: A Woman's Experience on the Frontline of the War on Terror* (London: Biteback, 2011). General Pervez Musharraf granted the author unparalleled access to the army, including its installations, operations, training schools, and even a tailored uniform.

117. Some scholars argue that Pakistan inherited the most militarized parts of the British Empire, particularly the Punjab, and that this explains the postcolonial militarization of its politics. See Tan Tai Yong, *The Garrison State: The Military, Government and Society in Punjab, 1849–1947* (London: Sage, 2005). See also Christophe Jaffrelot, "India and Pakistan: Interpreting the Divergence of Two Political Trajectories," *Cambridge Review of International Affairs* 15, no. 2 (2002): 251–267; Clive Dewey, "The Rural Roots of Militarism in Pakistan," in Low, *Political Inheritance of Pakistan,* 255–283. Colonial legacies may have contributed to the militarization of politics in Pakistan. But as I noted earlier, Pakistan's colonial inheritance was not immutable, nor was its adverse political impact inevitable. Understanding why colonial imbalances continued to shape politics after Pakistan's independence is an empirical question that requires scrutinizing the first decade of its history, which was shaped in no small measure by elite responses to the threat from India and problems of national cohesion.

118. Cultural arguments focus on the presumed linkage between "Islam's affinity for militarism" and military dictatorships in Pakistan, and are especially highlighted by Indian authors, who contrast it with Hinduism's "vague and individualistic" nature as a barrier against authoritarianism in India. See Taya Zinkin, "Military Dictatorship in India," *Pacific Affairs* 32, no. 1 (March 1959): 89–91; Apurba Kundu, *Militarism in India: Army and Civil Society in Consensus* (London: I. B. Taurus, 1998), 93. Such cultural arguments, however, fall flat when we consider Muslim-majority countries that have embraced competitive democratic institutions, such as Indonesia, Bangladesh, and Turkey.

119. These works invoke either the political and economic strength of feudalism (landlords) or the weakness of the middle classes in Pakistan. See Robert Stern, *Democracy and Dictatorship in South Asia: Dominant Classes and Political Outcomes in India, Pakistan and Bangladesh* (London: Praeger, 2001); Tudor, *Promise of Power;* and Aitzaz Ahsan, "Why Pakistan Is Not a Democracy" in *Divided by Democracy,* by Meghnad Desai and Aitzaz Ahsan (New Delhi: Roli Books, 2005), 82–98.

120. See, for instance, Rizvi, *Military and Politics in Pakistan,* 269–270; Oldenburg, *India, Pakistan, and Democracy,* 21–22; and Stephen P. Cohen, *Pakistan Army,* 107–108. See also Callard, *Pakistan,* 21, 49, 328–329; Khalid Bin Sayeed, "Collapse of Parliamentary Democracy in Pakistan," *Middle East Journal* 13, no. 4 (1959): 389–406. More recent works focus on the ideology and mobilization strategy of the Muslim League in locating the roots of authoritarianism in Pakistan. See Sumit Ganguly and C. Christine Fair, "The Structural Origins of Authoritarianism in Pakistan," *Commonwealth and Comparative Politics* 51, no. 1 (2013): 122–142.

121. For a theoretically elegant statement emphasizing the role of weak civilian institutions in encouraging military interventions in Pakistan, and the opposite effect of stronger institutions on civil-military relations in India, see Paul Staniland, "Explaining Civil-Military Relations in Complex Political Environments: India and Pakistan in Comparative Perspective," *Security Studies* 17, no. 2 (April 2008): 322–362.

122. William R. Thompson, "Regime Vulnerability and the Military Coup," *Comparative Politics* 7, no. 4 (July 1975): 466.

123. Alfred Stepan, *Rethinking Military Politics: Brazil and the Southern Cone* (Princeton, NJ: Princeton University Press, 1988), 10.

124. Krasner, "Approaches to the State," 224–225. As William R. Thompson observed almost four decades ago, social scientists have a tendency to view military officers "as obediently enacting the roles assigned to

them by vague and impersonal systemic forces." Thompson, "Regime Vulnerability and the Military Coup," 466.

125. Siddiqa, *Military Inc.*, 19–20, 57, 248.

126. Talcott Parsons, "Professions," in *International Encyclopedia of the Social Sciences*, vol. 12 (New York: Macmillan, 1968), 539.

127. Aziz, *Military Control in Pakistan*, 86.

128. Countrywide interviews of military officers by the author, 2008–2013. See also Nawaz, *Crossed Swords*, 582.

129. Nordlinger, *Military Coups and Governments*, 66.

130. John Samuel Fitch, "Military Attitudes toward Democracy in Latin America: How Do We Know If Anything Has Changed?," in *Civil-Military Relations in Latin America: New Analytical Perspectives*, ed. David Pion-Berlin (Chapel Hill, NC: University of North Carolina Press, 2002), 83.

131. I do not know of any book-length work on the role of the Pakistani military's norms and attitudes in its political interventions or extrications. My own work owes much to the existing political science scholarship on military norms and beliefs. John Samuel Fitch has meticulously studied the role of military role beliefs in Latin America (especially Argentina and Ecuador) in shaping military politics. See, for instance, Fitch, *The Armed Forces and Democracy in Latin America* (Baltimore: Johns Hopkins University Press, 1996), esp. 61–105. See also Fitch, "Military Attitudes toward Democracy." Similarly, in his theoretically rigorous study of the Russian army, Brian Taylor uses an organizational culture approach to explain the absence of military coups in Russia. See Taylor, *Politics and the Russian Army: Civil-Military Relations, 1689–2000* (New York: Cambridge University Press, 2003).

132. Horowitz, *Coup Theories and Officers' Motives*, 147.

133. E. E. Schattschneider, *Party Government: American Government in Action* (New Brunswick, NJ: Transaction, 2004), 37. See also Kathryn Sikkink, *Ideas and Institutions: Developmentalism in Brazil and Argentina* (Ithaca, NY: Cornell University Press, 1991), 5–6.

134. Besides official army studies or officers' memoirs, various other works have documented the organizational history of the Pakistani military, including its battlefield performance. See, for instance, Nawaz, *Crossed Swords*. See also Brian Cloughley (former Australian military attaché to Pakistan), *A History of the Pakistan Army: Battles and Insurrections*, 3rd ed. (Karachi: Oxford University Press, 2006); Pervaiz Iqbal Cheema, *The Armed Forces of Pakistan* (Karachi: Oxford University Press, 2002).

1. WAGING WAR, BUILDING A NATION

1. Ayesha Jalal, *The State of Martial Rule: The Origins of Pakistan's Political Economy of Defense* (Lahore: Sang-e-Meel, 1999), 3. On the crucial importance of this period for Pakistan's democratic experiment, see also Mushtaq Ahmad, *Government and Politics in Pakistan* (New York: Praeger, 1963), 174–175.

2. In August 1947, the army of independent India was only marginally better off in regard to the number of senior officers; it had two major generals to Pakistan's one. See *Civil and Military Gazette* (Karachi), July 31, 1947.

3. Morris Janowitz, *Military Institutions and Coercion in the Developing Nations* (Chicago: University of Chicago Press, 1977), 89.

4. Ibid., 82, 85.

5. Alfred Stepan, "The New Professionalism of Internal Warfare," in *Arguing Comparative Politics* (New York: Oxford University Press, 2001), 23–28.

6. Daljit Singh, "Military Education in India: Changes from the British Tradition," *United Services Institution Journal,* January–March 1974, 229.

7. William F. Gutteridge, *Military Institutions and Power in the New States* (New York: Praeger, 1965), 148.

8. Stephen P. Cohen, *The Indian Army: Its Contribution to the Development of a Nation* (Berkeley: University of California Press, 1972), 29.

9. Lloyd L. Rudolph and Susanne H. Rudolph, "Generals and Politicians in India," *Pacific Affairs* 37, no. 1 (Spring 1964): 9.

10. Stephen P. Cohen, *The Pakistan Army,* 2nd ed. (Karachi: Oxford University Press, 1998), 117.

11. "General Report of the Burma Army Mission on the Military Establishments of India and Pakistan," June 19–September 14, 1952; quoted in Mary Callahan, "The Origins of Military Rule in Burma" (PhD diss., Cornell University, 1996), 23–24.

12. See, for instance, Harold D. Lasswell, "The Garrison State," *American Journal of Sociology* 46, no. 4 (January 1941): 455–468.

13. For example, see Stanislav Andreski, *Military Organization and Society,* 2nd ed. (New York: Routledge, 1968).

14. Cohen, *Indian Army,* 171.

15. The DCC was to "define . . . the task of the armed forces in accordance with overall policy of government and to call upon the Joint Staff Committee to produce appreciations and plans to carry out defense policy." Headed by the prime minister, it consisted of the home, defense, finance,

and foreign affairs ministers. The military service chiefs could attend by invitation when defense problems or plans were under consideration. See "Minutes of the Cabinet Meeting," September 23, 1948, File 172/CF/48 (Cabinet Secretariat, Government of Pakistan). See also "Formation of Subcommittees of the Defense Committee of the Cabinet," September 25, 1948, in the same file.

16. Most scholars believe that a civilian-led defense ministry is key to "unequivocally establishing the supremacy of civilian authority." See Felipe Agüero, *Soldiers, Civilians, and Democracy: Post-Franco Spain in Comparative Perspective* (Baltimore: Johns Hopkins University Press, 1995), 197. See also Samuel Huntington, *The Soldier and the State: The Theory and Politics of Civil-Military Relations* (Cambridge, MA: Belknap Press of Harvard University Press, 1957), 80–87.

17. Shuja Nawaz, *Crossed Swords: Pakistan, Its Army, and the Wars Within* (Karachi: Oxford University Press, 2008), 64.

18. Ashutosh Varshney, "Why Democracy Survives in India," *Journal of Democracy* 9, no. 3 (1998): 39.

19. This is not to say that the idea of India as a nation was universally shared across the country, or that the process of Indian nation building was wholly peaceful and consensual (e.g., the Indian military occupied Hyderabad in 1948). In fact, there were violent agitations in the South over linguistic autonomy, as well as against Hindi as a national language. On India's subnational, fissiparous tendencies at the time, see Selig Harrison, *India: The Most Dangerous Decades* (Princeton, NJ: Princeton University Press, 1960).

20. The Muslim League won 425 of the 496 seats reserved for Muslims (and about 89.2 percent of Muslim votes) in the provincial legislatures. In British India, the vote was granted at the provincial level in 1909, but the franchise was restricted on the basis of landownership and literacy. Fourteen percent of the Indian adult population was eligible to vote in the 1946 elections. See Granville Austin, *The Indian Constitution: Cornerstone of a Nation* (Oxford: Clarendon Press, 1966), 10.

21. The League had mobilized mass support in the terminal stages of British rule. Even then, the core parts of what was to become Pakistan, especially the Punjab, were ruled by the cross-religious (Hindu, Muslim, and Sikh), nonconfessional Unionist Party until the eve of independence.

22. Mohammad Waseem, *Politics and the State in Pakistan* (Islamabad: National Institute of Historical and Cultural Research, 1994), 106–107.

23. The resolution enunciated the Muslim League's principal demand that "geographically contiguous units are demarcated into regions which should be constituted, with such territorial readjustments as may be neces-

sary that the areas in which the Muslims are numerically in a majority as in the North Western and Eastern Zones of India should be grouped to constitute 'independent states' in which the constituent units should be autonomous and sovereign." See text of the Resolution of the Lahore Session of the All India Muslim League, in *Muslim League Session 1940 and the Lahore Resolution* (Documents), vol. 6 of Historical Studies Series, compiled by Ikram Ali (Islamabad: National Institute of Historical and Cultural Research, 1990), 298–301.

24. Gyanendra Pandey, *The Ascendancy of the Congress in Uttar Pradesh: Class, Community and Nation in Northern India, 1920–1940* (London: Anthem, 2002), 126.

25. *Report of the Inquiry Committee Appointed by the Council of the All India Muslim League to Inquire into Muslim Grievances in Congress Provinces* (Delhi, 1939); A. K. Fazlul Haq, "Muslim Sufferings under Congress Rule," press statement (Calcutta: Bengal Provincial Muslim League, 1939).

26. Interview between Khawaja Nazimuddin and Lord Mountbatten, April 17, 1947, in *Quaid-i-Azam Mohammad Ali Jinnah Papers: Prelude to Pakistan*, ed. Z. H. Zaidi, February 20–June 2, 1947, vol. 1, pt. 2 (Islamabad: Quaid-i-Azam Papers Project, National Archives of Pakistan, Distributed by Oxford University Press, 1993), 659. See also record of interview between Lord Mountbatten and M. A. Jinnah, April 26, 1947, ibid., 669.

27. Jalal, *State of Martial Rule.*

28. Cohen, *Pakistan Army,* 36.

29. Jalal, *State of Martial Rule,* 42.

30. Cohen, *Pakistan Army,* 58–161; A. A. K. Niazi, *The Betrayal of East Pakistan* (Karachi: Oxford University Press, 1998), 12.

31. Stephen P. Cohen, *The Idea of Pakistan* (Washington, DC: Brookings Institution Press, 2004), 101.

32. Cohen, *Pakistan Army,* 60.

33. Ayub Khan notes bitterly in his autobiography, "We were entitled to 160 trainloads of military equipment and weapons. . . . Little of that ever arrived and when the wagons did arrive they were full of stones and wrecked equipment." See Mohammad Ayub Khan, *Friends Not Masters: A Political Autobiography* (Islamabad: Mr. Books, 2006), 36. Field Marshal Sir Claude Auchinleck, the supreme commander responsible for the partition of the BIA, confirmed in a note to the British prime minister that the Indian government had decided to "prevent Pakistan receiving her just share, or indeed anything of the large stock of reserve arms, equipment, and stores, etc., held in the arsenals and depots of India." John Connell, *Auchinleck* (London:

Cassell, 1959), 930–931. See also Chaudhri Muhammad Ali, *The Emergence of Pakistan* (Lahore: Research Society of Pakistan, University of the Punjab, 2001), 189–192.

34. Proximity raises the likelihood of war when states are embroiled in territorial conflict. See John A. Vasquez, "Why Do Neighbors Fight? Proximity, Interaction, or Territoriality," *Journal of Peace Research* 32, no. 3 (1995): 277–293.

35. General Aslam Beg (retd.), former chief of the army staff, and Lieutenant General K.M. Arif (retd.), former vice chief of the army staff, cited in Julian Schofield, "Militarized Decision-Making for War in Pakistan: 1947–1971," *Armed Forces and Society* 27, no. 1 (Fall 2000): 139.

36. James Fearon, "Rationalist Explanations for War," *International Organization* 49 (1995): 390.

37. Junagadh and Hyderabad, both located in the territories of the Indian state, were Hindu-majority states ruled by Muslim rulers. The nizam of Hyderabad desired independence, but the nawab of Junagadh used the state's sea access to Pakistan to legitimate his decision to accede to that country on August 15, 1947. India refused to accept that accession, occupied the state by force in September 1947, and held a plebiscite in February 1948 in which over 90 percent of the population voted in favor of joining India. India also incorporated Hyderabad into the Indian union by the use of force in September 1948, on the eve of Jinnah's death.

38. The Hindu maharajah of Kashmir had intended to sign a Standstill Agreement with both Pakistan and India. The Standstill Agreement provided for in the India Independence Act, 1947, was designed to preserve the status quo between the princely states and the dominions of India and Pakistan until new administrative arrangements/agreements could be made. Pakistan signed the agreement on August 15, 1947, whereas India asked the maharajah to send a representative to negotiate an agreement. The Pakistani leadership viewed the Indian government's apparent prevarication as an indication that India was seeking the state's immediate accession. The entry of Pakistani raiders into Kashmir drastically altered the situation, and the maharajah decided to accede to India. See C. Dasgupta, *War and Diplomacy in Kashmir, 1947–1948* (New Delhi: Sage, 2002), 36.

39. Akbar Khan, *Raiders in Kashmir* (Lahore: Jang, 1992), 22–24.

40. Ibid., 21.

41. Ibid., 25.

42. On January 1, 1948, Indian prime minister Nehru sought the intervention of the UN Security Council against Pakistani aggressors, a decision

that internationalized the dispute and involved the United Nations in the conflict.

43. Quoted in Major General Sher Ali Pataudi (retd.), *The Story of Soldiering and Politics in India and Pakistan* (Lahore: Wajidalis, 1978), 116–117.

44. Major General Fazal Muqeem Khan, *The Story of the Pakistan Army* (Karachi: Oxford University Press, 1963), 115–119. See also Ayub Khan, *Friends Not Masters*, 54; Brigadier A. R. Siddiqi (retd.), *The Military in Pakistan: Image and Reality* (Lahore: Vanguard, 1996), 10–11; Lieutenant General Jahandad Khan (retd.), *Pakistan: Leadership Challenges* (Karachi: Oxford University Press, 1999), 33.

45. See Pataudi, *Story of Soldiering*, 133; Ayub Khan, *Friends Not Masters*, 54–55.

46. Ayub Khan, *Friends Not Masters*, 54.

47. Ibid.

48. "Judgment in the Rawalpindi Conspiracy Case," File 23 (34)-PMS/53 (Cabinet Secretariat, Government of Pakistan), 25–26.

49. *Dawn* (Karachi), April 17, 1951.

50. Foreign Ministry to the Prime Minister, March 9, 1951, in "Judgment in the Rawalpindi Conspiracy Case," 71.

51. The conspiracy is the subject of only one book-length study, Hassan Zaheer, *The Times and Trial of the Rawalpindi Conspiracy, 1951: The First Coup Attempt in Pakistan* (Lahore: Sang-e-Meel, 2007). Zaheer, a former Pakistani bureaucrat, mischaracterizes the plot as a coup attempt. In addition, he focuses on the genesis and planning of the conspiracy, the trial, and the subsequent judgment and does not deal adequately with the impact of the event on the military institution. Shuja Nawaz acknowledges in passing that the Rawalpindi conspiracy marked the "beginning of Bonapartism in Pakistan" but does not analyze it any further. See Nawaz, *Crossed Swords*, 71. See also Cohen, *Idea of Pakistan*, 102.

52. Jalal, *State of Martial Rule*, 120–121.

53. "Pakistan Links a 'Certain Foreign Country' to Conspiracy to Set Up Communist Government," *New York Times*, March 22, 1951.

54. Akbar Khan, *Raiders in Kashmir*, 23.

55. Ibid.

56. Meeting of [Brigadier] Habibullah with Akbar in October 1949, in "Judgment in the Conspiracy Case," 8; Piffer's Week, in ibid., 10.

57. Testimony of Lt. Col. Gul Muwaz, *Proceedings of the Rawalpindi Conspiracy Tribunal* (Cabinet Secretariat, Government of Pakistan), 429–430. Muwaz disagreed with Akbar Khan's views and did not join the conspiracy

because, in his view, the "army was the instrument of policy, and not the policymaker." See Gul Muwaz–Akbar Khan meeting at Murree, in "Judgment in the Conspiracy Case," 7.

58. Testimony of Major Eusoph Sethi, *Proceedings of the Rawalpindi Conspiracy Tribunal,* July 27, 1951, 459–466.

59. Testimony of Siddiq Raja, in ibid., July 30, 1951, 488. Habibullah-Akbar Meeting, in "Judgment in the Conspiracy Case," 8.

60. Akbar Khan, quoted in "Judgment in the Conspiracy Case," 10.

61. Sadiq Khan, quoted in ibid.

62. "Judgment in the Conspiracy Case," 2–7.

63. Ibid., 8–10.

64. See Air Commodore Janjua to PM, "Breaches of Security and Major Policy," Top Secret, Prime Minister's Secretariat, January 17, 1949 (Cabinet Secretariat, Government of Pakistan).

65. See Fazal Muqeem Khan, *Story of the Pakistan Army,* 117.

66. Ayub Khan attributed the plot to the civilian government's inability to do its job properly. See *Friends Not Masters,* 54. See also Pataudi, *Story of Soldiering,* 132–133.

67. Jalal, *State of Martial Rule.*

68. Amos Perlmutter, "The Praetorian State and the Praetorian Army: Toward a Taxonomy of Civil-Military Relations in Developing Polities," *Comparative Politics* 1, no. 3 (April 1969): 384.

69. Note from Finance Advisor Military to Finance Minister, "Interim Review of Requirements for the Armed Forces," October 16, 1949, File 15 (2), PMS/50 (Prime Minister's Secretariat, Government of Pakistan).

70. "Appreciation and Outline Plan for Defense of Pakistan against Attack by India, 1949–1950," quoted in ibid.

71. "Purchase of Tanks for the Armored Brigade: Summary for the DCC," File 280/CF/49 (Cabinet Division, Government of Pakistan).

72. Ilhan Niaz, *The Culture of Power and Governance of Pakistan* (Karachi: Oxford University Press, 2010), 164.

73. Military spending as a percentage of total government expenditure averaged 59.5 percent between 1947 and 1959. Hasan-Askari Rizvi, *The Military and Politics in Pakistan, 1947–1997* (Lahore: Sang-e-Meel, 2000), 57.

74. The military oath of service, adapted from British India, read, "I solemnly affirm, in the presence of Almighty God, that I owe allegiance to the Constitution and Dominion of Pakistan and that I will as in duty bound honestly and faithfully serve in the Dominion of Pakistan Forces . . .

and that I will observe and obey all commands of any officer set over me." See File 94/CF/48 (Cabinet Secretariat, Government of Pakistan).

75. "Responsibility of the Defence Forces," Staff College (Quetta), June 14, 1948, in *Mahomed Ali Jinnah: Speeches and Statements, 1947–1948,* ed. S. M. Burke (Karachi: Oxford University Press, 2000), 224.

76. See K. B. Sayeed, *Pakistan: The Formative Phase* (London: Oxford University Press, 1968), 259–260, 299–300. After independence, the governor general, like his counterparts in Australia and Canada, was to act on the advice of the cabinet on all matters of public policy. Keith Callard, *Pakistan: A Political Study* (London: Allen and Unwin, 1957), 130–131.

77. When doubts arose about the specific competent governmental authority in relation to the armed forces, the government added a special section to the Government of India Act empowering the governor general to grant military commissions, appoint military service chiefs, and determine their pay and allowances. See "Additions to Government of India Act to Provide for Raising of Defence Forces," File 304/CF/49. It was enacted into law in 1950. See Government of India (Second Amendment Act, 1950), in ibid.

78. Sharifuddin Pirzada, interview by the author, Islamabad, July 2009.

79. Allen McGrath, *The Destruction of Pakistan's Democracy* (Karachi: Oxford University Press, 1996), 41.

80. See Sayeed, *Pakistan,* 259–260, 279–300.

81. Ibid., 299.

82. In early August, Jinnah had asked viceroy Lord Mountbatten to instruct then NWFP governor Sir Rob Lockhart to dismiss the Congress ministry. Mountbatten informed Jinnah that under provisions of the Independence of India Act and the Governors' Instruments of Accession, such a step would be unconstitutional. Jinnah then insisted that Section 93 of the Independence Act be adapted in Pakistan to empower the governor general to order the provincial governor to take over the administration of a province in case of a grave threat to peace and security. Mountbatten consulted the secretary of state for India, who advised him that such a step would be legally questionable and that Jinnah should leave it to the Constituent Assembly to enact such special emergency powers. See "Report for the Secretary of State [for Commonwealth Relations] on Events in India and Pakistan for the Period 15th August to 26th August," September 3, 1947 (ID 3054/47), India Office Records, L/I/1/42.

83. Callard, *Pakistan,* 27, 185; McGrath, *Destruction of Pakistan's Democracy,* 46–47.

84. McGrath, *Destruction of Pakistan's Democracy,* 57.

85. Callard, *Pakistan*, 160.

86. Ayesha Jalal, *Democracy and Authoritarianism in South Asia: A Comparative and Historical Perspective* (Lahore: Sang-e-Meel, 1995), 18.

87. See Ayesha Jalal, "Inheriting the Raj: Jinnah and the Governor-Generalship Issue," *Modern Asian Studies* 19 (1985): 29–53.

88. M. A. H. Isphahani, *Quaid-e-Azam Jinnah as I Knew Him* (Karachi: Royal Book Company, 1970), 277.

89. McGrath, *Destruction of Pakistan's Democracy*, 41.

90. Philip Oldenburg, "A Place Insufficiently Imagined: Language, Belief, and the Pakistan Crisis of 1971," *Journal of Asian Studies* 44, no. 4 (August 1985): 712.

91. Ibid.

92. Ralph Braibanti, *Research on the Bureaucracy of Pakistan* (Durham, NC: Duke University Press, 1966), 49.

93. The Sindhis and Baloch too were grossly underrepresented. In 1947, 2.2 percent of the army was from Sindh and only 0.06 percent from Balochistan. See Cohen, *Pakistan Army*, 44.

94. The martial-races theory, codified after the 1857 mutiny, was based on the colonial categorization and recruitment of selected Indian races on the basis of their innate soldierly skills and political loyalty. The rest were declared nonmartial and unsuitable for military service. The main martial races were the Sikhs, the Dogras, the Rajputs, the Jats, the Gurkhas of Nepal, the Punjabi Muslims, and the Pashtuns. In the words of one of the theory's most ardent supporters, Lord Roberts, the C in C of the Bengal army, "No comparison can be made between the martial values of a regiment recruited amongst the Ghurkhas of Nepal or the warlike races of Northern India [the Punjab and the North-West Frontier Province], and those recruited from the effeminate peoples of the South." See Earl Frederick Sleigh Roberts, *Forty-One Years in India: From Subaltern to Commander-in-Chief*, vol. 2 (London: Richard Bentley and Sons, 1897), 441–442.

95. Rounaq Jahan, *Pakistan: Failure in National Integration* (New York: Columbia University Press, 1972), 20.

96. By 1958, Bengalis constituted 41.7 percent of the gazetted civil officers, but top positions continued to be under West Pakistani control because of the initial disparities. Of the nineteen secretaries, not even one was Bengali. Only three of the thirty-eight joint secretaries were from East Pakistan. Braibanti, *Research on the Bureaucracy of Pakistan*, 48; Jahan, *Pakistan*, 25–26.

97. *Constituent Assembly Debates* 1 (March 1, 1948): 127.

98. Cohen, *Pakistan Army*, 43.

99. Jahan, *Pakistan*, 5.

100. Ibid., 23–24; Jalal, *State of Martial Rule*, 60.

101. The Muslim League had staked its claim as the sole representative of the Indian Muslim nation in British India on the basis of a Muslim civilization with Urdu as its lingua franca distinct from Hindu culture and Hindi. It had considered making Urdu the official party language during its Lucknow session in 1937 but had retreated after opposition from Bengali delegates. See Sayeed, *Pakistan*, 210.

102. *Constituent Assembly Debates* 2 (February 25, 1948), 15.

103. For the genesis of the Bengali language movement, see Badruddin Umar, *The Language Movement in East Pakistan* (Dhaka: Jatiya Grontha Prakashan, 2000), 46–50.

104. Tariq Rahman, "Language and Ethnicity in Pakistan," *Asian Survey* 37, no. 9 (September 1997): 833.

105. Address by Muhammad Ali Jinnah, Governor General of Pakistan, March 21, 1948, in *The Nation's Voice, Vol. 7: Launching the State and the End of the Journey* (August 1947–September 1948), ed. Waheed Ahmad (Karachi: Quaid-i-Azam Academy, 2003), 252.

106. Ibid., 254–255.

107. Speech at Dhaka University Convocation, March 24, 1948, in Mohammad Ali Jinnah, *Speeches as Governor General of Pakistan, 1947–1948* (Karachi: Pakistan Publications, 1976), 90.

108. Jahan, *Pakistan*, 37.

109. Rafiqul Islam, "The Bengali Language and the Emergence of Bangladesh," *Contributions to Asian Studies* 11 (1978): 146.

110. For discussions of the early regional conflict over constitutional issues, see Callard, *Pakistan*, 85–123, 172–193; and Richard Sisson and Leo E. Rose, *War and Secession: Pakistan, India, and the Creation of Bangladesh* (Berkeley: University of California Press, 1990), 8–28.

111. *Constituent Assembly Debates* 8, no. 5 (November 21, 1950): 183.

112. Anwar Dil and Afia Dil, *Bengali Language Movement to Bangladesh* (Lahore: Ferozsons, 2000), 636–637; Badruddin Umar, *The Emergence of Bangladesh: Class Struggles in East Pakistan, 1947–1958* (New York: Oxford University Press, 2004), 163–166.

113. Jahan, *Pakistan*, 43.

114. Dil and Dil, *Bengali Language Movement*, 633.

115. Popularized as Ekushey (Bengali for "twenty-one"), the date February 21, 1952, had a "formative and profound influence" on shaping the

Bengali collective consciousness. Syed Nazrul Islam, *Essays on Ekushey, the Language Movement, 1952* (Dhaka: Bangla Academy, 1994), 13.

116. Callard, *Pakistan*, 183.

117. Maya Tudor, *The Promise of Power: The Origins of Democracy in India and Autocracy in Pakistan* (New York: Cambridge University Press, 2013), 32–34.

118. Umar, *Language Movement in East Pakistan*, 46.

119. In Anderson's words, a nation is "imagined because the members of even the smallest nation will never know most of their fellow-members, meet them, or even hear of them, yet in the minds of each lives the image of their communion . . . and it is imagined as a community, because, regardless of the actual inequality and exploitation that may prevail in each, the nation is always conceived as a deep, horizontal comradeship." Benedict Anderson, *Imagined Communities: Reflections on the Nature and Origins of Nationalism* (London: Verso, 1991), 5–7.

120. Jahan, *Pakistan*, 44.

121. Juan Linz, Alfred Stepan, and Yogendra Yadav, *Crafting State-Nations: India and Other Multinational Democracies* (Baltimore: Johns Hopkins University Press, 2010), 1–38; Dunkart Rustow, "Transitions to Democracy: Toward a Dynamic Model," *Comparative Politics* 2, no. 3 (April 1970): 350.

122. McGrath, *Destruction of Pakistan's Democracy*, 68.

123. *Constituent Assembly Debates* (March 1, 1948), 82.

124. *Gazette of Pakistan*, July 9, 1949.

125. Saad Akbar Babrak, an Afghan Pashtun reportedly living in exile in Pakistan, assassinated Liaquat at a public rally in Rawalpindi on October 16, 1951. He was shot dead by police soon after, so his motives remain unclear. The official inquiry into the assassination remained inconclusive.

126. Callard, *Pakistan*, 49.

127. Jahan, *Pakistan*, 41–42.

128. Ayub Khan's staff officer and biographer, Colonel Mohammad Ahmed, noted with regret that there was no "full-time defense minister to handle the enormous defense problems at cabinet level. . . . The Defense portfolio had always been held by the Prime Minister himself, who being the leader of the ruling party, had mostly been busy in consolidating his party position. . . . His successors . . . never found time to attend to the real problems of the defense ministry." See Ahmed, *My Chief* (Lahore: Longmans, Green, 1960), 46–47.

129. Ibid., 50.

130. Lieutenant General Mohammad Atiqur Rehman (retd.), *Leadership: Senior Commanders* (Lahore: Ferozsons, 1973), 13.

131. Pataudi, *Story of Soldiering*, 158. This view is corroborated in Rehman, *Leadership*, 6. A former air force chief notes that "all power in the army and indeed all those powers that a government wields over an army were in the hands of one man." Air Marshal Asghar (retd.), *Generals in Politics: Pakistan, 1958–1982* (New Delhi: Vikas, 1983), 128. See also Major General Fazal Muqeem Khan, *Pakistan's Crisis in Leadership* (Islamabad: National Book Foundation, 1973), 264–265.

132. "Minutes of Cabinet Meeting," January 23, 1953, File 26/CF/50-1 (Cabinet Secretariat, Government of Pakistan).

133. See Pataudi, *Story of Soldiering*, 138–139. See also Altaf Gauhar, *Pakistan's First Military Ruler* (Lahore: Sang-e-Meel, 1993).

134. One official memo noted that the DCC had stopped meeting despite a cabinet decision that mandated a meeting at least once every two months. See "Reorganization of the Existing Joint Services Machinery," November 6, 1951, File 172/CF/48 (Cabinet Secretariat, Government of Pakistan).

135. Ibid.

136. Finance Minister Ghulam Mohammad to Prime Minister Liaquat Ali Khan, D.O. H.M.F. 1287/1949, December 14, 1949 (Ministry of Finance, Government of Pakistan).

137. Mohammad to Liaquat, H.M.F. 289/50, February 28, 1950 (Ministry of Finance, Government of Pakistan).

138. Gwynne Dyer, "Pakistan," in *World Armies*, ed. John Keegan (London: Macmillan, 1979), 530.

139. See "Pakistan Army: An Update, August 1948 to 14 August 1949" (Prime Minister's Secretariat, Government of Pakistan). See also "Report of the Nationalisation Committee, 1950" (Cabinet Secretariat, Government of Pakistan).

140. "Summary for the Cabinet: Substantive Promotion of Army Officers," Ministry of Defense, File 227/CF-49 (Cabinet Secretariat, Government of Pakistan).

141. See Ayub Khan, *Friends Not Masters*, 36.

142. Fazal Muqeem Khan, *Story of the Pakistan Army*, 26. Pakistan did receive compensation and aid from the United Kingdom to start building its first ordnance factory in 1948.

143. Commander-in-Chief, Indian Army General Sir Rob Lockhart's Comment, "Minutes of the Defense Committee of the Cabinet," October 7,

1947, File 245, Roll 30, Mountbatten Papers, Nehru Memorial Museum and Library, New Delhi.

144. High military allocations did not translate into speedy release of funds, however. In fact, bureaucratic red tape often hindered the timely procurement of military stores and supplies. Ahmed, *My Chief,* 50–52.

145. For details of the process of army reorganization from the divisional level down to the unit level, see the army's official history, Major General Shaukat Riza, *Pakistan Army, 1947–1949,* reprint ed. (Dehradun: Natraj, 2003), 145–262. See also Fazal Muqeem Khan, *Story of the Pakistan Army,* 137–151; Brian Cloughley, *A History of the Pakistan Army: Battles and Insurrections,* 3rd ed. (Karachi: Oxford University Press, 2006), 22–24, 29–32; and Pervaiz Iqbal Cheema, *The Armed Forces of Pakistan* (Karachi: Oxford University Press, 2002), 46–85.

146. Pakistan inherited most of the infantry training centers. Fazal Muqeem Khan, *Story of the Pakistan Army,* 49–52.

147. The initial intake consisted of cadets from the third post–World War II Indian Military Academy course, the First Graduates Course (for university graduates) at the Pakistan Military Academy (PMA), and the first PMA Long Course. Riza, *Pakistan Army,* 228–229.

148. Ayub Khan, *Friends Not Masters,* 63.

149. Fazal Muqeem Khan, *Story of the Pakistan Army,* 139–143.

150. Ayub Khan, *Friends Not Masters,* 59.

151. Fazal Muqeem Khan, *Story of the Pakistan Army,* 150–151.

152. Ibid. See also Donald Horowitz, *Coup Theories and Officers' Motives: Sri Lanka in Comparative Perspective* (Princeton, NJ: Princeton University Press, 1980), 160.

153. Fazal Muqeem Khan, *Story of the Pakistan Army,* 149–150. See also Pataudi, *Story of Soldiering,* 146, 158–159.

154. Ahmed, *My Chief,* 86, claims that the plan was the brainchild of Ayub Khan. In fact, the idea of the One Unit did not originate with Ayub, but he did become its most powerful proponent by virtue of his position as C in C of the army. See Ayub Khan, *Friends Not Masters,* 216.

155. Mazhar Aziz, *Military Control in Pakistan: The Parallel State* (London: Routledge, 2008), 64.

156. Memo of Conversation between General Ayub Khan, Commander in Chief, Pakistan Army, and Raleigh A. Gibson, American Consul General, Embassy of the United States of America, Karachi, Foreign Service Dispatch no. 105, December 23, 1952, www.icdc.com/~paulwolf/pakistan /ayubkhan23dec1952.htm (accessed May 6, 2009).

157. Aziz, *Military Control in Pakistan*, 64.

158. Memo of conversation between Ayub and Gibson, December 23, 1952.

159. Memo of conversation between General Ayub Khan, Commander in Chief, Pakistan Army and Raleigh A. Gibson, American Consul General, Embassy of the United States of America, Karachi, Foreign Service Dispatch No. 135, February 13, 1953, www.icdc.com/~paulwolf/pakistan/ayubkhan13feb1952.htm (accessed May 6, 2009).

160. Pataudi, *Story of Soldiering*, 146.

161. The Pakistani military's only legally permitted nonmilitary task was providing "aid to the civil power." This was inherited from colonial rule, when the military served primarily as an internal stabilizing force. Governed by the Code of Criminal Procedure, the provision for "aid to the civil power" was designed as a mechanism to seek the assistance of the armed forces when civil authorities failed to maintain public order in a specific locality. However, in carrying out their assigned task, the armed forces "were their own masters." Penderel Moon, *Divide and Quit* (Berkeley: University of California Press, 1961), 141.

162. Raymond A. Moore Jr., "The Role of the Pakistan Army in Nation-Building," *Asian Survey* 9, no. 6 (June 1969): 447.

163. Rizvi, *Military and Politics in Pakistan*, 78–79.

164. Memo of Conversation between General Ayub Khan, Commander in Chief, Pakistan Army, and Charles D. Withers, First Secretary, American Embassy, Foreign Service Dispatch no. 851, February 28, 1953, www.icdc.com/~paulwolf/pakistan/ayub28feb1953.htm (accessed May 6, 2009).

165. Fazal Muqeem Khan, *Story of the Pakistan Army*, 182–183.

166. Ibid., 186. See also Rizvi, *Military and Politics in Pakistan*, 78–79.

167. Siddiqi, *Military in Pakistan*, 33.

168. Ibid., 25.

169. Ibid., 29.

170. See Department of State, "Policy of the United States with Respect to Pakistan," *Foreign Relations of the United States* 5 (1950): 1491, http://digicoll.library.wisc.edu/cgi-bin/FRUS/FRUS-idx?id=FRUS.FRUS1950v05 (accessed September 17, 2010).

171. Ayub Khan's biographer claims that "US military aid . . . was made possible through the initiative and efforts of General Ayub. The idea was born in his mind and it was through his negotiations with American political and military leaders that the US invited Pakistan to enter into a Mutual Defense Pact." See Ahmed, *My Chief,* 73–74.

172. Ibid., 75.

173. Department of State, "Policy of the United States with Respect to Pakistan," 1491–1492.

174. Ibid., 1492. See also William J. Barnds, *India, Pakistan, and the Great Powers* (New York: Praeger, 1972), 91.

175. *Foreign Relations of the United States* 11 (1952–1954): 1845. To assuage Indian concerns about arming Pakistan, the agreement emphasized that the assistance would be part of a regional defense initiated by Turkey.

176. Between 1954 and 1965, Pakistan received US arms worth $700 to $800 million. Barnds, *India, Pakistan, and the Great Powers*, 323.

177. Stephen P. Cohen, "U.S. Weapons and South Asia: A Policy Analysis," *Pacific Affairs* 49, no. 1 (Spring, 1976): 49–69.

178. Ministry of Defense, "Summary for the DCC: U.S. Aid to Pakistan," File 34/CF/58 (Cabinet Secretariat, Government of Pakistan).

179. See Fazal Muqeem Khan, *Story of the Pakistan Army*, 159–161.

180. Ibid.

181. See Guillermo O'Donnell, "Modernization and Military Coups: Theory, Comparisons, and the Argentine Case," in *Armies and Politics in Latin America*, ed. Abraham F. Lowenthal and J. Samuel Fitch (New York: Holmes and Meier, 1986), 96–133. See also O'Donnell, *Bureaucratic Authoritarianism: Argentina, 1966–1973, in Comparative Perspective* (Berkeley: University of California Press, 1988), 51–58.

182. Rehman, *Leadership*, 5.

2. MARCHING TOWARD MARTIAL LAW

1. "Question of the Adoption of Bengali as a State Language and the Division of Powers between the Provinces and the Center," Minutes of Cabinet Meeting held on April 24, 1954, File CF/74/54 (Cabinet Secretariat, Government of Pakistan).

2. East Pakistan, Planning Department, *Economic Disparities between East and West Pakistan* (1963), 18, 21, cited in Rounaq Jahan, *Pakistan: Failure in National Integration* (New York: Columbia University Press, 1972), 34–35.

3. Richard Sisson and Leo E. Rose, *War and Secession: Pakistan, India, and the Creation of Bangladesh* (Berkeley: University of California Press, 1990), 10.

4. Katharine Adeney, *Federalism and Ethnic Conflict Regulation in India and Pakistan* (London: Palgrave Macmillan, 2007), 138.

5. The UF received 65.72 percent of the vote and secured 223 of the 237 seats reserved for Muslims. The League's share of the vote was 19.57 percent,

and it could win only 9 seats. Craig Baxter and Syedur Rehman, *Historical Dictionary of Bangladesh,* 3rd ed. (Lanham, MD: Scarecrow Press, 2003), 90.

6. Richard L. Park, "East Bengal: Pakistan's Troubled Province," *Far Eastern Survey* 23, no. 5 (May 1954): 72–73.

7. "State Language: Discussion with [Maulvi] Abdul Haq and His Colleagues," Minutes of Cabinet Meeting held on April 24, 1954.

8. See Minutes of Cabinet Meetings held on April 7 and 10, 1954, File CF/74/54 (Cabinet Secretariat, Government of Pakistan). The Bengali Muslim League members of the Constituent Assembly were also pressuring the central government to take a hard line against the UF government and not to concede anything lest it embolden the UF's radical demands. Instead, they wanted the government to quickly resolve the issues of the distribution of power between the center and the provinces and the adoption of Bengali as a state language. Some of them even suggested to then prime minister Mohammad Ali Borga that if Arabic was adopted as a state language instead of Urdu, they would drop the demand for the state recognition of the Bengali language.

9. "Communist Situation in Pakistan," Minutes of Cabinet Meeting held on May 12, 1954, File 458/37/54 (Cabinet Secretariat, Government of Pakistan).

10. Ministry of Interior, "Summary for the Cabinet: The Communist Problem," in ibid.

11. There were two precipitating events. First, clashes between Bengalis and non-Bengalis at the Adamjee Jute Mills in Narayanganj reportedly killed over 400 people. Second, UF chief minister A. K. Fazlul Haq made several statements about the indivisibility of the two Bengals that the central government interpreted as treason. However, Haq and his cabinet members strongly denied the allegations, claiming that they "were true Pakistanis who stood for the unity and strength of our dearly beloved Pakistan . . . [whose] safety lies in our unity." "Pak General Leaving for Dacca Today," *Times of India* News Service, May 29, 1954; "East Pakistan Ministry Dismissed," *Times of India* News Service, May 31, 1954.

12. The military dispatched some 10,000 troops and a naval frigate with more troops and arms to East Pakistan to back the government's action. Richard L. Park and Richard S. Wheeler, "East Bengal under Governor's Rule," *Far Eastern Survey* 23, no. 9 (September 1954): 132; Hamza Alavi, "Class and State," in *Pakistan: The Roots of Dictatorship: The Political Economy of a Praetorian State,* ed. Hassan Gardezi and Jamil Rashid (London: Zed Press, 1983), 81.

13. Sisson and Rose, *War and Secession*, 12.

14. Colonel Mohammad Ahmed, *My Chief* (Lahore: Longmans, Green, 1960), 86–93.

15. Morris Janowitz, *Military Institutions and Coercion in the Developing Nations* (Chicago: University of Chicago Press, 1977), 83.

16. Hasan-Askari Rizvi, *The Military and Politics in Pakistan, 1947–1997* (Lahore: Sang-e-Meel, 2000), esp. 62–66, 172–187.

17. "U.S. Policy toward South Asia," NSC 5409, February 19, 1954, *Foreign Relations of the United States* 11, pt. 2 (1952–1954): 1103.

18. Despite the charges of incompetence against the government, Ghulam Mohammad reappointed most members of the sacked cabinet. Allen McGrath, *The Destruction of Pakistan's Democracy* (Karachi: Oxford University Press, 1996), 96–97.

19. Raleigh A. Gibson, American Consul General, Lahore, to the Department of State, April 28, 1953, 790 D.00/4-2853, Department of State Records, cited in Robert J. McMahon, *The Cold War on the Periphery: The United States, India, and Pakistan* (New York: Columbia University Press, 1994), 376.

20. McGrath, *Destruction of Pakistan's Democracy*, 96.

21. "Minutes of Cabinet Meeting," January 23, 1953, File 26/CF/50-1 (Cabinet Secretariat, Government of Pakistan).

22. McGrath, *Destruction of Pakistan's Democracy*, 137. Ayesha Jalal claims that military outlays were, in fact, reduced by one-third in the 1953 budget. See Jalal, *The State of Martial Rule: The Origins of Pakistan's Political Economy of Defense* (Lahore: Sang-e-Meel, 1999), 178. However, estimated budgetary figures from the time do not support this claim. See Rizvi, *Military and Politics in Pakistan*, 57–58.

23. McGrath, *Destruction of Pakistan's Democracy*, 123–124; Louis D. Hayes, *The Struggle for Legitimacy in Pakistan* (Lahore: Vanguard, 1986), 88.

24. "Interests of the Country above All," *Dawn* (Karachi), October 25, 1954.

25. Editorial, *Dawn*, August 11, 1957.

26. Keith Callard, *Pakistan: A Political Study* (London: Allen and Unwin, 1957), 186.

27. K. B. Sayeed, *Politics in Pakistan: The Nature and Direction of Change* (New York: Praeger, 1980), 43; G. W. Choudhury, *The Last Days of United Pakistan* (London: Hurst, 1974), 46; M. Rafique Afzal, *Pakistan: History and Politics, 1947–1971* (Karachi: Oxford University Press, 2009), 216.

28. K. J. Newman, "Pakistan's Preventive Autocracy and Its Causes," *Pacific Affairs* 32, no. 1 (March 1959): 26.

29. 1956 Constitution of the Islamic Republic of Pakistan, Article 37.

30. Mohammad Ayub Khan, *Friends Not Masters: A Political Autobiography* (Islamabad: Mr. Books, 2006), 71.

31. See, for instance, Rizvi, *Military and Politics in Pakistan,* 62–70.

32. Newman, "Pakistan's Preventive Autocracy," 31.

33. Mirza, like Ayub a graduate of the Royal Military Academy at Sandhurst, was deputed to the colonial Indian Political Service before independence and was defense secretary between 1947 and 1954. In this position, he was the principal civilian liaison between the government and army headquarters. During this time, Mirza developed close links to Ayub and the military, and he strongly backed the military's efforts to seek US military assistance. Mirza also had close family ties to the then US ambassador to Pakistan, Horace Hildreth, whose daughter was married to Mirza's son.

34. "Gen. Mirza in Favor of Controlled Democracy," *Times of India* News Service, November 15, 1954; Callard, *Pakistan,* 142.

35. Sayeed, *Politics in Pakistan,* 45.

36. Ayub Khan, *Friends Not Masters,* 53.

37. Ministry of Defense, "Summary for the DCC Meeting Held on 17th November, 1958," File 34/CF/58 (Cabinet Secretariat, Government of Pakistan). See also Ayub Khan, *Friends Not Masters,* 41–42.

38. "Minutes of the DCC Meeting, 17th November 1958," File 34/CF/58 (Cabinet Secretariat, Government of Pakistan).

39. Ahmed, *My Chief,* 97.

40. Shaista Suhrawardy Ikramullah, *Huseyn Shaheed Suhrawardy: A Biography* (Karachi: Oxford University Press, 1991), 91.

41. Mazhar Aziz, *Military Control in Pakistan: The Parallel State* (London: Routledge, 2007), 59–60; Rounaq Jahan, *Pakistan,* 53.

42. Of the 229 successful or unsuccessful coups between 1946 and 1970, 31 percent were carried out to preempt individuals or groups who were perceived as detrimental to military corporate interests from coming to power. William R. Thompson, *The Grievances of Military Coup Makers* (Beverly Hills, CA: Sage, 1973), 132–139.

43. Afzal, *Pakistan,* 212–213.

44. As John Samuel Fitch argues, officers' belief in the "legitimacy of military intervention in politics" is a key factor in the decision to overthrow a government. John Samuel Fitch, *The Military Coup d'État as a Political Process: Ecuador, 1948–1966* (Baltimore: Johns Hopkins University Press, 1977), 9.

45. Cynthia Enloe, *Ethnic Soldiers: State Security in Ethnically Divided Societies* (London: Penguin Books, 1980), 159.

46. Memo of Conversation between General Ayub Khan, Commander in Chief, Pakistan Army, and Charles D. Withers, First Secretary, American Embassy, Foreign Service Dispatch no. 851, February 28, 1953, www.icdc.com /~paulwolf/pakistan/ayub28feb1953.htm (accessed May 6, 2009).

47. Major General Fazal Muqeem Khan, *The Story of the Pakistan Army* (Karachi: Oxford University Press, 1963), 190.

48. The cabinet responded that political matters should be of no concern to the Ministry of Defence and should be avoided. Relaying the opinion of the GHQ authorities, the ministry informed the cabinet that the military's field formations routinely reported the troops' reaction to political events up the chain of command every month, and that this practice serves a useful purpose and ought to be continued. See Minutes of Cabinet Meeting held on November 21, 1957; excerpt from the Fortnightly Summary of the Ministry of Defense, October 16–31, 1957; and Ministry of Defence, "Summary for the Cabinet," March 12, 1958, Accession No. 2234, Min/Def No.6/178/D-8 (Cabinet Secretariat, Government of Pakistan).

49. Fazal Muqeem Khan, *Story of the Pakistan Army*, 189–190.

50. Ayub Khan, *Friends Not Masters*, 75.

51. Fazal Muqeem Khan, *Story of the Pakistan Army*, 175; Ahmed, *My Chief*, 101.

52. Fazal Muqeem Khan, *Story of the Pakistan Army*, 176–177; Mushtaq Ahmad, *Government and Politics in Pakistan* (New York: Praeger, 1963), 125.

53. Ahmed, *My Chief*, 101.

54. Fazal Muqeem Khan, *Story of the Pakistan Army*, 177.

55. Ahmed, *My Chief*, 102.

56. Ibid., 101–103.

57. "General Ayub Khan's First Broadcast to the Nation," October 8, 1958, reproduced in Rizvi, *Military and Politics in Pakistan*, 290–294.

58. Eric Nordlinger, *Soldiers in Politics: Military Coups and Governments* (Englewood Cliffs, NJ: Prentice-Hall, 1977), 19.

59. Fazal Muqeem Khan, *Story of the Pakistan Army*, 189–191.

60. Jahan, *Pakistan*, 53.

61. "General Ayub Khan's First Broadcast to the Nation."

62. Government of Pakistan, *Three Years of Progress under the Revolutionary Government of Pakistan: 1958–1961* (Karachi: Department of Films and Publications, 1961), 2.

63. Wayne Wilcox, "The Pakistan Coup d'Etat of 1958," *Pacific Affairs* 38, no. 2 (1965): 149.

64. Multiple interviews of civilian and military officers on active duty in 1957–1958 by the author, Islamabad and Lahore, 2008. For instance,

Roedad Khan, who was then deputy commissioner in Dera Ismail Khan, claims that there was no serious breakdown in public order, and he was surprised when the assistant martial law administrator, an army colonel, summoned him and the superintendent of the police and instructed them to collect all unlicensed arms. Interview by the author, Islamabad, June 2008.

65. Kalat was the largest princely state in Balochistan. Pakistan deployed its army troops to the state and coerced the khan into acceding to Pakistan in March–April 1948.

66. Wayne Wilcox argues that the alleged secession announced by the khan of Kalat was fabricated by the coup makers because they needed a dramatic example of a threat to national unity to justify the coup. See Wayne Wilcox, *Pakistan: The Consolidation of a Nation* (New York: Columbia University Press, 1963), 262–267.

67. Lewis Coser, *The Functions of Social Conflict* (Glencoe, IL: Free Press, 1956), 107.

68. Other incidents that appeared to the military as cues for immediate action were the fatal injuries sustained by the deputy speaker of East Pakistan's provincial legislature in a parliamentary brawl in September 1958 and a massive demonstration in Karachi on October 6, 1958, by the Muslim League against the banning of its National Guards as part of a broader government ban on private paramilitary organizations. See Fazal Muqeem Khan, *Story of the Pakistan Army*, 194.

69. Ayub Khan, *Friends Not Masters*, 75. See also L. F. Rushbrook Williams, *State of Pakistan* (London: Faber, 1966), 186. Williams had interviewed key senior military officers at the time.

70. Edwin Lieuwan, *Generals vs. Presidents: Neo-militarism in Latin America* (New York: Praeger, 1964), 98.

71. Ayub Khan, *Friends Not Masters*, 70.

72. Bilal Hashmi, "Dragon Seed: Military in the State," in Gardezi and Rashid, *Pakistan*, 164.

73. McMahon, *Cold War on the Periphery*, 267.

74. See the declassified documents on Chile and Iran compiled by the National Security Archive, George Washington University, for example, "CIA Notes on Meeting with the President on Chile, September 5, 1970"; and "Genesis of Project FUBULT, September 16, 1970," Department of Defense, U.S. Milgroup, Situation Report #2, October 1, 1973, http://www2 .gwu.edu/~nsarchiv/NSAEBB/NSAEBB8/nsaebb8i.htm. On Iran, see "CIA, Memo from Kermit Roosevelt to [Excised], July 15, 1953"; and "CIA, Note to Mr. [John] Waller, July 22, 1953," http://www2.gwu.edu/~nsarchiv /NSAEBB/NSAEBB435/ (accessed August 20, 2013).

75. "U.S. Policy toward South Asia," 1094–1095.

76. "Minutes of the DCC Meeting," May 19, 1958.

77. The State Department was gratified by such privileged access to the government, but it instructed its officials in Pakistan to "avoid semblance of tutelage of Pakistani leadership" as a "matter of principle." See Department of State to the U.S. Embassy in Pakistan, February 4, 1958, *Foreign Relations of the United States* XV, *South and Southeast Asia* (1958–1960): 621. .

78. Hildreth went on to remind the Department of State that "one should not forget that with the tide of communist advance in Southeast Asia, East Bengal might offer an attractive and little noticed target to the planners of the Asian Cominform." See Ambassador in Pakistan [Hildreth] to the Department of State, July 10, 1954, *Foreign Relations of the United States* XI, pt. 2 (1952–1954): 1852.

79. Ibid.

80. Department of State to the U.S. Embassy in Pakistan, 621.

81. Letter from President Eisenhower to President Mirza, October 11, 1958, *Foreign Relations of the United States* XV (1958–1960): 673–674.

82. Department of State, Central Files, 611.90D/10–1258, Telegram 833 to Karachi, October 13, 1958.

83. Ibid., 611.90D/10–1358.

84. Letter from Secretary of State Dulles to President Mirza, October 17, 1958, *Foreign Relations of the United States* XV (1958–1960): 677.

85. *Pakistan Forum* 2, nos. 7/8 (April–May 1972): 9.

86. McMahon, *Cold War on the Periphery*, 267.

87. Bruce Riedel, *Deadly Embrace: Pakistan, America, and the Future of the Global Jihad* (Washington, DC: Brookings Institution Press, 2011), 13.

3. "REVOLUTION" TO REVOLT

1. Ayesha Jalal, *Democracy and Authoritarianism in South Asia: A Comparative and Historical Perspective* (Lahore: Sang-e-Meel, 1995), 55.

2. Major General Fazal Muqeem Khan, *The Story of the Pakistan Army* (Karachi: Oxford University Press, 1963), 199.

3. "General Ayub Khan's First Broadcast to the Nation," October 8, 1958, reproduced in Hasan-Askari Rizvi, *The Military and Politics in Pakistan, 1947–1997* (Lahore: Sang-e-Meel, 2000), 290–294.

4. Ralph Braibanti, *Research on the Bureaucracy of Pakistan* (Durham, NC: Duke University Press, 1966), 45.

5. This was done through the Elective Bodies Disqualification Order, 1959. The number of people affected by the order is unclear and often dis-

puted. Estimates range from 500 to 6,000. See Rizvi, *Military and Politics in Pakistan,* 101–102.

6. On the structure and functioning of General Ayub's military-led government, see Lawrence Ziring, *The Ayub Era: Politics in Pakistan, 1958–1969* (Syracuse, NY: Syracuse University Press, 1971).

7. Gerald H. Heeger, "Politics in the Post-military State: Some Reflections on the Pakistani Experience," *World Politics* 29, no. 2 (January 1977): 250.

8. Karl Von Vorys, *Political Development in Pakistan* (Princeton, NJ: Princeton University Press, 1965), 146–147.

9. Raymond A. Moore, *Nation Building and the Pakistan Army, 1947–1969* (Ann Arbor: University of Michigan Press, 1979), 32.

10. Ziring, *Ayub Era,* 12.

11. *Dawn of a New Era: Basic Democracies in Pakistan* (Karachi: Bureau of National Reconstruction, Government of Pakistan, 1960), 8.

12. Field Marshal Mohammed Ayub Khan, "A New Experiment in Democracy," *Annals of the American Academy of Political and Social Science* 358 (March 1965): 111.

13. Ziring, *Ayub Era,* 15–16.

14. *Dawn of a New Era,* 10–12.

15. Ibid., 14.

16. "A Constitution for Pakistan," *Round Table* 52, no. 207 (June 1, 1962): 228.

17. Samuel Huntington, *Political Order in Changing Societies* (New Haven, CT: Yale University Press, 1968), 250–254. In 1969, a year after *Political Order* was published, Ayub and his BD system were swept aside when he had to relinquish power in the face of an antiregime movement, in good part because he had denied the movement's members meaningful political participation. In fact, the BD system was one of the main sources of public alienation and opposition to the regime.

18. Heeger, "Politics in the Post-military State," 250.

19. Interviews by the author, Peshawar, Islamabad, and Lahore, June–December 2008.

20. Interview by the author, Lahore, December 2008. Lieutenant General Mohammad Tariq (retd.) recalled that he and his colleagues and contemporaries had faith in the system until he discovered that most BDs, who were in the "pocket" of the local administration and the police, would dare not elect anyone but Ayub Khan as president. Interview by the author, Lahore, November 2008.

21. Ayub Khan, "New Experiment in Democracy," 111.

22. Ibid.

23. Ziring, *Ayub Era*, 18.

24. Ayub Khan, "New Experiment in Democracy," 111–112. However, Ayub ignored the commission's recommendations, which conflicted directly with his vision of controlled democracy. Among the recommendations were discarding the BD system in favor of direct presidential elections (albeit with restricted franchise), a strong legislature, and the revival of political parties. See Ziring, *Ayub Era*, 24–25.

25. For instance, its powers of legislation were limited by the president's ability to make laws through ordinances (Article 29) and to veto legislation even when passed by the National Assembly with a two-thirds majority (Article 27). The Constitution of the Republic of Pakistan, 1962.

26. "Constitution for Pakistan," 228–237.

27. Article 238, The Constitution of the Republic of Pakistan.

28. Ziring, *Ayub Era*, 27–28.

29. Richard Sisson and Leo E. Rose, *War and Secession: Pakistan, India, and the Creation of Bangladesh* (Berkeley: University of California Press, 1990), 18–19.

30. "Franchise Commission Report, 1963," *Gazette of Pakistan Extraordinary*, August 23, 1963, 637a.

31. *Franchise Commission Report: An Analysis* (Islamabad: Ministry of Law, Government of Pakistan, 1964), 10–11.

32. Ibid., 12–13.

33. Ibid., 13.

34. Ibid., 12.

35. Ibid.

36. Ibid., 13.

37. Sean P. Winchell, "Pakistan's ISI: The Invisible Government," *International Journal of Intelligence and Counterintelligence* 16, no. 3 (2003): 375.

38. Sisson and Rose, *War and Secession*, 19.

39. Rounaq Jahan, *Bangladesh Politics: Problems and Issues* (Dhaka: University Press, 1980), 30.

40. Mahbubul Haq, "The System Is to Blame for the 22 Wealthy Families," *Times* (London), March 22, 1973.

41. *National Assembly of Pakistan Debates* 1 (March 8, 1963): 30–31.

42. Brian Cloughley, *A History of the Pakistan Army: Battles and Insurrections*, 3rd ed. (Karachi: Oxford University Press, 2006), 64.

43. General K.M. Arif, *Khaki Shadows: Pakistan, 1947–1997* (Karachi: Oxford University Press, 2004), 47–49; Cloughley, *History of the Pakistan Army,* 57–58.

44. Lieutenant General Gul Hassan Khan, *Memoirs* (Karachi: Oxford University Press, 1993), 182.

45. Ibid., 178.

46. G.W. Choudhury, *The Last Days of United Pakistan* (London: Hurst, 1974), xii.

47. Gyasuddin Molla, "Awami League: From Charismatic Leadership to Political Party," in *Political Parties in South Asia,* ed. Subrata Kumar Mitra, Mike Enskat, and Clemens Spiess (Westport, CT: Praeger, 2004), 219.

48. War Directive No. 4, August 9, 1967, quoted in *The Report of the Hamoodur Rehman Commission of Inquiry into the 1971 War* as declassified by the Government of Pakistan (Lahore: Vanguard, 2000), 166–168.

49. The six points were as follows: (1) a federal government, parliamentary in form, was to be established by free and fair elections on the basis of universal adult franchise; (2) the federal government was to have responsibilities only for defense and foreign policy; (3) there were to be separate currencies or other alternate means of preventing the transfer of resources from the East to the West; (4) each federating unit was to have powers of taxation; (5) each federating unit was to have control over its foreign exchange earnings and the power of negotiating foreign aid and trade; and (6) each unit was to raise its own paramilitary force.

50. *Report of the Hamoodur Rehman Commission,* 49.

51. Haq, "System Is to Blame."

52. Bhutto founded the PPP in 1967 with the explicit goal of establishing a socialist government in Pakistan. The party's declared basic principles were as follows: "Islam is our faith. Democracy is our politics. Socialism is our economy. All power to the people." On the PPP's birth and evolution, see Philip Edward Jones, *The Pakistan People's Party: Rise to Power* (New York: Oxford University Press, 2003); see also K.B. Sayeed, *Politics in Pakistan: The Nature and Direction of Change* (New York: Praeger, 1980); Anwar H. Syed, "The Pakistan People's Party," in *Pakistan: The Long View,* ed. Lawrence Ziring, Ralph Braibanti, and Howard Wriggins (Durham, NC: Duke University Center for Commonwealth and Comparative Politics, 1977), 70–116.

53. Omar Noman, *Pakistan: A Political and Economic History since 1947* (London: Kegan Paul, 1990), 43.

54. Ziring, *Ayub Era*, 112.

55. Ibid., 109.

56. Ibid., 112–113.

57. President General Yahya Khan, "Address to the Nation," March 26, 1969, in Sheelendra Kumar Singh, *Bangladesh Documents*, vol. 1 (Dhaka: University Press Limited, 1999), 275–277.

58. Herbert Feldman, *The End and the Beginning: Pakistan, 1969–1971* (London: Oxford University Press, 1975), 18.

59. Lieutenant General Fazal Muqeem Khan (retd.), *Pakistan's Crisis in Leadership* (Islamabad: National Book Foundation, 1973), 150.

60. Choudhury, *Last Days of United Pakistan*, 52–53.

61. See the salient points of the Legal Framework Order, President's Order No. 2 of March 30, 1970, in Feldman, *End and the Beginning*, 62–66.

62. Legal Framework Order, Clauses 24–25.

63. Altaf Gauhar, "How Intelligence Agencies Run Our Politics," *Nation* (Lahore), August 17, 1997.

64. *Report of the Hamoodur Rehman Commission*, 352.

65. Hussain Haqqani, *Pakistan: Between Mosque and Military* (Washington, DC: Carnegie Endowment for International Peace, 2005), 57.

66. G. W. Choudhury, *Pakistan: Transition from Military to Civilian Rule* (Essex: Scorpion, 1988), 8.

67. Bhutto desired a PPP-AL grand coalition because "neither majority party had any representation in the National Assembly from the other Wing. . . . A coalition would also avoid further polarization between the two Wings of the country. In the circumstances, such a coalition would conform to the democratic principle of giving proper representation to, and combining the views of, the majorities of both Wings in a national government." See Z. A. Bhutto, *The Great Tragedy* (n.d.), 17, www.bhutto.org (accessed July 8, 2012).

68. Jahan, *Bangladesh Politics*, 56.

69. Lieutenant General Kamal Matinuddin, *Tragedy of Errors: The East Pakistan Crisis, 1968–1971* (Lahore: Wajidalis, 1994), 156. Brigadier A. R. Siddiqi, the head of the army's public relations department at the time, described the generals' dilemma: "The armed forces had suddenly lost their power to act. . . . Gulliver bound by Bengali Lilliputians. . . . They continued to drift from . . . crisis to crisis in the vague expectation of perpetuating their power without ostensibly striving for it." See A. R. Siddiqi, *The Military in Pakistan: Image and Reality* (Lahore: Vanguard, 1996), 180.

70. Choudhury, *Last Days of United Pakistan*, 148.

71. Gauhar, "How Intelligence Agencies Run Our Politics."

72. *Report of the Hamoodur Rehman Commission,* 79.

73. Quoted in Brigadier Siddiq Salik, *Witness to Surrender* (Karachi: Oxford University Press, 1977), 53.

74. The military had reportedly started a military buildup in East Pakistan in mid-February under the pretext of tensions with India, which increased after March 1. Feldman, *End and the Beginning,* 129; Jahan, *Bangladesh Politics,* 58.

75. Jahan, *Bangladesh Politics,* 47.

76. Yaqub Khan ultimately resigned from the army when Yahya Khan did not heed his advice. Fazal Muqeem Khan, *Pakistan's Crisis in Leadership,* 59–60; Gul Hassan Khan, *Memoirs,* 266.

77. On March 17, after holding talks with Mujib, Yahya told the new commander of the Eastern Command, Lieutenant General Tikka Khan, "The bastard is not behaving. Get ready." Salik, *Witness to Surrender,* 62. See also Feldman, *End and the Beginning,* 112–113.

78. Sisson and Rose, *War and Secession,* 3.

79. Ibid., 157–158.

80. Gul Hassan Khan, *Memoirs,* 244.

81. Fazal Muqeem Khan, *Pakistan's Crisis in Leadership,* 51.

82. *Report of the Hamoodur Rehman Commission,* 79.

83. Fazal Muqeem Khan, *Pakistan's Crisis in Leadership,* 51.

84. Yahya Khan, "Address to the Nation."

85. A. A. K. Niazi, *The Betrayal of East Pakistan* (Karachi: Oxford University Press, 1998), 78–79.

86. There is considerable controversy about the number of people killed by the Pakistani army, ranging from the official Bangladeshi claim of 3 million Bengalis to the official Pakistani figure of 26,000 civilian casualties. Both sides obviously had an incentive to misrepresent the death toll for domestic and international consumption. More recently, the Indian-Bengali scholar Sharmila Bose has claimed that Bengali nationalists, who themselves committed appalling and widespread atrocities against non-Bengalis, have grossly exaggerated the alleged mass killings committed by the Pakistani army. However, as the Bangladeshi author Naeem Mohieman wrote in a sharp rebuke of Bose, a "distinction needs to be made between the violence of a chaotic, freelance mob" against non-Bengalis and "the systematic violence of the [Pakistani] military" and its sponsored "death squads." Mohieman asks poignantly, "Whether the death toll was 3 million or 30,000 or less, does that make it any less of a genocide?" See "Mujib Charges 3 Million Slaughtered by Pakistan,"

Associated Press, January 15, 1972; *Report of the Hamoodur Rehman Commission*, 513; Sarmila Bose, *Dead Reckoning: Memories of the 1971 Bangladesh War* (London: Hurst, 2011), 13, 180, 183, 191; and Naeem Mohieman, "Flying Blind: Waiting for a Real Reckoning," *Economic and Political Weekly*, September 3, 2011, 41, 46.

87. Ian Talbot, *Pakistan: A Modern History* (London: Hurst, 2005), 213.

88. These events are documented by the then chief of general staff, Lieutenant General Gul Hassan Khan, in *Memoirs*, 339–344. See also Hassan Abbas, *Pakistan's Drift into Extremism: Allah, the Army, and America's War on Terror* (London: M. E. Sharpe, 2005), 67–68.

89. For the role of founding leaders in imprinting their legacy on organizations, see John R. Kimberley, "Environmental Constraints and Organizational Culture: A Comparative Analysis of Rehabilitation Organizations," *Administrative Sciences Quarterly* 20 (1975): 1–9.

90. Gul Hassan Khan, *Memoirs*, 248–249.

91. Interview by the author, Lahore, December 2008.

92. Ibid.

93. Interview of Lieutenant General Moinuddin Haider (retd.) by the author, Lahore, November 2008.

94. Interview by the author, Peshawar, June 2008.

95. Lieutenant General Talat Masood (retd.), interview by the author, Islamabad, April 2008.

96. Lieutenant General Mohammad Tariq (retd.), interview by the author, Lahore, November 2008.

97. Matinuddin, *Tragedy of Errors*, 155; Fazal Muqeem Khan, *Pakistan's Crisis in Leadership*, 51.

98. Niazi, *Betrayal of East Pakistan*, 178.

99. Fazal Muqeem Khan, *Pakistan's Crisis in Leadership*, 146.

100. "Journey from Scratch to Nuclear Power," www.pakistanarmy.gov.pk (the Pakistani army's official website) (accessed September 3, 2011).

4. RECAPTURING THE STATE

1. See Stephen P. Cohen, "Arms and Politics in Bangladesh, India, and Pakistan" (Special Studies no. 49, Council on International Studies, State University of New York, 1974), 41–42. Cohen's study covers the early 1970s.

2. Khurshid Hyder, "Pakistan under Bhutto," *Current History* 63, no. 735 (1972): 202.

3. See Lieutenant General Gul Hassan Khan, *Memoirs* (Karachi: Oxford University Press, 1993), 349–350.

4. Ibid., 353–359.

5. James Q. Wilson, *Bureaucracy: What Government Agencies Do and Why They Do It* (New York: Basic Books, 1989), 110.

6. Gul Hassan Khan, *Memoirs,* 363–364.

7. For the civilian government, the most alarming instance of military defiance came during a police strike in major urban centers in the North-West Frontier Province and the Punjab. The army chief, who flatly refused to aid the government, suspected that the PPP had organized the strike to drag the army in and further defame it in the public's eyes. See Gul Hassan Khan, *Memoirs,* 362. PPP leaders suspected that the army had a hand in the police crisis, which was meant to create an impression of civilian incompetence. Interviews of then Punjab governor Ghulam Mustafa Khar and the federal finance minister and PPP secretary general, Dr. Mubashir Hassan, by the author, December and June 2008.

8. Gul Hassan Khan, *Memoirs,* 357.

9. In his view, the minister of state for defense was trying to "lord it over the army" by summoning the chief of staff to meetings. Ibid., 353.

10. Interview of Dr. Mubashir Hassan by the author.

11. G.W. Chaudhury, *The Last Days of United Pakistan* (London: Hurst, 1974), 148; Shahid Javed Burki, *Pakistan under Bhutto* (London: Macmillan, 1980), 70.

12. Mubashir Hassan, *The Mirage of Power: An Inquiry into the Bhutto Years, 1971–1977* (Karachi: Oxford University Press, 2000), 80.

13. Interview of Ghulam Mustafa Khar by the author, Lahore, December 2008.

14. Rafi Raza, then the minister for production, cites one incident when, on the way back from an official visit to Ankara, Bhutto received an urgent message from Pakistan to delay his departure. Bhutto read it as a sure sign of a military putsch, even though it turned out not to be one. See Raza, *Zulfiqar Ali Bhutto and Pakistan, 1967–1977* (Karachi: Oxford University Press, 1998), 162.

15. Interview, *Times of India,* March 14, 1972.

16. Gul Hassan Khan confirms these events. He also claims that he could not mobilize the army to forestall his ouster, perhaps because he had been effectively sequestered from his troops. See Gul Hassan Khan, *Memoirs,* 368–372.

17. Zulfiqar Ali Bhutto, *Speeches and Statements, 20 December 1971 to 31 March 1972* (Karachi: Films and Publications Department, Government of Pakistan, 1972), 371–372.

18. Shirin Tahir-Kheli, "The Military in Contemporary Pakistan," *Armed Forces and Society* 6, no. 4 (Summer 1980): 646.

19. Hasan-Askari Rizvi, *Military, State, and Society in Pakistan* (Lahore: Sang-e-Meel, 2003), 144; A. A. K. Niazi, *The Betrayal of East Pakistan* (Karachi: Oxford University Press, 1998), 221.

20. The officers were court-martialed, dismissed from service, and given prison sentences ranging from three months to life. See details in Hassan Abbas, *Pakistan's Drift into Extremism: Allah, the Army, and America's War on Terror* (London: M. E. Sharpe, 2005), 73–77; and Shuja Nawaz, *Crossed Swords: Pakistan, Its Army, and the Wars Within* (Karachi: Oxford University Press, 2008), 335–337.

21. Gul Hassan Khan, *Memoirs,* 360–361.

22. *Constitution of the Islamic Republic of Pakistan* (Islamabad: National Assembly of Pakistan, 2004), Article 245(1).

23. Article 6(1) of the constitution declares the abrogation or subversion of the constitution "by the use of force or show of force or any other unconstitutional means" to be "high treason." Ibid.

24. In September 1973, the parliament passed the High Treason (Punishment) Act, which provided the death penalty or life imprisonment for the crime.

25. Every member of the armed forces has to take this oath at the time of commission: "I do solemnly swear that I will bear true faith and allegiance to Pakistan and uphold the Constitution of the Islamic Republic of Pakistan which embodies the will of the people, that I will not engage myself in any political activities whatsoever and that I will honestly and faithfully serve Pakistan in the Pakistan Army (or Navy or Air Force) as required by and under the law." The previous oath of service included a pledge of allegiance to the constitution but did not explicitly proscribe military involvement in politics.

26. As noted in Chapter 1, the Defense Committee of the Cabinet was created in 1948. It fell into disuse in the 1950s and became virtually redundant under military rule from 1958 to 1971.

27. The committee's members included the minister of state for defense and the ministers of interior, finance, foreign affairs, information, communications, and commerce. The Chairman Joint Chiefs of Staff Committee, the three service chiefs, and the secretaries general and secretaries of defense, finance, and foreign affairs were in attendance. See *White Paper on Higher Defense Organization* issued in October 1976, reproduced in Hasan-Askari Rizvi, *The Military and Politics in Pakistan, 1947–1997* (Lahore: Sang-e-Meel, 2000), 1, 311–319.

28. Defense Division, Ministry of Defense, Government of Pakistan, www.mod.gov.pk (accessed April 4, 2012).

29. Zulfiqar Ali Bhutto, "Address to the Nation," March 3, 1972; reproduced in Bhutto, *Speeches and Statements,* 110–111.

30. The term "steel frame" was first used by British prime minister David Lloyd George in a speech to the House of Commons in 1922. While defending the colonial civil service in India, he said, "I can see no period when they can dispense with the guidance and the assistance of this small nucleus of the British Civil Service, of British officials in India. . . . They are the steel frame of the whole structure . . . if you take that steel frame out, the fabric will collapse." *Parliamentary Debates,* House of Commons (official report), 5th series 157, column 1513.

31. The service was renamed the District Management Group (DMG) and was made part of the unified Central Superior Services, which was divided into different occupational groups (e.g., police, customs, and income tax). For an in-depth discussion of Bhutto's civil service reforms, see Charles Kennedy, *Bureaucracy in Pakistan* (Karachi: Oxford University Press, 1987). See also Burki, *Pakistan under Bhutto,* 98–103.

32. *The Report of the Hamoodur Rehman Commission of Inquiry into the 1971 War* as declassified by the Government of Pakistan (Lahore: Vanguard, 2000), 353–354. The need for a military joint staff was also felt in the military after the 1965 and 1971 wars with India, which revealed poor coordination among the different military services. Interview of Lieutenant General Kamal Matinuddin (retd.), director general at the Joint Staff Headquarters (1976–1977), by the author, Rawalpindi, June 2008.

33. *White Paper on Higher Defense Organization.*

34. Ibid.

35. Ayesha Siddiqa, *Military Inc.: Inside Pakistan's Military Economy* (London: Pluto Press, 2007), 62.

36. *White Paper on Higher Defense Organization.*

37. Interview of Chishti by the author, Rawalpindi, June 2008. In his capacity as the military secretary, Chishti was responsible for putting together files of the officers qualified to become chief of army staff.

38. Shahid Javed Burki, "Zia's Eleven Years," in *Pakistan under the Military: Eleven Years of Ziaul Haq,* by Shahid Javed Burki and Craig Baxter (Boulder, CO: Westview Press, 1991), 6.

39. Rizvi, *Military, State, and Society in Pakistan,* 147.

40. Burki, *Pakistan under Bhutto,* 105.

41. "Statement by Begum Nusrat Bhutto," *National Assembly of Pakistan Debates* 6, no. 11 (June 20, 1977): 108.

42. Kamal Hossain, Bangladesh's first law minister (1972–1973) and former foreign minister (1973–1975), contends that Bhutto dissuaded Mujib from his demand for war-crimes trials by essentially telling him that trying Pakistani military officers would be politically impossible and would lead to his "beheading" and the "end of democracy" in Pakistan. Interview of Kamal Hossain by the author, Dhaka, November 2012.

43. Clive Dewey, "The Rural Roots of Pakistani Militarism," in *The Political Inheritance of Pakistan*, ed. D. A. Lowe (London: Macmillan, 1991), 259.

44. Rizvi, *Military and Politics in Pakistan*, 218.

45. Stephen P. Cohen, *The Pakistan Army*, 2nd ed. (Karachi: Oxford University Press, 1998), 73.

46. The Commission also issued a supplemental report in October 1974 after recording the testimony of returned Pakistani POWs and civilians who had been interned in India. The report was declassified by the Pakistani government in 2000 after it was leaked in the Indian press.

47. *Report of the Hamoodur Rehman Commission*, Supplemental Report, 24.

48. *Report of the Hamoodur Rehman Commission*, 518.

49. Ibid., 542.

50. See Zulfiqar Ali Bhutto, "Rejoinder in the Supreme Court," October 31, 1977, www.bhutto.org (accessed February 8, 2010).

51. Abbas, *Pakistan's Drift into Extremism*, 72.

52. *Report of the Hamoodur Rehman Commission*, 518.

53. Gerald Heeger, "Politics in the Post-military State: Some Reflections on the Pakistani Experience," *World Politics* 29, no. 2 (January 1977): 253; Ian Talbot, *Pakistan: A Modern History* (London: Hurst, 2005), 244; and Stanley Wolpert, *Zulfi Bhutto of Pakistan* (Karachi: Oxford University Press, 1993), 3–4.

54. Ayesha Jalal, *Democracy and Authoritarianism in South Asia: A Comparative and Historical Perspective* (Lahore: Sang-e-Meel, 1995), 80–83.

55. Heeger, "Politics in the Post-military State," 253.

56. Burki, *Pakistan under Bhutto*, 184–189.

57. Talbot, *Pakistan*, 218–220; Raza, *Zulfiqar Ali Bhutto and Pakistan*, 323.

58. Under the provisions of the act, individuals involved in aiding or advocating treasonous or secessionist activities could be imprisoned for up to seven years, and associations suspected of similar acts could be proscribed and have their assets frozen. The act is available at http://www.ma-law.org.pk/pdflaw/THE%20PREVENTION%20OF%20ANTI.pdf (accessed September 3, 2012).

59. Talbot, *Pakistan*, 243; Burki, *Pakistan under Bhutto*, 106–107; Herbert Feldman, "Pakistan in 1974," *Asian Survey* 15, no. 2 (February 1975): 113, 115; and Feldman, "Pakistan—1973," *Asian Survey* 14, no. 2 (February 1974): 137, 141.

60. Bhutto himself subscribed to this theory.

61. Saeed Shafqat, *Civil-Military Relations: From Zulfiqar Ali Bhutto to Benazir Bhutto* (Boulder, CO: Westview Press, 1997), 177.

62. Nawaz, *Crossed Swords*, 328–330.

63. "Secret GHQ Report on the Indo-Pakistan 1971 War," quoted in ibid., 310.

64. Interview of a brigadier, directing staff, at the National Defence University, by the author, December 2009.

65. Eric A. Nordlinger, *Soldiers in Politics: Military Coups and Governments* (Englewood Cliffs, NJ: Prentice-Hall, 1977), 75–77. See also Edwin Lieuwan, *Generals vs. Presidents: Neo-militarism in Latin America* (New York: Praeger, 1964); and Martin Needler, *Anatomy of a Coup d'État: Ecuador, 1963* (Washington, DC: Institute for the Comparative Study of Political Systems, 1964).

66. Bhutto wrote forebodingly to his chief security officer, "Once the armed forces intervene" in civil administration, "they play the game according to their own rules. It is necessary for a civilian government to avoid seeking the assistance of the armed forces in dealing with its responsibilities and problems." See "Z. A. Bhutto's Directive for the Creation of the FSF," Annexure 26, *White Paper on the Performance of the Bhutto Regime*, vol. 3 (Islamabad: Government of Pakistan, 1979), A-68.

67. The FSF was equipped with semiautomatic rifles, submachine guns, mortars, grenades, vehicles, and communications gear. In 1974, its strength was 13,785 men, which had risen to 18,563 by 1976. See ibid., 26.

68. Shafqat, *Civil-Military Relations*, 180–181, 185.

69. Shirin Tahir-Kheli, *The United States and Pakistan: The Evolution of an Influence Relationship* (London: Praeger, 1982), 69.

70. Rizvi, *Military, State, and Society in Pakistan*, 146; Shafqat, *Civil-Military Relations*, 180.

71. Claude E. Welch, "Civilian Control of the Military: Myth and Reality," in *Civilian Control of the Military: Theory and Cases from Developing Countries*, ed. Claude E. Welch (Albany: State University of New York Press, 1976), 4.

72. In several Latin American countries (e.g., Honduras, Ecuador, and Chile in the 1960s and 1970s), the raising of armed militias and paramilitaries

prompted military coups because leftist governments intended to replace the regular military with these irregular forces.

73. Raju Thomas, *Indian Security Policy* (Princeton, NJ: Princeton University Press, 1986), 22–23. See also "National Security Paper" (Rawalpindi: National Defence College, 1988), 39.

74. T. V. Paul, "Causes of India-Pakistan Rivalry," in *The India-Pakistan Conflict: An Enduring Rivalry*, ed. T. V. Paul (New York: Cambridge University Press, 2005), 11.

75. Simla Agreement, http://www.stimson.org/research-pages/simla -agreement/ (accessed March 5, 2011).

76. Jalal, *Democracy and Authoritarianism in South Asia*, 81. See also Tahir-Kheli, "Military in Contemporary Pakistan," 645.

77. See General Pervez Musharraf, *In the Line of Fire: A Memoir* (New York: Free Press, 2006), 72.

78. Rizvi, *Military and Politics in Pakistan*, 217–218.

79. The Islamists were acceptable to Pakistan because they did not support Kabul's position on the Durand Line, Pakistan's contested border with Afghanistan. Rizwan Hussain, *Pakistan and the Emergence of Islamic Militancy in Afghanistan* (London: Ashgate, 2005), 97.

80. Zulfikar Ali Bhutto, *If I Am Assassinated* (Lahore: Classic, n.d.), 97. For the ISI's inflated assessments of a PPP electoral victory, see Husain Haqqani, *Pakistan: Between Mosque and Military* (Washington, DC: Carnegie Endowment for International Peace, 2005), 115–117.

81. Dominated by Islamists, the component parties in the coalition were the Jamiatul Ulema Islam, headed by Maulana Mufti Mehmud; the Jamaate Islami (JI), led by Mian Tufail Mohammad; the Jamiatul Ulema Pakistan of Maulana Shah Ahmed Noorani; the Tehreeke Istiqlal of former air marshal Asghar Khan; the Pakistan Muslim League (Pir Pigaro); the Pakistan Democratic Party (Nawabzada Nasrullah Khan); the Kashmiri Muslim Conference (Sardar Abdul Qayyum); the National Democratic Party (Sherbaz Khan Mazari); and the Khaksar Tehrik (Khan Mohammad Ashraf Khan).

82. Marvin G. Weinbaum, "The March 1977 Elections in Pakistan: Where Everyone Lost," *Asian Survey* 17, no. 7 (July 1977): 606.

83. The extent to which the election was rigged remains disputed, but, as Marvin Weinbaum notes, "Whatever the extent of irregularities, in just a matter of days, the legitimacy of the entire electoral exercise had been lost." Ibid., 614.

84. "Re-polling Wherever Irregularities Proved," *Pakistan Times* (Lahore), March 22, 1977.

85. Talbot, *Pakistan*, 240–241.

86. Weinbaum, "March 1977 Elections in Pakistan," 616.

87. "Arson and Rioting by Demonstrators," *Pakistan Times*, April 10, 1977.

88. "Shariat Law in Six Months: Total Prohibition, Ban on Gambling Forthwith," *Pakistan Times*, April 18, 1977; "Weekly Holiday on Friday from July 1," *Pakistan Times*, May 26, 1977.

89. See Maulana Kausar Niazi, *Zulfiqar Ali Bhutto: The Last Days* (Delhi: Vikas, 1992), 84–86. Niazi was the federal minister for information and broadcasting and one of the two members of the PPP team negotiating with the PNA.

90. "Martial Law Imposed: Karachi, Hyderabad, Lahore under Curfew," *Pakistan Times*, April 24, 1977.

91. The Constitution (7th) Amendment Bill, *National Assembly of Pakistan Debates* 4, no. 9 (May 16, 1977): 309–311.

92. Bhutto's address to parliament, reported in *Pakistan Times*, April 29, 1977.

93. "Statement by Prime Minister Zulfiqar Ali Bhutto on the Adjournment Motion re: Nuclear Reprocessing Plant," *National Assembly of Pakistan Debates* 5 (June 10, 1977): 110.

94. Dennis Kux, *The United States and Pakistan: Disenchanted Allies, 1947–2000* (Karachi: Oxford University Press, 2001), 229–230. The conversation, which took place over an insecure phone line, apparently referred to Bhutto's exit from a reception at the US consulate in Karachi.

95. "Statement by Prime Minister Zulfiqar Ali Bhutto on the Adjournment Motion," 115; "US Offers to Hold Talks on Grievances," *Pakistan Times*, May 1, 1977.

96. Kux, *United States and Pakistan*, 229.

97. "U.S. Withholds Sale of Jets to Pakistan," *New York Times*, June 3, 1977.

98. Despite claiming to have concrete evidence of foreign involvement, the PPP government did not produce any substantial proof that the United States or any other foreign power was conspiring to destabilize it by supporting the PNA. "Evidence Available of Foreign Involvement," *Pakistan Times*, April 29, 1977; Kux, *United States and Pakistan*, 230–231.

99. See "Saudi Envoy Delivers PNA's Letter to the Prime Minister," *Pakistan Times*, May 29, 1977. See also "PLO Envoy Meets PM, Mufti," *Pakistan Times*, May 26, 1977.

100. "PNA Central Leaders Freed: Both Sides Agree to Suspend Processions and Rallies," *Pakistan Times*, June 4, 1977.

101. See "Asghar Threatens to Launch Movement," *Pakistan Times*, June 8, 1977.

102. "Government and Opposition Conclude Agreement," *Pakistan Times*, June 16, 1977.

103. General Ziaul Haq, speech, July 5, 1977, http://www.youtube.com /watch?v=pJIFbJX-cY8&feature=related (accessed March 7, 2012).

104. See Alfred Stepan, *The Military in Politics: Changing Patterns in Brazil* (Princeton, NJ: Princeton University Press, 1971), 61–80.

105. Mohammad Asghar Khan, *Generals in Politics: Pakistan, 1958–1982* (New Delhi: Vikas, 1983), 116–118.

106. Interview of Maulana Ghafoor Ahmed by the author, Karachi, July 2008.

107. Raza, *Zulfiqar Ali Bhutto*, 359; see also General K. M. Arif, *Working with Zia: Pakistan's Power Politics, 1977–1988* (Karachi: Oxford University Press, 1995), 86. Bhutto alleged from his death cell that "jawans [soldiers] dressed in civilian clothes were sent to PNA demonstrations to swell the crowds and incite public provocation." See Bhutto, *If I Am Assassinated*, 165.

108. Quoted in Haqqani, *Pakistan*, 124–125. Ghafoor Ahmed confirmed this claim in an interview by the author.

109. Niazi, *Zulfiqar Ali Bhutto*, 79.

110. Weinbaum, "March 1977 Elections in Pakistan," 617.

111. "Forces to Back Government as Constitutional Obligation," *Pakistan Times*, April 28, 1977.

112. General Zia's press conference, July 14, 1977, quoted in Lieutenant General Faiz Ali Chishti, *Betrayals of Another Kind: Islam, Democracy and the Army in Pakistan* (Cincinnati: Asia Publishing House, 1990), 68.

113. Talbot, *Pakistan*, 224.

114. Mohammad Waseem, *The Politics of Pakistan* (Islamabad: National Institute of Historical Research, 1994), 327; see also Shafqat, *Civil-Military Relations*, 90–106.

115. Presidential proclamation, cited in Raza, *Zulfiqar Ali Bhutto*, 268.

116. Ibid.; interview of Major General Naseerullah Babar (retd.) by the author, Peshawar, June 2008.

117. Haqqani, *Pakistan*, 102–103.

118. Note by Special Secretary, Prime Minister's Secretariat, "General Situation in Baluchistan," July 13, 1976, in *White Paper on the Conduct of the General Elections in March 1977* (Rawalpindi: Government of Pakistan, July 1978), A-271.

119. Donald Horowitz, *Coup Theories and Officers' Motives: Sri Lanka in Comparative Perspective* (Princeton, NJ: Princeton University Press, 1980), 148.

120. See "Pre-curfew Prices Only: Martial Law Warning to Profiteers" and "Military Courts Established," *Pakistan Times*, April 25, 1977.

121. For the military's account of the events, I have relied on Chishti, *Betrayals of Another Kind*, 8–78; and Arif, *Working with Zia*, 61–96. Chishti was commander of the Army's X Corps in Rawalpindi that executed the coup through its 111th Infantry Brigade, which is also responsible for security of the prime minister's and president's houses. Then Major General Arif was one of the six principal staff officers in army headquarters, heading the Military Secretary Branch responsible for army postings, transfers, and promotions. After the coup, Zia appointed Arif his chief of staff (1977–1984) and later vice chief of the army staff (1984–1987). I have supplemented these written accounts through extensive interviews with both Chishti and Arif, as well as over half a dozen officers on active duty at the time of the 1977 coup.

122. Raza, *Zulfiqar Ali Bhutto*, 360. See Niazi, *Zulfiqar Ali Bhutto*, 82–83; Arif, *Working with Zia*, 87; Gul Hassan Khan, *Memoirs*, 417; and Mazhar Aziz, *Military Control in Pakistan: The Parallel State* (London: Routledge, 2007), 71.

123. Chishti, *Betrayals of Another Kind*, 66–67.

124. Interview of Lieutenant General Abdul Majid Malik by the author, Islamabad, June 2011.

125. A similar logic was at work in the failed Sri Lankan coup of 1962. See Horowitz, *Coup Theories and Officers' Motives*, 148.

126. Interview of a retired lieutenant general by the author, Rawalpindi, June 2008.

127. This view was shared by several PNA leaders, including the hard-liner and former commander-in-chief of the air force, Air Marshal Asghar Khan (retd.).

128. Interview of Faiz Ali Chishti by the author, Rawalpindi, June 2008.

129. Chishti, *Betrayals of Another Kind*, 62.

130. *White Paper on the Conduct of the General Elections in March 1977*, 395–399. Bhutto flatly refuted the charge, arguing that a prescribed number of arms licenses were issued to PPP members of the National Assembly and provincial assemblies only after police endorsement. See Bhutto, "Rejoinder in the Supreme Court," 31–32.

131. Arif, *Working with Zia*, 80–81. See also Burki, *Pakistan under Bhutto*, 199.

132. Interview of Chishti by the author, Rawalpindi, June 2008.

133. For instance, Brazil's 1946 constitution entrusted the military with the task of maintaining a balance between the executive, the legislature, and the judiciary.

134. Even when the civilian authorities seek its assistance in "aid of civil power," say, to control a law-and-order situation in a particular locality, the military is expected to operate under instructions from the civilian district magistrate for the arrest or confinement of a person.

135. Raza, *Zulfiqar Ali Bhutto,* 360; interview of Ghafoor Ahmed by the author.

136. Raza, *Zulfiqar Ali Bhutto,* 355.

137. Niazi, *Zulfiqar Ali Bhutto,* 189–190, 195.

138. Victoria Schofield, *Bhutto: Trial and Execution* (London: Cassell, 1979), 8; Bhutto later claimed that "on four separate occasions I had laid down a time table for the winding up of the military operation," but each time, the army "impressed upon the Government" that its "presence in the field was considered absolutely necessary to protect the integrity of the country against the insurgents." See Bhutto, "Rejoinder in the Supreme Court," 17.

139. Arif, *Working with Zia,* 82. Asghar Khan corroborates this view. See Asghar Khan, *Generals in Politics,* 126–127.

140. Interview of Ghafoor Ahmed by the author; Chishti, *Betrayals of Another Kind,* 62.

141. Interview of Chishti by the author, Rawalpindi, January 2013.

142. Ibid.

143. Arif, *Working with Zia;* Chishti, *Betrayals of Another Kind,* 66.

144. Chishti, *Betrayals of Another Kind,* 62; Raza, *Zulfiqar Ali Bhutto,* 360; and Arif, *Working with Zia,* 88. General Arif contends that Bhutto was "too weak, isolated and unsure of himself" to have sacked Zia.

145. Juan Linz, *The Breakdown of Democratic Regimes* (Baltimore: Johns Hopkins University Press, 1978), 17.

146. Nordlinger, *Soldiers in Politics.*

147. See Rizvi, *Military, State, and Society in Pakistan,* 164.

148. Interview by the author, Rawalpindi, June 2008.

149. Arif, *Working with Zia,* 73.

150. Stepan, *Military in Politics,* 118–121.

151. This observation is based on my interviews with Pakistani army officers who were recruited in the 1960s and 1970s. The opposition to parliamentary democracy persisted into the twenty-first century. In the words of

one active-duty officer, Pakistan's problems stem from "the flawed West-minster constitutional model," and "checks and balances" are necessary for good governance. Lieutenant Colonel Raashid Wali Janjua, "Army's Role in Nation-Building," in *Pakistan Army Green Book* (Rawalpindi: General Head-quarters, 2000), 61.

152. Arif, *Working with Zia*, 93.

153. John Samuel Fitch, *The Military Coup d'État as a Political Process: Ecuador, 1948–1966* (Baltimore: Johns Hopkins University Press, 1977), 9.

154. Arthur T. Denzau and Douglass C. North, "Shared Mental Mod-els: Ideologies and Institutions," *Kyklos* 47, no. 1 (1994): 1.

155. Walter J. Powell, "Expanding Institutional Analysis," in *The New Institutionalism in Organizational Analysis,* ed. Walter W. Powell and Paul J. DiMaggio (Chicago: University of Chicago Press, 1991), 189.

156. Interview of Chishti by the author, Rawalpindi, June 2008.

157. Interviews of army officers by the author, Lahore and Rawalpindi, June–December 2008. See also Chishti, *Betrayals of Another Kind,* 42, 44, 56, 65; and Arif, *Working with Zia,* 72–74.

158. Samuel E. Finer, *The Man on Horseback: The Role of the Military in Politics,* 5th ed. (London: Transaction Press, 2002), 32.

159. Chishti, *Betrayals of Another Kind,* 58–59.

160. Interview by the author, Rawalpindi, June 2008.

161. Interview by the author, Islamabad, August 2008.

162. Interview of Lieutenant General Faiz Ali Chishti by the author, Rawalpindi, January 2013.

163. Niazi's record of a meeting between the army's corps command-ers and the prime minister held on June 14, 1977. See Niazi, *Zulfiqar Ali Bhutto,* 194–195. See also Mohammad Asghar Khan, *Generals in Politics,* 113.

164. Arif, *Working with Zia,* 80.

165. Zia also cited the public ridicule and criticism of the military as a reason for the coup. "Martial Law Proclaimed," *Pakistan Times,* July 6, 1977.

166. Tahir-Kheli, *United States and Pakistan,* 69.

167. Chishti, *Betrayals of Another Kind,* 65.

168. Interviews of Arif and Chishti by the author, Rawalpindi, June 2008.

169. Bhutto claimed that "the Brigadiers were not court-martialed. They were not even dismissed from service. They were transferred to Rawalpindi, given a pat for their role in the game and told to remain out of sight." He also

cited other manufactured incidents of impending military revolt: "Junior officers were ordered to heckle Mr. Aziz Ahmed, the Minister of State for Foreign Affairs, when he addressed them in Karachi." See Bhutto, *If I Am Assassinated*, 165.

5. FROM ZIA TO MUSHARRAF

1. Feroze Ahmed, *Ethnicity and Politics in Pakistan* (Karachi: Oxford University Press, 1999), 118.

2. This observation is based on my interviews with Pakistani military officers. The opposition to parliamentary democracy persisted into the twenty-first century. In the words of one active-duty officer, Pakistan's problems stem from "the flawed Westminster constitutional model," and "checks and balances" are necessary for good governance. *Pakistan Army Green Book: Nation-Building* (Rawalpindi: General Headquarters, 2000), 61.

3. General Ziaul Haq, speech, July 5, 1977, http://www.youtube.com /watch?v=pJIFbJX-cY8 (accessed September 2, 2010).

4. John L. Esposito, "Islam, Ideology and Politics in Pakistan," in *The State, Religion, and Ethnic Politics in Afghanistan, Iran, and Pakistan*, ed. Ali Banuazizi and Myron Wiener (Syracuse, NY: Syracuse University Press, 1986), 343.

5. *Revival of Islamic Values in Pakistan* (Islamabad: Ministry of Information and Broadcasting, n.d.), 8–9.

6. See details in Esposito, "Islam," 343–359. The impact of these polices on economic management, taxation, legal reforms, and women's status is discussed in *Islamic Reassertion in Pakistan*, ed. Anita M. Wiess (Syracuse, NY: Syracuse University Press, 1986). A sympathetic view of the Hudood ordinances is found in Muhammad Taqi Usmani, "The Islamization of Laws in Pakistan: The Case of *Hudud* Ordinances," *Muslim World* 96, no. 2 (April 2006): 287–304. For a critical empirical assessment of the adverse impact of the Hudood ordinances on criminal law, women's status, and judicial procedures, see Charles Kennedy, "Islamization in Pakistan: Implementation of the Hudood Ordinances," *Asian Survey* 28, no. 3 (March 1988): 307–316.

7. See Shahid Javed Burki, "Zia's Eleven Years," in *Pakistan under the Military: Eleven Years of Ziaul Haq*, by Shahid Javed Burki and Craig Baxter (Boulder, CO: Westview Press, 1991), 16.

8. Ibid.

9. Saeed Shafqat, *Civil-Military Relations: From Zulfiqar Ali Bhutto to Benazir Bhutto* (Boulder, CO: Westview Press, 1997), 204–206; Burki, "Zia's Eleven Years," 17.

10. General K.M. Arif, *Working with Zia: Pakistan's Power Politics* (Karachi: Oxford University Press, 1995), 154–156.

11. Zia had initially appointed the four high-court chief justices as governors in the provinces. Rodney W. Jones, "The Military and Security in Pakistan," in *Zia's Pakistan: Politics and Stability in a Frontline State,* ed. Craig Baxter (Boulder, CO: Westview Press, 1985), 76.

12. Arif, *Working with Zia,* 110.

13. The summary courts dealt with specific emergencies concerning law and order, whereas the regular courts enforced martial law regulations, such as the ban on political assembly.

14. In his capacity as commander of X Corps, Chishti controlled the 111th infantry brigade, nicknamed the "Coup Brigade." Zia's lack of confidence in Chishti was revealed when he removed the commander of the 111th Brigade, Brigadier Mohammad Khan, and replaced him with Brigadier Rahat Latif without Chishti's knowledge. Interview of Lieutenant General Faiz Ali Chishti by the author, Rawalpindi, January 2013.

15. Shafqat, *Civil-Military Relations,* 201; Hasan-Askari Rizvi, *The Military and Politics in Pakistan, 1947–1997* (Lahore: Sang-e-Meel, 2000), 257.

16. Ayesha Siddiqa, *Military Inc.: Inside Pakistan's Military Economy* (London: Pluto Press, 2007), 139–151.

17. Stephen P. Cohen, *The Pakistan Army,* 2nd ed. (Karachi: Oxford University Press, 1998), 73.

18. Secretary of State Alexander Haig to Senator Mark Hatfield (R-OR), November 21, 1981, Confidential, State Department FOIA release, http://www.gwu.edu/~nsarchiv/nukevault/ebb377/ (accessed April 11, 2012).

19. U.S. Department of State, Paul H. Kreisberg to Mr. Newsom, "Presidential Letter on Pakistan Nuclear Program to Western Leaders," March 30, 1979, Secret Source, RG 59, Records of Anthony Lake, box 5, TL 3/16–3/31/79, http://www.gwu.edu/~nsarchiv/nukevault/ebb333/index.htm#4 (accessed April 11, 2012).

20. "Pakistan Is Offered a Choice on A-Arms," *New York Times,* April 16, 1979, A3.

21. "Pakistan Dismisses $400 Million in Aid Offered by U.S. as Peanuts," *New York Times,* January 18, 1980, A1.

22. "Pakistan Agrees to a U.S. Aid Plan and F-16 Delivery," *New York Times,* September 16, 1981.

23. U.S. Embassy Pakistan cable 15696 to State Department, "Pakistan Nuclear Issue: Meeting with General Zia," October 17, 1982, Secret,

http://www.gwu.edu/~nsarchiv/nukevault/ebb377/ (accessed March 9, 2012).

24. From 1982 to 1989, President Ronald Reagan and his successor, George H.W. Bush (1989–1993), gave Pakistan presidential waivers, required under the Pressler Amendment to the Foreign Assistance Act, 1961, certifying that the country did not possess a nuclear device.

25. For a useful analysis of defense policy in the wake of the Soviet occupation of Afghanistan, see Shirin Tahir-Kheli, "Defense Planning in Pakistan," in *Defense Planning in Less Industrialized States: The Middle East and South Asia,* ed. Stephanie Neuman (Lexington, MA: Lexington Books, 1984), 209–238.

26. Rizwan Hussain, *Pakistan and the Emergence of Islamic Militancy in Afghanistan* (London: Ashgate, 2005), 103–107.

27. "The Mullahs and the Military" (Asia Report no. 49, International Crisis Group, March 20, 2003), 8.

28. Ibid., 13.

29. Testimony of the former director general of the ISI, Lieutenant General Ahmed Shuja Pasha (retd.), before the Abbottabad Inquiry Commission, 192, www.aljazeera.com (accessed July 25, 2013).

30. Steve Coll, *The Secret History of the CIA, Afghanistan, and bin Laden: From the Soviet Invasion to September 10, 2001* (New York: Penguin, 2004), 238.

31. Interview of a former ISI officer by the author, Islamabad, December 2012.

32. The Jamiat rose to political prominence in the 1970s after winning student union elections in universities across Pakistan. It formed the backbone of the opposition to the PPP government of Zulifqar Ali Bhutto, including in the PNA agitation in 1977. On the origins and development of the Jamiat from the JI's student wing into a relatively autonomous militant organization, see Seyyed Vali Reza Nasr, *The Vanguard of the Islamic Revolution: The Jama'at-i-Islami of Pakistan* (London: I. B. Tauris, 1994), esp. 64–70.

33. Ziul Haq, interview with the BBC, http://www.youtube.com/watch?v=w48W2qgO9wk (accessed September 7, 2012).

34. *White Paper on the Performance of the Bhutto Regime,* 4 vols. (Islamabad: Government of Pakistan, 1979), vol. 1, *Mr. Z.A. Bhutto, His Family and Associates;* vol. 2, *Treatment of Fundamental State Institutions;* vol. 3, *Misuse of the Instruments of State Power;* vol. 4, *The Economy.*

35. Craig Baxter, "Restructuring the Political System," in Burki and Baxter, *Pakistan under the Military,* 32–33.

36. "Pakistan's Ruler Looks Unbeatable," *New York Times,* January 5, 1984.

37. Government sources claimed that there were 60 casualties in total, of which over 12 to 15 were security personnel. In September, the MRD leadership believed that the death toll was possibly over 100. Some independent observers claimed that 150 people were killed during the thirteen-week-long movement. See "Pakistanis Charge 22 Were Slain by Army," *New York Times,* October 21, 1983, A5; "Pak Agitation Enters Second Month," *Times of India,* September 15, 1983; and *Sydney Morning Herald,* October 1, 1983.

38. The referendum asked the people to support his Islamization program, and a yes vote was considered popular approval of his presidency.

39. Seyyed Vali Reza Nasr, "Democracy and the Crisis of Governability in Pakistan," *Asian Survey* 32, no. 6 (1992): 528.

40. For an excellent discussion of the politicization of Muhajir ethnic identity, the rise of the MQM, and the role of the Zia government in exploiting ethnic rivalries in urban Sindh, see Feroze Ahmed, *Ethnicity and Politics in Pakistan,* 89–125.

41. Superior-court judges were required to take a new oath of office under Ziaul Haq's Provisional Constitutional Order of 1981.

42. The Eighth Amendment Act of 1985, clause 58(2)b, allowed the president to "dissolve the National Assembly in his discretion where, in his opinion, a situation has arisen in which the Government of the Federation cannot be carried on in accordance with the provisions of the Constitution and an appeal to the electorate is necessary." Constitution of the Islamic Republic of Pakistan.

43. Sartaj Aziz, *Between Dreams and Reality: Some Milestones in Pakistan's History* (Karachi: Oxford University Press, 2013), 238–239.

44. Rizvi, *Military and Politics in Pakistan,* 265.

45. Nusrat Javed, "Ojhri Camp Ki Tabahi Ka Zimadar Kaun?" [Who Was Responsible for the Ojhri Camp Disaster?], *Express News* (Islamabad/Lahore/Karachi), June 1, 2013.

46. Zia's C-130 Hercules plane was headed back to Rawalpindi from Bahawalpur, where he had gone to attend a test of the Abrahams tank, when it crashed soon after takeoff. Aboard the plane were the American ambassador, Arnold Raphael, the CJCSC, General Akhtar Abdur Rehman, and other military officers. Conspiracy theories about the cause of the crash, involving the Soviet KGB, India's Research and Analysis Wing, the CIA, and even elements of the Pakistani army, abound. Pakistani and American members of a joint investigation reportedly reached different conclusions,

with the former blaming sabotage and the latter concluding that the cause was a mechanical failure. See James Bon and Zahid Hussain, "As Pakistan Comes Full Circle, a Light Is Shone on Ziaul Haq's Death," *Times* (London), August 16, 2008.

47. Stephen P. Cohen, "State Building in Pakistan," in Banuazizi and Wiener, *State, Religion, and Ethnic Politics*, 317.

48. See Cohen, *Pakistan Army*, 93–103.

49. Ibid., 96.

50. Brigadier S. K. Malik, *The Quranic Concept of War* (Delhi: Adam, 1992), esp. 72–141.

51. Ibid., 30.

52. Ibid., i.

53. Cohen, *Pakistan Army*, 88–89.

54. Ibid.

55. Seyyed Vali Reza Nasr, "Military Rule, Islamism and Democracy in Pakistan," *Middle East Journal* 58, no. 2 (Spring 2004): 201.

56. Samuel E. Finer, *The Man on Horseback: The Role of the Military in Politics*, 5th ed. (London: Transaction Press, 2002).

57. For instance, the US House of Representatives passed a resolution in August 1988 that declared that "the United States, in determining future levels of assistance, should consider whether Pakistan has held such elections and continued its progress toward a full-fledged democracy." See "A Resolution to Encourage the Establishment of Genuine Democracy in Pakistan," H.R. Res. 484, 100th Cong. (1988), http://www.govtrack.us/congress/bills/100/hres484 (accessed August 8, 2012). See also "Pakistan Risks Loss of Billions of Dollars in Aid," *Chicago Tribune*, June 13, 1988.

58. Robert Dahl, *Polyarchy: Participation and Opposition* (New Haven, CT: Yale University Press, 1971), 15. See also Michael Hoffman, "Military Extrication and Temporary Democracy: The Case of Pakistan," *Democratization* 18, no. 1 (January 2011): 75–99.

59. Hasan-Askari Rizvi, "The Legacy of Military Rule in Pakistan," *Survival* 31, no. 3 (May–June 1989): 255.

60. Samina Ahmed, "Military and Ethnic Politics," in *Pakistan: 1995*, ed. Charles Kennedy and Rasul Bakhsh Rais (Lahore: Vanguard, 1995), 116.

61. Interview of Lieutenant General Khawaja Ziauddin (retd.), who was then a brigadier serving as Personal Secretary to army chief General Aslam Beg, by the author, Lahore, December 2008.

62. Interview of former corps commander (V Corps, Karachi) Lieutenant General Naseer Akhtar (retd.) by the author, Lahore, December 2008.

63. Husain Haqqani, *Pakistan: Between Mosque and Military* (Washington, DC: Carnegie Endowment for International Peace, 2005), 235.

64. E-mail correspondence with the former COAS, General Aslam Beg, by the author, June 2008.

65. Interview by the author, Rawalpindi, March 2011.

66. Tahir Mehdi, "The Politics of ID Cards," *Dawn* (Karachi), June 17, 2012. See also *Pakistan Elections: Foundation for Democracy* (Washington, DC: National Democratic Institute for International Affairs, 1989), 26–28.

67. Interview of a former ISI officer by the author, Islamabad, August 2008.

68. "Hamid Gul Admits He Had Role in IJI Formation," *Daily Times* (Lahore), January 5, 2010.

69. Rizvi, "Legacy of Military Rule in Pakistan," 265–266.

70. Shuja Nawaz, *Crossed Swords: Pakistan, Its Army, and the Wars Within* (Karachi: Oxford University Press, 2008), 430.

71. Abbas Nasir, "The Empire Strikes Back," *Herald* (Karachi), August 1990; "The Invisible War," *Herald*, January 2008, 85–87.

72. Interview of a former resident editor of *Dawn* by the author, Islamabad, June 2008.

73. Nasr, "Democracy and the Crisis of Governability in Pakistan," 527.

74. Dependent on the MQM's support, Bhutto had accepted the party's demands in the Karachi agreement of December 1988, including the repatriation of Bihari refugees from Bangladesh and the introduction of Sindhi and Muhajir categories in place of urban and rural Sindh for employment quotas in the civil service. Samina Ahmed, "Military and Ethnic Politics," 116.

75. See Affidavit of Brigadier Hamid Saeed (retd.), Supreme Court Detailed Judgement in the Asghar Khan Case, HRC 19/1996, 12, www.supremecourt.gov.pk/web/user_files/File/H.R.C.19of1996[AsgharKhanCase]DetailedReasons.pdf (accessed April 1, 2013).

76. Samina Ahmed, "Military and Ethnic Politics," 117.

77. Naeem Ahmed Goraya, "And Now, General Janjua," *Newsline* (Karachi), July 1991, 42.

78. Affidavit of Brigadier Hamid Saeed, 13.

79. Ibid. See also "Bhutto Says She Is Silent Because of National Interest," *Asian Tribune*, March 9, 2005, http://www.asiantribune.com/news/2005/03/09/bhutto-says-she-silent-because-national-interest (accessed January 2, 2012).

80. In December 1988, less than a month after assuming office, Bhutto formally signed a nuclear risk-reduction agreement with then Indian prime minister Rajiv Gandhi to exchange lists of their nuclear installations and to refrain from attacks on the listed sites. In July 1989, Bhutto and Gandhi met in Islamabad, issued a joint communiqué, and agreed to work toward a comprehensive settlement of disputes and to reduce the chances of conflict. They also set up the first prime-ministerial hotline. See P. R. Chari, Pervaiz Iqbal Cheema, and Stephen P. Cohen, *Four Crises and a Peace Process: American Engagement in South Asia* (Washington, DC: Brookings Institution Press, 2007), 34.

81. When Bhutto complained, the ISPR reportedly issued a statement that "under the law, the COAS was not obliged to seek anyone's permission for conducting training exercises in any part of the country." Affidavit of Brigadier Hamid Saeed, 13.

82. Quoted in Zahid Hussain, *Frontline Pakistan: The Struggle with Militant Islam* (New York: Columbia University Press, 2007), 24.

83. The report was never made public.

84. Bhutto used the pretext of a failed mujahideen operation backed by the CIA and the ISI and designed to install the Afghan Interim Government in power by capturing Jalalabad to remove Gul from his post in April 1989. For details of the operation, see Steve Coll, *The Secret History of the CIA, Afghanistan, and bin Laden: From the Soviet Invasion to September 10, 2001* (New York: Penguin, 2004), 192–194.

85. Interview of the former defense secretary, Ijlal Haider Zaidi, by the author, Islamabad, August 2008. General Beg denies that the military was upset with the prime minister's decision to appoint her own man. E-mail correspondence with General Beg, June 2008.

86. Maleeha Lodhi and Zahid Hussain, "The Army's Long Shadow," *Newsline*, July 1990, 24.

87. Nawaz, *Crossed Swords*, 425–426.

88. Ishaq used his presidential authority (under the Eighth Amendment) to appoint and retire armed services chiefs and the CJCSC to block Sirohey's retirement.

89. Then US ambassador Robert Oakley, quoted in Dennis Kux, *The United States and Pakistan: Disenchanted Allies, 1947–2000* (Karachi: Oxford University Press, 2001), 303.

90. Conversations of Imtiaz and Amir with some PPP members of the National Assembly were recorded in a sting operation by the Intelligence Bureau (IB). Incensed, the PPP government shared the tapes with General Beg. Beg ordered a summary inquiry that resulted in the compulsory retirement of both officers. See "Night of the Jackals," *Newsline,* October 1992, reprinted in Maleeha Lodhi, *Pakistan's Encounter with Democracy* (Lahore: Vanguard, 1995), 146–147. See also "Operation Midnight Jackals," *Nation* (Lahore), September 30, 1992.

91. Clive Dewey, "The Rural Roots of Pakistani Militarism," in *The Political Inheritance of Pakistan,* ed. D. A. Low (New York: Macmillan, 1991), 259.

92. The army retired Mehsud and replaced him with another general in clear disregard of the prime minister's wishes.

93. Benazir Bhutto, *Reconciliation: Islam, Democracy, and the West* (New York: Harper Collins, 2008), 202–203.

94. This decision was reportedly made in a corps commanders' meeting held on October 10–11. See Maleeha Lodhi, "The New Old Order," *Newsline,* November 1990.

95. General Beg's explanation of his disagreement with the civilian governments is that "I felt very strongly that the support to USA in first Gulf War was a wrong policy. If the government wanted to take action against me, it could. I would have no regrets. But I was clear in my mind that if USA is not discouraged to attack Iraq, the next target would be Iran and then possibly Pakistan. I did disagree with the government but no tension was created because of my disagreement." E-mail correspondence with author, June 2008.

96. The military launched its operation on the grounds that it had discovered maps in the MQM's party headquarters that depicted Jinnahpur, an independent state for the Muhajirs to be carved out of urban areas of Sindh. See "Jinnahpur Key Naqhsay Fauji Record Mein Mehfuz Hain" [Jinnahpur Maps Part of Army Record], *Daily Ummat* (Karachi), August 31, 2011; and "Asif Nawaz Janjua: The Man behind the 1992 Operation," *News* (Rawalpindi), September 4, 2009.

97. "60 MQM Men Buried in Margalla Hills in 1997: Shujaat," *News,* August 27, 2009.

98. "Pakistani Government Ousted," *Washington Post,* April 19, 1993.

99. President Ghulam Ishaq Khan, "Address to the Nation on the Dissolution of the National Assembly," April 18, 1993, http://www.youtube.com /watch?v=iUG-4JJDIjk (accessed January 12, 2012).

100. Samina Ahmed, "Military and Ethnic Politics," 120.

101. Ishaq Khan, "Address to the Nation."

102. Nawaz, *Crossed Swords*, 471–472.

103. Interview of Lieutenant General Naseer Akhtar by the author, Lahore, December 2008.

104. Zahid Hussain, "Back to the Future," *Newsline,* September 1993, 36.

105. "1993 Elections: A Pile of Dirty Linen," *Dawn,* April 4, 2013.

106. The PPP won a plurality of seats and formed a government at the center and in the Punjab with the help of the PML-Chattha and independents.

107. By 1994, the ISI's favored proxy, Gulbaddin Hekmatyar, had failed to make any military breakthrough to capture Kabul, which was now under the control of the Tajik leader, Burhanuddin Rabbani.

108. Ahmed Rashid, *The Taliban: Militant Islam, Oil, and Fundamentalism in Central Asia* (New Haven, CT: Yale University Press, 2001), 21–30.

109. Kamran Khan, "Bhutto out as Premier in Pakistan; President Charges Corruption, Dissolves National Assembly," *Washington Post,* November 5, 1996.

110. "Leghari's Law," *Outlook India,* December 25, 1996.

111. Interview of Lieutenant General Ali Kuli Khan by the author, Rawalpindi, August 2012.

112. Interviews of Lieutenant Generals Moinuddin Haider and Mohammad Tariq by the author, Lahore, December 2008; interview of Najam Sethi, editor of the weekly *Friday Times* and adviser in the caretaker government, by the author, Lahore, October 2002.

113. Interview of former president Farooq Leghari by the author, Islamabad, July 2009.

114. Its members included the prime minister, the CJCSC, the three military services chiefs, and the ministers of foreign affairs, interior, and finance.

115. Interview of former caretaker defense minister Shahid Hamid by the author, Lahore, August 2008.

116. Sharif's PML-N won 137 of the 217 national assembly seats. In the 1997 elections, Sharif was able to successfully appropriate the right-of-center Islamic vote by projecting the PML-N as a conservative but moderate right-of-center Muslim democratic party, edging the Islamists out of the electoral arena. See Vali Nasr, "Rise of Muslim Democracy," *Journal of Democracy* 16, no. 2 (April 2005): 13–25.

117. Hasan-Askari Rizvi, "National Security Council: A Comparative Study of Pakistan and other Selected Countries" (background paper, Paki-

stan Institute for Legislative Development and Transparency, August 2005), 14.

118. "Nawaz Couldn't Have Impeached Me: Leghari," *Dawn*, August 6, 2003.

119. "Pakistan President Resigns, Raising Fears of a Military Takeover," *Associated Press*, December 2, 1997; Nawaz, *Crossed Swords*, 489.

120. "Advani Tells Pak to Roll Back India Policy, or Else," May 18, 1998, http://www.rediff.com/news/1998/may/18advani.htm (accessed February 24, 2011).

121. Interview of a former senior official of the prime minister's secretariat by the author, May 2010.

122. Interview of then finance minister Sartaj Aziz by the author, Lahore, August 2008; interview of Ahsan Iqbal, then deputy chairman of the Planning Commission, by the author, Islamabad, September 2008.

123. Hasan-Askari Rizvi, "Pakistan in 1998: The Polity under Pressure," *Asian Survey* 39, no. 1 (January–February 1999): 181.

124. Kamran Khan, "PM's Bolt from the Blue Actions Cause Army's NSC Move," *News* (Lahore), October 7, 1998.

125. Interview of Ali Kuli Khan by the author; interview of the adjutant general, Lieutenant General Khawaja Ziauddin, by the author, Lahore, December 2008.

126. Jehangir Karamat, e-mail to the author, July 2009.

127. For instance, the US NSC is chaired by the president. Its regular attendees (both statutory and nonstatutory) are the vice president, the secretaries of state, the Treasury, and defense, and the assistant to the president for the NSC. The chairman of the Joint Chiefs of Staff is the military adviser to the council. http://www.whitehouse.gov/administration/eop/nsc/ (accessed September 7, 2010).

128. According to Ali Kuli Khan, "We had informed the Prime Minister through the COAS and the ISI of our reservations about poor governance, corruption and deteriorating law and order. But to no avail." Interview by the author.

129. Karamat, e-mail to the author, July 2009.

130. Ali Kuli Khan denies that he advised Karamat to defy or challenge the prime minister. Instead, he told his army chief that he should not resign. Interview by the author. General Musharraf asserted in his autobiography that Ali Kuli Khan was in fact a strong advocate of martial law. See *In the Line of Fire: A Memoir* (New York: Free Press, 2006), 83. Lieutenant General Ziauddin corroborated Musharraf's claim in an interview by the author, Lahore, December 2008.

131. Karamat's version is that "he said what needed to be said," and that he left "in the best interest of his institution." Note again that in his view, publicly criticizing the elected government and advocating a formal governmental role for the army were the right things to do. Karamat, e-mail to the author, July 2009.

132. Owen Bennett Jones, "Resignation Shifts Balance of Power," *BBC News Online,* October 8, 1998, http://news.bbc.co.uk/2/hi/south_asia/189233 .stm (accessed July 5, 2009). See also Ihtashamul Haq, "Karamat Retired, Musharraf Takes Over as COAS," *Dawn,* October 10, 1998.

133. Interview of Mohammad Tariq by the author.

134. Interview of Moinuddin Haider by the author.

135. See Musharraf, *In the Line of Fire,* 84.

136. Interview of Lieutenant General Tauqir Zia (retd.) by the author, Lahore, June 2008.

137. Musharraf, *In the Line of Fire,* 86.

138. Interview of the former chief of naval staff, Admiral Fasih Bokhari (retd.), by the author, Islamabad, January 2009. One close aide of Sharif revealed in an interview by the author in Islamabad, June 2010, that the prime minister was also keen to forge normal relations with India because he wanted to puncture military domestic political power.

139. Lahore Declaration, February 21, 1999, http://www.usip.org/sites /default/files/file/resources/collections/peace_agreements/ip_lahore19990221 .pdf (accessed September 7, 2010).

140. Interview with General Musharraf in Urdu, *Kal Tak,* Express TV, January 30, 2013, http://www.youtube.com/watch?v=9BjxFkmnbvU (accessed May 1, 2013).

141. For a good accounting of the military origins, logic, and objectives behind the conflict, see Feroze Hassan Khan, Peter Lavoy, and Chris Clary, "Pakistan's Calculations and Motivations for the Kargil Conflict," in *Asymmetric Warfare in South Asia: The Causes and Consequences of the Kargil Conflict,* ed. Peter Lavoy (New York: Cambridge University Press, 2009), 64–91. See also Zafar Iqbal Cheema, "The Strategic Context of the Kargil Conflict: A Pakistani Perspective," ibid., 39–63; Nawaz, *Crossed Swords,* 510–520; and Hassan Abbas, *Pakistan's Drift into Extremism: Allah, the Army, and America's War on Terror* (London: M. E. Sharpe, 2005), 169–174.

142. See Maleeha Lodhi, "The Anatomy of a Debacle," *Newsline,* July 1999. According to the then deputy director general (analysis) of the ISI, Lieutenant General Shahid Aziz (retd.), Kargil was "an unsound military plan based on invalid assumptions, launched with little preparations and in total

disregard to the regional and international environment, [and] was bound to fail." "Putting Our Children in the Line of Fire," *Nation,* January 6, 2013. See also interview of Brig Shahid Hussain (retd.), *The News Hour,* Times Now, http://www.youtube.com/watch?v=N1yPwbNOQCo (accessed June 1, 2013).

143. Owen Bennett Jones, *Pakistan: Eye of the Storm,* 2nd ed. (New Haven, CT: Yale University Press, 2003), 93.

144. Musharraf, *In the Line of Fire,* 95–96.

145. Sohail Warraich, *Ghaddar Kaun?* [Who Is the Traitor?] (Lahore: Sagar, 2006), 142.

146. Sartaj Aziz, *Between Dreams and Reality,* 253.

147. Ibid., 255.

148. "India Gave Kargil Tapes to Sharif a Week before Release," *Indian Express,* October 25, 1999; "I Have a Tape of Musharraf-Aziz Phone Call on Kargil: Nawaz," *Daily Times,* October 21, 2006.

149. See transcript of conversations between General Pervez Musharraf and Lieutenant General Mohammad Aziz, May 26 and May 29, 1999, *India Today,* July 1, 2008, http://web.archive.org/web/20080701220255/http://www.india-today.com/kargil/audio.html (accessed September 1, 2010).

150. See, for instance, "G-8 Condemns Violation of the LoC," *Hindu,* June 21, 1999. In late June, President Clinton dispatched the commander of the US Central Command, Anthony Zinni, to persuade the Pakistani military to withdraw its forces.

151. Thomas W. Lippman, "India Hints at Attack in Pakistan," *Washington Post,* June 27, 1999, A26; John Lancaster, "Kashmir Crisis Was Defused on the Brink of War," *Washington Post,* July 26, 1999, A1.

152. "Press Briefing by Senior Administration Official on President's Meeting with Prime Minister Sharif of Pakistan," Office of the Press Secretary, The White House, July 4, 1999, http://www.fas.org/news/pakistan/1999/990704-pak-wh2.htm (accessed June 27, 2010).

153. See Bruce Riedel, "American Diplomacy and the 1999 Kargil Summit at Blair House" (Policy Paper Series, Center for the Advanced Study of India, University of Pennsylvania, May 2002).

154. Interview of Fasih Bokhari by the author.

155. Assistant Chief of Air Staff (Operations) Air Commodore Abid Rao, quoted in Air Commodore Kaiser Tufail (retd.), "Himalayan Showdown: Kargil Crisis, Ten Years On," *Air Forces Monthly* 22, no. 6 (June 2009): 93.

156. Warraich, *Ghaddar Kaun,* 146–147. On the basis of interviews with "insiders," Jones claims that "Musharraf was in full agreement with Sharif's decision to go to Washington." Jones, *Pakistan,* 40.

157. Interview of a former major general by the author, Islamabad, July 2008.

158. Musharraf, *In the Line of Fire*, 95.

159. Musharraf had been given acting charge of the Joint Chiefs of Staff when he was promoted to the post of army chief in October 1998. See "Musharraf to Stay On as CJCSC, Army Chief," *Dawn*, September 29, 1999.

160. See also Musharraf, *In the Line of Fire*, 112.

161. Interview of Sartaj Aziz by the author, Lahore, August 2008.

162. Musharraf admits in his autobiography, "I had already conveyed an indirect warning to the prime minister through several intermediaries: I am not Jehangir Karamat." Musharraf also told Sharif's brother and Punjab chief minister Shahbaz Sharif to warn the prime minister that "I would not agree to give up my present position of army chief of staff and be kicked upstairs as CJCSC before my term was up." See Musharraf, *In the Line of Fire*, 110–112.

163. Aziz contacted then brigadier (later major general) Faisal Alavi, commandant of the army's Special Services Group. Alavi deployed a company of the group's commandos to the Dhamial aviation camp in Rawalpindi under the cover of providing the prime minister extra security in case of a breakdown of law and order. Interview of Faisal Alavi by the author, Islamabad, July 2008.

164. Tariq Pervez reportedly passed on the information to the prime minister through his relative, Raja Nadir Pervez, a minister in Sharif's cabinet. Jones, *Pakistan*, 39.

165. Musharraf, *In the Line of Fire*, 112.

166. Interview in Urdu with Lieutenant General Shahid Aziz (retd.), who was director general of military operations at the time of the coup, *Islamabad Tonight*, Aaj TV, May 13, 2010, http://www.youtube.com/watch?v=x6kpHJTh9hU (accessed April 1, 2012).

167. Speech of the Chief Executive of Pakistan, General Pervez Musharraf, October 17, 1999, http://presidentmusharraf.wordpress.com/2007/07/10/address-nation-7-point-agenda/ (accessed May 1, 2012).

168. Interview with Shahid Aziz, *Islamabad Tonight*, May 13, 2010.

169. Many politically informed and important civilians were also wary of Sharif's allegedly dictatorial tendencies. Particularly alarming for them was the Fifteenth Amendment, the Shariah Bill, passed by the National Assembly (but blocked in the Senate, where the PML-N was in the minority). The bill mandated the government "to take steps to enforce the Shariah, to establish Salat [prayer], to administer Zakat, to promote amr

bil nahi anil munkar [to prescribe what is right and to forbid what is wrong] . . . in accordance with the principles of Islam, as laid down in the Holy Quran."

170. Asad Durrani, e-mail to the author, July 2008.

171. Musharraf, *In the Line of Fire*, 110.

172. Interview of Ziauddin by the author.

173. Musharraf, *In the Line of Fire*, 110.

174. Interview of Lieutenant General Tauqir Zia by the author, Lahore, June 2008.

175. Musharraf, *In the Line of Fire*, 109.

176. Interview of Ziauddin by the author.

6. MUSHARRAF AND MILITARY PROFESSIONALISM

1. Proclamation of Emergency, October 14, 1999, http://news.bbc.co .uk/2/hi/south_asia/475415.stm (accessed September 6, 2012).

2. Sharif had reportedly ordered the Civil Aviation Authority to divert the plane carrying Musharraf to Muscat. Since the plane was low on fuel, the pilot was then instructed to refuel at Nawabshah airport in Sindh, where Musharraf was to be detained by the police. However, Musharraf directed the pilot to circle around the airport. Once the army took control of the airport, the plane landed safely. See "Sharif Diverted Aircraft," *BBC News Online*, February 9, 2000, http://news.bbc.co.uk/2/hi/south_asia /636396.stm (accessed October 26, 2013).

3. Sharif returned to Pakistan in 2007 and appealed his conviction in the Supreme Court. In July 2009, the Court overturned both his conviction and the life sentence. See "Pakistan Court Quashes Sharif Hijacking Conviction," *Reuters Online*, http://www.reuters.com/article/2009/07/17/us -pakistan-sharif-idUSTRE56G2VO20090717 (accessed August 19, 2012).

4. *Syed Zafar Ali Shah v. General Pervez Musharraf, Chief Executive of Pakistan* (PLD 2000 S.C. 869).

5. US Foreign Assistance Act, 1961, Section 508, http://www.usaid .gov/sites/default/files/documents/1868/faa.pdf (accessed June 14, 2012).

6. Interviews by the author, Lahore, December 2008.

7. Speech of the Chief Executive of Pakistan, General Pervez Musharraf, October 17, 1999, http://presidentmusharraf.wordpress.com/2007/07 /10/address-nation-7-point-agenda/ (accessed May 1, 2011).

8. Ibid.

9. C.E. Order No. 6 under the Provisional Constitutional Order, 1999, *Dawn* (Karachi), October 31, 1999.

10. These included Omar Asghar Khan, the head of the well-known SUNGI Development Foundation, and the education activist Zubeida Jalal.

11. Speech of the Chief Executive of Pakistan.

12. See US Department of State, cable, "Deputy Secretary Armitage's Meeting with General Mahmud: Actions and Support Expected of Pakistan in Fight against Terrorism," secret, September 14, 2001, http://www.gwu.edu/~nsarchiv/NSAEBB/NSAEBB358a/doc05.pdf (accessed April 22, 2012).

13. Interview of the then interior minister, Lieutenant General Moinuddin Haider (retd.), by the author, Lahore, December 2008.

14. On October 27, 2001, President Bush signed into law a congressional bill to exempt Pakistan from the application of Section 508 of the Foreign Assistance Act, provided the president determines that making foreign assistance available "facilitates the transition to democratic rule in Pakistan" and "is important to United States efforts to respond to, deter, or prevent acts of international terrorism." See A Bill to Authorize the President to Exercise Waivers of Foreign Assistance Restrictions with Respect to Pakistan, S. 1465, 107th Cong. (2001), http://www.govtrack.us/congress/bills/107/s1465 (accessed March 27, 2009).

15. US Department of State, "Deputy Secretary Armitage's Meeting with General Mahmud."

16. Interview of Lieutenant General Abdul Qadir Baloch (retd.) by the author, Lahore, October 2008.

17. "58-(2) b Back, NSC Formed," *Nation* (Lahore), August 22, 2002.

18. "Musharraf Defends Power to Sack Government," *News* (Rawalpindi), June 23, 2002.

19. Chief Executive's Order No. 12 of 2002, *Nation*, April 10, 2002.

20. Most of those who voted were captive voters, such as prisoners, factory workers, and government officials. See "Referendum 2002: Interim Report" (Human Rights Commission of Pakistan, April 30, 2002).

21. The MMA originated from the Afghan Defense Council, which consisted of over twenty religious parties and sectarian groups and was formed in October 2001 to oppose the US invasion of Afghanistan and Pakistan's support of the US-led War on Terror. See "The Mullahs and the Military" (Asia Report no. 49, International Crisis Group, March 20, 2003), 5.

22. The political and electoral manipulations of the military government are documented in "Pakistan: Transition to Democracy" (Asia Report no. 40, International Crisis Group, October 3, 2002). See also Aqil Shah,

"Pakistan's 'Armored' Democracy," *Journal of Democracy* 14, no. 4 (October 2003): 26–40.

23. Alfred Stepan and Aqil Shah, "Pakistan's Real Bulwark," *Washington Post,* May 5, 2004.

24. For instance, in February 2005, the army reached a six-point peace agreement with Baitullah Mehsud of the Pakistani Taliban in Srarogha, South Waziristan. According to the terms, Mehsud and his associates were given amnesty, and they pledged not to attack government functionaries or forces or to provide shelter to foreign terrorists. See details in "Pakistan's Tribal Areas: Appeasing the Militants," (Asia Report no. 125, International Crisis Group, December 11, 2006), 8.

25. Many civilians share the view of one veteran scholar that "the overwhelming illiteracy of the general public . . . precluded constructive evolution of public opinion and allowed the public to fall easy prey to organized divisive maneuvers." Pervaiz Iqbal Cheema, *The Armed Forces of Pakistan* (Karachi: Oxford University Press, 2002), 135–136.

26. Brigadier Muhammad Khurshid Khan, "A Stable Pakistan: Proposed Model of National Security," *Margalla Papers* (National Defence University, 2011), 85.

27. See Brigadier Ahmed Shuja Pasha, "The Role of the Army in Building the Primary Education Base," in *Pakistan Army Green Book: Nation Building* (Rawalpindi: Army General Headquarters, 2000), 245.

28. Pervez Musharraf, *In the Line of Fire: A Memoir* (New York: Free Press, 2006), 172.

29. "CE Announces Holding of Local Government Elections," Associated Press of Pakistan, March 24, 2000.

30. Local Government Plan 2000 (Government of Pakistan: National Reconstruction Bureau), 1.

31. Zaffar Abbas, "Musharraf Unveils Local Election Plan," *BBC News Online,* August 14, 2000, http://news.bbc.co.uk/2/hi/south_asia/880655.stm (accessed March 21, 2012).

32. See, for instance, "HRCP Rejects Devolution Plan of CE," *Dawn,* March 25, 2000; "Devolution in Pakistan: Reform or Regression?" (Asia Report no. 77, International Crisis Group, March 22, 2004); and Mohammad Waseem, comments made at the seminar "Conduct of Local Government Election 2005 and Prospects of the Next General Election," organized by the Pakistan Institute of Legislative Development and Transparency, Islamabad, September 5, 2005.

33. "HRCP Rejects Devolution Plan of CE."

34. NDC Individual Research Papers (IRPs).

35. Brigadier Javed Iqbal Sattar, "Empowering the People," *NDC Journal* (2001): 54.

36. Ibid., 61, 63.

37. Cited in Ian Talbot, *Pakistan: A Modern History* (London: Hurst, 2005), 401.

38. National Security Council Act, 2004.

39. *Pakistan Army Green Book* (2000), 9.

40. Ibid., 60.

41. The strength of this institutionally inculcated preference can be gauged from the fact that even after his exit from the army and government, Musharraf continues to believe that "if you want stability, checks and balances in the democratic structure of Pakistan, the military ought to have some sort of role." *Dawn,* September 30, 2010.

42. Interview by the author, Rawalpindi, June 2008.

43. "Local Government Elections," Associated Press of Pakistan, March 23, 2000.

44. *Pakistan Army Green Book* (2000), 23.

45. See *Report on the Work of the Government: October 12, 1999 to January 2000* (Islamabad: Ministry of Information, 2000), quoted in *Reform or Repression: Post-coup Abuses in Pakistan* (New York: Human Rights Watch, October 2000), http://www.hrw.org/reports/2000/pakistan/ (accessed June 4, 2008).

46. *Local Government (Proposed Plan): Devolution of Power and Responsibility Establishing the Foundations for Genuine Democracy* (Islamabad: National Reconstruction Bureau, May 2000), 1.

47. *Structural Analysis of National Reconstruction* (Government of Pakistan, National Reconstruction Bureau, May 27, 2000).

48. "1,027 Civilian Posts Occupied by Servicemen," *Dawn,* October 3, 2002; Massoud Ansari, "The Militarisation of Pakistan," *Newsline* (Karachi), October 2004, http://www.newslinemagazine.com/2004/10/the-militarisation-of-pakistan/ (accessed April 15, 2012).

49. Shuja Nawaz, *Crossed Swords: Pakistan, Its Army, and the Wars Within* (Karachi: Oxford University Press, 2008), 532.

50. Editorial, in *Pakistan Army Green Book* (2000), ii.

51. Message of General Pervez Musharraf, in *Pakistan Army Green Book* (2000), i.

52. According to its website, the origins of the NDC can be traced to the first War Course organized by the Command Staff College at Quetta in 1963. The NDC was established in 1971. http://www.ndu.edu.pk/courses_nswc.php (accessed April 29, 2010).

53. In 2010, the two courses (along with the Allied Officers War Course) were merged into a single, forty-six-week-long National Security and War Course. The new course has two components: National Security (twenty weeks) and Military Strategy (twenty-six weeks). By this integration, the NDU hopes to achieve comprehensive training in the "entire spectrum of national security as well as military strategy." http://www.ndu.edu .pk/courses_nswc.php (accessed March 26, 2012).

54. National Defence Course Syllabus, 2008–2009, National Defence College.

55. Ibid., iv.

56. Ibid., 56.

57. Ibid.

58. Ibid., 59. See also *Pakistan Army Green Book* (2000), 240–241, 245–250.

59. National Defence Course Syllabus, 59, 70, 79, 81–82.

60. Ibid., 38, 67.

61. Speech of the Chief Executive of Pakistan.

62. Major General Asif Duraiz Akhtar, "Nation-Building," in *Pakistan Army Green Book* (2000), 2.

63. Brigadier Sardar Mahmood Khan, "Army Employment in Nation Building: A Concept," in *Pakistan Army Green Book* (2000), 22.

64. Editorial, in *Pakistan Army Green Book* (2000), ii.

65. Akhtar, "Nation Building," 1.

66. Another brigadier's solution to these problems is that "ethnic elements should be dealt with an iron hand." *Pakistan Army Green Book* (2000), 60.

67. Brigadier Usman Ghani, "Good Governance: Reasons for Failure; Strategy for Future," *NDC Journal* (2001): 39; Khurshid Khan, "Stable Pakistan," 94.

68. Interview of Major General Tahir Ali (retd.) by the author, Rawalpindi, August 2012.

69. Akhtar, "Nation Building," 1.

70. Mahmood Khan, "Army Employment in Nation Building," 21–22.

71. With the exception of three Baloch sardars, the Mengals, Marris, and Bugtis, the rest of the seventy or so sardars support the federal government and rely on its patronage to further their social and political power.

72. See "Pakistan: The Forgotten Conflict in Baluchistan" (Asia Report no. 69, International Crisis Group, October 22, 2007).

73. Attacks on government installations and troops began in summer 2004, but were intensified after army personnel raped a female doctor in Sui

in January 2005. Bugti's killing was the final nail in the coffin. On the revival of Baloch insurgency under Musharraf's rule, see Frédéric Grare, *Pakistan: The Resurgence of Baluch Nationalism* (Washington, DC: Carnegie Endowment for International Peace, 2006). Military officers allege that Bugti
committed suicide by blowing himself up, and that the blast also killed
five army officers who had gone to arrest him. Interview with a colonel on
active duty in Balochistan at the time, Rawalpindi, July 2008. See also
"Akbar Bugti Committed Suicide, Claims Musharraf," *Dawn*, March 14,
2012; "Musharraf, Army Chief Want Independent Probe into Bugti's
Death," *News*, September 29, 2012.

74. See Selig S. Harrison, "Pakistan's Baluch Insurgency," *Le Monde
Diplomatique*, October 2006, http://mondediplo.com/2006/10/05baluchistan
(accessed July 3, 2010).

75. Alfred Stepan, *Military Politics: Changing Patterns in Brazil*
(Princeton, NJ: Princeton University Press, 1971), 229.

76. *Pakistan Army Green Book* (2000), 2, 8–9, 60.

77. General Ashfaq Pervez Kayani, quoted in "50 Most Powerful People of the World," *Newsweek*, December 19, 2008, http://www.thedaily
beast.com/newsweek/2008/12/19/20-gen-ashfaq-parvez-kayani.html (accessed
November 27, 2012).

78. *Pakistan Army Green Book* (2000), 34.

79. Ibid., e.g., 34, 56, 240–241, 258, 262.

80. Ibid., 2. See also 43–44.

81. Juan J. Linz, *Totalitarian and Authoritarian Regimes* (Boulder, CO:
Lynne Rienner, 2000), 205.

82. Brigadier Raashid Wali Janjua, "The Impact of Internal and Exter-
nal Factors in Shaping the Balance of Civil and Military Power," *NDU
Journal* (2010): 40; Brigadier Shafqat Asghar, "Army-Police Cooperation," in
A Report on Stabilizing Pakistan through Police Reform, ed. Hassan Abbas
(New York: Asia Society), 82.

83. Interview with a major general posted in the NDU, Islamabad,
August 2012.

84. Lieutenant General Tanvir Naqvi (retd.), comments made at the
seminar "Parliamentary Oversight of the Security Sector," organized by the
Pakistan Institute of Legislative Development and Transparency, February
25, 2005, http://www.pildat.org/eventsdel.asp?detid=70 (accessed March 7,
2011).

85. Senator Farhatullah Babar, comments made at the seminar "Parliamentary Oversight of the Security Sector," February 25, 2005, http://www
.pildat.org/eventsdel.asp?detid=70 (accessed March 7, 2011).

7. THE MILITARY AND DEMOCRACY

1. Guillermo O'Donnell and Philippe C. Schmitter, *Transitions from Authoritarian Rule: Tentative Conclusions about Uncertain Democracies* (Baltimore: Johns Hopkins University Press, 1996), 49.

2. Shoaib A. Ghias, "Miscarriage of Chief Justice: Judicial Power and the Legal Complex in Pakistan under Musharraf," *Law and Social Inquiry* 35, no. 4 (Fall 2010): 999.

3. Ibid., 991.

4. Under the 1973 constitution, an electoral college comprising both houses of the parliament and the four provincial assemblies indirectly elects the president.

5. Article 41(1) of the 1973 constitution bars the president from holding any other public office. Musharraf had secured a one-time waiver from the Supreme Court in 2002.

6. Also present were the Director of the Intelligence Bureau, Brigadier Ijaz Shah (retd.) and Musharraf's Chief of Staff, Lieutenant General Hamid Javed. See text of the affidavit filed by Iftikhar Mohammad Chaudhry in the Supreme Court, May 29, 2007, http://www.humanrights.asia/news/forwarded-news/FS-023-2007/?searchterm= (accessed August 29, 2013).

7. "Nationwide Protest by Lawyers: 40 Hurt in Lahore Baton Charge," *Dawn*, March 13, 2007.

8. "SCBA Terms Removal Assault on Independence of Judiciary," *Dawn*, March 10, 2007.

9. "Daylong Running Battles across Capital" and "Opposition Flexes Muscles on Protest Day," *Dawn*, March 17, 2007.

10. Helene Cooper and Mark Mazzetti, "Backstage, US Nurtured Pakistan Rivals' Deal," *New York Times*, October 20, 2007.

11. Benazir Bhutto details her on-again, off-again negotiations with Musharraf in her posthumously published book, *Reconciliation: Islam, Democracy, and the West* (New York: HarperCollins, 2008), 225–230; see also "Benazir Defends Deal with Musharraf," *News*, April 26, 2007; "Bhutto Close to Deal with Musharraf," *Guardian*, August 29, 2007.

12. Section 2 of the NRO empowered the federal and provincial governments to withdraw cases against those accused in absentia due to "political reasons or through political victimization" in any case initiated between January 1, 1986, and October 12, 1999. Under section 7, the federal government withdrew pending cases against public officials initiated before October 12, 1999. See National Reconciliation Ordinance (Government

of Pakistan: Ministry of Law, Justice and Human Rights, October 5, 2007).

13. Opposition parties resigned from the national and provincial assemblies to protest Musharraf's reelection by the same parliament that had elected him in 2002. As it had assured Musharraf, the PPP remained in parliament but did not vote for his candidacy.

14. See "Proclamation of Emergency," *Dawn*, November 4, 2007.

15. The Provisional Constitutional Order mandated that all superior court justices take a new oath pledging unconditional obedience to the regime, or lose their office. The almost sixty judges who refused to comply were sacked and placed under house arrest.

16. See "Text of the Charter of Democracy," *Dawn*, May 16, 2006.

17. Interview with a retired army major general by author, Rawalpindi, September 2012. See also Jay Solomon and Zahid Hussain, "Army Grows Cooler to Musharraf," *Wall Street Journal*, February 13, 2008.

18. Declan Walsh, "Bush Tells Musharraf to Choose Ballot Box or Uniform," *Guardian*, November 7, 2007.

19. In accordance with their respective strengths in each provincial assembly, the PPP led the provincial government in Sindh, the PML-N in the Punjab, and the Awami National Party in the North-West Frontier Province.

20. Interview, Islamabad, September 2008. See also "Kayani Looks Musharraf in the Eye," *News*, May 29, 2008; "Army to Avoid Involvement in Politics," *Times of India*, August 8, 2008.

21. "Pakistan Army to Ask Musharraf to Resign," *Telegraph*, August 8, 2008.

22. "West's Diplomats Rush to Save Musharraf from Impeachment," *Guardian*, August 13, 2008.

23. *Pakistan Army Green Book* (Rawalpindi: General Headquarters, 2008), 51.

24. *Report of the United Nations Commission of Inquiry into the Facts and Circumstances of the Assassination of Former Pakistani Prime Minister Mohtarma Benazir Bhutto*, 59, http://www.un.org/News/dh/infocus/Pakistan/UN_Bhutto_Report_15April2010.pdf (accessed September 2, 2011) (hereafter cited as *UN Inquiry Report*).

25. The former chief of the ISI's political cell, Major General Ehtisham Zameer (retd.), has disclosed that he rigged the 2002 elections on General Musharraf's orders. See "The Man, Who Rigged the Polls, Spills the Beans," *News* (Rawalpindi), February 24, 2008.

26. See, for instance, "Musharraf Successor Kayani Boosts Pakistan Army's Image," *Christian Science Monitor,* February 23, 2008; and Raza Rumi, "Good Luck, General Kayani," *Express Tribune* (Karachi), July 24, 2010. The US government was not far behind in applauding Kayani's professionalism. In the words of the then American ambassador to Pakistan, Anne Patterson, "We should praise Kayani's efforts to support civilian rule." See US Embassy, "Scene-Setter for General Kayani's Visit to Washington," February 19, 2009, http://www.theguardian.com/world/us-embassy-cables-documents/192895 (accessed November 4, 2011).

27. Wendy Hunter, "Civil-Military Relations in Argentina, Brazil, and Chile: Past Trends, Future Prospects," in *Fault Lines of Democracy in Post-transition Latin America,* ed. Felipe Agüero and Jeffrey Stark (Coral Gables, FL: North-South Center/University of Miami Press, 1998), 313.

28. PML-N cabinet ministers had resigned from the cabinet in May 2008 after the first mutually agreed deadline to restore the judges passed.

29. The Pakistan Tehreek-e-Insaaf is a right-of-center party led by Imran Khan, the charismatic former captain of the Pakistani cricket team. The party has tried to present itself as an alternative to the two major parties, the PPP and the PML-N, on the basis of its nondynastic and presumably honest leadership, as well as a virulent anti-Americanism popular with Pakistan's urban middle classes. In the 2008 elections, Khan won the sole National Assembly seat for the party.

30. "Governor Rule in Punjab," *Nation* (Lahore), February 26, 2009.

31. General Ashfaq Pervez Kayani, quoted in "50 Most Powerful People of the World," *Newsweek,* December 19, 2008, http://www.thedailybeast.com/newsweek/2008/12/19/20-gen-ashfaq-parvez-kayani.html (accessed November 27, 2012).

32. "Political Deal Worked Out," *News,* March 13, 2009.

33. Declan Walsh, "Pakistan Army Chief Demands Removal of Zardari Loyalists from Cabinet," *Guardian,* October 1, 2010.

34. "Corps Commanders Concerned about Karachi Violence," *Nation,* August 8, 2011; "Kayani, Malik Discuss Judicial Crisis in Meeting," *Nation,* February 20, 2010. Karachi has become a seething cauldron of interacting ethnic, political, sectarian, and criminal violence for many reasons, including its complex and changing ethnic demography, army intelligence manipulation of ethnic identities, the proliferation of sophisticated arms since the 1980s, poor urban planning and competition over resources, and the growing presence of terrorist groups like the Tehrike

Taliban Pakistan. According to the Human Rights Commission of Pakistan, 800 people died in 2011 in ethnopolitically motivated shootings. "800 Killed in Karachi This Year: HRCP," *Express Tribune*, August 5, 2011. The violence has only escalated since. In the first six months of 2012, 1,215 people were killed in sectarian, ethnopolitical, or other violence. For the same period in 2013, the number of fatalities was 1,726. See "Six-month HRCP Report: 1,726 People Killed in Karachi," *Nation* (Lahore), July 16, 2013.

35. "First Secretaries' Meeting Chaired by Army Chief," *Dawn* (Karachi), March 17, 2010.

36. See, for instance, "Inside the Secret U.S.-Pakistan (Army) Meeting in Oman," http://thecable.foreignpolicy.com/posts/2011/02/24/inside_the _secret_us_pakistan_meeting_in_oman (accessed August 3, 2012).

37. The CIA has reportedly doled out to the ISI funds that equal up to one-third of the agency's budget, as well as hundreds of millions of dollars in bounty money for the capture of wanted al-Qaeda militants. See Greg Miller, "CIA Pays for Support in Pakistan," *Los Angeles Times*, November 15, 2009.

38. Testimony of the former ISI director general, Lieutenant General Ahmed Shuja Pasha (retd.), before the Abbottabad Inquiry Commission, 200, http://www.aljazeera.com/indepth/spotlight/binladenfiles/ (accessed July 9, 2013).

39. Bruce Riedel, *Deadly Embrace: Pakistan, America, and the Future of the Global Jihad* (Washington, DC: Brookings Institution Press, 2011), 121.

40. "General Kayani Gets 3-Year Extension," *Nation*, July 23, 2010.

41. "Kayani Gives One More Extension," *News*, February 21, 2010; "ISPR Chief Clarifies Only Promotions Require Ratification," *News*, February 21, 2010.

42. In prior years, the military's budget was just a lump-sum figure.

43. "ISPR Chief Decries Criticism of Defense Budget," *News*, March 14, 2011.

44. Omar Warraich, "Pakistan's Spies Elude Its Government," *Time*, July 31, 2008, http://www.time.com/time/world/article/0,8599,1828207,00. html (accessed October 19, 2011).

45. Headed by Justice Javed Iqbal of the Supreme Court, the commission's members included the former diplomat Jehangir Ashraf Qazi; a retired police inspector general, Abbas Khan; and Lieutenant General Nadeem Ahmad (retd.).

46. Testimony of Ahmed Shuja Pasha, 204.

47. Ibid., 193.

48. See, for instance, the commission's observations on the testimony of the garrison commander/commandant of the Pakistan Military Academy at Kakul. The commission concluded that the commander took charge of the site of Osama bin Laden's death and prevented the police from performing their mandated function of collecting evidence. Moreover, Military Intelligence collected the initial forensic evidence from Osama bin Laden's compound and then handed it over to the ISI, which took over the investigation. See Abbottabad Inquiry Commission, 70, 186, 190.

49. Adjutant General's testimony before the Abbottabad Inquiry Commission, 172. See also testimony of the Director General of Military Intelligence before the same commission, 186.

50. "Despite Promises to Talk, New Pakistan PM Gets Tough on Insurgents," Reuters, July 23, 2013, http://www.reuters.com/article/2013/07/23/us-pakistan-security-idUSBRE96M12Z20130723 (accessed July 25, 2013).

51. "Civilians, Military Consulted on Trade with India," *Dawn*, November 5, 2011; "No Immediate Plan to Grant India MFN Status," *Nation*, August 12, 2013.

52. "There Is a Bit of India in Every Pakistani: Zardari," *Hindustan Times*, November 22, 2008.

53. US Embassy, "Scene-Setter for General Kayani's Visit to Washington."

54. Elizabeth Bumiller and Jane Perlez, "Pakistan's Spy Agency Is Tied to Attack on U.S. Embassy," *New York Times*, September 22, 2011.

55. "Zardari Vows Operation against Haqqanis," *Dawn*, November 9, 2011.

56. See A. R. Siddiqi, *The Military in Pakistan: Image and Reality* (Lahore: Vanguard, 1996).

57. *Pakistan Army Green Book* (2008), 8.

58. Huma Yusuf, "Conspiracy Fever: The US, Pakistan and Its Media," *Survival* 53, no. 4 (2011): 105.

59. National Defence University, http://www.ndu.edu.pk (accessed September 6, 2012).

60. ISPR press release PR396/2009-ISPR, October 7, 2009, http://ispr.gov.pk/front/main.asp?o=t-press_release&id=914&search=1 (accessed September 2, 2010).

61. As reported by then US ambassador to Pakistan, Anne Patterson, these civilian control provisions "rankled COAS Kayani" because "he had

no intention of taking over the government . . . and was receiving criticism on the bill from the Corps Commanders." See "Ambassador Meets with Kayani and Pasha about Kerry-Lugar Bill," October 7, 2009, http://www.theguardian.com/world/us-embassy-cables-documents/228747 (accessed March 13, 2011).

62. Farrukh Saleem, "Drones Not Public Enemy No. 1," *News*, April 26, 2011.

63. Yusuf, "Conspiracy Fever," 97.

64. "Names of 55 Suspects on the Loose," *News*, March 12, 2011, http://www.thenews.com.pk/TodaysPrintDetail.aspx?ID=4553&Cat=13 (accessed February 4, 2012).

65. "Leak of CIA Officer Name Sign of Rift with Pakistan," *New York Times*, May 9, 2011.

66. See *Aaj Kamran Khan Key Saath* [Tonight with Kamran Khan], Geo TV, May 4, 2011, http://www.youtube.com/watch?v=C_88jfndamw (accessed February 9, 2012). See also Talat Hussain, "The Problem Within," *Dawn*, June 13, 2011.

67. ISPR press release, "139th Corps Commanders Conference," June 9, 2011.

68. Although the ISI has denied involvement in his murder, there is strong circumstantial evidence implicating the military agency in this heinous act, including thinly veiled death threats given to Shehzad by senior officers of its media wing, the disappearance of Shehzad's cell-phone record from a cell-phone company's database, and the agency's intimidation of other journalists who spoke out against its involvement. Even more damning are reported American intelligence intercepts that directly link the army chief to the murder. See Dexter Felkins, "The Journalist and the Spies," *New Yorker*, September 19, 2011. See also "Admiral Links Pakistan to Journalist's Murder," *New York Times*, July 7, 2011.

69. Saleem Shehzad, "Al-Qaeda Had Warned of Pakistan Strike," *Asia Times Online*, May 27, 2011, http://www.atimes.com/atimes/South_Asia/ME27Df06.html (accessed June 22, 2011).

70. Mansoor Ijaz, "Time to Take on Pakistan's Jihadist Spies," *Financial Times*, October 10, 2011.

71. The ISI's director general, Lieutenant General Ahmed Shuja Pasha, secretly visited Ijaz in London and reportedly collected incriminating transcripts of text messages exchanged between Haqqani and Ijaz. See Fasih Ahmed, "When Mansoor Ijaz Met General Pasha," *Newsweek* (Pakistan), November 20, 2011.

72. "Memogate: COAS Submits Rejoinder to SC," *News*, December 21, 2011.

73. The commission was ordered to investigate the authenticity of the memo and to determine whether sending the memo to senior American officials was tantamount to compromising the sovereignty, security, and independence of Pakistan. See "Memogate Probe: Full Text of the SC Decision to Form Commission," *Express Tribune*, December 3, 2011.

74. "State within a State Not Acceptable: PM Gillani," Associated Press of Pakistan, December 22, 2011.

75. ISPR press release, January 11, 2012.

76. "Commander 111 Brigade Changed," *News*, January 11, 2012.

77. The last time a civilian government tried to prematurely retire an army chief (in October 1999), the army executed a coup.

78. "Government Does Not Want to Sack Army, ISI Chiefs," *Nation*, January 20, 2012; "Court Admits Petition on Saving Army and ISI Chiefs," *Express Tribune*, February 28, 2012.

79. "Adiala Missing Inmates: ISI and MI Not Superior to Civilians, Says SC," *Express Tribune*, March 1, 2012.

80. "Disband Agencies' Death Squads," *News*, September 28, 2012.

81. "SC Seeks Progress Report on Missing Persons," *Daily Times* (Lahore), February 9, 2012; "Missing Persons: ISI, MI Counsel Says RAW and Mossad Involved," *Express Tribune*, March 16, 2012; "SC Seeks Report in Missing Persons' Case," *Frontier Post* (Peshawar), July 23, 2013.

82. "Two Bodies of Missing Persons Found in Balochistan," *Express Tribune*, May 1, 2012.

83. "Supreme Court Takes U-Turn on Arrest of ISI Brigadier," *Daily Times*, July 24, 2013.

84. *Pakistan Army Green Book* (2011), 7.

85. "Kayani Decries Military Bashing," *News*, March 15, 2012.

86. *UN Inquiry Report*, 1; "Limited Mandate Hinders UN Effort," *Dawn*, December 31, 2009.

87. *UN Inquiry Report*, 33.

88. "Military Slammed UN Report on Benazir Assassination," *Dawn*, December 25, 2010.

89. The National Logistics Cell is a monopolistic army-run freight, construction, and engineering agency, even though it falls under the administrative purview of the National Logistics Board, an attached department of the federal Planning and Development Division.

90. "NLC Scam: Army to Investigate Retired Generals under Army Act," *Express Tribune*, September 14, 2012. It is unclear whether the internal inquiry was ever completed.

91. See Pakistan Army Amendment Ordinance, 2007, http://www.na .gov.pk/uploads/documents/1302673360_974.pdf, March 1, 2012 (accessed March 21, 2012).

92. "New Regulations Give Legal Cover to Detentions in Tribal Areas," *Dawn*, July 11, 2011.

93. "Peshawar High Court Judge Says Missing Persons Killed after Courts Pressure Agencies," *News*, July 24, 2013; "ISI Denies Torturing Man to Death in Custody," *Express Tribune*, September 28, 2011; *Globalizing Torture: CIA Secret Detention and Extraordinary Rendition* (New York: Open Society Foundations, 2013).

94. Human Rights Watch, "Enforced Disappearances by Pakistan Security Forces in Balochistan," July 28, 2011.

95. Quoted in ibid.

96. Observers saw PML-N president and Punjab chief minister Shahbaz Sharif's call to include the military and the judiciary in a proposed all-parties conference to tackle Pakistan's many crises as an indication of the party's permissive attitude toward a temporary military intervention. See, for instance, "Call for Intervention," *Dawn*, March 9, 2011. See also "MQM to Back Martial Law Like Steps: Altaf," *Express Tribune*, August 23, 2010; and "Altaf Again Invokes 'Patriotic' Generals," *Dawn*, February 12, 2011.

97. Interviews by the author, June–August 2008.

98. See "Text of the Charter of Democracy," *Dawn*, May 16, 2006.

99. The only constitutional way to remove a government is if the National Assembly passes a no-confidence motion against it.

100. The higher judiciary has traditionally legitimized military intervention and rule by applying the doctrine of necessity. See Paula Newberg, *Judging the State: Courts and Constitutional Politics in Pakistan* (New York: Cambridge University Press, 1995), chaps. 2, 3, and 6.

101. The caretaker prime minister is appointed by the president in consultation with the incumbent prime minister and the leader of the opposition in the outgoing National Assembly. In case of a deadlock, the prime minister and the opposition leader forward two names each to an eight-member parliamentary committee consisting of four members each from the treasury and opposition benches within three days of the assembly's dissolution. If the committee is unable to reach a decision in the next three days,

the Election Commission has to appoint the caretaker prime minister from the committee's short list within two days. See Constitution of the Islamic Republic of Pakistan, Articles 224 and 224A.

102. However, the prime minister's power to appoint military service chiefs is constrained because the pool of candidates is determined by the military. Before the 1999 military coup, appointing its chief used to be the main civilian prerogative with regard to the army, but it lost much of its force once a new COAS assumed office.

103. EU Election Observation Mission, "Preliminary Statement," May 13, 2013, http://www.eueom.eu/files/dmfile/eom-pakistan-preliminary-state ment-13052013-en.pdf (accessed May 19, 2013).

104. On the attitudinal and behavioral dimensions of democratic consolidation, see Juan Linz and Alfred Stepan, *Problems of Democratic Transition and Consolidation: Southern Europe, South America, and Eastern Europe* (Baltimore: Johns Hopkins University Press), 5–6.

105. National Defence University, Islamabad, Syllabus, 2012–2013, vi, 6–7.

106. National Defence College, Dhaka, Syllabus, 2012–2013, 11.

107. "COAS Address on the Eve of the Yaum-e-Shuhhada [Martyrs' Day]," April 30, 2013, http://www.ispr.gov.pk/front/main.asp?o=t-press_re lease&date=2013/4/30 (accessed June 1, 2013).

108. *Pakistan Army Green Book* (2008), 26.

109. Ibid., 3.

110. *Pakistan Army Green Book* (Rawalpindi: General Headquarters, 2011), 49–50. See also Brigadier Muhammad Khurshid Khan, "A Stable Pakistan: Proposed Model of National Security," *Margalla Papers* (National Defence University, 2011), 85, 93–94.

111. *Pakistan Army Green Book* (2011), 50.

112. Testimony of Ahmed Shuja Pasha, 203.

113. Interview by the author, Islamabad, August 2012.

114. Affidavit of Brigadier Hamid Saeed (retd.), Supreme Court Detailed Judgement in the Asghar Khan Case, HRC 19/1996, 12, www.supremecourt .gov.pk/web/user_files/File/H.R.C.19of1996[AsgharKhanCase]Detaile dReasons.pdf (accessed April 1, 2013).

115. *Pakistan Army Green Book* (2008), 3.

116. Interviews by the author, June–September 2012.

117. *Pakistan Army Green Book* (2011), 20.

118. *Pakistan Army Green Book* (2008), 52.

119. *Pakistan Army Green Book* (2011), 49.

120. "COAS Address."

121. Brigadier Farooq Ahmed Khan (retd.), "Countdown to May 11: Kayani Clears the Cloud," *News*, May 4, 2013.

122. Concerned with improving the image of the army, some officers hold the opinion that the armed forces should stay out of politics and focus on their primary task of combat preparedness. See, for instance, *Pakistan Army Green Book* (2008), 89.

123. Interview of a civilian academic who delivers lectures at the NDU by the author, Islamabad, September 2012.

124. Interviews of military officers by the author, August–October, 2012.

125. Christine Fair, "The Pakistani Military's New Coup Playbook," *Foreign Affairs*, March 14, 2013, http://www.foreignaffairs.com/articles/139054 /c-christine-fair/the-pakistani-militarys-new-coup-playbook (accessed July 4, 2013).

126. *Pakistan Army Green Book* (Rawalpindi: General Headquarters, 2000), 240; Khurshid Khan, "A Stable Pakistan," 82–109.

127. Khurshid Khan, "A Stable Pakistan"; Brigadier Javed Iqbal Sattar, "Empowering the People," *NDC Journal*, 2001, 54–65.

128. Testimony of Ahmed Shuja Pasha, 199.

129. Brigadier Shafqat Asghar, "Army-Police Cooperation," in *A Report on Stabilizing Pakistan through Police Reform*, ed. Hassan Abbas (New York: Asia Society, July 2012), 83.

130. Ibid., 82–84.

131. Testimony of Ahmed Shuja Pasha, 199.

132. *National Strategy Paper, 2012: Non-kinetic Challenges to the State of Pakistan* (Islamabad: National Defence University, February 2012), 25–32; *Pakistan Army Green Book* (2008), 7, 55, 131, 134.

133. Khurshid Khan, "A Stable Pakistan," 91.

134. Interview of Major General Tahir Ali by the author, 2012; interview of Lieutenant General Asad Durrani (retd.) by author, 2009.

135. *Pakistan Army Green Book* (2011), 214. See also *Pakistan Army Green Book* (2008); 134.

136. Adam Przeworski's comment on the dust jacket of *The Soldier and the Changing State: Building Democratic Armies in Africa, Asia, Europe and the Americas*, by Zoltan Barany (Princeton, NJ: Princeton University Press, 2012).

137. "Message of General Ashfaq Pervez Kayani, Chief of Army Staff," in *Pakistan Army Green Book* (2011), i.

138. Testimony of the Deputy Chief of Air Staff, and Chief of Air Staff, Air Marshal Rao Qamar Suleman, before the Abbottabad Commission of Inquiry, 142–143, 153.

139. *Pakistan Army Green Book* (2008), 6.

140. Major General Shaukat Iqbal, "Security Politics of the Region: The Indo-US Nexus," in *Pakistan Army Green Book* (2011), 111; *Pakistan Army Green Book* (2011), 46; *Pakistan Army Green Book* (2008), 4; *NDU Strategy Paper, 2012,* 16; and "South and Central Asia," *Opinion: A Journal of the Armed Forces War College* (National Defence University) 1, no. 1 (June 2013): 6–8.

141. *National Strategy Paper, 2012,* 17; *Pakistan Army Green Book* (2011), 48, 85, 93.

142. See, for example, *Pakistan Army Green Book* (2011), 150–157, 192.

143. *Pakistan Army Green Book* (2008), 4.

144. For instance, under the doctrine of collective and territorial responsibility, the FCR empowers the political agent (local head of the administration answerable to the NWFP/KPK governor) to punish a tribe for individual crimes committed on its territory by fines, arrests, property seizures and blockades. The PA's decisions cannot be legally challenged because the constitution bars the judiciary from enforcing fundamental rights in the FATA.

145. "Governance of Specially Administered Areas and Their Impact on National Security (National Strategy Paper—2007–08)," *NDU Journal* 2 (2008): 37–40.

146. "National Strategy for Countering Extremism and Terrorism (National Security Paper–2009–10)," *NDU Journal* (2010): 135–140.

147. *Pakistan Army Green Book* (2008), 4–5, 53 54.

148. "Governance of Specially Administered Areas," 24–25; *Pakistan Army Green Book* (2011), 47. See also roundtable talk, "The Pakistan Dilemma: Why the World Should Care," National Defence University (June 11, 2012), 11–13, http://www.ndu.edu.pk/issra/issra_pub/Interactions/ (accessed January 9, 2013).

149. *Pakistan Army Green Book* (2011), 31–32, 111, 150.

150. "South and Central Asia," 6.

151. *Pakistan Army Green Book* (2008), 5.

152. *National Strategy Paper, 2012,* 57.

153. *Pakistan Army Green Book* (2008), 5.

154. *Pakistan Army Green Book* (2011), 5–6, 109–111.

155. Ibid., 46–47.

156. *National Strategy Paper, 2012,* 15–16, 20; *Pakistan Army Green Book* (2011), 45.

157. *National Strategy Paper, 2012.* See also *Pakistan Army Green Book* (2011), 111–113; *Pakistan Army Green Book* (2008), 52–54.

158. *National Strategy Paper, 2012,* 52–55. See also *Pakistan Army Green Book* (2008), 3–4, 45–46, 240–241; *Pakistan Army Green Book* (2011), 6, 122, 150, 188.

159. Lieutenant Colonel Mohammad Khan, "Kashmir Dispute and the Prospects of India-Pakistan Peace," *NDU Journal* 2 (2008): 49–89.

160. *Pakistan Army Green Book* (2011), 148–150. See also *National Strategy Paper,* 2012, 20–22.

161. Lieutenant Colonel Lodhi, "Kashmir Policy: Options for Pakistan," *NDU Journal* (2007): 141; *Pakistan Army Green Book* (2011), 46–47; *Pakistan Army Green Book* (2008), 7.

162. Mohammad Khan, "Kashmir Dispute," 82; Lodhi, "Kashmir Policy," 128–129.

163. Brigadier Naeem Ahmed Salik, "Confidence Building Measures between India and Pakistan," *NDU Journal* (2010): 59–60; Lieutenant Colonel Sahir Shamshad Mirza, "Subcontinental Security and Its Impact on World Security: Challenges and the Way Forward," *NDU Journal* (2009): 99; Lodhi, "Kashmir Policy."

164. *Pakistan Army Green Book* (2008), 55.

165. *Pakistan Army Green Book* (2011), 47–48, 95.

166. *Pakistan Army Green Book* (2008), 46–48.

167. Interview by author, August 2012.

168. *National Strategy Paper, 2012,* 11–12.

169. Ibid., 25.

170. NDU Syllabus, 2012–2013, 38–43.

171. Frederick M. Nunn, "The South American Military and (Re) Democratization: Professional Thought and Self-Perception," *Journal of Inter-American Studies and World Affairs* 37, no. 2 (1995): 20.

172. *Pakistan Army Green Book* (2008), 8–9, 14–16.

173. Colonel Muhammad Yahya Effendi, "The World of the Secret Services: Intelligence, Espionage, and Special Operations," *Pakistan Defence Review* 7 (1995): 27–28.

CONCLUSION

1. I use the term "postauthoritarian" to describe the period after the end of military government so as to better distinguish the latter from the

transition period. I do not claim that the military's exit from control over direct power means that the Pakistani state and society are free of authoritarian features. At the same time, it is important to acknowledge that even the most advanced or established democracies can contain some authoritarian elements in their governments or political culture. Still, for both normative and analytical reasons, we would be remiss to lump democratically elected governments with military-authoritarian ones. Insofar as democracy is a system of government in which universally enfranchised, competitive elections determine "who governs," and elected officials are not de jure accountable to nor have to formally share their power with the administrative institutions of the state (including the military), I use democracy, democratic government, and civilian rule interchangeably for governments that meet these procedural minima. By this yardstick, the PPP government (2008–2013) was democratic, but Musharraf's government was authoritarian despite its civilianization between 2002 and 2007.

2. In such a coalition, the military is a key political actor, and civilian governments can stay in power only with military acquiescence or active support. Morris Janowitz, *Military Institutions and Coercion in the Developing Nations* (Chicago: University of Chicago Press, 1977), 83.

3. See Michael C. Desch, *Civilian Control of the Military: The Changing Security Environment* (Baltimore: Johns Hopkins University Press, 1997), 13–14.

4. Dunkart Rustow, "Transitions to Democracy: Toward a Dynamic Model," *Comparative Politics* 2, no. 3 (April 1970): 350.

5. Amos Perlmutter, "The Praetorian State and the Praetorian Army: Toward a Taxonomy of Civil-Military Relations in Developing Polities," *Comparative Politics* 1, no. 3 (April 1969): 384.

6. E-mail exchange with John Samuel Fitch, November 11, 2012.

7. The democratic peace has been described as being "as close as anything we have to an empirical law in international relations." Jack S. Levy, "The Causes of War: A Review of Theories and Evidence," in *Behavior, Society, and Nuclear War,* ed. Philip E. Tetlock et al. (Oxford: Oxford University Press, 1989), 270.

8. Julian Schofield, "Militarized Decision-Making for War," *Armed Forces and Society* 27, no. 1 (Fall 2000): 139.

9. Scholars like Michael Doyle argue that the democratic peace obtains between liberal democracies. Some would argue that in 1999, Pakistan was at best what Fareed Zakaria termed an "illiberal democracy" because of Prime Minister Nawaz Sharif's violations of basic liberal tenets, such as the

rule of law and freedom of speech. See Michael Doyle, "Liberalism and World Politics," *American Political Science Review* 80, no. 4 (December 1986): 1151–1169; Fareed Zakaria, "The Rise of Illiberal Democracy," *Foreign Affairs* 76, no. 6 (November–December 1997): 22–43. However, Pakistan scored +7 on the authoritative Annual Polity IV dataset, which categorizes political regimes on a scale from −10 to +10. Countries that score −6 and below are coded as autocracies and those with a score of +10 as democracies. India's score was +9 in 1999. See Monty G. Marshall, *Polity IV Project: Political Regime Characteristics and Transitions, 1800–2012* (College Park, MD: Integrated Network for Societal Conflict Research, 2013). Others have questioned whether Kargil was, in fact, a war. For instance, Bruce Russet and John R. O'Neal argue that Kargil was not a war because it involved "Islamic guerillas" rather than regular Pakistani troops. See their *Triangulating Peace: Democracy, Interdependence, and International Organizations* (New York: Norton, 2001), 48. However, the Kargil war involved over a thousand total battle fatalities, the criteria used in the Correlates of War (COW) dataset to classify a conflict as war. See COW 4.0., http://www.correlatesofwar.org/ (accessed September 19, 2013). Subsequent research also shows that Pakistani combatants were in fact regular troops from the Northern Light Infantry, a paramilitary force that was inducted as the army's sixth infantry regiment after the war.

10. Richard Kohn, "How Democracies Control the Military," *Journal of Democracy* 8, no. 4 (1997): 142.

11. See Deborah L. Norden, *Military Rebellion in Argentina: Between Coups and Consolidation* (Lincoln: University of Nebraska Press, 1996).

12. "Egypt Leader Morsi Orders Army Chief Tantawi to Resign," *BBC Online News*, August 12, 2012, http://www.bbc.co.uk/news/world-africa-19234763 (accessed December 21, 2012).

13. See Narcís Serra, *The Military Transition: Democratic Reform of the Armed Forces*, trans. Peter Bush (New York: Cambridge University Press, 2010), esp. 66–89.

14. Ibid., 33.

15. Samuel Huntington, *The Third Wave: Democratization in the Late Twentieth Century* (Norman: University of Oklahoma Press, 1993), 267.

16. It is important to note that the turnover effect is not set in stone. Two democratic alternations in power may or may not make countries immune from regression into overt or behind-the-scenes authoritarianism. For instance, Bangladesh had three transfers of power—1991, 1996, and 2001—in which the losers yielded power to the winners. However, in 2007, the mili-

tary stepped in to impose emergency rule amid preelection violence fomented by the Awami League's refusal to accept elections under a progovernment caretaker adviser (who oversees elections) appointed by the ruling Bangladesh National Party.

17. Terry Lynn Karl, "From Democracy to Democratization and Back: Before Transitions from Authoritarian Rule" (Occasional Paper no. 45, Center for Democracy, Development, and the Rule of Law, Stanford University, September 2005), 9.

18. Larry Diamond, "Democracy in Latin America: Degrees, Illusions and Directions for Consolidation," in *Beyond Sovereignty: Collectively Defending Democracy in the Americas,* ed. Tom Farer (Baltimore: Johns Hopkins University Press, 1996), 87.

19. Ibid.

20. See, for instance, Samuel Huntington, *The Soldier and the State: Theory and Practice of Civil-Military Relations* (Cambridge, MA: Belknap Press, 1957), 80–87; Felipe Agüero, *Soldiers, Civilians, and Democracy: Post-Franco Spain in Comparative Perspective* (Baltimore: Johns Hopkins University Press, 1995).

21. Defense Division, Ministry of Defense, Government of Pakistan, www.mod.gov.pk (accessed April 4, 2012).

22. The MoD also has a Military Accounts Department, which is responsible for internal audits of military spending. In addition, a special Finance Division (Military) of the federal Ministry of Finance deals with the preparation and monitoring of defense allocations to ensure compliance with budgetary regulations.

23. Testimony of the PPP Defence Minister Chaudhry Ahmed Mukhtar before the Abbottabad Commission of Inquiry, 224–225, http://www.aljazeera .com/indepth/spotlight/binladenfiles/ (accessed July 9, 2011).

24. Serra, *Military Transition*, 81.

25. Mazhar Aziz, *Military Control in Pakistan: The Parallel State* (London: Routledge, 2007), 95.

26. It is pertinent to note that many politicians (and generals) have abused this provision to induct favored military officers into the civil services.

27. Janowitz, *Military Institutions and Coercion*, 114.

28. On the difficulties involved in, and the reforms intended to facilitate, the transition from repressive authoritarian police forces to a more democratic model of policing based on serving and protecting the citizenry, see Michael D. Wiatrowski and Jack A. Goldstone, "The Ballot and the Badge: Democratic Policing," *Journal of Democracy* 21, no. 2 (April 2010): 72–92.

29. Successive civil and military governments have formed commissions for police reform, only to ignore their recommendations. This is in good part because of the incentive to retain control over the police as a tool for achieving political ends, including the intimidation and suppression of regime opponents. Ironically, the most radical changes in the structure and functioning of the police were introduced under General Musharraf through the Police Order, 2002. With the exception of a democratically problematic essay by one active-duty brigadier who would like to clone the Pakistani police in the image of the country's army, an excellent collection of papers written by active-duty and former police officers, as well as scholars and journalists, on the problems, prescriptions, and prospects of police reform in Pakistan is Hassan Abbas, ed., *A Report on Stabilizing Pakistan through Police Reform* (New York: Asia Society, July 2012).

30. For instance, one analysis of ninety insurgencies since 1945 has shown that the capacity of police forces is a key variable in the success of counterinsurgency operations. See Seth Jones, *Counterinsurgency in Afghanistan* (Santa Monica, CA: Rand Corporation, 2008).

31. "COAS to Call the Shots in Military Action," *News*, June 26, 2008.

32. For a useful analysis of the army's COIN training and capabilities based on close observation of its training operations, see Shuja Nawaz, *Learning by Doing: The Pakistan Army's Experience with Counterinsurgency* (Washington, DC: Atlantic Council, February 2011).

33. Eric Schmitt and Jane Perlez, "Distrust Slows U.S. Training of Pakistanis," *New York Times*, July 11, 2010.

34. Clause 201 (4), "Rules of Procedure and Conduct of Business in the National Assembly of Pakistan, 2007," www.na.gov.pk (accessed April 1, 2012).

35. Pakistan Institute of Legislative Development and Transparency, "Performance of the Parliamentary Committees on Defense and National Security, March 15, 2008–March 15, 2011," May 2011, http://www.pildat .org/publications/publication/CMR/Report-PerformanceoftheParliamen taryCommitteesofDefenceandNationalSecurityMar08toMar11.pdf (accessed May 10, 2012).

36. "ISI, Army to Brief NA, Senate Committees," *Dawn*, October 11, 2011.

37. Instead of calling the military to account, the joint session strongly condemned US unilateral actions on Pakistani territory and reposed "full confidence in the defense forces . . . in safeguarding Pakistan's sovereignty, independence and territorial integrity and in overcoming any challenge to security." National Assembly of Pakistan, "Resolution on Unilateral U.S.

Forces Action in Abbottabad," May 14, 2011, http://www.na.gov.pk/en/reso lution_detail.php?id=52 (accessed April 2, 2012).

38. National Assembly of Pakistan, "Consensus Resolution of the In-Camera Joint Sitting of Parliament," October 22, 2008, http://www.na.gov .pk/en/resolution_detail.php?id=39 (accessed April 2, 2012).

39. See "Parliamentary National Security Committee Refuses to Attend GHQ Briefing," *Dawn*, October 11, 2011.

40. National Assembly of Pakistan, "Resolution on Unilateral U.S. Forces Action."

41. On the Brazilian intelligence system, see Alfred Stepan, *Rethinking Military Politics: Brazil and the Southern Cone* (Princeton, NJ: Princeton University Press, 1988), 13–29.

42. Report of the Abbottabad Inquiry Commission, http://www.al jazeera.com/indepth/spotlight/binladenfiles/, 181 (accessed July 9, 2013).

43. "Farhatullah Babar Moves Bill to Control, Govern ISI," *News*, July 10, 2012; "Farhatullah Withdraws Bill in Senate about ISI Control," *News*, July 13, 2012.

44. See the Report of the Abbottabad Inquiry Commission, 187.

45. Zoltan Barany, *The Soldier and the Changing State: Building Democratic Armies in Africa, Asia, Europe, and the Americas* (Princeton, NJ: Princeton University Press, 2012), 353.

46. www.ndu.edu (accessed October 10, 2013).

47. Testimony of the Secretary of Defence, Abbottabad Inquiry Commission, http://www.aljazeera.com/indepth/spotlight/binladenfiles/, 222 (accessed July 9, 2013). The NDU's National Strategy Paper, 2012, discussed in Chapter 7, is a prototype of such a policy, which laments the lack of a comprehensive national security strategy. It covers a host of internal and external threats and offers a series of solutions, including the creation of a central "national security management system" with a permanent secretariat to institutionalize national security policy planning and making. See *National Strategy Paper* (Islamabad: National Defence University, 2012), e.g., 29–32.

48. Barany, *Soldier and the Changing State*, 353.

49. See, for instance, Testimony of the former ISI director general, Lieutenant General Ahmed Shuja Pasha (retd.), before the Abbottabad Inquiry Commission, http://www.aljazeera.com/indepth/spotlight/binladenfiles/, 192–208 (accessed July 9, 2013).

50. Editorial, "Judicial Coup?" *Express Tribune* (Karachi), June 20, 2012.

51. See, for instance, *International Dimensions of Democratization: Europe and the Americas,* ed. Laurence Whitehead (New York: Oxford University Press, 2001).

52. Susan Epstein and Alan Kronstadt, "Pakistan: U.S. Foreign Assistance" (Congressional Research Service Report, July 1, 2013), 4–5.

53. The term "Af-Pak" was coined by the former US special envoy for Afghanistan and Pakistan, the late Richard Holbrooke, to signal the Obama administration's focus on Pakistan as part of its first major review of US policy in Afghanistan in March 2009. The term was later dropped or fell into disuse primarily because of objections from Pakistan, which disliked the implied close association with Afghanistan and exclusion of India.

54. "Afghanistan and Pakistan Regional Stabilization Strategy" (Office of the Special Representative for Afghanistan and Pakistan, US State Department, February 2010).

55. See Interview, Secretary of State John Kerry, Islamabad, Pakistan, August 1, 2013, http://www.state.gov/secretary/remarks/2013/08/212626.htm (accessed August 29, 2013).

56. "Kayani Meets Kerry, Karzai for Afghan Talks," *Dawn* (Karachi), April 24, 2013.

57. Huntington, *Third Wave,* 45, 56.

58. "PM's Address to the Nation: Nawaz Sharif Dreams of Making Pakistan an 'Asian Tiger,'" *Express Tribune,* August 19, 2013.

59. "No Immediate Plan to Grant India MFN Status: Dar," *Nation* (Lahore), August 12, 2013.

60. The DCC was the highest governmental forum for defense policy making.

61. "DCC Reconstituted as CCNS," *Associated Press of Pakistan,* August 22, 2013, http://www.app.com.pk/en_/index.php?option=com_content&task=view&id=247202&Itemid=1 (accessed August 24, 2013).

62. Interview by author, Lahore, October 2000. See also Sartaj Aziz, *Between Dream and Realities: Some Milestones in Pakistan's History* (Karachi: Oxford University Press, 2009), 242–245.

ACKNOWLEDGMENTS

This book started out as a project at Columbia University and was completed at Harvard University. Then, as now, Alfred Stepan has been a constant source of warm encouragement and invaluable advice. Jack Snyder and Sheri Berman have been most generous with their time, support, and feedback.

I am particularly grateful to Stephen P. Cohen for sharing his intimate knowledge of Pakistan and its army over the years, even though we sometimes disagreed about the nature and limits of military interventions in politics. He also diligently read the entire manuscript and provided detailed comments. Christophe Jaffrelot was also kind enough to read the manuscript, raise provocative questions, and offer many useful suggestions. My wife, Bushra Asif, read several drafts in full and often offered trenchant criticism in the politest way possible. For that, and for her unwavering affection and support, especially during frustrating moments in the process of writing, I am forever thankful. Samina Ahmed, Zoltan Barany, Larry Diamond, J. Samuel Fitch, and Arun Swamy read individual or multiple chapters and with their vast knowledge of both theory and actual countries provided insightful comments. For comments on earlier versions of chapters and papers derived from the book, I want to thank participants at Comparative Politics and other seminars at Columbia, the University of Chicago, Harvard, and Stanford, as well as Timothy Frye, Sumit Ganguly, Andrew Nathan, Philip Oldenburg, Peter Purdue, and Vickie Langohr. I must also acknowledge the assistance and guidance of many serving and retired military officers in Pakistan, without which this book would not have been possible. Some of my interviewees were not comfortable signing a release form given the sensitive nature of the topic. All interviewees consented verbally to being interviewed for publication and knew that their words might be reproduced in print. Some of the interviewees wished to remain anonymous; in such cases, I have not used their names. Portions of Chapter 7 appeared in "Constraining Consolidation: Military Politics and Democracy in Pakistan," *Democratization*, April 29, 2013, and are reprinted here courtesy of Taylor & Francis (www.tandfonline.com).

At the National Documentation Center in Islamabad, the director, Saleemullah Khan, was very helpful and facilitated archival research by cutting proverbial red tape. Staff at the British Army Museum in London and the Nehru Memorial Museum Library in New Delhi were quick to respond and provide materials. I am also grateful to Hamza Khan, Amel Zahid, Rushna Shahid, and Umair Rasheed for their excellent research assistance. A very warm thank-you to my older brother Aimal Shah, who was always on hand to help acquire information and materials from Pakistan, often at short notice. I must also express my gratitude to my family, especially my mother, Mumtaz Begum, and Bushra's parents, Drs. Muhammad and Farida Asif, for their support and hospitality during our several trips to Pakistan. Last, and definitely not least, my son Sahir Shah was an inimitable source of much-needed distraction and joy. In his infinite toddler wisdom, he would often tell me, "Don't worry, baba [father in Urdu/Pashtu], your book will be awesome."

The Harvard University William F. Milton Fund provided funding for additional field research in Pakistan. At Harvard University Press, Kathleen McDermott's unflinching support, patience, and guidance helped me see the project through to the end. Katherine Brick was most helpful with her rapid-fire editorial feedback on several chapters at the tail end of the project. I am also grateful to Brian Ostrander and Barbara Goodhouse at Westchester Publishing Services for their assistance and persistence in keeping the production of the book on track. Finally, I owe special gratitude to the Harvard Society of Fellows, particularly its senior fellows Amartya Sen and Nur Yalman, for an intellectually stimulating environment and generous financial support while I tried to convert my manuscript into a book useful to both scholars and informed general readers. If I have not succeeded in that endeavor, the fault is solely mine.

INDEX

Abbas, Hassan, 25, 332n20
Abbassi, Zaheerul Islam, 164
Abbottabad Inquiry Commission, 225, 273–274
Accelerated promotions, 43
Accountability, 278; avoiding, 232–234
Actions in Aid of Civil Power Regulation (2011), 233
Adamjee Jute Mills, 319n11
Administrative control, 140
Adultery (*zina*), 152
Advani, L. K., 176
Afghan Defense Council, 356n21
Afghanistan, 13, 246, 249, 261; regional influence in, 10; Soviets in, 19, 156–157, 161, 189; Islamists and, 133; Taliban in, 174, 187
Afghan National Army, 249
Agartala conspiracy, 104
Agência Brasileira de Inteligência (ABIN). *See* Brazilian Intelligence Agency
Ahmadi Muslims, 68
Ahmed, Aziz, 95, 342n169

Ahmed, Ghafoor, 137, 144
Ahmed, Imtiaz, 123, 170–171
Ahmed, Mahmud, 179, 182–184
Ahmed, Mian Nadeem Ijaz, 233
Ahmed, Nazir, 45
Ahsan, S. M., 106, 110
Aid of civil power, 135, 340n134
Air Force Security Service, US, 92
Akbar Khan, Mohammed, 33, 41–45, 256
Akhtar, Naseer, 173
Akram, Mohammad, 183–184
Alavi, Faisal, 354n163
Alavi, Hamza, 290n7
Alfonsin, Raul, 262
Ali, F. B., 113
Ali Kuli Khan, 177–178
All-Pakistan Education Conference, 57
All Pakistan Muhajir Students Organization, 169
Alternative power, 278–280
Anderson, Benedict, 59
Andreski, Stanislav, 9
Ansar (volunteer civil force), 74

Anti-Muslim policies (Congress), 38

Apolitical professionalism, 33–34

Appointments, 224; controlling, 275–276

Appointments Committee (India), 276

Argentina, 32, 71, 262, 282–283

Arif, Khalid Mahmud, 142, 145, 339n121

"Armed Revolt in Kashmir" (Akbar Khan), 41

Armored Corps Training School, 64

Army Act (1952), 233

Assimilation: military/professional, 7–8, 21, 195, 214; nation-state, 34

Asymmetric warfare, 11, 180, 296n46

Attock conspiracy, 123

Auchinleck, Claude, 307n33

Authoritarianism, 1–2, 98–102, 150, 211, 216, 227; sources of, 3; centralization of, 16; origins of, 29; civil-military relations and, 48; delegated, 98; of Zulfiqar Ali Bhutto, 128; postauthoritarian period, 372n1

Awami League (AL), 58, 61, 82, 86, 108–111, 242; elections and, 74, 137; Suhrawardy and, 82–83; Zulfiqar Ali Bhutto and, 116

Awami National Party, 168, 220, 236, 260, 362n19

Azad (free) territory (Kashmir), 42

Aziz, Mazhar, 26, 84, 294n32, 354n63

Aziz, Sartaj, 180, 286

Aziz, Shahid, 183

Aziz, Tariq, 218

Babar, Farhatullah, 213, 273

Babar, Naseerullah Khan, 115, 174

Babrak, Said Akbar, 314n125

al-Badr (Islamist militia), 112

Baghdad Pact, 89

Baloch (ethnic group), 14, 104, 132–133, 312n93

Baloch, Bashir Azeem, 234

Balochistan, 132, 139, 143, 208–209, 234, 248

Balochistan Liberation Army, 248

Baloch Republican Party, 234

Bangladesh National Defence College, 238

Bangladesh National Party, 242

Barany, Zoltan, 12–13, 277, 298n72

Basic Democracies (BD), 96–97, 193–194, 196

Basic Principles Committee, 58–59

Battle of Badr, 163

Beg, Mirza Aslam, 93, 166, 170–172, 232, 349nn90,95

Bengal Army, 54

Bengalis (ethnic group), 51–55, 82–84, 109–113, 298n67; elites, 14; linguistic heritage of, 14; national unification project and, 15–16; nation-state policies and, 34; Lahore Resolution and, 37, 52; nationalism and, 54, 58–61, 112; language and, 56, 59, 74, 79; constitution and, 57, 79, 99; imagined community and, 60; CAP and, 72, 78–79; exclusion of, 73; UF and, 74, 99; Mirza and, 75; autonomy and, 76, 86; US and, 89; Six Points movement and, 104; numerical majority of, 108; Zulfiqar Ali Bhutto and, 116; India and, 117

Bharatiya Janata Party, 176

Bhutto, Begum Nusrat, 126, 159

Bhutto, Benazir, 159, 168, 234; PPP and, 165, 169, 174; ISI and, 170–171; Musharraf and, 215, 217–219; assassination of, 220, 233

Bhutto, Zulfiqar Ali, 123–130, 140–141, 347n74; PPP and, 29, 104, 116–117, 119, 257; Six Points movement and, 109; Bengalis and, 116; PNA and, 120; Gul Hassan and, 121; Ziaul Haq and, 125–126, 135–137, 141–144, 148; India and, 126–127, 169, 171; authoritarianism of, 128; political crisis and, 133–138

bin Laden, Osama, 187, 189, 270–271, 365n48

Bogra, Mohammad Ali, 79, 319n8

Bokhari, Fasih, 181

Bonapartism, 122–123

Border Security Force (India), 268

Bose, Sharmila, 329n86

Brazil, 19, 272, 283

Brazilian Intelligence Agency, 272

British Cabinet Mission Plan (1946), 39

British India, 1, 38–40, 49

British Indian Army (BIA), 5, 31–33, 39–40, 63–64

Bugti, Akbar Khan, 209, 360n73

Bureaucracy, 72, 95–96, 124, 154, 212, 290n7; civil, 14; promotion and, 20, 23; depoliticizing, 22; recruitments and, 23; centralized, 49; elites, 75; policing, dividing, and militarizing of, 197–200; Musharraf and, 221; MoD and, 267

Burki, Shahid Javed, 126, 152

Bush, George H. W., 344n24

Bush, George W., 189, 219, 356n14

Cabinet Committee on National Security (CCNS), 285–286

Cabinet of talents, 79–80, 85

Caretaker adviser, 375n16

Caretaker government, 175, 236

Caretaker prime minister, 173, 236, 368–369n101

Carter, Jimmy, 136, 156

Cawthome, R., 300n89

Central Committee of Democratic Federation, 58

Central Industrial Security Force (India), 268

Central Intelligence Agency (CIA), 92, 228, 274; ISI and, 19, 157; in FATA, 223

Centralization, 255; of authoritarianism, 16; of bureaucracy, 49; decentralization of power, 84, 109

Central Nacional de Informaciones. See National Information Center

Central Police Organizations (India), 268

Central Selection Board, 200

Central Superior Services, 333n31

Central Treaty Organization, 70

Chairman Joint Chiefs of Staff Committee (CJCSC), 125, 138, 153, 161, 182

Charter of Democracy, 234, 273

Chaudhry, Iftikhar Muhammad, 216–217, 222, 231

Checks and balances, authoritarian, 195–197, 341n151, 342n2

Chilean Directorate of National Intelligence (Dirección de Inteligencia Nacional), 19

Chishti, Faiz Ali, 141–144, 146, 154, 339n121, 343n14

Choudhury, G. W., 109
Chundrigar, I. I., 83
Civil Aviation Authority, 355n2
Civil disobedience movement, 111
Civilian administration, 121;
demilitarizing, 267–270
Civilian control, 9; objective,
292n16; subjective, 292n16
Civilian democratic control, 11–12,
99
Civilian oversight, 35–36
Civilian political loyalty, 234–237
Civilian supremacy, 9, 28, 61, 120,
131, 221, 261; external security
threats and, 35; formal structures
and, 62; legal-institutional
framework for, 123; MPs and,
212–213; consolidation of, 236; US
and, 281; Kashmir and, 284;
Nawaz Sharif and, 285; norms of,
297n55
Civil-military coalition, 3, 77,
299n83
Civil-military relations, 9–10, 30, 35,
62, 262–263, 268; NSC and, 23;
India and, 32; authoritarianism
and, 48; Nawaz Sharif and,
178–179; configuring, 202; judicial
sanction and, 216; civilian
supremacy and, 236; reforming,
264
Civil Service of Pakistan, 95,
124, 197
Civil Services Academy, 200
Civil war, 95–113, 257; authoritarian
politics and, 98–102; waging,
103–106; military government and,
106–113
Clausewitz, Carl von, 296n48
Clinton, Bill, 176, 181

Code of Criminal Procedure,
317n161
Code of ethics, 206
Coercion, 4, 11–13, 34, 226, 278
Cohen, Stephen P., 9, 35, 119,
162–163
Cold War, 4, 6, 29, 34, 281, 287;
security assistance and, 17; new
professionalism and, 32; geopo-
litical imperatives and, 35;
Eisenhower and, 70; ML and, 84;
stability and, 90
Collective action, 23
Colonial inheritance, 50, 302n117
Combined Opposition Parties,
101, 170
Command and Staff College, 32, 48,
64, 162, 269
Commission of Inquiry, UN, 233
Communist Party, 43–44, 75
Complex threat environment,
245–251
Comprehensive national security
paradigm, 212, 251
Conduct: codes of, 7–8; rules of, 33
Congress Party, 36–37, 48
Consolidation phase, of reform,
263
Constituent Assembly of Pakistan
(CAP), 16, 47, 55, 86, 319n8;
consensus constitution and, 36;
Government of India Act and, 50;
Objectives Resolution and, 58;
Bengalis and, 72, 78–79; second, 81
Constitution, 142, 148, 160, 238, 268,
332n23; delayed process of making,
4, 16, 73; Government of India Act
and, 49; of independent states, 51;
Bengalis and, 57, 79, 99; Objectives
Resolution and, 58; Ayub Khan

and, 76, 79–80, 98, 151; unicameral legislature and, 99; LFO and, 107; Six Points movement and, 109; civilian supremacy and, 123; martial law and, 135; crisis and, 145–146; impartial elections and, 159; NSC and, 177; Musharraf and, 186–187, 192, 202, 215, 218–219; PPP and, 257. *See also specific amendments*
Corporate autonomy, 11
Corps Headquarters, 169, 182
Correlates of War (COW), 374n9
Coser, Lewis, 14, 88
Council for Defense and National Security (CDNS), 175
Council of Administration, 106
Counterinsurgency (COIN), 269; operations, 121, 139, 143
Counterinsurgency Capability Fund, 269
Counterterrorism, 271, 274, 281
Counterterrorism Wing (ISI), 274. *See also* Inter-Services Intelligence (ISI)
Coup Brigade (111th Brigade), 184, 230, 339n121, 343n14
Coups, 27, 33, 41, 81–87, 93, 122, 182, 241; of 1999, 1, 24; Rawalpindi conspiracy, 42–46; domestic threats and, 88–92; external influences and, 88–92; of 1977, 120, 126, 140–145; Attock conspiracy, 123; prelude to, 171–185; extrication, 215
Criminal Investigation Department, 43
Crises: Suez, 82; of 1977, 140–145; constitution and, 145–146
Cunningham, George, 49

Curtailed democracy, 165–171
Customs Intelligence, 164

Dahl, Robert, 12–13
Dar, Ishaq, 284
Daud, Sardar Mohammad, 133
David, Paul, 289n4
Davis, Raymond, 228, 248
Death squads of the ISI and MI, 231
Decade of development, 116
Defense Committee of the Cabinet (DCC), 62, 235, 267, 305n15, 332n26; creation of, 35–36; air force and, 63; revival of, 124; NDU and, 250; CCNS and, 285–286
Defense Council, 36
Defense expenditures, 126, 129
Defense of Pakistan Ordinance (1965), 129
Defense policy, 22–23, 35–36
Delegated authoritarianism, 98
Demilitarization, of civilian administration and security forces, 267–270
Democratic consolidation, 276, 285
Democratic resocialization, 276–278
Democratic transition, 150, 165, 356n14
Democratization, 47, 251, 261, 264, 280, 284
Department for International Development (UK), 199
Department of State, US, 69, 90–91, 136, 324nn77,78
Desch, Michael C., 295n41, 373n3
Devolution, 193; despotism and, 193–195
Dhaka University, 57
Dharna (sit-in), 222

Dirección de Inteligencia Nacional. *See* Chilean Directorate of National Intelligence

Directorate General of Training, 65;

Dirty War, 262

District Management Group (DMG), 197, 199, 267, 333n31

Domestic factors, 264–280; ministerial regulation, 266–267; demilitarizing civilian administration and security forces, 267–270; parliamentary scrutiny, 270–271; military intelligence sector, 272–275; controlling appointments, 275–276; democratic resocialization, 276–278; alternative power, 278–280

Domestic political restructuring, 158–162

Domestic threats and 1958 coup, 88–92

Doyle, Michael, 373n9

Dulles, John Foster, 91–92

Durand Line, 336n79

Durrani, Asad, 183, 232

East Bengal Regiment, 112

East India Company, 54

East Pakistan Rifles, 112

East-West integration, 94

Economics, 73, 106; deterioration of, 88; inequalities of, 101–102

Education, 276; nationalization of, 128; expansion of, 155; illiteracy and, 193; standardized qualifications for, 206

Egypt, 24, 263, 281–282, 287

Eighteenth Amendment, 235, 260, 265

Eisenhower, Dwight D., 70, 91

Elahi, Chaudhry Fazal, 146

Election Commission, 174, 369n101

Elections, 74–76, 86, 96, 116, 204, 236, 260, 265; rigging of, 19, 29, 145, 336n83; universally enfranchised, 37–38, 107–108; Bengalis and, 84; indirect, 99; direct, 100; opposition parties and, 101, 221; Six Points movement and, 109; PPP and, 119, 159, 167, 171, 173–174; PNA and, 120, 128, 141, 143; parliamentary, 133–140, 161, 192, 220; domestic political restructuring and, 158–159; Ziaul Haq and, 158–159; PML-N and, 175, 220; legitimacy of, 240

Elective Bodies Disqualification Order (1959), 324n5

Electoral college, 100, 361n4

Electoral democracy, 30, 258

Elites, 37–38, 59–60, 116, 241, 255; Bengalis and, 14; nation-state policies and, 15; India and, 35; ethnoregional, 74; bureaucracy and, 75; politicians, 239

Emergency (1975–1977), India, 131, 186

Enhanced Partnership Act (2009), 227, 281–282

Ethnic groups, 14–15, 51–54; identity and, 34; recruitment and, 53–55; parties, 206. *See also specific groups*

Ethnoregional elite, 74

External factors, 280–284; US as, 280–283

External influences and 1958 coup, 88–92

External security, 11; environment of, 131–133

External threats, 9, 132–133, 207

Extraregional forces (ERFs), 246

Faisal II (king), 89
Faiz, Faiz Ahmed, 42–43
Falklands War, 283
Fauji Foundation, 154
Fearon, James, 41
Feaver, Peter, 297n52
Federal Inspection Commission, 153
Federal Investigation Agency, 232, 243
Federalism, 194, 205
Federally Administered Tribal Areas (FATA), 223, 226, 234, 246–247, 269
Federal Public Service Commission, 200
Federal Security Force (FSF), 129–131, 134, 335n67
Federal Shariat Court, 152
Feroze Khan Noon, Malik, 83, 86
Fifteenth Amendment, 354n169
Fifth Amendment. *See* Government of India Act
Financial Times, 229
Finer, Samuel, 5, 146, 297n55
First-use policy, 226
Fitch, John Samuel, 304n131, 321n44
Force Command Northern Areas, 180
Foreign Assistance Act (1961), 187, 344n24, 356n14
Foreign policy, 67, 153, 164, 189, 207; Islamists and, 25; US and, 82, 89–90, 156; Bengalis and, 84; management of, 129; continuity in, 168; Nawaz Sharif and, 179; nuclear weapons and, 281
Foreign Service, 267
Foundational project, 96
Franchise Commission, 99–100

Frontier Corps, 231–232, 268–269
Frontier Crimes Regulation (1901), 247

Gandhi, Indira, 131
Gandhi, Mohandas, 36
Gandhi, Rajiv, 348n80
Garrison-state argument, 9, 290n7
General Headquarters (GHQ), 45, 64–65, 113, 117, 168, 174, 184, 270
General staff, 20, 202, 219
Geneva Accords (1988), 161
George, David Lloyd, 333n30
Gillani, Yousaf Raza, 224, 230, 280
Government of India Act (1935), 48–50, 78, 311n77
Great Sepoy Mutiny (1857), 54
Gross national product (GNP), 101, 126
Ground lines of communication (GLOCs), 271
Guerrilla warfare, 296n46
Gul, Hamid, 170
Gutteridge, William F., 32
Gwadar, 209

Habib, Younis, 171
Haider, Moinuddin, 178
Haider, Saleem, 184
Hamoodur Rehman Commission of Inquiry, 111, 124, 127
Haq, A. K. Fazlul, 319n11
Haq, Ehsanul, 183
Haq, Mehbubul, 101
Haqqani, Husain, 25, 167, 229–230
Haqqani, Jalaluddin, 226
Haqqani network, 226, 262, 281
Harkatul Jihadul Islami, 164
Hartal (strike), 110

Hassan, Gul, 109, 111, 113–114, 121–123, 331n16
Hassan, Javed, 180
Hassan, Mubashir, 122
Heeger, Gerald, 95, 97
Hekmetyar, Gulbadin, 133, 157
High Treason (Punishment) Act, 332n24
Hildreth, Horace, 90, 324n78
Hindi (language), 38, 306n19, 313n101
Hindus, 37–40, 56, 86, 255, 303n118, 308n38
Hizbe Islami, 157
Holbrooke, Richard, 378n53
Home Ministry (India), 268
Hossain, Kamal, 334n42
Hudood punishments, 152
Human Rights Commission, 194
Human rights violations, 155, 231; in Balochistan, 231, 274; in Argentina, 262, 283
Human Rights Watch, 198
Huntington, Samuel, 5, 9, 97, 256–257, 292n16
Hussain, Raja Khadim, 110

Iftikharuddin, Mian, 45–46
Ijaz, Mansoor, 229
Illiberal democracy, 373n9
Imagined community, 60
Income transfers, 128
Independence, significance for the military, 40
Independence of India Act, 311n82
India, 41, 61, 70, 84, 131, 181, 207–214, 249–250; British, 1, 38–40, 49; security threat from, 4, 22, 34–35, 47, 55, 67, 73, 131–132, 255–256; BIA, 5, 31–33, 39–40, 63–64; professionalism and, 5, 34; Kashmir and, 10,

13, 19, 42; military superiority of, 11; 1971 war with, 20, 29; civil-military relations and, 32; institutional structures in, 36; Lahore Resolution and, 37; Government of India Act, 48–50, 78, 311n77; ethnic groups and, 51–54; nationalist movement of, 54; two-nation theory and, 56; conflict with, 102–105, 117; intervention of, 112; Zulfiqar Ali Bhutto and, 126–127, 169, 171; nuclear tests of, 176; Nawaz Sharif and, 179; PPP and, 226; US and, 246–248; asymmetric warfare and, 252
India Independence Act (1947), 308n38
Indian Civil Service, 53, 95, 298n67
Indian Military Academy, 32, 64
Indian National Congress, 38, 49
Indian Political Service, 53, 298n67, 321n33
India-Pakistan war (1965), 70
Individual research papers (NDU), 201–202
Indoctrination, military, 23–24
Industrial Development Corporation, 95
Industry, nationalization of, 128
Inequality, 73; economic, 101–102
Influences, external (1958 coup), 88–92
Information Management Wing (ISI), 228. *See also* Inter-Services Intelligence (ISI)
Information warfare, 251
Inspector General Training and Evaluation, 294n31

Institutional approach, 243–244
Institutions, 6–11, 69; development of, 17, 63–67; beliefs and motives of, 29; norms and, 221; regulatory, 266; total, 293n25
Instruments of Accession, 311n82
Intelligence and Security Committee, 273
Intelligence Bureau (IB), 75, 122, 123, 243, 349n90
Internal fragmentation, 34, 37
Internal security, 243
Internal Security Wing (ISI), 158, 170. *See also* Inter-Services Intelligence (ISI)
International security, 10
Inter-Services Intelligence (ISI), 101, 139, 173, 218, 224–225, 228, 260; Ayub Khan and, 18; CIA and, 19, 157; Tikka and, 123; PNA and, 138; Ziaul Haq and, 158; PPP and, 167, 174; Benazir Bhutto and, 170–171; Taliban and, 189; PML-Q and, 191; Kayani and, 232; PML-N and, 273
Inter-Services Intelligence Agency (Functions, Powers and Regulation) Act (2012), 273
Inter-Services Public Relations (ISPR), 68, 227, 279, 348n81
Inter-Services Selection Board (ISSB), 300n94
Interventions, 2, 66, 88, 145, 205, 211, 216; precedent of, 20; pull and push factors and, 25–27; corporate grievances and, 84; of India, 112; tutelary, 222–234
Interwing parity, 73
Islami Jamhoori Ittehad (IJI), 167, 170–171

Islami Jamiat Talaba (Jamiat), 134, 158, 344n32
Islamists, 68, 134, 162, 208, 226, 230; militancy, 2, 10, 164; terrorism by, 25; electoral campaign of, 108; militias, 112; Afghanistan and, 133; opposition groups, 157; MMA and, 191
Islamization, 152, 157, 162, 163, 258; of the military, 162–165

Jaffrelot, Christophe, 14
Jalal, Ayesha, 43, 47, 50, 291n9
Jamaate Islami (JI), 68, 137, 167, 336n81; PPP and, 133–134, 157; PML-N and, 222
Jamiat. *See* Islami Jamiat Talaba
Jamiat Ulema-e-Islam (JUI), 139, 157, 174, 192, 336n81
Janjua, Asif Nawaz, 169, 172
Janjua, M. K., 46
Janowitz, Morris, 17, 31, 77, 299n83
Jatoi, Mustafa, 171
Jinnah, Fatima, 101
Jinnah, Mohammad Ali, 37, 44, 48–51, 56, 255, 311n82; ML and, 3, 13; viceregalism and, 16; death of, 38, 60, 65; British India and, 39; two-nation theory of, 56
Joint-electorate system, 73–74
Joint Staff, 124, 125, 257
Joint Strategic Directive (2007), 246
Judicial activism, 217, 229–232
July-August military crisis (1951), 47
Junejo, Mohammad Khan, 161

Kakar, Waheed, 172–173
Kallu, Shamsur Rehman, 170
Karamat, Jehangir, 175–179, 196, 285
Kargil war, 150, 189, 262, 278, 374n9

Kashmir, 40–44, 47, 255, 283, 308n38; India and, 10, 13, 19, 42; asymmetric warfare and, 180; civilian supremacy and, 284

Kayani, Ashfaq Pervez, 218, 220–224, 230, 238, 241, 363n26; ISI and, 232; complex threat environment and, 245–246; Kerry and, 282

Kerry, John, 282

Kerry-Lugar-Berman Bill, 227, 229, 248

Khan, Abdul Hamid, 106, 109, 113

Khan, Ali Kuli, 177, 178, 351nn128,130

Khan, Dera Ismail, 323n64

Khan, Ghulam Ishaq, 166, 168, 171–173

Khan, Imran 363n29

Khan, Iqbal, 147, 153, 154

Khan, Liaquat Ali 56, 60–62, 65, 82, 314n125; Akbar Khan and, 33, 44; assassination of, 38; ML and, 60

Khan, Mohammad Asghar, 137, 144

Khan, Mohammad Ayub, 23, 62–67, 84–88, 94–98, 105, 257; professionalism and, 6; ISI and, 18; accelerated promotions and, 43; Training Advisory Staff and, 64; Planning Board and, 65; US and, 69–70, 90–91; constitution and, 76, 79–80, 98, 151; cabinet of talents and, 79–80; Suhrawardy and, 82–83; universal adult franchise and, 100; legitimacy and, 101; tutelary professionalism and, 113–116; Press and Publications Ordinance and, 129; Musa and, 152; Basic Democracy and, 193–194, 196; Civil Service of Pakistan and, 197

Khan, Mohammad Azam, 68

Khan, Mohammad Aziz, 179, 181–184

Khan, Nawabzada Nasrullah, 138, 336n81

Khan, Nur, 106–107

Khan, Rahim, 113, 122

Khan, Roedad, 323n64

Khan, Sadiq, 45

Khan, Sahibzada Yaqub, 110–111, 168

Khan, Sawar, 153, 154

Khan, Sher, 46

Khan, Tikka, 122–123, 125, 128–129

Khan, Yahya, 18, 20, 29, 105–109, 257; Bengalis and, 111–113; Zulfiqar Ali Bhutto and, 122; LFO and, 151

Khan, Zulfiqar Ali, 170

Khar, Ghulam Mustafa, 122

Khilnani, Sunil, 291n8

Khuhro, M. A., 50

Kier, Elizabeth, 7

Kill-and-dump operations in Balochistan, 231

Kissinger, Henry, 135

Kohn, Richard, 12–13, 262

Korean War, 70

Krishak Saramik Party, 74

Labor: unions, 105; reforms, 128

Lahore Declaration, 179

Lahore Resolution (1940), 37, 52, 58, 74

Lahore Session (Muslim League), 51

Land tax. See Ushr

Langley, James, 91

Language, 16, 36, 55–57, 74, 79–80; movement, 16, 60

Lashkare Tayyaba, 249, 262
Lasswell, Harold, 9, 290n7
Lateral entry, 124
Latif, Rahat, 343n14
Lawyers' movement, 217
Legal Framework Order (LFO), 107, 109–110, 151, 190–192, 196
Leghari, Farooq, 174–176, 178
Letelier, Orlando, 300n92
Liberalization, political, 216
Lieven, Anatol, 25
Line of Control (LoC), 180–181, 284
Local government, 159, 195
Lockhart, Rob, 311n82
Logic of appropriateness, 7, 9, 295n37
Low intensity conflict (LIC), 269
Loyalty: of civilians, 234–237; of military, 237–245

Majlise Ahrar, 68
Malik, S. K., 162
Malvinas War, 283
Man on Horseback, The (Finer), 297n55
Martial law, 68–69, 107, 144, 161, 187, 196
Martial Law Administrators' Conference, 153
Martial races, 54, 298n67; theory of, 312n94
Marxism, 89, 157
Massoud, Ahmed Shah, 133
Mazari, Sherbaz, 144
Media, 197, 216; suppression of, 129; broadcast news, 227; public opinion and, 227–229; alternative power and, 278–279
Mehmud, Maulana Mufti, 144, 336n81

Mehran Bank, 171, 232
Mehsud, Alam Jan, 171
Members of parliament (MPs), 212–213
Memogate affair, 229–230, 280
Menon, Krishna, 28
Messervy, Frank, 42
Militarization, 13, 34, 47; of bureaucracy, 154; of MoD, 267
Military Control in Pakistan: The Parallel State (Aziz), 294n32
Military corporate autonomy, 11
Military Council, 153
Military expenditures, 126, 129
Military Inc. (Siddiqa), 154
Military Intelligence (MI), 75, 164, 231–234, 272, 274, 365n48
Military loyalty, 237–245
Military mind-set, 8, 294n30
Military perceptions, 1977 elections and, 140–145
Military promotions, 23, 123, 224
Ministerial regulation, 266–267
Ministry of Defense (MoD), 36, 82, 85, 106, 230, 322n48; ministerial regulation and, 266–267; parliamentary scrutiny and, 270
Ministry of Defense Production, 124
Ministry of Economic Affairs, 106
Ministry of Finance, 63
Ministry of Foreign Affairs, 106
Ministry of Interior, 75, 224–225, 268, 274
Ministry of Law, 100
Ministry of Planning, 106
Mirza, Iskander, 75, 79–82, 86, 90–92, 321n33
Missing persons, 217, 231
ML-Conventional, 101

Modernization, 18, 94, 256; military and, 17, 47, 71, 132

Mohammad, Ghulam, 33, 62, 77, 79, 81

Mohammad, Mian Tufail, 336n81

Mohieman, Naeem, 329n86

Moore, Robert, 136

Morsi, Mohammad, 24, 263, 281

Mountbatten, Louis, 39, 311n82

Movement for the Restoration of Democracy (MRD), 159–160

Muhajir Qaumi Movement (MQM), 160, 168–170, 172, 236, 347n74

Muhajirs (ethnic group), 14, 51, 160

Mukti Bahini (liberation force), 112, 117

Musa, Mohammad, 95, 152

Musharraf, Pervez, 183–184, 216, 259, 279, 354n162; NDU and, 22; NSC and, 23, 188, 195–197; state power and, 150; Nawaz Sharif and, 176, 180–182, 184, 186, 217, 220; Karamat and, 178–179; Aziz Khan and, 181; Emergency and, 186; constitution and, 186–187, 192, 202, 215, 218–219; martial law and, 187; national reconstruction and, 188, 190; political restruc-turing and, 190–200; political liberalization and, 191; MMA and, 192; devolution project of, 194; DMG and, 197, 199; professional-ism and, 200; tutelage and, 200–214; Benazir Bhutto and, 215, 217–219; bureaucracy and, 221

Muslim League (ML), 15, 37, 61, 99, 167, 173, 255; Mohammad Ali Jinnah and, 3, 13; assimilation policies of, 34; Indian National Congress and, 38; Lahore Session of, 51; nation-state building policies of, 55; Working Commit-tee of, 57; Dhaka session of, 59; Liaquat and, 60; elections and, 74–75; Nazimuddin and, 77; Cold War and, 84; ML-Convention, 101; Islamists of, 108. See also Awami League; Pakistan Muslim League (Nawaz); Pakistan Muslim League (Quaid-e-Azam)

Muslims, 37–41, 51–53, 56–57; Ahmadi, 68; Quran and, 162–163

Mutahida Majlise Amal (MMA), 191–192, 196, 208

Muttahida Qaumi Movement. See Muhajir Qaumi Movement

Mutual Defense Assistance Agreement, 70

Muwaz, Gul, 309–310n57

Naqvi, Tanvir, 190, 212–213

Nasir, Javed, 172

National Accountability Bureau, 186, 233

National Assembly, 171, 220, 235, 240, 260, 273; constitution and, 99; AL and, 108; LFO and, 109–110; Zulfiqar Ali Bhutto and, 116–117; Public Accounts Com-mittee, 233

National Awami Party (NAP), 99

National Awami Party–Jamiat Ulema-e-Islam (NAP-JUI) government, 139

National Defence University (NDU), 8–9, 22, 51, 259, 277, 358n52; socialization and, 165; tutelage and, 201, 237; parliamen-tary government and, 205; national security and, 211–212;

media and, 227; DCC and, 250;
syllabus of, 251; LIC and, 269
National Defence Course, 201, 237
National Democratic Front, 99
National Information Center
(Central Nacional de Informacio-
nes, Chile), 300n92
National Information Service
(Serviço Nacional de Informa-
ções, Brazil), 19, 272
National Institutes of Public
Administration, 200
Nationalism, 14, 22, 165; secular, 40;
conflicting, 41; Bengalis and, 54,
59–60, 112; rural peasants and, 60;
linguistic, 72
National Logistics Cell, 154, 233,
367n89
National Reconciliation Ordinance
(NRO), 218
National reconstruction, 188
National Reconstruction Bureau
(NRB), 190, 194, 199
National Security and War Course,
237
National Security Council (NSC),
23, 151, 205, 235, 259, 285, 351n127;
Musharraf and, 23, 188, 195–197;
US and, 90; Yahya Khan and,
108; Ziaul Haq and, 160; compo-
sition of, 161; in constitution, 177;
Near East and South Asian
Affairs, 181; LFO and, 191–192;
Turkish model of, 202; abolish-
ment of, 245
National Security Workshop, 212
National Strategy Paper, 2007–2008,
246–247
National Strategy Paper, 2012
(NDU), 244, 248–250, 377n47

Nation-state policies, 15, 34
Naval mutiny (1946), 33
Naval War College, 177
Nawaz, Shuja, 25, 199
Nazimuddin, Khawaja, 39, 54, 59,
77–78
NDU Journal, 213–214
Nehru, Jawarhalal, 36, 78
New professionalism, 32
Niazi, Maulana Kausar, 337n89
9/11 terrorist attacks, 189, 225
Nizam e Mustafa (System of the
Prophet), 135
No-first-use policy, 226
Noncooperation, 111
Nongovernmental organizations,
197
Nonkinetic warfare, 251
Non-Proliferation Treaty, 247
Nonviolent civil disobedience
campaign, 111
Norms, 7–8, 21, 225, 237–238,
257–258, 294n30; institutions and,
221; of civilian supremacy, 297n55
Nuclear weapons, 132, 135–136,
155–156, 248, 348n80; tests of, 176,
179, 187; first-use policy for, 226;
foreign policy and, 281; Pressler
Amendment and, 344n24
Nunn, Frederick, 251

Oath of service, military, 310–311n74,
332n25
Obama, Barack, 227, 281, 378n53
Objective civilian control, 292n16
Objectives Resolution (1949), 58,
188, 237
O'Donnell, Guillermo, 71, 216
Officer corps, 6, 17, 131
Ojhri Camp, 161

Oldenburg, Phillip, 51–52
Omar, Ghulam, 108
O'Neal, John R., 374n9
One Unit, 16, 80, 104
Operation Close Door, 86
Operation Fairplay, 142
Operation Gibraltar, 103
Operation Grandslam, 103
Operation Searchlight, 112

Pakistan Administrative Staff
    College, 200
Pakistan Army Green Book, 196, 200,
    203, 213–214, 245–246, 294n31
Pakistan Democratic Party, 336n81
Pakistan International Airlines, 270
Pakistan Military Academy
    (PMA), 115, 119, 244, 295n36,
    300n94, 365n48
Pakistan Movement for Justice. *See*
    Pakistan Tehreek-e-Insaaf
Pakistan Muslim League (Nawaz)
    (PML-N), 185, 230, 278, 285,
    350n116, 362n19; Nawaz Sharif
    and, 167; elections and, 175, 220;
    Musharraf and, 186; political
    restructuring and, 190–192; PPP
    and, 219, 234, 236, 260; JI and,
    222; ISI and, 273
Pakistan Muslim League (Quaid-
    e-Azam) (PML-Q), 191–192,
    196, 218
Pakistan National Alliance (PNA),
    120, 133–138, 140–141, 143, 157, 257
Pakistan People's Party (PPP),
    140–143, 167–168, 223–226, 240,
    273, 362n19; Zulfiqar Ali Bhutto
    and, 29, 104, 116–117, 119, 257; AL
    and, 108–109; elections and, 119,
    159, 171, 173–174; factionalism of,

128; public support of, 129; JI and,
    133–134, 157; NAP-JUI and, 139;
    MRD and, 159–160; Benazir
    Bhutto and, 165, 169, 174; Mush-
    arraf and, 215, 218; PML-N and,
    219, 234, 236, 260; Zardari and,
    220; basic principles of, 327n52
Pakistan Provisional Constitutional
    Order (1947), 49
Pakistan Tehreek-e-Insaaf (Paki-
    stan Movement for Justice), 222,
    236–237, 260, 363n29
Pakistan Television, 127
Pakistan Times, 42
Paramilitary forces, demilitarizing
    of, 267–270
Parliamentary Committee on
    National Security (PCNS),
    230, 271
Parliamentary democracy, 22, 205,
    259, 340n151, 342n2
Parliamentary elections, 133–140,
    161, 192, 220
Parliamentary scrutiny, 270–271
Parliamentary system, 145, 190–191
Pasha, Ahmed Shuja, 193, 214, 225,
    239, 243, 270–271
Pashtuns (ethnic group), 14, 42,
    53–54, 55, 104
Pataudi, Sher Khan, 67
Path dependence, 289n4
Paul, T. V., 297–298n64
Peerzada, S. G. M., 106–107, 109
Pentagon, 269
People's Democratic Party of
    Afghanistan (PDPA), 157
People's Student Federation, 158, 169
Pervez, Tariq, 182, 183
Pinochet, Augusto, 19, 300n92
Pirzada, Sharifuddin, 49

Planning Board, 65

Police, 29, 243, 268, 331n7, 376nn29,30

Police Service of Pakistan, 268

Political liberalization, 216

Political neutrality, 222

Political parties, 15, 101, 158; reform of, 206–207

Political restructuring, 151, 190–200; domestic, 158–162; despotism and, 193–195; checks and balances and, 195–197; bureaucracy and, 197–200

Polyarchy, 12

Postauthoritarianism, 373n1

Postcolonial societies, 290n7

Power: transfer of, 1, 34, 106, 285, 374n16; of institutions, 7; new centers of, 30; central, 36–37; regional, 36–37; distribution of, 72; decentralization of, 84, 109; executive, 99; occupation, 102; aid of civil power, 135, 340n134; alternation of, 150; alternative, 278–280

Praetorianism, 43, 69, 85

Presidential system, 95

Press and Publications Ordinance (1963), 129

Pressler Amendment, 344n24

Prevention of Anti-national Activities Act (1974), 129

Professional army, 162–165, 294n27

Professionalism, 9, 17, 149, 213, 252, 256, 277; India and, 5, 34; Ayub Khan and, 6; politics and, 19–25; new, 32; apolitical, 33–34; tutelary, 46, 113–118; Musharraf and, 200; socialization and, 201–202

Protests, 134, 136, 242; by students, 56–57, 59, 105

Provincial Development Council, 97

Provisional Constitutional Order, 218

Przeworski, Adam, 245

Public Accounts Committee, 233

Public and Representative (Disqualification) Offices Act (1949), 60, 78

Public Offices Disqualification Order, 95

Public opinion, manufacturing, 226–229

Public Service Commission, 59

Pull and push factors, 25–28

Punjabis (ethnic group), 16, 34, 50–54, 80, 94, 256; military officers and, 51–54; bureaucracy and, 72; in Balochistan, 208

Qadri, Allama Tahirul, 242

al-Qaeda, 187, 192, 229, 271, 274, 281; 9/11 attacks by, 189; CIA and, 223

Qazi, Javed Ashraf, 173

Quran, 162–163

Quranic Concept of War, The (Malik), 162

Quyuum, Abdul, 162

Rabbani, Burhanuddin, 157

Rangers, 268

Rally-around-the-flag effect, 132

Raphael, Arnold, 345n46

Rashid, Ahmed, 174

Rational-choice theory, 27

Rawalpindi conspiracy (1951), 42–46, 82, 89, 113, 309n51

Raza, Rafi, 138, 331n14

Reagan, Ronald, 156, 344n24

Recruits: resocialization of, 7; bureaucracy and, 23; ethnicity and, 53–55

Reforms, 234–235, 262; of labor, 128; of political parties, 206–207; phases of, 263; of civil-military relations, 264; legal, 273

Regional hegemony, 207

Regional power, 36–37

Regulatory institutions, 266

Rehman, Akhtar Abdur, 345n46

Rehman, Fazlur, 57

Rehman, Sheikh Mujibur, 104, 110–112, 116, 126

Report of the Hamoodur Rehman Commission of Inquiry into the 1971 War, The, 333n32

Republican Party (Pakistan), 82–83

Resocialization: of recruits, 7; democratic, 276–278

Restructuring, 151, 190–200; domestic, 158–162; despotism and, 193–195; checks and balances and, 195–197; bureaucracy and, 197–200

Riedel, Bruce, 181

Rival armed forces, 130–131

Roles: expanding, 67–71; moderating, 77

Royal Military Academy, 32, 321n33

Rules of business (1973), 124, 170

Russet, Bruce, 374n9

Sahib, Khan, 49

Saifullah, Qari, 164

Sardars (tribal chiefs), 209

Satti, Salahuddin, 184

Schaffer, Howard B., 136

Schattschneider, E. E., 28

Schiff, Rebecca, 296–297n52

Schmitter, Philippe C., 216

School of Artillery, 64

School of Infantry and Tactics, 269

School of Military Intelligence, 244

Secession, of East Pakistan, 104

Second Basic Principles Committee Report (Nazimuddin report), 78

Senate, 206, 240, 273

Senate Committee on Defense and Defense Production, 270

September 11, 2001 terrorist attacks, 189, 225

Serra, Narcís, 263–264

Service extensions, 224

Serviço Nacional de Informações. *See* National Information Service

Seven-point national reconstruction plan, 188

Seventeenth Amendment, 192

Shafqat, Saeed, 131

Shah, Sajjad Ali, 175

Shahabuddin, Muhammad, 98

al-Shams (Islamist militia), 112

Shariah Bill, 354n169

Sharia law, 135, 152

Sharif, Nawaz, 171–177, 234, 259, 266, 284, 355n2; PML-N and, 167; Musharraf and, 176, 180–182, 184, 186, 217, 220; civil-military relations and, 178–179; civilian supremacy and, 285

Sharif, Shahbaz, 222

Shehzad, Saleem, 229, 366n68

Sheikh, Farzana, 290n6

"Short Appreciation of Present and Future Problems of Pakistan, A" (Ayub Khan), 76

Siddiqa, Ayesha, 26–27, 154

Siddiqi, A. R., 68, 328n69

Simla Agreement, 131–132

Simmel, Georg, 298n70
Sindhis (ethnic group), 14, 50, 55, 104, 159–160, 312n93
Single-party regimes, 289n1
Sino-Indian war (1962), 28, 102
Sirohey, Iftikhar, 170
al-Sisi, Abdel-Fattah, 24
Sit-in. *See Dharna*
Six Points movement, 104, 109
Socialization, 7, 20–21, 23, 214, 259; informal, 32; secular, 165; professional, 201–202. *See also* Resocialization
Sociological institutionalism, 9
South Asian Association for Regional Cooperation, 250
Southeast Asia Treaty Organization, 70
Special Forces, US, 270
Special Services Group, 102, 113
Standstill Agreement, 308n38
State breakup, 95–113; authoritarian politics and, 98–102; waging war and, 103–106; military government and, 106–113
State Department, US, 69, 77, 90–91, 136, 324nn77,78
State-nation policies, 15
State necessity, 187
Steel frame, 333n30
Stepan, Alfred, 32, 77
Strikes, 105, 110, 134
"Structural Analysis of National Reconstruction" (NRB), 199
Student protests, 56–57, 59, 105
Subjective civilian control, 292n16
Subnational identities, 55
Suez crisis (1956), 82
Suharto, 32
Suhrawardy, H. S., 82–83, 95, 99

Supreme Council of the Armed Forces (SCAF), 263
Supreme Court, 175, 187, 215–218, 230–232, 275, 278–280
Supreme Court Bar Association, 217
Symington Amendment, 156
System of the Prophet. *See* Nizam e Mustafa

Tablighi Jamaat, 163
Taliban (Tehrike Taliban Pakistan), 236, 247, 260, 269, 271, 282; coercion and, 11; in Afghanistan, 174, 187; US and, 189; CIA and, 223
Tariq, Mohammad, 325n20
Tashkent Agreement, 103
Taylor, Brian, 304n131
Tehreeke Istiqlal, 336n81
Tehrike Taliban Pakistan. *See* Taliban
Tehsil (subdistrict), 97
Territorial rivalry, 40, 47
Terrorism, 11, 223, 243, 247, 249, 261–262; by Islamists, 25; War on Terror, 162, 217, 219, 274, 302n116, 356n21; September 11, 2001 attacks, 189, 225; counterterrorism, 271, 274, 281
Thana (subdistrict, East Pakistan), 97
Third-wave democracy, 264
Thirteenth Amendment, 175–176
Threat-based theories, 9–10
Tilly, Charles, 13, 297n64
Times and Trial of the Rawalpindi Conspiracy, 1951: The First Coup Attempt in Pakistan, The (Zaheer, H.), 309n51
Total institution, 293n25

Toynbee, Arnold, 97–98
Training Advisory Staff, 64
Transition phase, of reform, 263
Tribal chiefs. *See* Sardars
Tribal militias, 42
Tripartite defense policy, 22
Turkey, 109, 122, 142, 202
Tutelage: mentality, 17, 21, 77, 121; professionalism and, 46, 113–118; training for, 200–214; NDU and, 201, 237; interventions of, 222–234
Twelfth Division, 103
Twentieth Amendment, 236
Two-front war, 208
Two-nation theory, 52, 56

United Action Front. *See* Mutahida Majlise Amal
United Democratic Front, 133
United Front (UF), 8, 74–75, 80, 99, 318n5, 319n8
United Nations Development Programme, 198–199
United Provinces, 38
United States (US), 17, 44, 181, 187, 223, 229, 246–248, 256, 269; Ayub Khan and, 69–70, 90–91; foreign policy and, 82, 89–90, 156; Bengalis and, 89; coup and, 89–92; economic aid from, 101; Ziaul Haq and, 155–158; War on Terror by, 162, 217, 219, 274, 302n116, 356n21; strategic defiance of, 172; September 11, 2001 terrorist attacks and, 189, 225; Taliban and, 189; Benazir Bhutto and, 218; public opinion and, 227–228; bin Laden and, 270–271; as external factor, 280–283. *See also specific government agencies*

Unity of command, 190–200, 206; despotism and, 193–195; checks and balances and, 195–197; bureaucracy and, 197–200
Universal adult franchise, 97–100, 106–108, 327n49
Universally franchised elections, 37–38, 107–108
Urdu (language), 16, 55–59, 79, 313n101
Ushr (Islamic land tax), 152
Uttar Pradesh, 37

Vajpayee, Atal Behari, 179, 181
Vance, Cyrus, 136
Vande Mataram, 38
Viceregalism, 4–6, 16, 51, 74, 292n12
Viceregal-military coalition, 80

War Course, 51, 201, 204, 237, 358n52, 359n53
Wards, 97
War on Terror, 162, 217, 219, 274, 302n116, 356n21
Water and Power Development Authority, 95
Wattoo, Mian Manzoor, 173
Weinbaum, Marvin, 336n83
Welch, Claude, 131
White Paper on Higher Defense Organization, 125
Wilcox, Wayne, 88, 323n66
Working Committee (Muslim League), 37, 39, 57
World Bank, 152
World War II, 120
Wyne, Ghulam Haider, 173

Zaheer, Hassan, 309n51
Zaheer, Sajjad, 43
Zakaria, Fareed, 373n9

Zakat (Islamic wealth tax), 152
Zarbe Momin (1989), 170
Zardari, Asif Ali, 218, 226, 229, 273, 280; ISI and, 171; Leghari and, 174–175; PPP and, 220; tutelary interventions and, 222–223
Zero-error syndrome, 23
Zia, Tauqir, 184
Zia generation, 163
Ziauddin, Khawaja, 182, 183, 184, 185

Ziaul Haq, Muhammad, 18, 30, 129, 193–199, 257–258, 345n46; Zulfiqar Ali Bhutto and, 125–126, 135–137, 141–144, 148; military government of, 151–155; US and, 155–158; domestic political restructuring and, 158–162; NSC and, 160; death of, 165–166
Zina (adultery), 152
Zonal martial law, 107